Six Months in Hawaii

Six Months in Hawaii , set in the islands in 1873, is the compelling account of the true life adventures that transformed a quiet English lady into the darling and dashing world traveller Isabella Bird, whose exploits held the world enthralled. She spent six months journeying through the islands, cantering through lush forests and grasslands on spirited ponies, drifting over the rolling blue seas on raffish schooners, and finally making her way to the fiery volcano of Mauna Loa. This is a book of singular charm, guaranteed to produce a thirst for adventure and travel. Here, all the beauties of Hawaii and the island way of life are seen through the eyes of one who is, for the first time, tasting life to the full.

Six Months in Hawaii

Isabella Bird

Routledge
Taylor & Francis Group

LONDON AND NEW YORK

SIX MONTHS IN HAWAII
First published in 1875 as Hawaiian archipelago. By John Murray
Kegan Paul Limited

This edition first published in 2009 by
Routledge
2 Park Square, Milton Park, Abingdon, Oxfordshire OX14 4RN

Simultaneously published in the USA and Canada
by Routledge
711 Third Avenue, New York, NY 10017, USA

First issued in paperback 2016

Routledge is an imprint of the Taylor & Francis Group, an informa business

British Library Cataloguing in Publication Data
A catalogue record for this book is available from the British Library

ISBN 13: 978-1-138-98196-6 (pbk)
ISBN 13: 978-0-7103-0811-5 (hbk)

Publisher's Note
The publisher has gone to great lengths to ensure the quality of this reprint
but points out that some imperfections in the original copies may be
apparent. The publisher has made every effort to contact original copyright
holders and would welcome correspondence from those they have been
unable to trace.

TO

MY SISTER,

TO WHOM THESE LETTERS WERE ORIGINALLY WRITTEN,
THEY ARE NOW AFFECTIONATELY

𝕯𝖊𝖉𝖎𝖈𝖆𝖙𝖊𝖉.

A NIGHT SCENE IN THE CRATER OF THE VOLCANO OF KILAUEA, HAWAII.

PREFACE.

WITHIN the last century the Hawaiian islands have been the topic of various works of merit, and some explanation of the reasons which have led me to enter upon the same subject are necessary.

I was travelling for health, when circumstances induced me to land on the group, and the benefit which I derived from the climate tempted me to remain for nearly seven months. During that time the necessity of leading a life of open air and exercise as a means of recovery, led me to travel on horseback to and fro through the islands, exploring the interior, ascending the highest mountains, visiting the active volcanoes, and remote regions which are known to few even of the residents, living among the natives, and otherwise seeing Hawaiian life in all its phases.

At the close of my visit, my Hawaiian friends urged me strongly to publish my impressions and experiences, on the ground that the best books already existing, besides being old, treat chiefly of aboriginal customs and habits now extinct, and of the introduction of Christianity and subsequent historical events. They also represented that I had seen the islands more thoroughly than any foreign visitor, and the volcano of Mauna Loa under specially favourable circumstances, and that I had so completely lived the island life, and acquainted myself with the existing state of the country, as to be rather a *kamaina** than a stranger, and that consequently I should be able to write on Hawaii with a degree of intimacy as well as freshness. My friends at home, who were interested in my narratives, urged me to give them to a wider circle, and my inclinations led me in the same direction, with a sort of longing to make others share something of my own interest and enjoyment.

The letters which follow were written to a near relation, and often hastily and under great difficulties of circumstance, but even with these and other disadvantages, they appear to me the best form of conveying my impressions in their original vividness. With the exception of certain omissions and abridgments, they are printed as they were written, and for such demerits as arise from this mode of publication, I ask the kind indulgence of my readers.

ISABELLA L. BIRD.

January, 1875.

* A native word used to signify an old resident.

LIST OF ILLUSTRATIONS.

—•—

INTRODUCTION

THE SMALL, quietly-dressed English gentlewoman who dis-
embarked at Honolulu from the decrepit paddle-steamer *Nevada*
in January, 1873, must have looked thoroughly and dully conventional to the colourful, flower-bedecked Hawaiians waiting on
shore. They probably thought she was a missionary. Something of
the missionary spirit did indeed possess Miss Bird, but that was
only one aspect of her complex personality – and it was about to be
thrown to the warm, seductive Hawaiian winds; for other, wilder
hankerings also lurked beneath that sober, buttoned-up exterior.

Isabella Bird was forty-one years old when she reached the
Sandwich Islands and her life till then had been an unremitting and
painful struggle to conform to the role considered appropriate to
her social background. Elder daughter of Edward Bird, an English
clergyman, she had grown up in a pious home devoted to earnest
private study and public Christian philanthropy, and, being a
young woman of exceptional intelligence and energy, she had made
her mark even in that limited sphere. She studied widely (botany,
chemistry, biology as well as the more traditionally "feminine"
subjects), wrote for various scholarly periodicals, organised help
schemes for Scottish crofters and Edinburgh slum-dwellers, even
visited Canada and America and published a decorously anony-
mous collection of letters about her experiences.

But all this was small fry for one of Isabella's powerful talents,
and in between these bursts of activity she was prey to numerous
physical and mental ailments, most of them undoubtedly related to
the frustrations of a temperament hopelessly at odds with its

environment. Throughout this time Isabella's closest companion and emotional mainstay was her younger sister Henrietta, whose traditionally 'feminine' virtues – tranquillity, docility, simple unselfishness – Isabella conspicuously lacked. For years she had striven to accept her lot in life with Henrietta's cheerful contentment, but to no avail – her true nature would not be forever denied.

So, in her fortieth year, following further severe bouts of back trouble, insomnia and depression, she sailed for Australia in a desperate search for physical health and mental well-being. But the Antipodes did not provide immediate balm for her troubled spirit: a 'prosaic, hideous country' she soon decided, 'the golden calf its one deity' and 'its colonial young ladies all afflicted with hysteria.' That was the very last thing she needed, so, after several months of disappointment and still in hope of cure, she boarded the *Nevada*. There at last, unexpectedly invigorated by the very real perils of a hurricane in an unseaworthy vessel, her spirits soared, her aches and tensions vanished, she felt whole and well.

'It is so like living in a new world,' she wrote Hennie. 'So free, so fresh, so vital, so careless, so unfettered, so full of interest that one grudges being asleep; and instead of carrying cares and worries and thoughts of the morrow to bed that keep one awake, one falls asleep at once to wake up to another day in which one knows there can be nothing to annoy – no door-bells and "please mems", no dirt, no bills, no demands of any kind . . . Above all, no nervousness, no conventionalities, no dressing . . . I am often in tempestuous spirits. It seems a sort of brief resurrection of a girl of twenty-one.'

That, indeed, is the greatest delight of these remarkable letters from Hawaii: they combine the head-over-heel zest of a twenty-one-year-old who is seeing its tropical beauty for the first time, with the shrewdness of an older head that balances, assesses, puts experiences into a mature perspective. It was difficult, though, for Isabella to be quite rational about scenery so close to every westerner's vision of Paradise and of the kind which, nowadays, exists only in travel brochures. But, at that period, the archipelago was well off the beaten tourist track, seemingly the very antithesis of Victorian England and blissfully free from the squalor, noise and conventional formalities of urban life that Isabella so detested.

She returns to this theme several times, the glorious freedom of the present making her more acutely aware of how harassing, uncongenial and stultifying was her existence at home. The shibboleths of home are soon put aside however and she adapts herself quickly and easily to native ways, being neither irritated, frightened nor shocked by their strangeness. This adaptability, allied to her determined curiosity to find out how other peoples actually lived, were traits that would stand her in good stead during her many future, much harsher journeyings, and would make her a popular and welcome guest wherever she went. 'There is something soothing and gratifying in being so much liked,' she confessed to Hennie. 'It makes me such a nice, genial and pleasant person!'

For six months this pleasant little person dispatched to faithfully waiting Henrietta copious and colourful descriptions of her haphazard wanderings – the leisurely cantering through lush forests and grasslands; the drifting over rolling blue seas in the overcrowded inter-island schooners. She stayed in native grass-huts, on isolated sheep and cattle stations and busy sugar plantations and in a tent pitched 'precariously near' to the crater of the 13,650 feet high Mauna Loa volcano. This last was the culmination of a truly extraordinary feat of mountaineering, considering her age, physique and inexperience and was, in all senses, the dramatic high point of her visit.

When not on the move, Miss Bird usually stayed with the foreign settlers in Hilo and she offers many pleasing glimpses of their habitual pursuits – official gentlemen playing croquet on the Court House lawn, their wives engaged in fancywork or fern-printing, everyone enjoying a round of picnics, riding excursions, gossipy get-togethers. For a short while the simple, picturesque tenor of their uneventful lives appeals to her, though she knows it would not really suit her volatile temperament for long.

Most of the influential foreign inhabitants were Americans, either officials who headed the western-style constitutional government departments or missionaries bent on converting the local 'heathens'. Rather surprisingly, Isabella expresses more sympathy with the American Congregationalists (who preached, along with their brand of Christianity, the annexation of the islands to the United States) than with her compatriots, the Anglicans who, supported by the Anglophile royal family, wanted the islands to retain their independence.

On the religious front, this was probably because Miss Bird's own background was Evangelical (her family being closely related to the Wilberforces) and she was never of the High Church persuasion. Indeed in later years she often commented caustically about English clerics in the East who immured themselves inside imposing residences and churches at safe distances from their 'native flocks'. Politically, she foresaw that the eventual absorption of Hawaii into the United States was inevitable, though she realised sadly that this would be totally destructive of its traditional, feudal way of life. Feeling between the two factions was running high during the 1870s and Isabella has some shrewd observations to make on the issue; she also draws a sympathetic portrait of King Lunalilo who was caught between the two and without the strength to resist either.

But Isabella seldom had politics much in mind during this most carefree and irresponsible of all her many adventures. Returned from a splendid canter around Kauai, she told Hennie that she had 'done wild things which I can't do with white people,' such as 'hallooing and riding without stirrups' and that, when the surprised natives saw her, they'd thrown flowers after her calling *paniola, paniola* – which meant 'cowboy'. 'I thought of nothing all that day,' she concludes . . . And what a triumphant release *that* was for Miss Bird who, when at Home, always rode side-saddle, behaved decorously, never stopped thinking!

Throughout the rest of her long, eventful and courageous life Isabella remained unable to resolve the conflict of these two selves that dwelt within her dumpy frame: she who galloped recklessly to the furthest frontiers of the known world intoxicated by its natural splendours, and she who rode a quiet side-saddle, tamed and chastened by its conventional codes. For most of her stay in Hawaii the former is in the ascendant, but the severe, strait-laced tones of the latter are heard increasingly towards the end of the book, when the first rapturous enchantment has palled somewhat and there are hints of returning tensions and fretfulness. It was time to move on, even though, to the very end, one senses the deep pull the islands' magic exerted on her, the secret temptation, which she confessed only to Hennie, of continuing 'to riot most luxuriantly in the congenial life of the wilds,' perhaps forever.

But Miss Bird, a true-born traveller, never outstayed her welcome anywhere, so she packed her 'bloomer dress' and spurs (probably thinking, erroneously, that she would never wear them again) and left for America. There, in the untamed territory of Colorado, she was to brave new heights of physical derring-do and an emotional experience of greater intensity than any she'd yet known. Yet eventually she once again tore herself away from the seductive life of 'the wilds' and returned to home-loving Henrietta in early 1874.

The two books she wrote about her extended journey: *Six Months in Hawaii* (1875) and *A Lady's Life in the Rocky Mountains* (1879) were greeted with a degree of critical praise that genuinely surprised their author. 'A remarkable, fascinating and beautifully written book' applauded the *Spectator* of the first. And Miss Bird's early biographer, Anna Stoddart (who always emphasized her academic achievements), records that the periodical *Nature* reviewed it 'with warmth not unmixed with astonishment', while members of scientific societies congratulated her – quite rightly – on the accurate information and careful observation it contains. But neither literary success nor scholarly recognition were enough to satisfy Isabella's restive soul for long, and in 1879 she was off again – to Japan, Hong Kong, Malaya.

In the year following this second expedition her beloved sister died of typhoid and, soon afterwards while still stricken with grief, she married Dr John Bishop, the physician who had fought to save Henrietta's life. Obedient to the call of duty (as always when at Home) Mrs John Bishop tried to settle into the humdrum routine of a doctor's wife in Edinburgh; but she was not happy and suffered recurrent bouts of physical ill-health and 'nervous prostration'.

Oddly enough, King Kalakaua, whose succession to the Hawaiian throne Isabella describes in her final chapter, visited her and her husband in their Edinburgh home in 1882. While there, the king conferred upon her the Hawaiian Literary Order of Kapiolani – which suggests that the islanders truly appreciated this delightful book of hers which has filled many readers ever since with a longing to go and see their beautiful homeland for themselves! But Isabella herself never returned, probably preferring to keep intact that 'bright tropic dream' of a land where she first discovered how good a traveller she was and how her spirits could blossom into happiness.

Following her husband's premature death in 1886, Mrs Bishop undertook instead several far more rigorous and perilous journeys. Starting when she was fifty-eight years old, she spent the next decade making extensive explorations into the remote parts of Persia, Kurdistan, Ladakh, Korea, Manchuria and, by way of a grand finale, she made a spectacular three-thousand-mile expedition up the River Yangtze to the very borders of Tibet. The large volumes she wrote about her extraordinary adventures in these little-known parts of the world became travel classics in their day and brought her financial security and popular recognition. For the most part, they lack the spontaneous, enthusiastic sparkle of her earlier works, but there are glimpses of the younger *paniola* Isabella who loved a good gallop in the wilds above all things, who responded with rapture to the bounty, beauty and drama of Nature, who could adapt herself with perfect *sangfroid* to any style of life, whose brave, resourceful spirit never failed – except, that is, when faced with the lacklustre commonplaces of her own homeland. She returned to it reluctantly and finally in 1898 and continued to lecture on her travels and work in various humanitarian causes. At length, after several fruitless attempts to settle into ordinary domestic life, she returned to Edinburgh and died there aged seventy-three in 1904.

Pat Barr

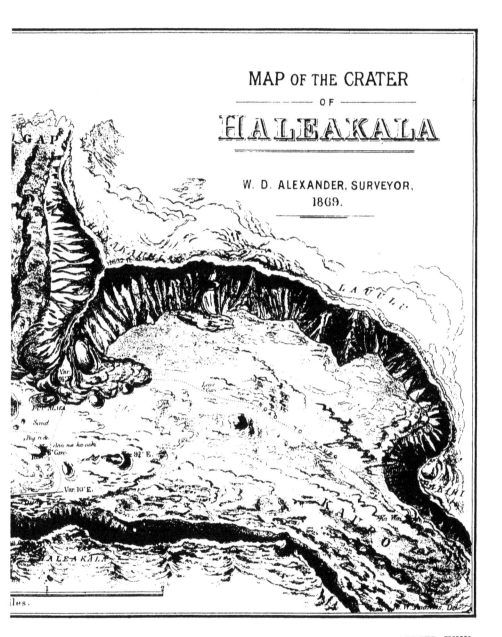

MAP OF THE CRATER

OF

HALEAKALA

W. D. ALEXANDER, SURVEYOR,
1869.

LETTER XXIV.

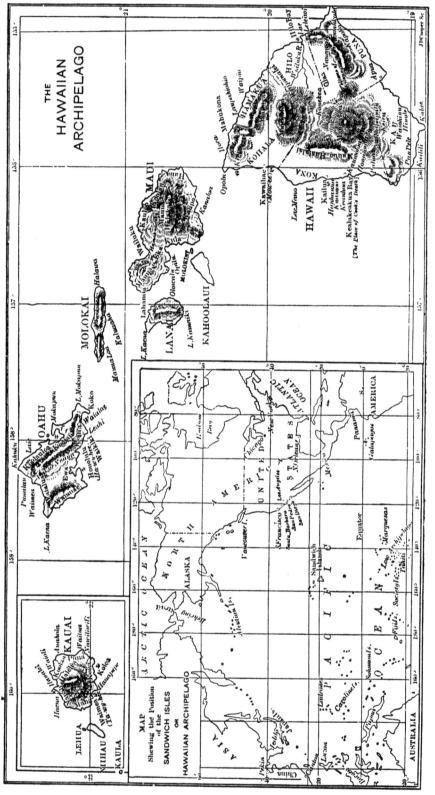

THE
HAWAIIAN
ARCHIPELAGO

MAP
Shewing the Position
of the
SANDWICH ISLES
OR
HAWAIIAN ARCHIPELAGO

To face page 1 of narrative.

TRAVELS

SANDWICH ISLANDS.

INTRODUCTORY CHAPTER.

CANON KINGSLEY, in his charming book on the West
Indies, says, "The undoubted fact is known I find to few
educated English people, that the Coco palm, which
produces coir rope, cocoanuts, and a hundred other useful
things, is not the same plant as the cacao bush which
produces chocolate, or anything like it. I am sorry to
have to insist upon this fact, but till Professor Huxley's
dream and mine is fulfilled, and our schools deign to
teach, in the intervals of Greek and Latin, some slight
knowledge of this planet, and of those of its productions
which are most commonly in use, even this fact may need
to be re-stated more than once."

There is no room for the supposition that the intelligence of Mr. Kingsley's "educated English" acquaintance is below the average, and I should be sorry to form

an unworthy estimate of that of my own circle, though I
have several times met with the foregoing confusion, as
well as the following and other equally ill-informed questions, one or two of which I reluctantly admit that I
might have been guilty of myself before I visited the
Pacific : "Whereabouts are the Sandwich Islands?
They are not the same as the Fijis, are they?   Are they
the same as Otaheite?   Are the natives all cannibals?
What sort of idols do they worship?   Are they as pretty
as the other South Sea Islands?   Does the king wear
clothes?   Who do they belong to?   Does any one live
on them but the savages?   Will anything grow on them?
Are the people very savage?" etc.   Their geographical
position is a great difficulty.   I saw a gentleman of very
extensive information looking for them on the map in the
neighbourhood of Tristran d'Acunha ; and the publishers
of a high-class periodical lately advertised, "Letters from
the Sandwich Islands" as "Letters from the South Sea
Islands."   In consequence of these and similar inter-
rogatories, which are not altogether unreasonable, considering the imperfect teaching of physical geography,
the extent of this planet, the multitude of its productions,
and the enormous number of islands composing Polynesia,
Micronesia, and Melanesia, it is necessary to preface the
following letters with as many preliminary statements as
shall serve to make them intelligible.

The Sandwich Islands do not form one of the South
Sea groups, and have no other connexion with them than
certain affinities of race and language.   They constitute
the only important group in the vast North Pacific Ocean,

in which they are so advantageously placed as to be pretty nearly equidistant from California, Mexico, China, and Japan. They are in the torrid zone, and extend from 18° 50′ to 22° 20′ north latitude, and their longitude is from 154° 53′ to 160° 15′ west from Greenwich. They were discovered by Captain Cook in 1778. They are twelve in number, but only eight are inhabited, and these vary in size from Hawaii, which is 4000 square miles in extent, and 88 miles long by 73 broad, to Kahoolawe, which is only 11 miles long and 8 broad. Their entire superficial area is about 6,100 miles. They are to some extent bounded by barrier reefs of coral, and have few safe harbours. Their formation is altogether volcanic, and they possess the largest perpetually active volcano and the largest extinct crater in the world. They are very mountainous, and two mountain summits on Hawaii are nearly 14,000 feet in height. Their climate for salubrity and general equability is reputed the finest on earth. It is almost absolutely equable, and a man may take his choice between broiling all the year round on the sea level on the leeward side of the islands at a temperature of 80°, and enjoying the charms of a fireside at an altitude where there is frost every night of the year. There is no sickly season, and there are no diseases of locality. The trade winds blow for nine months of the year, and on the windward coasts there is an abundance of rain, and a perennial luxuriance of vegetation.

The Sandwich Islands are not the same as Otaheite nor as the Fijis, from which they are distant about 4,000 miles, nor are their people of the same race. The natives

are not cannibals, and it is doubtful if they ever were so.
Their idols only exist in missionary museums. They
cast them away voluntarily in 1819, at the very time
when missionaries from America sent out to Christianize
the group were on their way round Cape Horn. The
people are all clothed, and the king, who is an educated
gentleman, wears the European dress. The official
designation of the group is " Hawaiian Islands," and
they form an independent kingdom.

The natives are not savages, most decidedly not. They
are on the whole a quiet, courteous, orderly, harmless,
Christian community. The native population has declined from 400,000 as estimated by Captain Cook in
1778 to 49,000, according to the census of 1872. There
are about 5,000 foreign residents, who live on very
friendly terms with the natives, and are mostly subjects
of Kalakaua, the king of the group.

The islands have a thoroughly civilized polity, and the
Hawaiians show a great aptitude for political organization.
They constitute a limited monarchy, and have a constitutional and hereditary king, a parliament with an upper
and lower house, a cabinet, a standing army, a police
force, a Supreme Court of Judicature, a most efficient
postal system, a Governor and Sheriff on each of the
larger islands, court officials, and court etiquette, a common school system, custom houses, a civil list, taxes, a
national debt, and most of the other amenities and ap-
pliances of civilization.

There is no State Church. The majority of the
foreigners, as well as of the natives, are Congregationalists.

The missionaries translated the Bible and other books into Hawaiian, taught the natives to read and write, gave the princes and nobles a high class education, induced the king and chiefs to renounce their oppressive feudal rights, with legal advice framed a constitution which became the law of the land, and obtained the recognition of the little Polynesian kingdom as a member of the brotherhood of civilized nations.

With these few remarks I leave the subject of the volume to develop itself in my letters. They have not had the advantage of revision by any one familiar with the Sandwich Islands, and mistakes and inaccuracies may consequently appear, on which, I hope that my Hawaiian friends will not be very severe. In correcting them, I have availed myself of the very valuable "History of the Hawaiian Islands," by Mr. Jackson Jarves, Ellis' "Tour Round Hawaii," Mr. Brigham's valuable monograph on "The Hawaiian Volcanoes," and sundry reports presented to the legislature during its present session. I have also to express my obligations to the Hon. E. Allen, Chief Justice and Chancellor of the Hawaiian kingdom, Mr. Manley Hopkins, author of "Hawaii," Dr. T. M. Coan, of New York, Professor W. Alexander, Daniel Smith, Esq., and other friends at Honolulu, for assistance most kindly rendered.

ISABELLA L. BIRD.

LETTER I.

Steamer Nevada, North Pacific,
January 19.

A white, unwinking, scintillating sun blazed down upon Auckland, New Zealand. Along the white glaring road from Onehunga, dusty trees and calla lilies drooped with the heat. Dusty thickets sheltered the cicada, whose triumphant din grated and rasped through the palpitating atmosphere. In dusty enclosures, supposed to be gardens, shrivelled geraniums scattered sparsely alone defied the heat. Flags drooped in the stifling air. Men on the verge of sunstroke plied their tasks mechanically, like automatons. Dogs, with flabby and protruding tongues, hid themselves away under archway shadows. The stones of the sidewalks and the brick of the houses radiated a furnace heat. All nature was limp, dusty, groaning, gasping. The day was the climax of a burning fortnight, of heat, draught, and dust, of baked, cracked, dewless land, and oily breezeless seas, of glaring days, passing through fierce fiery sunsets into stifling nights.

I only remained long enough in the capital to observe that it had a look of having seen better days, and that its business streets had an American impress, and, taking a boat at a wharf, in whose seams the pitch was melting, I went off to the steamer *Nevada*, which was anchored out in the bay, preferring to spend the night in her than in the unbearable heat on shore. She belongs to the Webb line, an independent mail adventure, now dying a natural death, undertaken by the New Zealand Government, as much probably out of jealousy of Victoria as anything else. She nearly foundered on her last voyage; her passengers unanimously signed a protest against her unseaworthy condition. She was condemned by the Government surveyor, and her mails were sent to Melbourne. She has, however, been patched up for this trip, and eight passengers, including myself, have trusted ourselves to her. She is a huge paddle-steamer, of the old-fashioned American type, deck above deck, balconies, a pilot-house abaft the foremast, two monstrous walking beams, and two masts which, possibly in case of need, might serve as jury masts.

Huge, airy, perfectly comfortable as she is, not a passenger stepped on board without breathing a more earnest prayer than usual that the voyage might end propitiously. The very first evening statements were whispered about to the effect that her state of disrepair is such that she has not been to her own port for nine months, and has been sailing for that time without a certificate; that her starboard shaft is partially fractured, and that to reduce the strain upon it the floats of her starboard wheel have been shortened five inches, the strain being further reduced by giving her a decided list to port; that her crank is " bandaged," that she is leaky, that her mainmast is sprung, and that with only four hours' steaming many of her boiler tubes, even some of those put in at Auckland, had already given way. I cannot testify concerning the mainmast, though it certainly does comport itself like no other mainmast I ever saw; but the other statements and many more which might be added, are, I believe, substantially correct. That the caulking of the deck was in evil case we véry soon had proof, for during heavy rain above, it was a smart shower in the saloon and state rooms, keeping four stewards employed with buckets and swabs, and compelling us to dine in waterproofs and rubber shoes.

In this dilapidated condition, when two days out from Auckland, we encountered a revolving South Sea hurricane, succinctly entered in the log of the day as "Encountered a very severe hurricane with a very heavy sea." It began at eight in the morning, and never spent its fury till nine at night, and the wind changed its direction eleven times. The *Nevada* left Auckland two feet deeper in the water than she ought to have been, and laboured heavily. Seas struck her under the guards with a heavy, explosive *thud*, and she groaned and strained as if she would párt asunder. It was a long weird day. We held no communication with each other, or with those who could form any rational estimate of the probabilities of our destiny; no officials appeared; the ordinary invariable routine of the steward department was suspended without notice; the sounds were tremendous, and a hot lurid obscurity filled the atmosphere. Soon after four the clamour increased, and the shock of a sea blowing up a part of the fore-guards made the groaning fabric reel and shiver throughout her whole huge bulk. At that time, by

common consent, we assembled in the deck-house, which
had windows looking in all directions, and sat there for
five hours.   Very few words were spoken, and very little
fear was felt.   We understood by intuition that if our
crazy engines failed at any moment to keep the ship's head
to the sea, her destruction would not occupy half-an-hour.
It was all palpable.   There was nothing which the most
experienced seaman could explain to the merest novice.
We hoped for the best, and there was no use in speaking
about the worst.   Nor, indeed, was speech possible, unless
a human voice could have outshrieked the hurricane.

In this deck-house the strainings, sunderings, and
groanings were hardly audible, or rather were overpowered
by a sound which, in thirteen months' experience of the
sea in all weathers, I have never heard, and hope never to
hear again, unless in a staunch ship, one loud, awful,
undying shriek, mingled with a prolonged relentless hiss.
No gathering strength, no languid fainting into momentary
lulls, but one protracted gigantic scream.   And this was
not the whistle of wind through cordage, but the actual
sound of air travelling with tremendous velocity, carrying
with it minute particles of water.   Nor was the sea running
mountains high, for the hurricane kept it down.   Indeed
during those fierce hours no sea was visible, for the whole
surface was caught up and carried furiously into the air,
like snow-drift on the prairies, sibilant, relentless.
There was profound quiet on deck, the little life which
existed being concentrated near the bow, where the
captain was either lashed to the foremast, or in shelter in
the pilot-house.   Never a soul appeared on deck, the force

of the hurricane being such that for four hours any man would have been carried off his feet. Through the swift strange evening our hopes rested on the engine, and amidst the uproar and din, and drifting spray, and shocks of pitiless seas, there was a sublime repose in the spectacle of the huge walking beams, alternately rising and falling, slowly, calmly, regularly, as if the *Nevada* were on á holiday trip within the Golden Gate. At eight in the evening we could hear each other speak, and a little later, through the great masses of hissing drift we discerned black water. At nine Captain Blethen appeared, smoking a cigar with nonchalance, and told us that the hurricane had nearly boxed the compass, and had been the most severe he had known for seventeen years. This grand old man, nearly the oldest captain in the Pacific, won our respect and confidence from the first, and his quiet and masterly handling of this dilapidated old ship is beyond all praise.

When the strain of apprehension was mitigated, we became aware that we had not had anything to eat since breakfast, a clean sweep having been made, not only of the lunch, but of all the glass in the racks above it; but all requests to the stewards were insufficient to procure even biscuits, and at eleven we retired supperless to bed, amidst a confusion of awful sounds, and were deprived of lights as well as food. When we asked for food or light, and made weak appeals on the ground of faintness, the one steward who seemed to dawdle about for the sole purpose [of making himself disagreeable, always replied, " You can't get anything, the stewards are on duty."

We were not accustomed to recognize that stewards had any other duty than that of feeding the passengers, but under the circumstances we meekly acquiesced. We were allowed to know that a part of the foreguards had been carried way, and that iron stanchions four inches thick had been gnarled and twisted like candy sticks, and the constant falling of the saloon casing of the main-mast, showed something wrong there. A heavy clang, heard at intervals by day and night, aroused some sus-picions as to more serious damage, and these were after-wards confirmed. As the wind fell the sea rose, and for some hours realized every description I have read of the majesty and magnitude of the rollers of the South Pacific.

The day after the hurricane something went wrong with the engines, and we were stationary for an hour. We all felt thankful that this derangement which would have jeopardised or sacrificed sixty lives, was then only a slight detention on a summer sea.

Five days out from Auckland we entered the tropics with a temperature of 80° in the water, and 85° in the air, but as the light head airs blew the intense heat of our two smoke stacks aft, we often endured a temperature of 110°. There were quiet heavy tropical showers, and a general misty dampness, and the Navigator Islands, with their rainbow-tinted coral forests, their fringe of coco palms, and groves of banyan and breadfruit trees, those sunniest isles of the bright South Seas, resolved them-selves into dark lumps looming through a drizzling mist. But the showers and the dampness were confined to that

region, and for the last fortnight an unclouded tropical
sun has blazed upon our crawling ship. The boiler
tubes are giving way at the rate of from ten to twenty
daily, the fracture in the shaft is extending, and so,
partially maimed, the old ship drags her 320 feet of length
slowly along. The captain is continually in the engine-room,
and we know when things are looking more unpropitious
than usual by his coming up puffing his cigar with unusual
strength of determination. It has been so far a very
pleasant voyage. The moral, mental, and social qualities
of my fellow-passengers are of a high order, and since
the hurricane we have been rather like a family circle
than a miscellaneous accidental group. For some time
our days went by in reading aloud, working, chess,
draughts and conversation, with two hours at quoits in
the afternoon for exercise; but four days ago the only son
of Mrs. Dexter, who is the only lady on board besides
myself, ruptured a blood vessel on the lungs, and lies in
a most critical state in the deck-house from which he has
not been moved, requiring most careful nursing, incessant
fanning, and the attention of two persons by day and
night. Mrs. D. had previously won the regard of everyone, and I had learned to look on her as a friend from whom
I should be grieved to part. The only hope for the young
man's life is that he should be landed at Honolulu, and
she has urged me so strongly to land with her there,
where she will be a complete stranger, that I have
consented to do so, and consequently shall see the Sandwich Islands. This severe illness has cast a great gloom
over our circle of six, and Mr. D. continues in a state of

so much exhaustion and peril that all our arrangements
as to occupation, recreation, and sleep, are made with
reference to a sick, and as we sometimes fear, a dying
man, whose state is much aggravated by the maltreatment
and stupidity of a dilapidated Scotch doctor, who must
be at least eighty, and whose intellects are obfuscated by
years of whiskey drinking. Two of the gentlemen not
only show the utmost tenderness as nurses, but possess
a skill and experience which are invaluable. They never
leave him by night, and scarcely take needed rest even in
the day, one or other of them being always at hand to
support him when faint, or raise him on his pillows.

It is not only that the *Nevada* is barely seaworthy, and
has kept us broiling in the tropics when we ought to have
been at San Francisco, but her fittings are so old. The
mattresses bulge and burst, and cockroaches creep in and
out, the deck is so leaky that the water squishes up under
the saloon matting as we walk over it, the bread swarms
with minute ants, and we have to pick every piece over
because of weevils. Existence at night is an unequal
fight with rats and cockroaches, and at meals with the
stewards for time to eat. The stewards outnumber the
passengers, and are the veriest riff-raff I have seen on
board ship. At meals, when the captain is not below,
their sole object is to hurry us from the table in order
that they may sit down to a protracted meal; they are
insulting and disobliging, and since illness has been on
board, have shown a want of common humanity which
places them below the rest of their species. The uncon-
cealed hostility with which they regard us is a marvellous

contrast to the natural or purchasable civility or servility which prevails on British steamers. It has its comic side too, and we are content to laugh at it, and at all the other oddities of this vaunted " Mail Line."

Our most serious grievance was the length of time that we were kept in the damp inter-island region of the Tropic of Capricorn. Early breakfasts, cold plunge baths, and the perfect ventilation of our cabins, only just kept us alive. We read, wrote, and talked like automatons, and our voices sounded thin and far away. We decided that heat was less felt in exercise, made up an afternoon quoit party, and played unsheltered from the nearly vertical sun, on decks so hot that we required thick boots for the protection of our feet, but for three days were limp and faint, and hardly able to crawl about or eat. The nights were insupportable. We used to lounge on the bow, and, retire late at night to our cabins, to fight the heat, and scare rats and kill cockroaches with slippers, until driven by the solar heat to rise again unrefreshed to wrestle through another relentless day. We read the " Idylls of the King " and talked of misty meres and reedy fens, of the cool north, with its purple hills, leaping streams, and life-giving breezes, of long northern winters, and ice and snow, but the realities of sultriness and damp scared away our coolest imaginations. In this dismal region, when about forty miles east of Tutuila, a beast popularly known as the " Flying fox " * alighted on our rigging, and was eventually captured

* A Frugiferous bat.

as a prize for the zoological collection at San Francisco. He is a most interesting animal, something like an exaggerated bat. His wings are formed of a jet black membrane, and have a highly polished claw at the extremity of each, and his feet consist of five beautifully polished long black claws, with which he hangs on head downwards. His body is about twice the size of that of a very large rat, black and furry underneath, and with red foxy fur on his head and back. His face is pointed, with a very black nose and prominent black eyes, with a savage, remorseless expression. His wings, when extended, measure forty-eight inches across, and his flying powers are prodigious. He snapped like a dog at first, but is now quite tame, and devours quantities of dried figs, the only diet he will eat.

We crossed the Equator in Long. 159° 44′, but in consequence of the misty weather it was not till we reached Lat. 10° 6′ N. that the Pole star, cold and pure, glistened far above the horizon, and two hours later we saw the coruscating Pleiades, and the starry belt of Orion, the blessed familiar constellations of "auld lang syne," and a "breath of the cool north," the first I have felt for five months, fanned the tropic night and the calm silvery Pacific. From that time we have been indifferent to our crawling pace, except for the sick man's sake. The days dawn in rose colour and die in gold, and through their long hours a sea of delicious blue shimmers beneath the sun, so soft, so blue, so dreamlike, an ocean worthy of its name, the

enchanted region of perpetual calm, and an endless
summer. Far off, for many an azure league, rims of
rock, fringed with the graceful coco palm, girdle still
lagoons, and are themselves encircled by coral reefs on
which the ocean breaks all the year in broad drifts of
foam. Myriads of flying fish and a few dolphins and
Portuguese men-of-war flash or float through the scarcely
undulating water. But we look in vain for the "sails
of silk and ropes of sendal," which are alone appropriate to this dream-world. The Pacific in this region is
an indolent blue expanse, pure and lonely, an almost
untraversed sea. We revel in these tropic days of tran-
scendent glory, in the balmy breath which just stirs the
dreamy blue, in the brief, fierce crimson sunsets, in the
soft splendour of the nights, when the moon and stars
hang like lamps out of a lofty and distant vault, and
in the pearly crystalline dawns, when the sun rising
through a veil of rose and gold "rejoices as a giant to
run his course," and brightens by no "pale gradations"
into the "perfect day."

P.S.—To-morrow morning we expect to sight land.
In spite of minor evils, our voyage has been a singularly pleasant one. The condition of the ship and her
machinery warrants the strongest condemnation, but her
discipline is admirable, and so are many of her regulations, and we might have had a much more disagreeable voyage in a better ship. Captain Blethen is beyond
all praise, and so is the chief engineer, whose duties

are incessant and most harassing, owing to the critical
state of the engines.   The *Nevada* now presents a
grotesque appearance, for within the last few hours she
has received such an added list to port that her starboard wheel looks nearly out of the water.

I. L. B.

LETTER II.

YESTERDAY morning at 6.30 I was aroused by the news that " The Islands " were in sight. Oahu in the distance, a group of grey, barren peaks rising verdureless out of the lonely sea, was not an exception to the rule that the first sight of land is a disappointment. Owing to the clear atmosphere, we seemed only five miles off, but in reality we were twenty, and the land improved as we neared it. It was the fiercest day we had had, the deck was almost too hot to stand upon, the sea and sky were both magnificently blue, and the unveiled sun turned every minute ripple into a diamond flash. As we approached, the island changed its character. There were lofty peaks, truly—grey and red, sun-scorched and wind-bleached, glowing here and there with traces of their fiery origin; but they were cleft by deep chasms and ravines of cool shadow and entrancing green, and falling water streaked their sides—a most welcome vision after eleven months of the desert sea and the dusty browns of Australia and New Zealand. Nearer yet, and the coast line came into sight, fringed by the feathery cocoanut tree of the tropics, and marked by a long line of surf. The grand promontory of Diamond Head, its fiery sides now softened by a haze of green, terminated the wavy line of palms ; then the Punchbowl, a very perfect extinct crater, brilliant with every shade of red volcanic ash, blazed against the green skirts of the mountains. We were close to the coral reef before the cry, " There's Honolulu ! " made us aware of the proximity of the capital of the island kingdom, and then, indeed, its existence had almost to be taken upon trust, for besides the lovely wooden and grass huts, with deep verandahs, which nestled under palms and bananas on soft green sward, margined by the bright sea sand, only two church spires and a few grey roofs appeared above the trees.

We were just outside the reef, and near enough to hear that deep sound of the surf which, through the ever serene summer years girdles the Hawaiian Islands with perpetual thunder, before the pilot glided alongside, bringing the news which Mark Twain had prepared us to receive with interest, that " Prince Bill " had been unanimously elected to the throne. The surf ran white and pure over the environing coral reef, and as we passed through the narrow channel, we almost saw the coral forests deep down under the *Nevada's* keel; the coral fishers plied their graceful trade ; canoes with outriggers rode the combers, and glided with inconceivable rapidity round our ship ; amphibious brown beings sported in the transparent waves ; and within the reef lay a calm surface of water of a wonderful blue, entered by a narrow, intricate passage of the deepest indigo. And beyond the reef and beyond the blue, nestling among cocoanut trees and bananas, umbrella trees and breadfruits, oranges, mangoes, hibiscus, algaroba, and passion-flowers, almost hidden in the deep, dense greenery, was Honolulu. Bright blossom of a summer sea! Fair Paradise of the Pacific!

Inside the reef the magnificent iron-clad *California* (the flag-ship) and another huge American war vessel, the *Benicia*, are moored in line with the· British corvette *Scout*, within 200 yards of the shore; and their boats were constantly passing and re-passing, among countless canoes filled with natives. Two coasting schooners were just leaving the harbour, and the inter-island steamer *Kilauea*, with her deck crowded with natives, was just coming in. By noon the great decrepit *Nevada*, which has no wharf at which she can lie in sleepy New Zealand, was moored alongside a very respectable one in this enterprising little Hawaiian capital.

We looked down from the towering deck on a crowd of two or three thousand people—whites, Kanakas, China-men—and hundreds of them at once made their way on board, and streamed over the ship, talking, laughing, and remarking upon us in a language which seemed without backbone. Such rich brown men and women they were, with wavy, shining black hair, large, brown, lustrous eyes, and rows of perfect teeth like ivory. Everyone was smiling. The forms of the women seem to be inclined towards obesity, but their drapery, which consists of a sleeved garment which falls in ample and unconfined folds from their shoulders to their feet, partly conceals this defect, which is here regarded as a beauty. Some of these dresses were black, but many of those worn by the younger women were of pure white, crimson, yellow, scarlet, blue, or light green. The men displayed their lithe, graceful figures to the best advantage in white trousers and gay Garibaldi shirts. A few of the women wore coloured handkerchiefs twined round their hair, but generally both men and women wore straw hats, which the men set jauntily on one side of their heads, and aggravated their appearance yet more by bandana handkerchiefs of rich bright colours round their necks, knotted loosely on the left side, with a grace to which, I think, no Anglo-Saxon dandy could attain. Without an exception the men and women wore wreaths and garlands of flowers, carmine, orange, or pure white, twined round their hats, and thrown carelessly round their necks, flowers unknown to me, but redolent of the tropics in fragrance and colour. Many of the young beauties wore the gorgeous blossom of the red hibiscus among their abundant, unconfined, black hair, and many, besides the garlands, wore festoons of a sweet-scented vine, or of an exquisitely beautiful fern, knotted behind and hanging half-way down their dresses. These adornments of natural flowers are most attractive. Chinamen, all alike, very yellow, with almond-shaped eyes, youthful, hairless faces, long pigtails, spotlessly clean clothes, and an expression of mingled cunning and simplicity, "foreigners," half-whites, a few negroes, and a very few dark-skinned Polynesians from the far-off South Seas, made up the rest of the rainbow-tinted crowd.

The "foreign" ladies, who were there in great numbers, generally wore simple light prints or muslins, and white straw hats, and many of them so far conformed to native custom as to wear natural flowers round their hats and throats. But where were the hard, angular, care-worn, sallow, passionate faces of men and women, such as form the majority of every crowd at home, as well as in America and Australia ? The conditions of life must surely be easier here, and people must have found rest from some of its burdensome conventionalities. The foreign ladies, in their simple, tasteful, fresh attire, inno-cent of the humpings and bunchings, the monstrosities and deformities of ultra-fashionable bad taste, beamed with cheerfulness, friendliness, and kindliness. Men and women looked as easy, contented, and happy as if care never came near them. I never saw such healthy, bright complexions as among the women, or such " sparkling smiles," or such a diffusion of feminine grace and gra-ciousness anywhere.

Outside this motley, genial, picturesque crowd about 200 saddled horses were standing, each with the Mexican saddle, with its lassoing horn in front, high peak behind, immense wooden stirrups, with great leathern guards, silver or brass bosses, and coloured saddle-cloths. The saddles were the only element of the picturesque that these Hawaiian steeds possessed. They were sorry, lean, undersized beasts, looking in general as if the emergen-cies of life left them little time for eating or sleeping. They stood calmly in the broiling sun, heavy-headed and heavy-hearted, with flabby ears and pendulous lower lips, limp and rawboned, a doleful type of the " creation which groaneth and travaileth in misery." All these belonged to the natives, who are passionately fond of riding. Every now and then a flower-wreathed Hawaiian woman, in her full radiant garment, sprang on one of these animals astride, and dashed along the road at full gallop, sitting on her horse as square and easy as a hussar. In the crowd and outside of it, and everywhere, there were piles of fruit for sale—oranges and guavas, strawberries, papayas, bananas (green and golden), cocoanuts, and other rich, fantastic productions of a prolific climate, where nature gives of her wealth the whole year round. Strange fishes, strange in shape and colour, crimson, blue, orange, rose, gold, such fishes as flash like living light through the coral groves of these enchanted seas, were there for sale, and coral divers were there with their treasures—branch coral, as white as snow, each perfect specimen weighing from eight to twenty pounds. But no one pushed his wares for sale—we were at liberty to look and admire, and pass on unmolested. No vexatious restrictions obstructed our landing. A sum of two dollars for the support of the Queen's Hospital is levied on each passenger, and the examination of ordinary luggage, if it exists, is a mere form. From the demeanour of the crowd it was at once apparent that the conditions of conquerors and conquered do not exist. On the contrary, many of the foreigners there were subjects of a Hawaiian king, a reversal of the ordinary relations between a white and a coloured race which it is not easy yet to appreciate.

Two of my fellow-passengers, who were going on to San Francisco, were anxious that I should accompany

them to the Pali, the great excursion from Honolulu;
and leaving Mr. M—— to make all arrangements for the
Dexters and myself, we hired a buggy, destitute of any
peculiarity but a native driver, who spoke nothing but
Hawaiian, and left the ship. This place is quite unique.
It is said that 15,000 people are buried away in these
low-browed, shadowy houses, under the glossy, dark-
leaved trees, but except in one or two streets of miscellaneous, old-fashioned looking stores, arranged with a
distinct leaning towards native tastes, it looks like a large
village, or rather like an aggregate of villages. As we
drove through the town we could only see our immediate
surroundings, but each had a new fascination. We drove
along roads with over-arching trees, through whose dense
leafage the noon sunshine only trickled in dancing, broken
lights; umbrella trees, caoutchouc, bamboo, mango,
orange, breadfruit, candlenut, monkey pod, date and coco
palms, alligator pears, "prides" of Barbary, India, and
Peru, and huge-leaved, wide-spreading trees, exotics from
the South Seas, many of them rich in parasitic ferns, and
others blazing with bright, fantastic blossoms. The air
was heavy with odours of gardenia, tuberose, oleanders,
roses, lilies, and the great white trumpet-flower, and myriads of others whose names I do not know, and verandahs
were festooned with a gorgeous trailer with magenta
blossoms, passion-flowers, and a vine with masses of
trumpet-shaped, yellow, waxy flowers. The delicate
tamarind and the feathery algaroba intermingled their
fragile grace with the dark, shiny foliage of the South
Sea exotics, and the deep red, solitary flowers of the

hibiscus rioted among dear familiar fuschias and geraniums, which here attain the height and size of large
rhododendrons.

Few of the new trees surprised me more than the
papaya. It is a perfect gem of tropical vegetation. It
has a soft, indented stem, which runs up quite straight to
a height of from 15 to 30 feet, and is crowned by a
profusion of large, deeply indented leaves, with long
foot-stalks, and among, as well as considerably below
these, are the flowers or the fruit, in all stages of development. This, when ripe, is bright yellow, and the size
of a musk melon. Clumps of bananas, the first sight of
which, like that of the palm, constitutes a new experience, shaded the native houses with their wonderful
leaves, broad and deep green, from five to ten feet long.
The breadfruit is a superb tree, about 60 feet high, with
deep green, shining leaves, a foot broad, sharply and
symmetrically cut, worthy, from their exceeding beauty
of form, to take the place of the acanthus in architectural
ornament, and throwing their pale green fruit into delicate contrast. All these, with the exquisite rose apple,
with a deep red tinge in its young leaves, the fan palm,
the chirimoya, and numberless others, and the slender
shafts of the coco palms rising high above them, with
their waving plumes and perpetual fruitage, were a perfect
festival of beauty.

In the deep shade of this perennial greenery the people
dwell. The foreign houses show a very various individuality. The peculiarity in which all seem to share is,
that everything is decorated and festooned with flowering

trailers. It is often difficult to tell what the architecture
is, or what is house and what is vegetation; for all angles,
and lattices, and balustrades, and verandahs are hidden
by jessamine or passion-flowers, or the gorgeous flame-
like **Bougainvillea.** Many of the dwellings straggle over
the ground without an upper story, and have very deep
verandahs, through which I caught glimpses of cool,
shady rooms, with matted floors. Some look as if they
had been transported from the old-fashioned villages of
the Connecticut Valley, with their clap-board fronts
painted white and jalousies painted green; but then the
deep verandah in which families lead an open-air life has
been added, and the chimneys have been omitted, and
the New England severity and angularity are toned down
and draped out of sight by these festoons of large-leaved,
bright-blossomed, tropical climbing plants. Besides the
frame houses there are houses built of blocks of a cream-
coloured coral conglomerate laid in cement, of *adobe*,
or large sun-baked bricks, plastered; houses of grass
and bamboo; houses on the ground and houses raised
on posts; but nothing looks prosaic, commonplace, or
mean, for the glow and luxuriance of the tropics rest on
all. Each house has a large garden or "yard," with
lawns of bright perennial greens and banks of blazing,
many-tinted flowers, and lines of Dracæna, and other
foliage plants, with their great purple or crimson leaves,
and clumps of marvellous lilies, gladiolas, ginger, and
many plants unknown to me. Fences and walls are
altogether buried by passion-flowers, the night-blowing
Cereus, and the tropæolum, mixed with geraniums,

fuschia, and jessamine, which cluster and entangle over them in indescribable profusion. A soft air moves through the upper branches, and the drip of water from miniature fountains falls musically on the perfumed air. This is midwinter! The summer, they say, is thermometrically hotter, but practically cooler, because of the regular trades which set in in April, but now, with the shaded thermo-meter at 80° and the sky without clouds, the heat is not oppressive.

The mixture of the neat grass houses of the natives with the more elaborate homes of the foreign residents has a very pleasant look. The " aborigines " have not been crowded out of sight, or into a special " quarter." We saw many groups of them sitting under the trees outside their houses, each group with a mat in the centre, with calabashes upon it containing *poi*, the national Hawaiian dish, a fermented paste made from the root of the *kalo*, or *arum esculentum*. As we emerged on the broad road which leads up the Nuuanu Valley to the mountains, we saw many patches of this *kalo*, a very handsome tropical plant, with large leaves of a bright tender green. Each plant was growing on a small hillock, with water round it. There were beautiful vegetable gardens also, in which Chinamen raise for sale not only melons, pineapples, sweet potatoes, and other edibles of hot climates, but the familiar fruits and vegetables of the temperate zones. In patches of surpassing neatness, there were strawberries, which are ripe here all the year, peas, carrots, turnips, asparagus, lettuce, and celery. I saw no other plants or trees which grow at home, but

recognized as hardly less familiar growths the Victorian
Eucalyptus, which has not had time to become gaunt
and straggling, the Norfolk Island pine, which grows
superbly here, and the handsome Moreton Bay fig.   But
the chief feature of this road is the number of residences;
I had almost written of pretentious residences, but the
term would be a base slander, as I have jumped to the
conclusion that the twin vulgarities of ostentation and
pretence have no place here.   But certainly for a mile
and a half or more there are many very comfortable-
looking dwellings, very attractive to the eye, with an ease
and imperturbable serenity of demeanour as if they had
nothing to fear from heat, cold, wind, or criticism.   Their
architecture is absolutely unostentatious, and their one
beauty is that they are embowered among trailers,
shadowed by superb exotics, and surrounded by banks
of flowers, while the stately cocoanut, the banana, and
the candlenut, the aborigines of Oahu, are nowhere
displaced.   One house with extensive grounds, a perfect
wilderness of vegetation, was pointed out as the summer
palace of Queen Emma, or Kaleleonalani, widow of
Kamehameha IV., who visited England a few years ago,
and the finest garden of all as that of a much respected
Chinese merchant, named Afong.   Oahu, at least on this
leeward side, is not tropical looking, and all this tropical
variety and luxuriance which delight the eye result from
foreign enthusiasm and love of beauty and shade.

When we ascended above the scattered dwellings and
had passed the tasteful mausoleum, with two tall Kahilis,*

* The kahili is shaped like an enormous bottle brush.   The fines

THE NUUANU PALI, OR PRECIPICE, NEAR HONOLULU. [*Page* 29.

or feather plumes, at the door of the tomb in which the last of the Kamehamehas received Christian burial, the glossy, redundant, arborescent vegetation ceased. At that height a shower of rain falls on nearly every day in the year, and the result is a green sward which England can hardly rival, a perfect sea of verdure, darkened in the valley and more than half way up the hill sides by the foliage of the yellow-blossomed and almost impenetrable hibiscus, brightened here and there by the pea-green candlenut. Streamlets leap from crags and ripple along the roadside, every rock and stone is hidden by moist-looking ferns, as aerial and delicate as marabout feathers, and when the windings of the valley and the projecting spurs of mountains shut out all indications of Honolulu, in the cool green loneliness one could image oneself in the temperate zones. The peculiarity of the scenery is, that the hills, which rise to a height of about 4,000 feet, are wall-like ridges of grey or coloured rock, rising precipitously out of the trees and grass, and that these walls are broken up into pinnacles and needles. At the Pali (wall-like precipice), the summit of the ascent of 1,000 feet, we left our buggy, and passing through a gash in the rock the celebrated view burst on us with

are sometimes twenty feet high, with handles twelve or fifteen feet long, covered with tortoiseshell and whale tooth ivory. [The upper part is formed of a cylinder of wicker work about a foot in diameter, on which red, black, and yellow feathers are fastened. These insignia are carried in procession instead of banners, and used to be fixed in the ground near the temporary residence of the king or chiefs. At the funeral of the late king seventy-six large and small kahilis were carried by the retainers of chief families.

overwhelming effect. Immense masses of black and ferruginous volcanic rock, hundreds of feet in nearly perpendicular height, formed the pali on either side, and the ridge extended northwards for many miles, presenting a lofty, abrupt mass of grey rock broken into fantastic pinnacles, which seemed to pierce the sky. A broad, umbrageous mass of green clothed the lower buttresses, and fringed itself away in clusters of coco palms on a garden-like stretch below, green with grass and sugarcane, and dotted with white houses, each with its palm and banana grove, and varied by eminences which looked like long extinct tufa cones. Beyond this enchanted region stretched the coral reef, with its white wavy line of endless surf, and the broad blue Pacific, ruffled by a breeze whose icy freshness chilled us where we stood. Narrow streaks on the landscape, every now and then disappearing behind intervening hills, indicated bridle tracks connected with a frightfully steep and rough zigzag path cut out of the face of the cliff on our right. I could not go down this on foot without a sense of insecurity, but mounted natives driving loaded horses descended with perfect impunity into the dreamland below.

This pali is the scene of one of the historic tragedies of this island. Kamehameha the Conqueror, who after fierce fighting and much ruthless destruction of human life united the island sovereignties in his own person, routed the forces of the King of Oahu in the Nuuanu Valley, and drove them in hundreds up the precipice, from which they leaped in despair and madness, and their bones lie bleaching 800 feet below.

THE PAU' OR HAWAIIAN LADIES' HOLIDAY RIDING DRESS. [*Page* 31

The drive back here was delightful, from the wintry height, where I must confess that we shivered, to the slumbrous calm of an endless summer, the glorious tropical trees, the distant view of cool chasm-like valleys, with Honolulu sleeping in perpetual shade, and the still blue ocean, without a single sail to disturb its profound solitude. Saturday afternoon is a gala-day here, and the broad road was so thronged with brilliant equestrians, that I thought we should be ridden over by the reckless laughing rout. There were hundreds of native horsemen and horsewomen, many of them doubtless on the dejected quadrupeds I saw at the wharf, but a judicious application of long rowelled Mexican spurs, and a degree of emulation, caused these animals to tear along at full gallop. The women seemed perfectly at home in their gay, brass-bossed, high peaked saddles, flying along astride, barefooted, with their orange and scarlet riding dresses streaming on each side beyond their horses' tails, a bright kaleidoscopic flash of bright eyes, white teeth, shining hair, garlands of flowers and many-coloured dresses ; while the men were hardly less gay, with fresh flowers round their jaunty hats, and the vermilion-coloured blossoms of the *Ohia* round their brown throats. Sometimes a troop of twenty of these free-and-easy female riders went by at a time, a graceful and exciting spectacle, with a running accompaniment of vociferation and laughter. Among these we met several of the *Nevada's* officers, riding in the stiff, wooden style which Anglo-Saxons love, and a horde of jolly British sailors from H.M.S. *Scout*, rushing helter skelter, colliding with

everybody, bestriding their horses as they would a topsail-
yard, hanging on to manes and lassoing horns, and
enjoying themselves thoroughly. In the shady tortuous
streets we met hundreds more of native riders, dashing
at full gallop without fear of the police. Many of the
women were in flowing riding-dresses of pure white, over
which their unbound hair, and wreaths of carmine-tinted
flowers fell most picturesquely.

All this time I had not seen our domicile, and when
our drive ended under the quivering shadow of large
tamarind and algaroba trees, in front of a long, stone,
two-storied house with two deep verandahs festooned
with clematis and passion flowers, and a shady lawn in
front, I felt as if in this fairy land anything might be
expected.

This is the perfection of an hotel. Hospitality seems
to take possession of and appropriate one as soon as one
enters its never-closed door, which is on the lower
verandah. There is a basement, in which there are a
good many bedrooms, the bar, and billiard-room. This
is entered from the garden, under two semicircular flights
of stairs which lead to the front entrance, a wide corridor
conducting to the back entrance. This is crossed by
another running the whole length, which opens into a very
large many-windowed dining-room which occupies the
whole width of the hotel. On the same level there is a
large parlour, with French windows opening on the
verandah. Upstairs there are two similar corridors on
which all the bedrooms open, and each room has one or
more French windows opening on the verandah, with

doors as well, made like German shutters, to close instead
of the windows, ensuring at once privacy and coolness.
The rooms are tastefully furnished with varnished pine
with a strong aromatic scent, and there are plenty of
lounging-chairs on the verandah, where people sit and
receive their intimate friends. The result of the construction of the hotel is that a breeze whispers through
it by day and night.

Everywhere, only pleasant objects meet the eye. One
can sit all day on the back verandah, watching the play
of light and colour on the mountains and the deep blue
green of the Nuuanu Valley, where showers, sunshine,
and rainbows make perpetual variety. The great dining-
room is delicious. It has no curtains, and its decorations
are cool and pale. Its windows look upon tropical trees
in one direction, and up to the cool mountains in the other.
Piles of bananas, guavas, limes, and oranges, decorate
the tables at each meal, and strange vegetables, fish, and
fruits vary the otherwise stereotyped American hotel fare.
There are no female domestics. The host is a German,
the manager an American, the steward an Hawaiian, and
the servants are all Chinamen in spotless white linen, with
pigtails coiled round their heads, and an air of super-
abundant good-nature. They know very little English,
and make most absurd mistakes, but they are cordial,
smiling, and obliging, and look cool and clean. The
hotel seems the great public resort of Honolulu, the
centre of stir—club-house, exchange and drawing-room
in one. Its wide corridors and verandahs are lively with
English and American naval uniforms, several planters'

families are here for the season ; and with health seekers
from California, resident boarders, whaling captains,
tourists from the British Pacific Colonies, and a stream
of townspeople always percolating through the corridors
and verandahs, it seems as lively and free-and-easy as a
place can be, pervaded by the kindliness and bonhommie
which form an important item in my first impressions of
the islands. The hotel was lately built by government
at a cost of $120,000, a sum which forms a considerable
part of that token of an advanced civilization, a National
Debt. The minister whose scheme it was seems to be
severely censured on account of it, but undoubtedly it
brings strangers and their money into the kingdom, who
would have avoided it had they been obliged as formerly
to cast themselves on the hospitality of the residents.
The present proprietor has it rent-free for a term of
years, but I fear that it is not likely to prove a successful
speculation either for him or the government. I dislike
health resorts, and abhor this kind of life, but for those
who like both, I cannot imagine a more fascinating
residence. The charges are $15 a week, or $3 a day,
but such a kindly, open-handed, system prevails that
I am not conscious that I am paying anything! This
sum includes hot and cold plunge baths *ad libitum*, justly
regarded as a necessity in this climate.

Dr. McGrew has hope that our invalid will rally in this
healing, equable atmosphere. Our kind fellow-passengers
are here, and take turns in watching and fanning him.
Through the half-closed jalousies we see bread-fruit
trees, delicate tamarinds and algarobas, fan-palms, date-

palms and bananas, and the deep blue Pacific gleams here
and there through the plumage of the cocoanut trees.   A
soft breeze, scented with a slight aromatic odour, wanders
in at every opening, bringing with it, mellowed by
distance, the hum and clatter of the busy cicada.   The
nights are glorious, and so absolutely still, that even the
feathery foliage of the algaroba is at rest.   The stars
seem to hang among the trees like lamps, and the crescent
moon gives more light than the full moon at home.   The
evening of the day we landed, parties of officers and ladies
mounted at the door, and with much mirth disappeared
on moonlight rides, and the white robes of flower-crowned
girls gleamed among the trees, as groups of natives went
by speaking a language which sounded more like the
rippling of water than human speech.   Soft music came
from the ironclads in the harbour, and from the royal
band at the king's palace, and a rich fragrance of dewy
blossoms filled the delicious air.   These are indeed the
" isles of Eden," the " sun lands," musical with beauty.
They seem to welcome us to their enchanted shores.
Everything is new but nothing strange ; for as I enjoyed
the purple night, I remembered that I had seen such
islands in dreams in the cold gray North.   " How
sweet," I thought it would be, thus to hear far off, the
low sweet murmur of the " sparkling brine," to rest, and

> " Ever to seem
> Falling asleep in a half-dream."

A half-dream only, for one would not wish to be quite
asleep and lose the consciousness of this delicious outer

world. So I thought one moment. The next I heard a droning, humming sound, which certainly was not the surf upon the reef. It came nearer—there could be no mistake. I felt a stab, and found myself the centre of a swarm of droning, stabbing, malignant mosquitos. No, even this is not paradise ! I am ashamed to say that on my first night in Honolulu I sought an early refuge from this intolerable infliction, in profound and prosaic sleep behind mosquito curtains.

I. L. B.

LETTER III.

SUNDAY was a very pleasant day here. Church bells rang, and the shady streets were filled with people in holiday dress. There are two large native churches, the Kaumakapili, and the Kaiwaiaho, usually called the stone church. The latter is an immense substantial building, for the erection of which each Christian native brought a block of rock-coral. There is a large Roman Catholic church, the priests of which are said to have been somewhat successful in proselytizing operations. The Reformed Catholic, or English temporary cathedral, is a tasteful but very simple wooden building, standing in pretty grounds, on which a very useful institution for boarding and training native and half-white girls, and the reception of white girls as day scholars, also stands. This is in connection with Miss Sellon's Sisterhood at Devonport. Another building, alongside the cathedral, is used for English service in Hawaiian. There are two Congregational churches : the old "Bethel," of which the Rev. S. C. Damon, known to all strangers, and one of the oldest and most respected Honolulu residents, is the minister; and the "Fort St. Church," which has a large and influential congregation, and has been said to " run the government," because its members compose the majority of the Cabinet. Lunalilo, the present king, has cast in his lot with the Congregationalists, but queen Emma is an earnest member of the Anglican Church, and attends the Liturgical Hawaiian Service in order to throw the weight of her influence with the natives into the scale of that communion. Her husband spent many of his later days in translating the Prayer-Book. As is natural, most of the natives belong to the denomination from which they or their fathers received the Christian faith, and the majority of the foreigners are of the same persuasion. The New England Puritan influence, with its rigid Sabbatarianism, though considerably worn away, is still influential enough to produce a general appearance of Sabbath observance. The stores are closed, the church-going is very demonstrative, and the pleasure-seeking is very unobtrusive. The wharves are profoundly quiet.

I went twice to the English Cathedral, and was interested to see there a lady in a nun's habit, with a number of brown girls, who was pointed out to me as Sister Bertha, who has been working here usefully for many years. The ritual is high. I am told that it is above the desires and the comprehension of most of the island episcopalians, but the zeal and disinterestedness of Bishop Willis will, in time, I doubt not, win upon those who prize such qualities. He called in the afternoon, and took me to his pretty, unpretending residence up the Nuuanu Valley. He has a training and boarding school there for native boys, some of whom were at church in the morning as a surpliced choir. The bishop, his sister, the schoolmaster, and fourteen boys take their meals together in a refectory, the boys acting as servitors by turns. There is service every morning at 6.30 in the private chapel attached to the house, and also in the cathedral a little later. Early risers, so near the equator, must get up by candlelight all the year round.

This morning we joined our kind friends from the *Nevada* for the last time at breakfast. I have noticed that there is often a centrifugal force which acts upon passengers who have been long at sea together, dispersing them on reaching port. Indeed, the temporary enforced cohesion is often succeeded by violent repulsion. But in this instance we deeply regret the dissolution of our pleasant fraternity ; the less so, however, that this wonderful climate has produced a favourable change in Mr. D., who no longer requires the hourly attention they have hitherto shown him. The mornings here, dew-bathed and rose-flushed, are, if possible, more lovely than the nights, and people are astir early to enjoy them. The American consul and Mr. Damon called while we were sitting at our eight-o'clock breakfast, from which I gather that formalities are dispensed with. After spending the morning in hunting among the stores for things which were essential for the invalid, I lunched in the *Nevada* with Captain Blethen and our friends.

Next to the advent of " national ships " (a euphemism or men-of-war), the arrivals and departures of the New Zealand mail-steamers constitute the great excitement of Honolulu, and the failures, mishaps, and wonderful un-punctuality of this Webb line are highly stimulating in a region where "nothing happens." The loungers were saying that the *Nevada's* pumps were going for five days before we arrived, and pointed out the clearness of the water which was running from them at the wharf as an evidence that she was leaking badly.* The crowd of natives was enormous, and the foreigners were there in hundreds. She was loading with oranges and green bananas up to the last moment,—those tasteless bananas which, out of the tropics, misrepresent this most delicious and ambrosial fruit.

There was a far greater excitement for the natives, for King Lunalilo was about to pay a state visit to the American flag-ship *California*, and every available place along the wharves and roads was crowded with kanakas anxious to see him. I should tell you that the late king, being without heirs, ought to have nominated his successor; but it is said that a sorceress, under whose influence he was, persuaded him that his death would follow upon this act. When he died, two months ago, leaving the succession unprovided for, the duty of electing a sovereign, according to the constitution, devolved upon the people through their representatives, and they exercised it with a combination of order and enthusiasm which reflects great credit on their civilization. They chose the highest chief on the islands, Lunalilo (Above All), known among foreigners as "Prince Bill," and at this time letters of

---

* A week after her sailing, this unlucky ship put back with some mysterious ailment, and on her final arrival at San Francisco, her condition was found to be such that it was a marvel that she had made the passage at all.

congratulation are pouring in upon him from his brethren, the sovereigns of Europe.

The spectacular effect of a pageant here is greatly heightened by the cloudless blue sky, and the wealth of light and colour. It was very hot, almost too hot for sight-seeing, on the *Nevada's* bow. Expectation among the lieges became tremendous and vociferous when Admiral Pennock's sixteen-oared barge, with a handsome awning, followed by two well-manned boats, swept across the strip of water which lies between the ships and the shore. Outrigger canoes, with garlanded men and women, were poised upon the motionless water or darted gracefully round the ironclads, as gracefully to come to rest. Then a stir and swaying of the crowd, and the American Admiral was seen standing at the steps of an English barouche and four, and an Hawaiian imitation of an English cheer rang out upon the air. More cheering, more excitement, and I saw nothing else till the Admiral's barge, containing the Admiral, and the King dressed in a plain morning suit with a single decoration, swept past the *Nevada*. The suite followed in the other boats,— brown men and white, governors, ministers, and court dignitaries, in Windsor uniforms, but with an added resplendency of plumes, epaulettes, and gold lace. As soon as Lunalilo reached the *California*, the yards of the three ships were manned, and amidst cheering which rent the air, and the deafening thunder of a royal salute from sixty-three guns of heavy calibre, the popular descendant of seventy generations of sceptred savages stepped on board the flag-ship's deck. No higher honours could

have been paid to the Emperor " of all the Russias." I
have seen few sights more curious than that of the representative of the American Republic standing bare-headed
before a coloured man, and the two mightiest empires on
earth paying royal honours to a Polynesian sovereign,
whose little kingdom in the North Pacific is known to
many of us at home only as " the group of islands where
Captain Cook was killed." Ah! how lovely this Queen
of Oceans is! Blue, bright, balm-breathing, gentle in
its supreme strength, different both in motion and colour
from the coarse " vexed Atlantic ! "

STEAMER KILAUEA,
Jan. 29th.

I was turning homewards, enjoying the prospect of a
quiet week in Honolulu, when Mr. and Mrs. Damon
seized upon me, and told me that a lady friend of theirs,
anxious for a companion, was going to the volcano on
Hawaii, that she was a most expert and intelligent traveller, that the *Kilauea* would sail in two hours, that
unless I went now I should have no future opportunity
during my limited stay on the islands, that Mrs. Dexter
was anxious for me to go, that they would more than fill
my place in my absence, that this was a golden opportunity, that in short I *must* go, and they would drive me
back to the hotel to pack! The volcano is still a myth
to me, and I wanted to "read up " before going, and
above all was grieved to leave my friend, but she had already made some needful preparations, her son with his
feeble voice urged my going, the doctor said that there

was now no danger to be apprehended, and the Damons' kind urgency left me so little choice, that by five I was with them on the wharf, being introduced to my travelling companion, and to many of my fellow-passengers. Such an unexpected move is very bewildering, and it is too experimental, and too much of a leap in the dark to be enjoyable at present.

The wharf was one dense, well-compacted mass of natives taking leave of their friends with much effusiveness, and the steamer's encumbered deck was crowded with them, till there was hardly room to move; men, women, children, dogs, cats, mats, calabashes of *poi*, cocoanuts, bananas, dried fish, and every dusky individual of the throng was wreathed and garlanded with odorous and brilliant flowers. All were talking and laughing, and an immense amount of gesticulation seems to emphasize and supplement speech. We steamed through the reef in the brief red twilight, over the golden tropic sea, keeping on the leeward side of the islands. Before it was quite dark the sleeping arrangements were made, and the deck and skylights were covered with mats and mattresses on which 170 natives sat, slept, or smoked,—a motley, parti-coloured mass of humanity, in the midst of which I recognized Bishop Willis in the usual episcopal dress, lying on a mattress among the others, a prey to discomfort and weariness! What would his episcopal brethren at home think of such a hardship?

There is a yellow-skinned, soft-voiced, fascinating Goa or Malay steward on board, who with infinite goodwill attends to the comfort of everybody. I was surprised

when he asked me if I would like a mattress on the skylight, or a berth below, and in unhesitating ignorance
replied severely, "Oh, below, of course, please," thinking
of a ladies' cabin, but when I went down to supper, my
eyes were enlightened.

The *Kilauea* is a screw boat of 400 tons, most unpre-
possessing in appearance, slow, but sure, and capable of
bearing an infinite amount of battering. It is jokingly
said that her keel has rasped off the branch coral round
all the islands. Though there are many inter-island
schooners, she is the only sure mode of reaching the
windward islands in less than a week; and though at
present I am disposed to think rather slightingly of her,
and to class her with the New Zealand coasting craft, yet
the residents are very proud of her, and speak lovingly of
her, and regard her as a blessed deliverance from the
horrors of beating to windward. She has a shabby, ob-
solete look about her, like a second-rate coasting collier,
or an old American tow-boat. She looks ill-found, too;
I saw two essential pieces of tackle give way as they were
hoisting the main sail.* She has a small saloon with a
double tier of berths, besides transoms, which give accommodation on the level of the lower berth. There is
a stern cabin, which is a prolongation of the saloon, and
not in any way separated from it. There is no ladies'
cabin; but sex, race, and colour are included in a promiscuous arrangement.

---

* Dear old craft! I would not change her now for the finest palace
which floats on the Hudson, or the trimmest of the Hutchesons' beautiful
West Highland fleet.

Miss Karpe, my travelling companion, and two agreeable ladies, were already in their berths very sick, but I did not get into mine because a cockroach, looking as large as a mouse, occupied the pillow, and a companion not much smaller was roaming over the quilt without any definite purpose. I can't vouch for the accuracy of my observation, but it seemed to me that these tremendous creatures were dark red, with eyes like lobsters', and antennæ two inches long. They looked capable of carrying out the most dangerous and inscrutable designs. I called the Malay steward; he smiled mournfully, but spoke reassuringly, and pledged his word for their innocuousness, but I never can believe that they are not the enemies of man; and I lay down on the transom, not to sleep, however, for it seemed essential to keep watch on the proceedings of these formidable vermin.

The grotesqueness of the arrangements of the berths and their occupants grew on me during the night, and the climax was put upon it when a gentleman coming down in the early morning asked me if I knew that I was using the Governor of Maui's head for a footstool, this portly native "Excellency" being in profound slumber on the forward part of the transom. This diagram represents one side of the saloon and the "happy family" of English, Chinamen, Hawaiians, and Americans :—

Governor Lyman.	Miss Karpe.	Miss ——.
Afong.	Vacant.	Miss ——.
Governor Nahaolelua.	Myself.	An Hawaiian.

I noticed, too, that there were very few trunks and

portmanteaus, but that the after end of the saloon was
heaped with Mexican saddles and saddlebags, which I
learned too late were the essential gear of every traveller
on Hawaii.

At five this morning we were at anchor in the roads of
Lahaina, the chief village on the mountainous island of
Maui. This place is very beautiful from the sea, for
beyond the blue water and the foamy reef the eye rests
gratefully on a picturesque collection of low, one-storied,
thatched houses, many of frame, painted white; others
of grass, but all with deep, cool verandahs, half hidden
among palms, bananas, kukuis, breadfruit, and mangoes,
dark groves against gentle slopes behind, covered with
sugar-cane of a bright pea-green. It is but a narrow
strip of land between the ocean and the red, flaring,
almost inaccessible, Maui hills, which here rise abruptly
to a height of 6,000 feet, pinnacled, chasmed, buttressed,
and almost verdureless, except in a few deep clefts, green
and cool with ferns and candlenut trees, and moist with
falling water. Lahaina looked intensely tropical in the
roseflush of the early morning, a dream of some bright
southern isle, too surely to pass away. The sun blazed
down on shore, ship, and sea, glorifying all things
through the winter day. It was again ecstasy " to dream,
and dream " under the awning, fanned by the light sea-
breeze, with the murmur of an unknown musical tongue
in one's ears, and the rich colouring and graceful group-
ing of a tropical race around one. We called at Maaleia,
a neck of sandy, scorched, verdureless soil, and at
Ulupalakua, or rather at the furnace seven times heated,

which is the landing of the plantation of that name, on whose breezy slopes cane refreshes the eye at a height of 2,000 feet above the sea. We anchored at both places, and with what seemed to me a needless amount of delay, discharged goods and natives, and natives, mats, and calabashes were embarked. In addition to the essential mat and calabash of *poi*, every native carried some pet, either dog or cat, which was caressed, sung to, and talked to with extreme tenderness; but there were hardly any children, and I noticed that where there were any, the men took charge of them. There were very few fine, manly dogs; the pets in greatest favour are obviously those odious weak-eyed, pink-nosed Maltese terriers.

The aspect of the sea was so completely lazy, that it was a fresh surprise as each indolent undulation touched the shore that it had latent vigour left to throw itself upwards into clouds of spray. We looked through limpid water into cool depths where strange bright fish darted through the submarine *chapparal*, but the coolness was imaginary, for the water was at 80.°* The air above

---

* This temperature is, of course, in shallow water. The United States surveying vessel, *Tuscarora*, lately left San Diego, California, shaping a straight course for Honolulu, and found a nearly uniform temperature of from 33° to 34° Fahrenheit at all depths below 1100 fathoms. The following table gives a good idea of the temperature of ocean water in this region of the Pacific :—

100	.	.	.	.	.	.	64°	7
200	.	.	.	.	.	.	48°	7
300	.	.	.	.	.	.	42°	4
400	.	.	.	.	.	.	40°	4
500	.	.	.	.	.	.	39°	4
600	.	.	.	.	.	.	38°	6
700	.	.	.	.	.	.	38°	3

the great black lava flood, which in prehistoric times had
flowed into the sea, and had ever since declined the
kindly draping offices of nature, vibrated in waves of
heat.   Even the imperishable cocoanut trees, whose tall,
bare, curved trunks rose from the lava or the burnt red
earth, were gaunt, tattered, and thirsty-looking, weary of
crying for moisture to the pitiless skies.   At last the
ceaseless ripple of talk ceased, crew and passengers slept
on the hot deck, and no sounds were heard but the
drowsy flap of the awning, and the drowsier creak of the
rudder, as the *Kilauea* swayed sleepily on the lazy undulations.   The flag drooped and fainted with heat.   The
white sun blazed like a magnesium light on blue water,
black lava, and fiery soil, roasting, blinding, scintillating,
and flushed the red rocks of Maui into glory.   It was a
constant marvel that troops of mounted natives, male and
female, could gallop on the scorching shore without being
melted or shrivelled.   It is all glorious, this fierce bright
glow of the Tropic of Cancer, yet it was a relief to look
up the great rolling featureless slopes above Ulupalakua
to a forest belt of perennial green, watered, they say, by
perpetual showers, and a little later to see a mountain
summit uplifted into a region of endless winter, above a
steady cloud-bank as white as snow.   This mountain,

800	37°	5
900	36°	6
1000	35°	6
1200	35°	4
3054	33°	2

The *Tuscarora* found the extraordinary depth of 3023 fathoms at a
distance of only 43 miles from Molokai.

Haleakala, the House of the Sun, is the largest extinct volcano in the world, its terminal crater being nineteen miles in circumference at a height of more than 10,000 feet. It, and its spurs, slopes, and clusters of small craters form East Maui. West Maui is composed mainly of the lofty picturesque group of the Eeka mountains. A desert strip of land, not much above high water mark, unites the twain, which form an island forty-eight miles long and thirty broad, with an area of 620 square miles.

We left Maui in the afternoon, and spent the next six hours in crossing the channel between it and Hawaii, but the short tropic day did not allow us to see anything of the latter island but two snow-capped domes uplifted above the clouds. I have been reading Jarves' excellent book on the islands as industriously as possible, as well as trying to get information from my fellow-passengers regarding the region into which I have been so suddenly and unintentionally projected. I really know nothing about Hawaii, or the size and phenomena of the volcano to which we are bound, or the state of society or of the native race, or of the relations existing between it and the foreign population, or of the details of the constitution. This ignorance is most oppressive, and I see that it will not be easily enlightened, for among several intelligent gentlemen who have been conversing with me, no two seem agreed on any matter of fact.

From the hour of my landing I have observed the existence of two parties of *pro* and *anti* missionary leanings, with views on all island subjects in grotesque

antagonism. So far, the former have left the undoubted
results of missionary effort here to speak for themselves ;
and I am almost disposed, from the pertinacious aggressiveness of the latter party, to think that it must be weak.
I have already been seized upon (a gentleman would write
" button-holed ") by several persons, who, in their anxiety
to be first in imprinting their own views on the *tabula rasa*
of a stranger's mind, have exercised an unseemly overhaste in giving the conversation an anti-missionary twist.
They apparently desire to convey the impression that the
New England teachers, finding a people rejoicing in the
innocence and simplicity of Eden, taught them the knowledge of evil, turned them into a nation of hypocrites,
and with a strange mingling of fanaticism and selfish-
ness, afflicted them with many woes calculated to accele-
rate their extinction, *clothing* among others. The animus
appears strong and bitter. There are two intelligent and
highly educated ladies on board, daughters of missionaries, and the candid and cautious tone in which
they speak on the same subject impresses me favourably.
Mr. Damon introduced me to a very handsome half white
gentleman, a lawyer of ability, and lately interpreter to
the Legislature, Mr. Ragsdale, or, as he is usually called,
" Bill Ragsdale," a leading spirit among the natives. His
conversation was eloquent and poetic, though rather
stilted, and he has a good deal of French mannerism; but
if he is a specimen of native patriotic feeling, I think that
the extinction of Hawaiian nationality must be far off. I
was amused with the attention that he paid to his dress
under very adverse circumstances. He has appeared in

three different suits, with light kid gloves to match, all
equally elegant, in two days.   A Chinese gentleman, who
is at the same time a wealthy merchant at Honolulu, and
a successful planter on Hawaii, interests me, from the
quiet keen intelligence of his face, and the courtesy and
dignity of his manner.   I hear that he possesses the
respect of the whole community for his honour and
integrity.   It is quite unlike an ordinary miscellaneous
herd of passengers.   The tone is so cheerful, courteous,
and friendly, and people speak without introductions,
and help to make the time pass pleasantly to each
other.

HILO, HAWAII.

The *Kilauea* is not a fast propeller, and as she lurched
very much in crossing the channel most of the passengers
were sea-sick, a casualty which did not impair their
cheerfulness and good humour.   After dark we called
at Kawaihae (pronounced To-wee-hye), on the north-
west of Hawaii, and then steamed through the channel
to the east or windward side.   I was only too glad on
the second night to accept the offer of "a mattrass on
the skylight," but between the heavy rolling caused by
the windward swell, and the natural excitement on
nearing the land of volcanoes and earthquakes, I could
not sleep, and no other person slept, for it was considered "a very rough passage," though there was hardly
a yachtsman's breeze.   It would do these Sybarites good
to give them a short spell of the howling horrors of
the North or South Atlantic, an easterly snowstorm off

Sable Island, or a winter gale in the latitude of Inaccessible Island! The night was cloudy, and so the glare from Kilauea which is often seen far out at sea was not visible.

When the sun rose amidst showers and rainbows (for this is the showery season), I could hardly believe my eyes. Scenery, vegetation, colour were all changed. The glowing red, the fiery glare, the obtrusive lack of vegetation were all gone. There was a magnificent coast-line of grey cliffs many hundred feet in height, usually draped with green, but often black, caverned, and fantastic at their bases. Into cracks and caverns the heavy waves surged with a sound like artillery, sending their broad white sheets of foam high up among the ferns and trailers, and drowning for a time the endless baritone of the surf, which is never silent through the summer years. Cascades in numbers took one impulsive leap from the cliffs into the sea, or came thundering down clefts or "gulches," which, widening at their extremities, opened on smooth green lawns, each one of which has its grass house or houses, *kalo* patch, bananas, and coco-palms, so close to the broad Pacific that its spray often frittered itself away over their fan-like leaves. Above the cliffs there were grassy uplands with park-like clumps of the screw-pine, and candle-nut, and glades and dells of dazzling green, bright with cataracts, opened up among the dark dense forests which for some thousands of feet girdle Mauna Kea and Mauna Loa, two vast volcanic mountains, whose snow-capped summits gleamed here and there above the clouds,

at an altitude of nearly 14,000 feet. Creation surely
cannot exhibit a more brilliant green than that which
clothes windward Hawaii with perpetual spring. I have
never seen such verdure. In the final twenty-nine miles
there are more than sixty gulches, from 100 to 700 feet
in depth, each with its cataracts, and wild vagaries of
tropical luxuriance. Native churches, frame-built and
painted white, are almost like mile-stones along the coast,
far too large and too many for the notoriously dwindling
population. Ten miles from Hilo we came in sight of
the first sugar plantation, with its patches of yet brighter
green, its white boiling house and tall chimney stack;
then more churches, more plantations, more gulches, more
houses, and before ten we steamed into Byron's, or as it
is now called Hilo Bay.

This is the paradise of Hawaii. What Honolulu
attempts to be, Hilo is without effort. Its crescent-
shaped bay, said to be the most beautiful in the Pacific,
is a semi-circle of about two miles, with its farther
extremity formed by Cocoanut Island, a black lava islet
on which this palm attains great perfection, and beyond
it again a fringe of cocoanuts marks the deep indenta-
tions of the shore. From this island to the north point
of the bay, there is a band of golden sand on which the
roar of the surf sounded thunderous and drowsy as it
mingled with the music of living waters, the Waiakea
and the Wailuku, which after lashing the sides of the
mountains which give them birth, glide deep and fern-
fringed into the ocean. Native houses, half hidden by
greenery, line the bay, and stud the heights above the

Wailuku, and near the landing some white frame houses
and three church spires above the wood denote the foreign
element. Hilo is unique. Its climate is humid, and the
long repose which it has enjoyed from rude volcanic
upheavals has mingled a great depth of vegetable mould
with the decomposed lava. Rich soil, rain, heat, sunshine,
stimulate nature to supreme efforts, and there is a
luxuriant prodigality of vegetation which leaves nothing
uncovered but the golden margin of the sea, and even
that above high-water-mark is green with the Convolvulus
maritimus. So dense is the wood that Hilo is rather
suggested than seen. It is only on shore that one
becomes aware of its bewildering variety of native and
exotic trees and shrubs. From the sea it looks one
dense mass of greenery, in which the bright foliage of
the candle-nut relieves the glossy dark green of the breadfruit—a maze of preposterous bananas, out of which
rise slender annulated trunks of palms giving their
infinite grace to the grove. And palms along the bay,
almost among the surf, toss their waving plumes in the
sweet soft breeze, not " palms in exile," but children
of a blessed isle where " never wind blows loudly."
Above Hilo, broad lands sweeping up cloudwards, with
their sugar cane, *kalo*, melons, pine-apples, and banana
groves suggest the boundless liberality of Nature. Woods
and waters, hill and valley are all there, and from the
region of an endless summer the eye takes in the domain
of an endless winter, where almost perpetual snow crowns
the summits of Mauna Kea and Mauna Loa. Mauna
Kea from Hilo has a shapely aspect, for its top is broken

into peaks, said to be the craters of extinct volcanoes, but my eyes seek the dome-like curve of Mauna Loa with far deeper interest, for it is as yet an unfinished mountain.   It has a huge crater on its summit 800 feet in depth, and a pit of unresting fire on its side; it throbs and rumbles, and palpitates; it has sent forth floods of fire over all this part of Hawaii, and at any moment it may be crowned with a lonely light, showing that its tremendous forces are again in activity.   My imagination is already inflamed by hearing of marvels, and I am beginning to think tropically.

Canoes came off from the shore, dusky swimmers glided through the water, youths, athletes, like the bronzes of the Naples Museum, rode the waves on their surf-boards, brilliantly dressed riders galloped along the sands and came trooping down the bridle-paths from all the vicinity till a many-coloured tropical crowd had assembled at the landing.   Then a whaleboat came off, rowed by eight young men in white linen suits and white straw hats, with wreaths of carmine-coloured flowers round both hats and throats.   They were singing a glee in honour of Mr. Ragsdale, whom they sprang on deck to welcome.   Our crowd of native fellow-passengers, by some inscrutable process, had re-arrayed themselves and blossomed into brilliancy.   Hordes of Hilo natives swarmed on deck, and it became a Babel of *alohas*, kisses, hand-shakings, and reiterated welcomes.   The glee singers threw their beautiful garlands of roses and *ohias* over the foreign passengers, and music, flowers, good-will and kindliness made us welcome to these enchanted

shores.   We landed in a whaleboat, and were hoisted
up a rude pier which was crowded, for what the arrival of
the Australian mail-steamer is to Honolulu, the coming
of the *Kilauea* is to Hilo.   I had not time to feel myself
a stranger, there were so many introductions, and so much
friendliness.   Mr. Coan and Mr. Lyman, two of the
most venerable of the few surviving missionaries, were on
the landing, and I was introduced to them and many
others.   There is no hotel in Hilo.   The residents
receive strangers, and Miss Karpe and I were soon in-
stalled in a large buff frame-house, with two deep
verandahs, the residence of Mr. Severance, Sheriff of
Hawaii.

Unlike many other places, Hilo is more fascinating on
closer acquaintance, so fascinating that it is hard to write
about it in plain prose.   Two narrow roads lead up from
the sea to one as narrow, running parallel with it.
Further up the hill another runs in the same direction.
There are no conveyances, and outside the village these
narrow roads dwindle into bridle-paths, with just room
for one horse to pass another.   The houses in which
Mr. Coan, Mr. Lyman, Dr. Wetmore (formerly of the
Mission), and one or two others live, have just enough
suggestion of New England about them to remind one of
the dominant influence on these islands, but the climate
has idealized them, and clothed them with poetry and
antiquity.

Of the three churches, the most prominent is the
Roman Catholic Church, a white frame building with
two great towers; Mr. Coan's native church with a spire

comes next; and then the neat little foreign church, also
with a spire. The Romish Church is a rather noisy
neighbour, for its bells ring at unnatural hours, and
doleful strains of a band which cannot play either in
time or tune proceed from it. The court-house, a large
buff painted frame-building with two deep verandahs,
standing on a well-kept lawn planted with exotic trees,
is the most imposing building in Hilo. All the foreigners
have carried out their individual tastes in their dwellings, and the result is very agreeable, though in picturesqueness they must yield the palm to the native
houses, which whether of frame, or grass plain or
plaited, whether one or two storeyed, all have the deep
thatched roofs and verandahs plain or fantastically
latticed, which are so in harmony with the surroundings.
These lattices and single and double verandahs are
gorgeous with trailers, and the general warm brown
tint of the houses contrasts pleasantly with the deep
green of the bananas which over-shadow them. There
are living waters everywhere. Each house seems to
possess its pure bright stream, which is arrested in
bathing houses to be liberated among *kalo* patches of
the brightest green. Every verandah appears a gathering place, and the bright *holukus* of the women, the
gay shirts and bandanas of the men, the brilliant wreaths
of natural flowers which adorn both, the hot-house
temperature, the new trees and flowers which demand
attention, the strange rich odours, and the low monotonous
recitative which mourns through the groves make me feel
that I am in a new world. Ah, this is all Polynesian!

This must be the land to which the " timid-eyed " lotos-eaters came.   There is a strange fascination in the languid air, and it is strangely sweet " to dream of fatherland " . . .

I. L. B.

LETTER IV.

HILO, HAWAII.

I FIND that I can send another short letter before leaving for the volcano. I cannot convey to you any idea of the greenness and lavish luxuriance of this place, where everything flourishes, and glorious trailers and parasitic ferns hide all unsightly objects out of sight. It presents a bewildering maze of lilies, roses, fuschias, clematis, begonias, convolvuli, the huge appalling looking granadilla, the purple and yellow water lemons, also varieties of passiflora, both with delicious edible fruit, custard apples, rose apples, mangoes, mangostein guavas, bamboos, alligator pears, oranges, tamarinds, papayas, bananas, breadfruit, magnolias, geraniums, candle-nut, gardenias, dracænas, eucalyptus, pandanus, *ohias,** *kamani* trees, *kalo,*† *noni,*‡ and quantities of other trees and flowers, of which I shall eventually learn the names, patches of pine-apple, melons, and sugar-cane for children to suck, *kalo* and sweet potatoes.

In the vicinity of this and all other houses, Chili peppers, and a ginger-plant with a drooping flower-stalk with a great number of blossoms, which when not fully developed have a singular resemblance to very pure porcelain tinted with pink at the extremities of the buds, are

* Metrosideros Polymorpha.　† Colocasia antiquorum (arum esculentum).
‡ Morinda Citrifolia.

to be seen growing in "yards," to use a most unfitting
Americanism. I don't know how to introduce you to
some of the things which delight my eyes here; but I must
ask you to believe that the specimens of tropical growths
which we see in conservatories at home are in general
either misrepresentations, or very feeble representations
of these growths in their natural homes. I don't allude
to flowers, and especially not to orchids, but in this
instance very specially to bananas, coco-palms, and the
pandanus. For example, there is a specimen of the
Pandanus odoratissimus in the palm-house in the Edinburgh Botanic Gardens, which is certainly a malignant
caricature, with its long straggling branches, and widely
scattered tufts of poverty stricken foliage. The bananas
and plantains in that same palm-house represent only the
feeblest and poorest of their tribe. They require not only
warmth and moisture, but the generous sunshine of the
tropics for their development. In the same house the
date and sugar-palms are tolerable specimens, but the
cocoa-nut trees are most truly " palms in exile."

I suppose that few people ever forget the first sight of
a palm-tree of any species. I vividly remember seeing
one for the first time at Malaga, but the coco-palm groves
of the Pacific have a strangeness and witchery of their own.
As I write now I hear the moaning rustle of the wind
through their plume-like tops, and their long slender
stems, and crisp crown of leaves above the trees with
shining leafage which revel in damp, have a suggestion
of Orientalism about them. How do they come too, on
every atoll or rock that raises its head throughout this

lonely ocean ? They fringe the shores of these islands.
Wherever it is dry and fiercely hot, and the lava is black
and hard, and nothing else grows, or can grow, there they
are, close to the sea, sending their root-fibres seawards
as if in search of salt water. Their long, curved, wrinkled,
perfectly cylindrical stems, bulging near the ground
like an apothecary's pestle, rise to a height of from
sixty to one hundred feet. These stems are never
straight, and in a grove lean and curve every way, and
are apparently capable of enduring any force of wind or
earthquake. They look as if they had never been young,
and they show no signs of growth, rearing their plumy
tufts so far aloft, and casting their shadows so far away,
always supremely lonely, as though they belonged to the
heavens rather than the earth. Then, while all else that
grows is green they are yellowish. Their clusters of nuts
in all stages of growth are yellow, their fan-like leaves,
which are from twelve to twenty feet long, are yellow, and
an amber light pervades and surrounds them. They
provide milk, oil, food, rope, and matting, and each tree
produces about one hundred nuts annually.

The pandanus, or *lauhala*, is one of the most striking
features of the islands. Its funereal foliage droops in Hilo,
and it was it that I noticed all along the windward coast
as having a most striking peculiarity of aërial roots which
the branches send down to the ground, and which I now
see have large cup-shaped spongioles. These air-roots
seem like props, and appear to vary in length from three
to twelve feet, according to the situation of the tree. There
is one variety I saw to-day, the " screw pine," which is

really dangerous if one approached it unguardedly. It is a whorled pandanus, with long sword-shaped leaves, spirally arranged in three rows, and hard, saw-toothed edges, very sharp. When unbranched as I saw them, they resemble at a distance pine-apple plants thirty times magnified. But the mournful looking trees along the coast and all about Hilo are mostly the Pandanus odoratissimus, a spreading and branching tree which grows fully twenty-five feet high, supports itself among inaccessible rocks by its prop-like roots, and is one of the first plants to appear on the newly-formed Pacific islands.* Its foliage is singularly dense, although it is borne in tufts of a quantity of long yucca-like leaves on the branches. The shape of the tree is usually circular. The mournful look is caused by the leaves taking a downward and very decided droop in the middle. At present each tuft of leaves has in its centre an object like a green pine-apple. This contains the seeds which are eatable, as is also the fleshy part of the drupes. I find that it is from the seeds of this tree and their coverings that the brilliant orange leis, or garlands of the natives, are made. The soft white case of the leaves and the terminal buds can also be eaten. The leaves are used for thatching, and their tough longitudinal fibres for mats and ropes. There is another

---

* I have since learned that it is the same as the Kaldera bush of Southern India, and that the powerful fragrance of its flowers is the subject of continual allusions in Sanskrit poetry under the name of Ketaka, and that oil impregnated with its odour is highly prized as a perfume in India. The Hawaiians also used it to give a delicious scent to the Tapa made for their chiefs from the inner bark of the paper mulberry.

kind, the Pandanus vacoa, the same as is used for making
sugar bags in Mauritius, but I have not seen it.

One does not forget the first sight of a palm.   I think
the banana comes next, and I see them in perfection here
for the first time, as those in Honolulu grow in "yards,"
and are tattered by the winds.   It transports me into the
tropics in feeling, as I am already in them in fact, and
satisfies all my cravings for something which shall represent   and   epitomize   their   luxuriance,   as   well   as   for
simplicity and grace in vegetable form.   And here it is
everywhere with its shining shade, its smooth fat green
stem, its crown of huge curving leaves from four to ten
feet long, and its heavy cluster of a whorl of green or
golden fruit, with a pendant purple cone of undeveloped
blossom below.   It is of the tropics, tropical; a thing of
beauty,   and   gladness,   and   sunshine.   It is   indigenous
here, and wild, but never bears seeds, and is propagated
solely by suckers, which spring up when the parent plant
has fruited, or by cuttings.   It bears seed, strange to say,
only (so far as is known) in the Andaman Islands, where,
stranger still, it springs up as a second growth wherever
the forests are cleared.   Go to the palm-house, find the
Musa   sapientum,   magnify   it   ten   times,   glorify   it
immeasurably, and you will have a laggard idea of the
banana groves of Hilo.

The ground is carpeted with a grass of preternaturally
vivid green and rankness of growth, mixed with a handsome   fern,   with   a   caudex   a   foot   high,   the   Sadleria
cyathoides, and another of exquisite beauty, the Micro-

pia tenuifolia, which are said to be the commonest ferns
on Hawaii. It looks Elysian.

Hilo is a lively place for such a mere village; so
many natives are stirring about, and dashing along
the narrow roads on horseback. This is a large airy
house, simple and tasteful, with pretty engravings and
water-colour drawings on the walls. There is a large
bath-house in the garden, into which a pure, cool stream
has been led, and the gurgle and music of many such
streams fill the sweet, soft air. There is a saying among
sailors, "Follow a Pacific shower, and it leads you to
Hilo." Indeed I think they have a rainfall of from
thirteen to sixteen feet annually. These deep verandahs
are very pleasant, for they render window-blinds unnecessary; so there is nothing of that dark stuffiness which
makes indoor life a trial in the closed, shadeless Australian
houses.

Miss Karpe, my travelling companion, is a lady of
great energy, and apparently an adept in the art of
travelling. Undismayed by three days of sea-sickness,
and the prospect of the tremendous journey to the
volcano to-morrow, she extemporised a ride to the
Anuenue Falls on the Wailuku this afternoon, and I
weakly accompanied her, a burly policeman being our
guide. The track is only a scramble among rocks and
holes, concealed by grass and ferns, and we had to cross
a stream, full of great holes, several times. The Fall
itself is very pretty, 110 feet in one descent, with a
cavernous shrine behind the water, filled with ferns.

There were large ferns all round the Fall, and a jungle of luxuriant tropical shrubs of many kinds.

Three miles above this Fall there are the Pei-pei Falls, very interesting geologically. The Wailuku River is the boundary between the two great volcanoes, and its waters, it is supposed by learned men, have often flowed over heated beds of basalt, with the result of columnar formation radiating from the bottom of the stream. This structure is sometimes beautifully exhibited in the form of Gothic archways, through which the torrent pours into a basin, surrounded by curved, broken, and half-sunk prisms, black and prominent amidst the white foam of the Falls. In several places the river has just pierced the beds of lava, and in one passes under a thick rock bridge, several hundred feet wide. Often, where the water flows over beds of dark grey basalt, masses of trachyte, closely resembling syenite, have formed "pot-holes," and by mutual action have been worn to pebbles. At Pei-pei there are three circular pools, each about fifty feet in diameter, and separated by walls six feet thick, in a bed of columnar basalt.* During freshets the river sometimes rises thirty feet, and hides these pools, but during the dry season the upper bed is bare, and after a succession of cascades of various heights the stream pours into the first basin, filling it with foam. From this there is no apparent outlet, but leaves thrown in soon appear in the second basin, whose tranquillity is only disturbed by a few bubbles. Between this and the third

* See Brigham, on the "Hawaiian Volcanoes."

there are two subterranean passages, and the water there leaps over a fall about forty feet high, nearly covering a perfect Gothic arch which is the entrance to a shallow cave. The scene is enclosed by high and nearly perpendicular walls.*

Near the Anuenue Fall we stopped at a native house, outside which a woman, in a rose-coloured chemise, was stringing roses for a necklace, while her husband pounded the *kalo* root on a board. His only clothing was the *malo*, a narrow strip of cloth wound round the loins, and passed between the legs. This was the only covering worn by men before the introduction of Christianity. Females wore the *pau*, a short petticoat made of *tapa*, which reached from the waist to the knees. To our eyes, the brown skin produces nearly the effect of clothing.

Everything was new and interesting, but the ride was spoiled by my insecure seat in my saddle, and the increased pain in my spine which riding produced. Once in crossing a stream the horses have to make a sort of downward jump from a rock, and I slipped round my horse's neck. Indeed on the way back I felt that on the ground of health I must give up the volcano, as I would never consent to be carried to it, like Lady Franklin, in a litter. When we returned, Mr. Severance suggested that it would be much better for me to follow the Hawaiian fashion, and ride astride, and put his saddle on the horse. It was only my strong desire to see the vol-

---

* In explorations some months later, I found nearly similar phenomena, in two other of the streams on the windward side of Hawaii.

cano which made me consent to a mode of riding against which I have so strong a prejudice, but the result of the experiment is that I shall visit Kilauea thus or not at all. The native women all ride astride, on ordinary occasions in the full sacks, or *holukus*, and on gala days in the *pau*, the gay, winged dress which I described in writing from Honolulu. A great many of the foreign ladies on Hawaii have adopted the Mexican saddle also, for greater security to themselves and ease to their horses, on the steep and perilous bridle-tracks, but they wear full Turkish trowsers and jauntily-made dresses reaching to the ankles.

It appears that Hilo is free from the universally admitted nuisance of morning calls. The hours are simple—eight o'clock breakfasts, one o'clock dinners, six o'clock suppers. If people want anything with you, they come at any hour of the day, but if they only wish to be sociable, the early evening is the recognized time for " calling." After supper, when the day's work is done, people take their lanterns and visit each other, either in the verandahs or in the cheerful parlours which open upon them. There are no door-bells, or solemn an-nouncements by servants of visitors' names, or " not-at-homes." If people are in their parlours, it is presumed that they receive their friends. Several pleasant people came in this evening. They seem to take great interest in two ladies going to the volcano without an escort, but no news has been received from it lately, and I fear that it is not very active as no glare is visible to-night. Mr. Thompson, the pastor of the small foreign congregation here, called on me. He is a very agreeable, accomplished man, and is acquainted with Dr. Holland and several of my New England friends. He kindly brought his wife's riding-costume for my trip to Kilauea. The Rev. Titus Coan, one of the first and most successful missionaries to Hawaii, also called. He is a tall, majestic-looking man, physically well fitted for the extraordinary exertions he has undergone in mission work, and intellectually also, I should think, for his face expresses great mental strength, and nothing of the weakness of a sanguine enthusiast. He has admitted about 12,000 persons into the Christian Church. He is the greatest authority on volcanoes on the islands, and his enthusiastic manner and illuminated countenance as he spoke of Kilauea, have raised my expectations to the highest pitch. We are prepared for to-morrow, having engaged a native named *Upa*, who boasts a little English, as our guide. He provides three horses and himself for three days for the sum of thirty dollars.

I. L. B.

LETTER V.

BRUISED aching bones, strained muscles, and over-whelming fatigue, render it hardly possible for me to undergo the physical labour of writing, but in spirit I am so elated with the triumph of success, and so thrilled by new sensations, that though I cannot com-municate the incommunicable, I want to write to you while the impression of Kilauea is fresh, and by "the light that never was on sea or shore."

By eight yesterday morning our preparations were finished, and Miss Karpe, whose conversance with the details of travelling I envy, mounted her horse on her own side-saddle, dressed in a short grey waterproof, and a broad-brimmed Leghorn hat tied so tightly over her ears with a green veil as to give it the look of a double spout. The only pack her horse carried was a bundle of cloaks and shawls, slung together with an umbrella on the horn of her saddle. Upa, who was most pic-turesquely got up in the native style with garlands of flowers round his hat and throat, carried our saddle-bags on the peak of his saddle, a bag with bananas, bread, and a bottle of tea on the horn, and a canteen of water round his waist. I had on my coarse Australian hat which serves the double purpose of sunshade and

umbrella, Mrs. Thompson's riding costume, my great
rusty New Zealand boots, and my blanket strapped
behind a very gaily ornamented brass-bossed *demi-pique*
Mexican saddle, which one of the missionary's daughters
had lent me. It has a horn in front, a low peak behind,
large wooden stirrups with leathern flaps the length of the
stirrup-leathers, to prevent the dress from coming in contact with the horse, and strong guards of hide which hang
over and below the stirrup, and cover it and the foot up to
the ancles, to prevent the feet or boots from being torn
in riding through the bush. Each horse had four fathoms
of tethering rope wound several times round his neck. In
such fashion must all travelling be done on Hawaii,
whether by ladies or gentlemen.

Upa supplied the picturesque element, we the grotesque.
The morning was moist and unpropitious looking. As
the greater part of the thirty miles has to be travelled at
a foot's-pace the guide took advantage of the soft grassy
track which leads out of Hilo, to go off at full gallop,
a proceeding which made me at once conscious of the
demerits of my novel way of riding. To guide the horse
and to clutch the horn of the saddle with both hands
were clearly incompatible, so I abandoned the first as
being the least important. Then my feet either slipped
too far into the stirrups and were cut, or they were
jerked out; every corner was a new terror, for at each
I was nearly pitched off on one side, and when at last
Upa stopped, and my beast stopped without consulting
my wishes, only a desperate grasp of mane and tethering
rope saved me from going over his head. At this ridi-

culous moment we came upon a bevy of brown maidens swimming in a lakelet by the roadside, who increased my confusion by a chorus of laughter. How fervently I hoped that the track would never admit of galloping again !

Hilo fringes off with pretty native houses, kalo patches and mullet ponds, and in about four miles the track, then formed of rough hard lava, and not more than 24 inches wide, enters a forest of the densest description, a burst of true tropical jungle. I could not have imagined anything so perfectly beautiful, nature seemed to riot in the production of wonderful forms, as if the moist hot-house air encouraged her in lavish excesses. Such endless variety, such depths of green, such an impassable and altogether inextricable maze of forest trees, ferns, and lianas! There were palms, breadfruit trees, *ohias*, eugenias, candle-nuts of immense size, *Koa* (acacia) bananas, *noni*, bamboos, papayas, (Carica papaya) guavas, *ti* trees (Cordyline terminalis), tree-ferns, climbing ferns, parasitic ferns, and ferns themselves the prey of parasites of their own species. The lianas were there in profusion climbing over the highest trees, and entangling them, with stems varying in size from those as thick as a man's arm to those as slender as whipcord, binding all in an impassable network, and hanging over our heads in rich festoons or tendrils swaying in the breeze. There were trailers, *ie*, (Freycinetia scandens) with heavy knotted stems, as thick as a frigate's stoutest hawser, coiling up to the tops of tall *ohias* with tufted leaves like yuccas, and crimson spikes

of gaudy blossom. The shining festoons of the yam
and the graceful trailers of the *mailé* (Alyxia Olivae-
formis), a sweet scented vine, from which the natives
make garlands, and glossy leaved climbers hung from
tree to tree, and to brighten all, huge morning glories of
a heavenly blue opened a thousand blossoms to the sun
as if to give a tenderer loveliness to the forest. Here
trees grow and fall, and nature covers them where they
lie with a new vegetation which altogether obliterates
their hasty decay. It is four miles of beautiful and
inextricable confusion, untrodden by human feet except
on the narrow track. "Of every tree in this garden
thou mayest freely eat," and no serpent or noxious
thing trails its hideous form through this Eden.

It was quite intoxicating, so new, wonderful, and
solemn withal, that I was sorry when we emerged from
its shady depths upon a grove of cocoanut trees and the
glare of day. Two very poor-looking grass huts, with a
ragged patch of sugar-cane beside them, gave us an
excuse for half an hour's rest. An old woman in a red
sack, much tattooed, with thick short grey hair bristling
on her head, sat on a palm root, holding a nude brown
child; a lean hideous old man, dressed only in a *malo*,
leaned against its stem, our horses with their highly
miscellaneous gear were tethered to a fern stump, and
Upa, the most picturesque of the party, served out tea.
He and the natives talked incessantly, and from the
frequency with which the words "*wahine haole*" (foreign
woman) occurred, the subject of their conversation was
obvious. Upa has taken up the notion from something

Mr. S—— said, that I am a " high chief," and related to
Queen Victoria, and he was doubtlessly imposing this
fable on the people.   In spite of their poverty and
squalor, if squalor is a term which can be applied to
aught beneath these sunny skies, there was a kindliness
about them which they made us feel, and the *aloha* with
which they parted from us had a sweet friendly sound.

From this grove we travelled as before in single file
over an immense expanse of lava of the kind called
pahoehoe, or satin rock, to distinguish it from the
a-a, or jagged, rugged, impassable rock.   Savants all use
these terms in the absence of any equally expressive.
in English.   The pahoehoe extends in the Hilo direction from hence about twenty-three miles.   It is the
cooled and arrested torrent of lava which in past ages
has flowed towards Hilo from Kilauea.   It lies in hummocks, in coils, in rippled waves, in rivers, in huge convolutions, in pools smooth and still, and in caverns
which are really bubbles.   Hundreds of square miles of
the island are made up of this and nothing more.   A
very frequent aspect of pahoehoe is the likeness on a
magnificent scale of a thick coat of cream drawn in
wrinkling folds to the side of a milk-pan.   This lava is
all grey, and the greater part of its surface is slightly
roughened.   Wherever this is not the case the horses slip
upon it as upon ice.

Here I began to realize the universally igneous origin
of Hawaii, as I had not done among the finely disintegrated lava of Hilo.   From the hard black rocks which
border the sea, to the loftiest mountain dome or peak,

every stone, atom of dust, and foot of fruitful or barren soil bears the Plutonic mark. In fact, the island has been raised heap on heap, ridge on ridge, mountain on mountain, to nearly the height of Mont Blanc, by the same volcanic forces which are still in operation here, and may still add at intervals to the height of the blue dome of Mauna Loa, of which we caught occasional glimpses above the clouds. Hawaii is actually at the present time being built up from the ocean, and this great sea of pahoehoe is not to be regarded as a vindictive eruption, bringing desolation on a fertile region, but as an architectural and formative process.

There is no water, except a few deposits of rain-water in holes, but the moist air and incessant showers have aided nature to mantle this frightful expanse with an abundant vegetation, principally ferns of an exquisite green, the most conspicuous being the Sadleria, the Gleichenia Hawaiiensis, a running wire-like fern, and the exquisite Microlepia tenuifolia, dwarf guava, with its white flowers resembling orange flowers in odour, and *ohelos* (Vaccinium reticulatum), with their red and white berries, and a profusion of small-leaved *ohias* (Metrosideros polymorpha), with their deep crimson tasselled flowers, and their young shoots of bright crimson, relieved the monotony of green. These crimson tassels deftly strung on thread or fibres, are much used by the natives for their *leis*, or garlands. The *ti* tree (Cordyline terminalis) which abounds also on the lava, is most valuable. They cook their food wrapped up in its leaves, the porous root when baked, has the taste and texture of molasses candy,

and when distilled yields a spirit, and the leaves form
wrappings for fish, hard *poi*, and other edibles.　Occasionally a clump of tufted coco-palms, or of the beautiful
candle-nut rose among the smaller growths.　To our left a
fringe of palms marked the place where the lava and the
ocean met, while, on our right, we were seldom out of
sight of the dense timber belt, with its fringe of tree-
ferns and bananas, which girdles Mauna Loa.

The track, on the whole, is a perpetual upward
scramble ; for, though the ascent is so gradual, that it is
only by the increasing coolness of the atmosphere that the
increasing elevation is denoted, it is really nearly 4,000
feet in thirty miles.　Only strong, sure-footed, well-shod
horses can undertake this journey, for it is a constant
scramble over rocks, going up or down natural steps, or
cautiously treading along ledges.　Most of the track is
quite legible owing to the vegetation having been worn
off the lava, but the rock itself hardly shows the slightest
abrasion.

Upa had indicated that we were to stop for rest at the
" Half Way House ; " and, as I was hardly able to sit on
my horse owing to fatigue, I consoled myself by visions
of a comfortable sofa and a cup of tea.　It was with real
dismay that I found the reality to consist of a grass hut,
much out of repair, and which, bad as it was, was locked.
Upa said we had ridden so slowly that it would be dark
before we reached the volcano, and only allowed us to
rest on the grass for half-an-hour.　He had frequently
reiterated " Half Way House, you wear spur ; " and, on
our remounting, he buckled on my foot a heavy rusty

Mexican spur, with jingling ornaments and rowels an inch
and a half long. These horses are so accustomed to be
jogged with these instruments that they won't move without them. The prospect of five hours more riding looked
rather black, for I was much exhausted, and my shoulders
and knee-joints were in severe pain. Miss K.'s horse
showed no other appreciation of a stick with which she
belaboured him than flourishes of his tail, so, for a time,
he was put in the middle, that Upa might add his more
forcible persuasions, and I rode first and succeeded in
getting my lazy animal into the priestly amble known at
home as "a butter and eggs trot," the favourite travelling
pace, but this not suiting the guide's notion of progress, he frequently rushed up behind with a torrent of
Hawaiian, emphasized by heavy thumps on my horse's
back, which so sorely jeopardised my seat on the animal,
owing to his resenting the interference by kicking, that
I "dropped astern" for the rest of the way, leaving Upa
to belabour Miss K.'s steed for his diversion.

The country altered but little, only the variety of trees
gave place to the *ohia* alone, with its sombre foliage.
There were neither birds nor insects, and the only travellers we encountered in the solitude compelled us to
give them a wide berth, for they were a drove of half wild
random cattle, led by a lean bull of hideous aspect, with
crumpled horns. Two picturesque native vaccheros on
mules accompanied them, and my flagging spirits were
raised by their news that the volcano was quite active.
The owner of these cattle knows that he has 10,000 head,
and may have a great many more. They are shot for

their hides by men who make shooting and skinning them a profession, and, near settlements, the owners are thankful to get two cents a pound for sirloin and rump-steaks. These, and great herds which are actually wild and ownerless upon the mountains, are a degenerate breed, with some of the worst peculiarities of the Texas cattle, and are the descendants of those which Vancouver placed on the islands and which were under *Tabu* for ten years. They destroy the old trees by gnawing the bark, and render the growth of young ones impossible.

As it was getting dark we passed through a forest strip, where tree-ferns from twelve to eighteen feet in height, and with fronds from five to seven feet long, were the most attractive novelties. As we emerged, " with one stride came the dark," a great darkness, a cloudy night, with neither moon nor stars, and the track was further obscured by a belt of *ohias*. There were five miles of this, and I was so dead from fatigue and want of food, that I would willingly have lain down in the bush in the rain. I most heartlessly wished that Miss K. were tired too, for her voice, which seemed tireless as she rode ahead in the dark, rasped upon my ears. I could only keep on my saddle by leaning on the horn, and my clothes were soaked with the heavy rain. " A dreadful ride," one and another had said, and I then believed them. It seemed an awful solitude full of mystery. Often, I only knew that my companions were ahead by the sparks struck from their horse's shoes.

It became a darkness which could be felt.

" Is that possibly a pool of blood ? " I thought in horror, as a rain puddle glowed crimson on the track. Not that indeed ! A glare brighter and redder than that from any furnace suddenly lightened the whole sky, and from that moment brightened our path. There sat Miss K. under her dripping umbrella as provokingly erect as when she left Hilo. There Upa jogged along, huddled up in his poncho, and his canteen shone red. There the *ohia* trees were relieved blackly against the sky. The scene started out from the darkness with the suddenness of a revelation. We felt the pungency of sulphurous fumes in the still night air. A sound as of the sea broke on our ears, rising and falling as if breaking on the shore, but the ocean was thirty miles away. The heavens became redder and brighter, and when we reached the crater-house at eight, clouds of red vapour mixed with flame were curling ceaselessly out of a huge invisible pit of blackness, and Kilauea was in all its fiery glory. We had reached the largest active volcano in the world, the " place of everlasting burnings."

Rarely was light more welcome than that which twinkled from under the verandah of the lonely crater-house into the rainy night. The hospitable landlord of this unique dwelling lifted me from my horse, and carried me into a pleasant room thoroughly warmed by a large wood fire, and I hastily retired to bed to spend much of the bitterly cold night in watching the fiery vapours rolling up out of the infinite darkness, and in dreading the descent into the crater. The heavy clouds were crimson with the reflection, and soon after midnight jets of flame of a most peculiar colour leapt fitfully into the air, accompanied by a dull throbbing sound.

This morning was wet and murky as many mornings are here, and the view from the door was a blank up to ten o'clock, when the mist rolled away and revealed the mystery of last night, the mighty crater whose vast terminal wall is only a few yards from this house. We think of a volcano as a cone. This is a different thing. The abyss, which really is at a height of nearly 4,000 feet on the flank of Mauna Loa, has the appearance of a great pit on a rolling plain. But such a pit! It is nine miles in circumference, and its lowest area, which not long ago fell about 300 feet, just as ice on a pond falls when the water below it is withdrawn, covers six square miles. The depth of the crater varies from 800 to 1,100 feet in different years, according as the molten sea below is at flood or ebb. Signs of volcanic activity are present more or less throughout its whole depth, and for some distance round its margin, in the form of steam cracks, jets of sulphurous vapour, blowing cones, accumulating deposits of acicular crystals of sulphur, &c., and the pit itself is constantly rent and shaken by earthquakes. Grand eruptions occur at intervals with circumstances of indescribable terror and dignity, but Kilauea does not limit its activity to these outbursts, but has exhibited its marvellous phenomena through all known time in a lake or lakes in the southern part of the crater three miles from this side.

This lake, the Hale-mau-mau, or House of Everlasting Fire of the Hawaiian mythology, the abode of the dreaded goddess Pele, is approachable with safety except during an eruption. The spectacle, however, varies almost daily, and at times the level of the lava in the pit within a pit is so low, and the suffocating gases are evolved in such enormous quantities, that travellers are unable to see anything. There had been no news from it for a week, and as nothing was to be seen but a very faint bluish vapour hanging round its margin, the prospect was not encouraging.

When I have learned more about the Hawaiian volcanoes, I shall tell you more of their phenomena, but to-night I shall only write to you my first impressions of what we actually saw on this January 31st. My highest expectations have been infinitely exceeded, and I can hardly write soberly after such a spectacle, especially while through the open door I see the fiery clouds of vapour from the pit rolling up into a sky, glowing as if itself on fire.

We were accompanied into the crater by a comical native guide, who mimicked us constantly, our Hilo guide, who " makes up " a little English, a native woman from Kona, who speaks imperfect English poetically, and her brother who speaks none. I was conscious that we foreign women with our stout staffs and grotesque dress looked like caricatures, and the natives, who have a keen sense of the ludicrous, did not conceal that they thought us so.

The first descent down the terminal wall of the crater is very precipitous, but it and the slope which extends to the second descent are thickly covered with *ohias, ohelos* (a species of whortleberry), sadlerias, polypodiums, silver grass, and a great variety of bulbous plants many of which bore clusters of berries of a brilliant turquoise blue. The " beyond " looked terrible. I could not help clinging to these vestiges of the kindlier mood of nature in which she sought to cover the horrors she had wrought. The next descent is over rough blocks and ridges of broken lava, and appears to form part of a break which extends irregularly round the whole crater, and which probably marks a tremendous subsidence of its floor. Here the last apparent vegetation was left behind, and the familiar earth. We were in a new Plutonic region of blackness and awful desolation, the accustomed sights and sounds of nature all gone. Terraces, cliffs, lakes, ridges, rivers, mountain sides, whirlpools, chasms of lava surrounded us, solid, black, and shining, as if vitrified, or an ashen grey, stained yellow with sulphur here and there, or white with alum. The lava was fissured and upheaved everywhere by earthquakes, hot underneath, and emitting a hot breath.

After more than an hour of very difficult climbing we reached the lowest level of the crater, pretty nearly a mile across, presenting from above the appearance of a sea at rest, but on crossing it we found it to be an expanse of waves and convolutions of ashy-coloured lava, with huge cracks filled up with black iridescent rolls of lava, only a few weeks old. Parts of it are very rough and ridgy, jammed together like field ice, or compacted by rolls of lava which may have swelled up from beneath, but the largest part of the area presents the appearance of huge coiled hawsers, the ropy formation of the lava

rendering the illusion almost perfect. These are riven
by deep cracks which emit hot sulphurous vapours.
Strange to say, in one of these, deep down in that black
and awful region, three slender metamorphosed ferns were
growing, three exquisite forms, the fragile heralds of the
great forest of vegetation, which probably in coming
years will clothe this pit with beauty. Truly they seemed
to speak of the love of God. On our right there was a
precipitous ledge, and a recent flow of lava had poured
over it, cooling as it fell into columnar shapes as sym-
metrical as those of Staffa. It took us a full hour to
cross this deep depression, and as long to master a steep
hot ascent of about 400 feet, formed by a recent lava-flow
from Hale-mau-mau into the basin. This lava hill is an
extraordinary sight—a flood of molten stone, solidifying
as it ran down the declivity, forming arrested waves,
streams, eddies, gigantic convolutions, forms of snakes,
stems of trees, gnarled roots, crooked water-pipes, all
involved and contorted on a gigantic scale, a wilderness
of force and dread. Over one steeper place the lava had
run in a fiery cascade about 100 feet wide. Some had
reached the ground, some had been arrested midway, but
all had taken the aspect of stems of trees. In some of
the crevices I picked up a quantity of very curious fila-
mentose lava, known as " Pelé's hair." It resembles
coarse spun glass, and is of a greenish or yellowish-
brown colour. In many places the whole surface of the
lava is covered with this substance seen through a glazed
medium. During eruptions, when fire-fountains play to
a great height, and drops of lava are thrown in all direc-

tions, the wind spins them out in clear green or yellow threads two or three feet long, which catch and adhere to projecting points.

As we ascended, the flow became hotter under our feet, as well as more porous and glistening. It was so hot that a shower of rain hissed as it fell upon it. The crust became increasingly insecure, and necessitated our walking in single file with the guide in front, to test the security of the footing. I fell through several times, and always into holes full of sulphurous steam, so malignantly acid that my strong dog-skin gloves were burned through as I raised myself on my hands.

We had followed a lava-flow for thirty miles up to the crater's brink, and now we had toiled over recent lava for three hours, and by all calculation were close to the pit, yet there was no smoke or sign of fire, and I felt sure that the volcano had died out for once for our especial disappointment. Indeed, I had been making up my mind for disappointment since we left the crater-house, in consequence of reading seven different accounts, in which language was exhausted in describing Kilauea.

Suddenly, just above, and in front of us, gory drops were tossed in air, and springing forwards we stood on the brink of Hale-mau-mau, which was about 35 feet below us. I think we all screamed, I know we all wept, but we were speechless, for a new glory and terror had been added to the earth. It is the most unutterable of wonderful things. The words of common speech are quite useless. It is unimaginable, indescribable, a sight to remember for ever, a sight which at once took possession of every faculty of sense and soul, removing one altogether out of the range of ordinary life. Here was the real "bottomless pit"—the "fire which is not quenched"—"the place of hell"—"the lake which burneth with fire and brimstone"—the "everlasting burnings"—the fiery sea whose waves are never weary. There were groanings, rumblings, and detonations, rushings, hissings, and splashings, and the crashing sound of breakers on the coast, but it was the surging of fiery waves upon a fiery shore. But what can I write! Such words as jets, fountains, waves, spray, convey some idea of order and regularity, but here there was none. The inner lake, while we stood there, formed a sort of crater within itself, the whole lava sea rose about three feet, a blowing cone about eight feet high was formed, it was never the same two minutes together. And what we saw had no existence a month ago, and probably will be changed in every essential feature a month hence.

What we did see was one irregularly-shaped lake, possibly 500 feet wide at its narrowest part and nearly half a mile at its broadest, almost divided into two by a low bank of lava, which extended nearly across it where it was narrowest, and which was raised visibly before our eyes. The sides of the nearest part of the lake were absolutely perpendicular, but nowhere more than 40 feet high; but opposite to us on the far side of the larger lake they were bold and craggy, and probably not less than 150 feet high. On one side there was an expanse entirely occupied with blowing cones, and jets of steam or vapour. The lake has been known to sink 400 feet, and a month ago it overflowed its banks. The prominent object was fire in motion, but the surface of the double lake was continually skinning over for a second or two with a cooled crust of a lustrous grey-white, like frosted silver, broken by jagged cracks of a bright rose-colour The movement was nearly always from the sides to the centre, but the movement of the centre itself appeared independent and always took a southerly direction. Before each outburst of agitation there was much hissing and a throbbing internal roaring, as of imprisoned gases. Now it seemed furious, demoniacal, as if no power on earth could bind it, then playful and sportive, then for a second languid, but only because it was accumulating fresh force. On our arrival eleven fire fountains were playing joyously round the lakes, and sometimes the six of the nearer lake ran together in the centre to go wallowing down in one vortex, from which they reappeared bulging upwards, till they formed a huge cone 30 feet high, which plunged downwards in a whirlpool only to reappear in exactly the previous number of fountains in different parts of the lake, high leaping, raging, flinging themselves upwards. Sometimes the whole lake, abandoning its usual centripetal motion, as if impelled southwards, took the form of mighty waves, and surging heavily against the partial barrier with a sound like the Pacific surf, lashed, tore, covered it, and threw itself over it in clots of living fire. It was all confusion, commotion, force, terror, glory, majesty, mystery, and even beauty. And the colour! "Eye hath not seen" it! Molten metal has not that crimson gleam, nor blood that living light!

Had I not seen this I should never have known that such a colour was possible.

The crust perpetually wrinkled, folded over, and cracked, and great pieces were drawn downwards to be again thrown up on the crests of waves. The eleven fountains of gory fire played the greater part of the time, dancing round the lake with a strength of joyousness which was absolute beauty. Indeed after the first half hour of terror had gone by, the beauty of these jets made a profound impression upon me, and the sight of them must always remain one of the most fascinating recollections of my life. During three hours, the bank of lava which almost divided the lakes rose considerably, owing to the cooling of the spray as it dashed over it, and a cavern of considerable size was formed within it, the roof of which was hung with fiery stalactites, more than a foot long. Nearly the whole time the surges of the further lake taking a southerly direction, broke with a tremendous noise on the bold craggy cliffs which are its southern boundary, throwing their gory spray to a height of fully forty feet. At times an overhanging crag fell in, creating a vast splash of fire and increased commotion.

Almost close below us there was an intermittent jet of lava, which kept cooling round what was possibly a blow-hole forming a cone with an open top, which when we first saw it was about six feet high on its highest side, and about as many in diameter. Up this cone or chimney heavy jets of lava were thrown every second or two, and cooling as they fell over its edge, raised it rapidly before our eyes. Its fiery interior, and the singular sound with which the lava was vomited up, were very awful. There was no smoke rising from the lake, only a faint blue vapour which the wind carried in the opposite direction. The heat was excessive. We were obliged to stand the whole time, and the soles of our boots were burned, and my ear and one side of my face were blistered. Although there was no smoke from the lake itself, there was an awful region to the westward, of smoke and sound, and rolling clouds of steam and vapour whose phenomena it was not safe to investigate, where the blowing cones are, whose fires last night appeared stationary. We were able to stand quite near the margin, and look down into the lake, as you look into the sea from the deck of a ship, the only risk being that the fractured ledge might give way.

Before we came away, a new impulse seized the lava. The fire was thrown to a great height; the fountains and jets all wallowed together; new ones appeared, and danced joyously round the margin, then converging towards the centre they merged into one glowing mass, which upheaved itself pyramidally and disappeared with a vast plunge. Then innumerable billows of fire dashed themselves into the air, crashing and lashing, and the lake dividing itself recoiled on either side, then hurling its fires together and rising as if by upheaval from below, it surged over the temporary rim which it had formed, passing downwards in a slow majestic flow, leaving the central surface swaying and dashing in fruitless agony as if sent on some errand it failed to accomplish.

Farewell, I fear for ever, to the glorious Hale-mau-
mau, the grandest type of force that the earth holds!
"Break, break, break," on through the coming years,

> " No more by thee my steps shall be,
>   No more again for ever !"

It seemed a dull trudge over the black and awful
crater, and strange, like half-forgotten sights of a world
with which I had ceased to have aught to do, were the
dwarf tree-ferns, the lilies with their turquoise clusters,
the crimson myrtle blossoms, and all the fair things
which decked the precipice up which we slowly dragged
our stiff and painful limbs. Yet it was but the exchange
of a world of sublimity for a world of beauty, the " place
of hell," for the bright upper earth, with its endless
summer, and its perennial foliage, blossom, and fruitage.

Since writing the above I have been looking over the
"Volcano Book," which contains the observations and
impressions of people from all parts of the world. Some
of these are painstaking and valuable as showing the
extent and rapidity of the changes which take place in
the crater, but there is an immense quantity of flippant
rubbish, and would-be wit, in which "Madam Pelé,"
invariably occurs, this goddess, who was undoubtedly
one of the grandest of heathen mythical creations, being
caricatured in pencil and pen and ink, under every
ludicrous aspect that can be conceived. Some of the
entries are brief and absurd, "Not much of a fizz," " a
grand splutter," "Madam Pelé in the dumps," and so
forth. These generally have English signatures. The
American wit is far racier, but depends mainly on the

profane use of certain passages of scripture, a species of wit which is at once easy and disgusting. People are all particular in giving the precise time of the departure from Hilo and arrival here, "making good time" being a thing much admired on Hawaii, but few can boast of more than three miles an hour. It is wonderful that people can parade their snobbishness within sight of Hale-mau-mau.

This inn is a unique and interesting place. Its existence is strikingly precarious, for the whole region is in a state of perpetual throb from earthquakes, and the sights and sounds are gruesome and awful both by day and night. The surrounding country steams and smokes from cracks and pits, and a smell of sulphur fills the air. They cook their *kalo* in a steam apparatus of nature's own work just behind the house, and every drop of water is from a distillery similarly provided. The inn is a grass and bamboo house, very beautifully constructed without nails. It is a longish building with a steep roof divided inside by partitions which run up to the height of the walls. There is no ceiling. The joists which run across are concealed by wreaths of evergreens, from among which peep out here and there stars on a blue ground. The door opens from the verandah into a centre room with a large open brick fire place, in which a wood fire is constantly burning, for at this altitude the temperature is cool. Some chairs, two lounges, small tables, and some books and pictures on the walls give a look of comfort, and there is the reality of comfort in perfection. Our sleeping-place, a neat room with a matted

floor opens from this, and on the other side there is a
similar room, and a small eating-room with a grass
cookhouse beyond, from which an obliging old Chinaman
who persistently calls us " sir," brings our food. We
have had for each meal, tea, preserved milk, coffee, *kalo*,
biscuits, butter, potatoes, goats' flesh, and *ohelos*. The
charge is five dollars a day, but everything except the
potatoes and *ohelos* has to be brought twenty or thirty
miles on mules' backs. It is a very pretty picturesque
house both within and without, and stands on a natural
lawn of brilliant but unpalatable grass, surrounded by a
light fence covered with a small trailing double rose. It
is altogether a most magical building in the heart of a
formidable volcanic wilderness. Mr. Gilman, our host,
is a fine picturesque looking man, half Indian, and speaks
remarkably good English, but his wife, a very pretty
native woman, speaks none, and he attends to us entirely
himself.

A party of native travellers rainbound are here, and
the native women are sitting on the floor stringing flowers
and berries for *leis*. One very attractive-looking young
woman, refined by consumption, is lying on some blankets, and three native men are smoking by the fire. Upa
attempts conversation with us in broken English, and the
others laugh and talk incessantly. My inkstand, pen,
and small handwriting amuse them very much. Miss K.,
the typical American travelling lady, who is encountered
everywhere from the Andes to the Pyramids, tireless, with
an indomitable energy, Spartan endurance, and a genius
for attaining everything, and myself, a limp, ragged,

shoeless wretch, complete the group, and our heaps of saddles, blankets, spurs, and gear tell of real travelling, past and future. It is a most picturesque sight by the light of the flickering fire, and the fire which is unquenchable burns without.

About 300 yards off there is a sulphur steam vapour-bath, highly recommended by the host as a panacea for the woeful aches, pains, and stiffness produced by the six-mile scramble through the crater, and I groaned and limped down to it : but it is a truly spasmodic arrangement, singularly independent of human control, and I have not the slightest doubt that the reason why Mr. Gilman obligingly remained in the vicinity was, lest I should be scalded or blown to atoms by a sudden freak of Kilauea, though I don't see that he was capable of preventing either catastrophe ! A slight grass shed has been built over a sulphur steam crack, and within this there is a deep box with a sliding lid and a hole for the throat, and the victim is supposed to sit in this and be steamed. But on this occasion the temperature was so high, that my hand, which I unwisely experimented upon, was immediately peeled. In order not to wound Mr. Gilman's feelings, which are evidently sensitive on the subject of this irresponsible contrivance, I remained the prescribed time within the shed, and then managed to limp a little less, and go with him to what are called the Sulphur Banks, on which sulphurous vapour is perpetually depositing the most exquisite acicular sulphur crystals ; these, as they aggregate, take entrancing forms, like the featherwork produced by the "frost-fall" in

Colorado, but, like it, they perish with a touch, and can only be seen in the wonderful laboratory where they are formed.

In addition to the natives before mentioned, there is an old man here who has been a bullock-hunter on Hawaii for forty years, and knows the island thoroughly. In common with all the residents I have seen, he takes an intense interest in volcanic phenomena, and has just been giving us a thrilling account of the great eruption in 1868, when beautiful Hilo was threatened with destruction. Three weeks ago, he says, a profound hush fell on Kilauea, and the summit crater of Mauna Loa became active, and amidst throbbings, rumblings, and earthquakes, broke into such magnificence that the light was visible 100 miles at sea, a burning mountain 13,750 feet high ! . The fires after two days died out as suddenly, and from here we can see the great dome-like top, snow-capped under the stars, serene in an eternal winter.

I. L. B.

LETTER VI.

My plans are quite overturned. I was to have ridden with the native mail-carrier to the north of the island to take the steamer for Honolulu, but there are freshets in the gulches on the road, making the ride unsafe. There is no steamer from Hilo for three weeks, and in the meantime Mr. and Mrs. S. have kindly consented to receive me as a boarder; and I find the people, scenery, and life so charming, that I only regret my detention on Mrs. Dexter's account. I am already rested from the great volcano trip.

We left Kilauea at seven in the morning of the 1st Feb. in a pouring rain. The natives decorated us with *leis* of turquoise and coral berries, and of crimson and yellow *ohia* blossoms. The saddles were wet, the crater was blotted out by mist, water dripped from the trees, we splashed through pools in the rocks, the horses plunged into mud up to their knees, and the drip, drip, of vertical, earnest, tepid, tropical rain accompanied us nearly to Hilo. Upa and Miss K. held umbrellas the whole way, but I required both hands for holding on to the horse whenever he chose to gallop. As soon as we left the crater-house Upa started over the grass at full speed, my horse of course followed, and my feet being jerked

out of the stirrups, I found myself ignominiously sitting
on the animal's back behind the saddle, and nearly slid
over his tail, before, by skilful efforts, I managed to
scramble over the peak back again, when I held on
by horn and mane until the others stopped. Happily
I was last, and I don't think they saw me. Upa
amused me very much on the way; he insists that I am
" a high chief." He said a good deal about Queen
Victoria, whose virtues seem well known here : " Good
Queen make good people," he said, " English very good ! "
He asked me how many chiefs we had, and supposing
him to mean hereditary peers, I replied, over 500.
" Too many, too many ! " he answered emphatically—
" too much chief eat up people ! " He asked me if all
people were good in England, and I was sorry to tell him
that this was very far from being the case. He was incredulous, or seemed so out of flattery, and said, " You
good Queen, you Bible long time, you good ! " I was
surprised to find how much he knew of European politics,
of the liberation of Italy, and the Franco-German war.
He expressed a most orthodox horror of the Pope, who,
he said, he knew from his Bible was the " Beast ! " He
said, " I bring band and serenade for good Queen sake,"
but this has not come off yet.

We straggled into Hilo just at dusk, thoroughly wet,
jaded, and satisfied, but half-starved, for the rain had
converted that which should have been our lunch into a
brownish pulp of bread and newspaper, and we had sub-
sisted only on some half-ripe guavas. After the black
desolation of Kilauea, I realized more fully the beauty of

Hilo, as it appeared in the gloaming. The rain had ceased, cool breezes rustled through the palm-groves and sighed through the funereal foliage of the pandanus. Under thick canopies of the glossy breadfruit and banana, groups of natives were twining garlands of roses and ohia blossoms. The lights of happy foreign homes flashed from under verandahs festooned with passion-flowers, and the low chant, to me nearly intolerable, but which the natives love, mingled with the ceaseless moaning of the surf and the sighing of the breeze through the trees, and a heavy fragrance, unlike the faint sweet odours of the north, filled the evening air. It was delicious.

I suffered intensely from pain and stiffness, and was induced to try a true Hawaiian remedy, which is not only regarded as a cure for all physical ills, but as the greatest of physical luxuries ; i.e. lomi-lomi. This is a compound of pinching, pounding, and squeezing, and Moi Moi, the fine old Hawaiian nurse in this family, is an adept in the art. She found out by instinct which were the most painful muscles, and subjected them to a doubly severe pounding, laughing heartily at my groans. However, I must admit that my arms and shoulders were almost altogether relieved before the lomi-lomi was finished. The first act of courtesy to a stranger in a native house is this, and it is varied in many ways. Now and then the patient lies face downwards, and children execute a sort of dance upon his spine.* Formerly, the chiefs, when not engaged in active pursuits, exacted lomi-lomi as a constant service from their followers.

* " Reef Rovings."

A number of Hilo folk came in during the evening to
inquire how we had sped, and for news of the volcano. I
think the proximity of Kilauea gives sublimity to Hilo,
and helps to lift conversation out of common-place
ruts. It is no far-off spectacle, but an immediate source
of wonder and apprehension, for it rocks the village with
earthquakes, and renders the construction of stone houses
and plastered ceilings impossible. It rolls vast tidal waves
with infinite destruction on the coast, and of late years
its fiery overflowings have twice threatened this paradise
with annihilation. Then there is the dead volcano of
Mauna Loa, from whose resurrection anything may be
feared. Even last night a false rumour that a light was
to be seen on its summit brought everyone out, but it was
only an increased glare from the pit of Hale-mau-mau.
It is most interesting to be in a region of such splendid
possibilities.

I. L. B.

LETTER VII.

THE white population here, which constitutes "society,' is very small. There are two venerable missionaries "Father Coan" and "Father Lyman," the former pastor of a large native congregation, which, though much shrunken, is not only self-sustaining, but contributes $1200 a year to foreign missions, and the latter, though very old and frail, the indefatigable head of an industrial school for native young men. Their houses combine the trimness of New England, with the luxuriance of the tropics; they are cool retreats, embowered among bread-fruit, tamarind, and bamboo, through whose graceful leafage the blue waters of the bay are visible. Innumerable exotics are domesticated round these fair home-steads. Two of "Father Lyman's" sons are influential residents, one being the Lieutenant-Governor of the island. Other sons of former missionaries are settled here in business, and there are a few strangers who have been attracted hither. Dr. Wetmore, formerly of the mission, is a typical New Englander of the old orthodox school. It is pleasant to see him brighten into almost youthful enthusiasm on the subject of Hawaiian ferns. My host, a genial, social, intelligent American, is sheriff of Hawaii, postmaster, &c., and with his charming wife

(a missionary's daughter), and some friends who live
with them, make their large house a centre of kindliness,
friendliness, and hospitality. Mr. Thompson, pastor of
the foreign church, is a man of very liberal culture, as
well as wide sympathies. The lady principal of the
Government school is a handsome, talented Vermont
girl, and besides being an immense favourite, well deserves her unusual and lucrative position.

There are hardly any young ladies, and very few young
men, but plenty of rosy, blooming children, who run
about barefoot all the year. Besides the Hilo residents,
there are some planters' families within seven miles, who
come in to sewing circles, church, &c. There is a small
class of reprobate white men who have ostracized themselves by means of drink and bad morals, and are a curse
to the natives. The half whites, among whom "Bill
Ragsdale" is the leading spirit, are not numerous. Hilo
has no carriage roads and no carriages : every one must
ride or travel in a litter. People are very kind to each
other. Horses, dresses, patterns, books, and articles of
domestic use, are lent and borrowed continually. The
smallness of the society and the close proximity are too
much like a ship. People know everything about the
details of each other's daily life, income, and expenditure, and the day's doings of each member of the little
circle are matters for conversation. Indeed, were it not
for the volcano and its doings, conversation might degenerate into gossip. There is an immense deal of personal talk; the wonder is that there is so little ill-nature.
Not only is what everybody does here common property,

but the sayings, doings, goings, comings, and purchases
of every one in all the other islands are common property
also, made so by letters and oral communication.　It is
all very amusing, and on the whole very kindly, and
human interests are always interesting; but it has its
perilous side.　They are very kind to each other.　There
is no distress which is not alleviated.　There is no nurse,
and in cases of sickness the ladies take it by turns to
wait on the sufferer by day and night for weeks, and even
months.　Such inevitable mutual dependence of course
promotes friendliness.

The foreigners live very simply.　The eating-rooms
are used solely for eating, the "parlours" are always
cheerful and tasteful, and the bedrooms very pretty,
adorned with all manner of knick-knacks made by the
ladies, who are indescribably deft with their fingers.
Light Manilla matting is used instead of carpets.　A
Chinese man-cook, who leaves at seven in the evening, is
the only servant, except in one or two cases, where, as
here, a native woman condescends to come in during the
day as a nurse.　In the morning the ladies, in their fresh
pretty wrappers and ruffled white aprons, sweep and dust
the rooms, and I never saw women look more truly graceful
and refined than they do, when engaged in the plain
prose of these domestic duties.　They make all their own
dresses, and when any lady is busy and wants a dress
in a hurry, two or three of them meet and make it for
her.　I never saw people live such easy pleasant lives.
They have such good health, for one thing, partly no
doubt because their domestic duties give them wholesome

exercise without pressing upon them. They have abounding leisure for reading, music, choir practising, drawing, fern-printing, fancy work, picnics, riding parties, and enjoy sociability thoroughly. They usually ride in dainty bloomer costumes, even when they don't ride astride. All the houses are pretty, and it takes little to make them so in this climate. One novel fashion is to decorate the walls with festoons of the beautiful fern Microlepia tenuifolia, which are renewed as soon as they fade, and every room is adorned with a profusion of bouquets, which are easily obtained where flowers bloom all the year. Many of the residents possess valuable libraries, and these, with cabinets of minerals, volcanic specimens, shells, and coral, with weapons, calabashes, ornaments, and cloth of native manufacture, almost furnish a room in themselves. Some of the volcanic specimens and the coral are of almost inestimable value, as well as of exquisite beauty.

The gentlemen don't seem to have near so much occupation as the ladies. There are two stores on the beach, and at these and at the Court-house they aggregate, for lack of club-house and exchange. Business is not here a synonym for hurry, and official duties are light; so light, that in these morning hours I see the governor, the sheriff, and the judge, with three other gentlemen, playing an interminable croquet game on the Court-house lawn. They purvey gossip for the ladies, and how much they invent, and how much they only circulate can never be known !

There is a large native population in the village, along

the beach, and on the heights above the Waikuku River. Frame houses with lattices, and grass houses with deep verandahs, peep out everywhere from among the mangoes and bananas. The governess of Hawaii, the Princess Keelikalani, has a house on the beach shaded by a large umbrella-tree and a magnificent clump of bamboos, 70 feet in height. The native life with which one comes constantly in contact, is very interesting.

The men do whatever hard work is done in cultivating the *kalo* patches and pounding the *kalo*. This *kalo*, the Arum esculentum, forms the national diet. A Hawaiian could not exist without his calabash of *poi*. The root is an object of the tenderest solicitude, from the day it is planted until the hour when it is lovingly eaten. The eating of *poi* seems a ceremony of profound meaning; it is like the eating salt with an Arab, or a Masonic sign. The *kalo* root is an ovate oblong, as bulky as a Californian beet, and it has large leaves, shaped like a broad arrow, of a singularly bright green. The best kinds grow entirely in water. The patch is embanked and frequently inundated, and each plant grows on a small hillock of puddled earth. The cutting from which it grows is simply the top of the plant, with a little of the tuber. The men stand up to their knees in water while cultivating the root. It is excellent when boiled and sliced; but the preparation of *poi* is an elaborate process. The roots are baked in an underground oven, and are then laid on a slightly hollowed board, and beaten with a stone pestle. It is hard work, and the men don't wear any clothes while engaged in it. It is

not a pleasant-looking operation. They often dip their
hands in a calabash of water to aid them in removing the
sticky mass, and they always look hot and tired. When
it is removed from the board into large calabashes, it is
reduced to paste by the addition of water, and set aside
for two or three days to ferment. When ready for use it
is either lilac or pink, and tastes like sour bookbinders'
paste. Before water is added, when it is in its dry state,
it is called *paiai*, or hard food, and is then packed in *ti*
leaves in 20 lb. bundles for inland carriage, and is exported to the Guano Islands. It is a prolific and nutri-
tious plant. It is estimated that forty square feet will
support an Hawaiian for a year.

The melon and *kalo* patches represent a certain
amount of spasmodic industry, but in most other things
the natives take no thought for the morrow. Why
should they indeed? For while they lie basking in the
sun, without care of theirs, the cocoanut, the breadfruit,
the yam, the guava, the banana, and the delicious
papaya, which is a compound of a ripe apricot with a
Cantaloupe melon, grow and ripen perpetually. Men
and women are always amusing themselves, the men
with surf-bathing, the women with making *leis*—both
sexes with riding, gossiping, and singing. Every man
and woman, almost every child, has a horse. There is a
perfect plague of badly bred, badly developed, weedy
looking animals. The beach and the pleasant lawn
above it are always covered with men and women riding
at a gallop, with bare feet, and stirrups tucked between
the toes. To walk even 200 yards seems considered a

degradation. The people meet outside each others' houses all day long, and sit in picturesque groups on their mats, singing, laughing, talking, and quizzing the *haoles*, as if the primal curse had never fallen. Pleasant sights of out-door cooking gregariously carried on greet one everywhere. This style of cooking prevails all over Polynesia. A hole in the ground is lined with stones, wood is burned within it, and when the rude oven has been sufficiently heated, the pig, chicken, breadfruit, or *kalo*, wrapped in *ti* leaves is put in, a little water is thrown on, and the whole is covered up. It is a slow but sure process.

Bright dresses, bright eyes, bright sunshine, music, dancing, a life without care, and a climate without asperities, make up the sunny side of native life as pictured at Hilo. But there are dark moral shadows, the population is shrinking away, and rumours of leprosy are afloat, so that some of these fair homes may be desolate ere long. However many causes for regret exist, one must not forget that only forty years ago the people inhabiting this strip of land between the volcanic wilderness and the sea were a vicious, sensual, shameless herd, that no man among them, except their chiefs, had any rights, that they were harried and oppressed almost to death, and had no consciousness of any moral obligations. Now, order and external decorum at least, prevail. There is not a locked door in Hilo, and nobody makes anybody else afraid.

The people of Hawaii-nei are clothed and civilized in their habits; they have equal rights; 6,500 of them have *kuleanas* or freeholds, equable and enlightened laws are impartially administered; wrong and oppression are unknown; they enjoy one of the best administered governments in the world; education is universal, and the throne is occupied by a liberal sovereign of their own race and election.

Few of them speak English. Their language is so easy that most of the foreigners acquire it readily. You know how stupid I am about languages, yet I have already picked up the names of most common things. There are only twelve letters, but some of these are made to do double duty, as K is also T, and L is also R. The most northern island of the group, Kauai, is as often pronounced as if it began with a T, and Kalo is usually Taro. It is a very musical language. Each syllable and word ends with a vowel, and there are none of our rasping and sibillant consonants. In their soft phraseology our hard rough surnames undergo a metamorphosis, as Fisk into Filikina, Wilson into Wilikina. Each vowel is distinctly pronounced, and usually with the Italian sound. The volcano is pronounced as if spelt Keel-ah-wee-ah, and Kauai as if Kah-wye-ee. The name Owhyhee for Hawaii had its origin in a mistake, for the island was never anything but Hawaii, pronounced Hah-wye-ee, but Captain Cook mistook the prefix O, which is the sign of the nominative case, for a part of the word. Many of the names of places, specially of those compounded with *wai*, water, are very musical; Wailuku, "water of destruction;" Waialeale, "rippling water;" *Waioli*, "singing water;" Waipio, "vanquished water;"

Kaiwaihae, "torn water." Mauna, "mountain," is a mere prefix, and though always used in naming the two giants of the Pacific, Mauna Kea, and Mauna Loa, is hardly ever applied to Hualalai, " the offspring of the shining sun ; " or to Haleakala on Maui, " the house of the sun."

I notice that the foreigners never use the English or botanical names of trees or plants, but speak of *ohias*, *ohelos*, *kukui* (candle-nut), *lauhala* (pandanus), *pulu* (tree fern), *mamané*, *koa*, &c. There is one native word in such universal use that I already find I cannot get on without it, *pilikia*. It means anything, from a down-right trouble to a slight difficulty or entanglement. "I'm in a pilikia," or "very pilikia," or "pilikia!" A revolution would be "a pilikia." The fact of the late king dying without naming a successor was pre-eminently a pilikia, and it would be a serious pilikia if a horse were to lose a shoe on the way to Kilauea. *Hou-hou,* meaning "in a huff," I hear on all sides ; and two words, *makai*, signify-ing "on the sea-side," and *mauka*, "on the mountain side." These terms are perfectly intelligible out of doors, but it is puzzling when one is asked to sit on " the *mauka* side of the table." The word *aloha*, in foreign use, has taken the place of every English equivalent. It is a greeting, a farewell, thanks, love, goodwill. *Aloha* looks at you from tidies and illuminations, it meets you on the roads and at house-doors, it is conveyed to you in letters, the air is full of it. " My *aloha* to you," " he sends you his *aloha*," " they desire their *aloha*." It already repre-sents to me all of kindness and goodwill that language can express, and the convenience of it as compared with other phrases is, that it means exactly what the receiver understands it to mean, and consequently, in all cases can be conveyed by a third person. There is no word for "thank you." *Maikai* "good," is often useful in its place, and smiles supply the rest. There are no words which express "gratitude" or "chastity," or some others of the virtues; and they have no word for "weather," that which we understand by "weather" being absolutely unknown.

Natives have no surnames. Our volcano guide is Upa, or Scissors, but his wife and children are anything else. The late king was Kamehameha, or the "lonely one." The father of the present king is called Kanaina, but the king's name is Lunalilo, or "above all." Nor does it appear that a man is always known by the same name, nor that a name necessarily indicates the sex of its possessor. Thus, in signing a paper the signature would be Hoapili *kanaka*, or Hoapili *wahine*, according as the signer was man or woman. I remember that in my first letter I fell into the vulgarism, initiated by the whaling crews, of calling the natives *Kanakas*. This is universally but very absurdly done, as *Kanaka* simply means man. If an Hawaiian word is absolutely necessary, we might translate native and have *maole*, pronounced *maori*, like that of the New Zealand aborigines. Kanaka is to me decidedly objectionable, as conveying the idea of canaille.

I had written thus far when Mr. Severance came in to say that a grand display of the national sport of surf-bathing was going on, and a large party of us went down to the beach for two hours to enjoy it. It is really a most exciting pastime, and in a rough sea requires immense nerve. The surf-board is a tough plank shaped like a coffin lid, about two feet broad, and from six to nine feet long, well oiled and cared for. It is usually made of the erythrina, or the breadfruit tree. The surf was very heavy and favourable, and legions of natives were swimming and splashing in the sea, though not more than forty had their *Papa-he-nalu*, or "wave sliding boards," with them. The men, dressed only in *malos*, carrying their boards under their arms, waded out from some rocks on which the sea was breaking, and, pushing their boards before them, swam out to the first line of breakers, and then diving down were seen no more till they re-appeared as a number of black heads bobbing about like corks in smooth water half a mile from shore.

What they seek is a very high roller, on the top of which they leap from behind, lying face downwards on their boards. As the wave speeds on, and the bottom strikes the ground, the top breaks into a huge comber. The swimmers but appeared posing themselves on its highest edge by dexterous movements of their hands and feet, keeping just at the top of the curl, but always apparently coming down hill with a slanting motion. So they rode in majestically, always just ahead of the breaker, carried shorewards by its mighty impulse at the rate of forty miles an hour, yet seeming to have a volition of their own, as the more daring riders knelt and even stood on their surf-boards, waving their arms and uttering exultant cries. They were always apparently on the verge of engulfment by the fierce breaker whose towering white

crest was ever above and just behind them, but just as
one expected to see them dashed to pieces, they either
waded quietly ashore, or sliding off their boards, dived
under the surf, taking advantage of the undertow, and were
next seen far out at sea preparing for fresh exploits.

The great art seems to be to mount the roller precisely
at the right time, and to keep exactly on its curl just
before it breaks. Two or three athletes, who stood erect
on their boards as they swept exultingly shorewards, were
received with ringing cheers by the crowd. Many of
the less expert failed to throw themselves on the crest,
and slid back into smooth water, or were caught in the
combers which were fully ten feet high, and after being
rolled over and over, ignominiously disappeared amidst
roars of laughter, and shouts from the shore. At first I
held my breath in terror, thinking the creatures were
smothered or dashed to pieces, and then in a few seconds
I saw the dark heads of the objects of my anxiety bobbing
about behind the rollers waiting for another chance. The
shore was thronged with spectators, and the presence of
the *élite* of Hilo stimulated the swimmers to wonderful
exploits.

These people are truly amphibious. Both sexes seem
to swim by nature, and the children riot in the waves from
their infancy. They dive apparently by a mere effort of
the will. In the deep basin of the Wailuku River, a
little below the Falls, the maidens swim, float, and dive
with garlands of flowers round their heads and throats.
The more furious and agitated the water is, the greater
the excitement, and the love of these watery exploits is

not confined to the young. I saw great fat men with
their hair streaked with grey, balancing themselves on
their narrow surf-boards, and riding the surges shorewards with as much enjoyment as if they were in their
first youth. I enjoyed the afternoon thoroughly.

Is it "always afternoon" here, I wonder? The sea
was so blue, the sunlight so soft, the air so sweet. There
was no toil, clang, or hurry. People were all holiday-
making (if that can be where there is no work), and enjoying themselves, the surf-bathers in the sea, and hundreds of gaily-dressed men and women galloping on the
beach. It was so serene and tropical. I sympathize
with those who eat thé lotus, and remain for ever on such
enchanted shores.

I am gaining health daily, and almost live in the open
air. I have hired the native policeman's horse and saddle,
and with a Macgregor flannel riding costume, which my
kind friends have made for me, and a pair of jingling
Mexican spurs am quite Hawaiianised. I ride alone once
or twice a day exploring the neighbourhood, finding some
new fern or flower daily, and abandon myself wholly to
the fascination of this new existence.

I. L. B.

LETTER VIII.

ONOMEA, HAWAII.
JUDGE AUSTIN'S.

MRS. A. has been ill for some time, and Mrs. S. her sister and another friend "plotted" in a very "clandestine" manner that I should come here for a few days in order to give her "a little change of society," but I am quite sure that under this they only veil a kind wish that I should see something of plantation life. There is a plan, too, that I should take a five days' trip to a remarkable valley called Waipio, but this is only a "castle in the air."

Mr. A. sent in for me a capital little lean rat of a horse which by dint of spirit and activity managed to keep within sight of two large horses, ridden by Mr. Thompson, and a very handsome young lady riding "cavalier fashion," who convoyed me out. Borrowed saddle-bags, and a couple of shingles for carrying ferns formed my outfit, and were carried behind my saddle. It is a magnificent ride here. The track crosses the deep, still, Wailuku River on a wooden bridge, and then after winding up a steep hill, among native houses fantastically situated, hangs on the verge of the lofty precipices which descend perpendicularly to the sea, dips into tremendous gulches, loses itself in the bright fern-fringed torrents which have cleft their way down from the mountains, and at last emerges on the delicious height on which this house is built.

This coast looked beautiful from the deck of the *Kilauea*, but I am now convinced that I have never seen anything so perfectly lovely as it is when one is actually among its details. Onomea is 600 feet high, and every yard of the ascent from Hilo brings one into a fresher and purer air. One looks up the wooded, broken slopes to a wild volcanic wilderness and the snowy peaks of Mauna Kea on one side, and on the other down upon the calm blue Pacific, wrinkled by the sweet trade-wind, till it blends in far-off loveliness with the still, blue, sky; and heavy surges break on the reefs, and fritter themselves away on the rocks, tossing their pure foam over *ti* and *lauhala* trees, and the exquisite ferns and trailers which mantle the cliffs down to the water's edge. Here a native house stands, with passion-flowers clustering round its verandah, and the great solitary red blossoms of the hibiscus flaming out from dark surrounding leafage, and women in rose and green *holukus*, weaving garlands, greet us with "*Aloha*" as we pass. Then we come upon a whole cluster of grass houses under *lauhalas* and bananas. Then there is the sugar plantation of Kaiwiki, with its patches of bright green cane, its flumes crossing the track above our heads, bringing the cane down from the upland cane-fields to the crushing-mill, and the shifting, busy scenes of the sugar-boiling season.

Then the track goes down with a great dip, along which we slip and slide in the mud to a deep broad stream. This is a most picturesque spot, the junction

of two clear bright rivers, and a few native houses and a
Chinaman's store are grouped close by under some palms,
with the customary loungers on horseback, asking and
receiving *nuhou*, or news, at the doors. Our accustomed horses leaped into a ferry-scow provided by Government, worked by a bearded female of hideous aspect, and
leaped out on the other side to climb a track cut on the
side of a precipice, which would be steep to mount on
one's own feet. There we met parties of natives, all
flower-wreathed, talking and singing, coming gaily down
on their sure-footed horses, saluting us with the invariable "*Aloha*." Every now and then we passed native
churches, with spires painted white, or a native school-
house, or a group of scholars all ferns and flowers. The
greenness of the vegetation merits the term " dazzling."
We think England green, but its colour is poor and pale
as compared with that of tropical Hawaii. Palms, candle-
nuts, *ohias*, hibiscus, were it not for their exceeding
beauty, would almost pall upon one from their abundance,
and each gulch has its glorious entanglement of breadfruit,
the large-leaved *ohia*, or native apple, a species of Eugenia
(*Eugenia Malaccensis*), and the pandanus, with its aerial
roots, all looped together by large sky-blue convolvuli and
the running fern, and is marvellous with parasitic growths.
　　The distracting beauty of this coast is what are called
gulches—narrow deep ravines or gorges, from 100 to 2,000
feet in depth, each with a series of cascades from 10 to
1,800 feet in height. I dislike reducing their glories to
the baldness of figures, but the depth of these clefts
(originally, probably, the seams caused by fire torrents),

cut and worn by the fierce streams fed by the snows of
Mauna Kea, and the rains of the forest belt, cannot otherwise be expressed. The cascades are most truly beautiful,
gleaming white among the dark depths of foliage far
away, and falling into deep limpid basins, festooned and
overhung with the richest and greenest vegetation of this
prolific climate, from the huge-leaved banana and shining
breadfruit to the most feathery of ferns and lycopodiums.
Each gulch opens on a velvet lawn close to the sea, and
most of them have space for a few grass houses, with
cocoanut trees, bananas, and *kalo* patches. There are
sixty-nine of these extraordinary chasms within a distance
of thirty miles !

I think we came through eleven, fording the streams
in all but two. The descent into some of them is quite
alarming. You go down almost standing in your stirrups,
at a right angle with the horse's head, and up, grasping
his mane to prevent the saddle slipping. He goes down
like a goat, with his bare feet, looking cautiously at
each step, sometimes putting out a foot and withdrawing
it again in favour of better footing, and sometimes gathering his four feet under him and sliding or jumping. The
Mexican saddle has great advantages on these tracks,
which are nothing better than ledges cut on the sides of
precipices, for one goes up and down not only in perfect
security but without fatigue. I am beginning to hope
that I am not too old, as I feared I was, to learn a new
mode of riding, for my companions rode at full speed
over places where I should have picked my way carefully
at a foot's pace ; and my horse followed them, galloping

and stopping short at their pleasure, and I successfully
kept my seat, though not without occasional fears of an
ignominious downfall. I even wish that you could see
me in my Rob Roy riding dress, with leather belt and
pouch, a *lei* of the orange seeds of the pandanus round
my throat, jingling Mexican spurs, blue saddle blanket,
and Rob Roy blanket strapped on behind the saddle!

This place is grandly situated 600 feet above a deep
cove, into which two beautiful gulches of great size run,
with heavy cascades, finer than Foyers at its best, and a
native village is picturesquely situated between the two.
The great white rollers, whiter by contrast with the dark
deep water, come into the gulch just where we forded the
river, and from the ford a passable road made for hauling
sugar ascends to the house. The air is something absolutely delicious; and the murmur of the rollers and the
deep boom of the cascades are very soothing. There is
little rise or fall in the cadence of the surf anywhere on
the windward coast, but one even sound, loud or 'soft,
like that made by a train in a tunnel.

We were kindly welçomed, and were at once "made at
home." Delicious phrase! the full meaning of which I
am learning on Hawaii, where, though everything has the
fascination of novelty, I have ceased to feel myself a
stranger. This is a roomy, rambling frame-house, with
a verandah, and the door, as is usual here, opens directly
into the sitting-room. The stair by which I go to my
room suggests possibilities, for it has been removed three
inches from the wall by an earthquake, which also brought
down the tall chimney of the boiling-house. Close by

there are small pretty frame-houses for the overseer, bookkeeper, sugar boiler, and machinist; a store, the factory, a pretty native church near the edge of the cliff, and quite a large native village below. It looks green and bright, and the atmosphere is perfect, with the cool air coming down from the mountains, and a soft breeze coming up from the blue dreamy ocean. Behind the house the uplands slope away to the colossal Mauna Kea. The actual, dense, impenetrable forest does not begin for a mile and a half from the coast, and its broad dark belt, extending to a height of 4,000 feet, and beautifully broken, throws out into greater brightness the upward glades of grass and the fields of sugar-cane.

This is a very busy season, and as this is a large plantation there is an appearance of great animation. There are five or six saddled horses usually tethered below the house; and with overseers, white and coloured, and natives riding at full gallop, and people coming on all sorts of errands, the hum of the crushing-mill, the rush of water in the flumes, and the grind of the waggons carrying cane, there is no end of stir.

The plantations in the Hilo district enjoy special advantages, for by turning some of the innumerable mountain streams into flumes the owners can bring a great part of their cane and all their wood for fuel down to the mills without other expense than the original cost of the woodwork. Mr. A. has 100 mules, but the greater part of their work is ploughing and hauling the kegs of sugar down to the cove, where in favourable weather they are put on board of a schooner for Honolulu. This plan-

tation employs 185 hands, native and Chinese, and turns
out 600 tons of sugar a year. The natives are much
liked as labourers, being docile and on the whole willing;
but native labour is hard to get, as the natives do not
like to work for a term unless obliged, and a pernicious
system of "advances" is practised. The labourers hire
themselves to the planters, in the case of natives usually
for a year, by a contract which has to be signed before a
notary public. The wages are about eight dollars a
month with food, or eleven dollars without food, and the
planters supply houses and medical attendance. The
Chinese are imported as coolies, and usually contract to
work for five years. As a matter of policy no less than
of humanity the "hands" are well treated; for if a single
instance of injustice were perpetrated on a plantation
the factory might stand still the next year, for hardly a
native would contract to serve again.

The Chinese are quiet and industrious, but smoke
opium, and are much addicted to gaming. Many of
them save money, and, when their turn of service is over,
set up stores, or grow vegetables for money. Each man
employed has his horse, and on Saturday the hands form
quite a cavalcade. Great tact, firmness, and knowledge
of human nature are required in the manager of a plantation. The natives are at times disposed to shirk work
without sufficient cause; the native *lunas*, or overseers,
are not always reasonable, the Chinamen and natives
do not always agree, and quarrels and entanglements arise,
and everything is referred to the decision of the manager,
who, besides all things else, must know the exact amount

of work which ought to be performed, both in the fields and factory, and see that it is done. Mr. A. is a keen, shrewd man of business, kind without being weak, and with an eye on every detail of his plantations. The requirements are endless. It reminds me very much of plantation life in Georgia in the old days of slavery. I never elsewhere heard of so many headaches, sore hands, and other trifling ailments. It is very amusing to see the attempts which the would-be invalids make to lengthen their brief smiling faces into lugubriousness, and the sudden relaxation into naturalness when they are allowed a holiday. Mr. A. comes into the house constantly to consult his wife regarding the treatment of different ailments.

I have made a second tour through the factory, and am rather disgusted with sugar making. "All's well that ends well," however, and the delicate crystalline result makes one forget the initial stages of the manufacture. The cane, stripped of its leaves, passes from the flumes under the rollers of the crushing-mill, where it is subjected to a pressure of five or six tons. One hundred pounds of cane under this process yield up from sixty-five to seventy-five pounds of juice. This juice passes, as a pale green cataract, into a trough, which conducts it into a vat, where it is dosed with quicklime to neutralize its acid, and is then run off into large heated metal vessels. At this stage the smell is abominable, and the turbid fluid, with a thick scum upon it, is simply disgusting. After a preliminary heating and skimming it is passed off into iron pans, several in a row, and boiled and skimmed, and ladled from one to the other till it reaches the last, which is nearest to the fire, and there it boils with the greatest violence, seething and foaming, bringing all the remaining scum to the surface. After the concentration has proceeded far enough, the action of the heat is suspended, and the reddish-brown, oily-looking liquid is drawn into the vacuum-pan till it is about a third full; the concentration is completed by boiling the juice in vacuo at a temperature of 150°, and even lower. As the boiling proceeds, the sugar boiler tests the contents of the pan by withdrawing a few drops, and holding them up to the light on his finger; and, by certain minute changes in their condition, he judges when it is time to add an additional quantity. When the pan is full, the contents have thickened into the consistency of thick gruel by the formation of minute crystals, and are then allowed to descend into an heater, where they are kept warm till they can be run into "forms" or tanks, where they are allowed to granulate. The liquid, or molasses, which remains after the first crystallization is returned to the vacuum pan and reboiled, and this reboiling of the drainings is repeated two or three times, with a gradually decreasing result in the quality and quantity of the sugar. The last process, which is used for getting rid of the treacle, is a most beautiful one. The mass of sugar and treacle is put into what are called "centrifugal pans," which are drums about three feet in diameter and two feet high, which make about 1,000 revolutions a minute. These have false interiors of wire gauze, and the mass is forced violently against their sides by centrifugal action, and they let the treacle whirl through, and retain the sugar crystals, which lie in a dry heap in the centre.

The cane is being flumed in with great rapidity, and the factory is working till late at night. The cane from which the juice has been expressed, called "trash," is dried and used as fuel for the furnace which supplies the steam power. The sugar is packed in kegs, and a cooper and carpenter, as well as other mechanics, are employed.

Sugar is now the great interest of the islands. Christian missions and whaling have had their day, and now people talk sugar. Hawaii thrills to the news of a cent up or a cent down in the American market. All the interests of the kingdom are threatened by this one, which, because it is grievously depressed and staggers under a heavy import duty in the American market, is now clamorous in some quarters for " annexation," and in others for a " reciprocity treaty," which last means the cession of the Pearl River lagoon on Oahu, with its adjacent shores, to America, for a Pacific naval station. There are 200,000 acres of productive soil on the islands, of which only a fifteenth is under cultivation, and of this large area 150,000 is said to be specially adapted for sugar culture. Herein is a prospective Utopia, and people are always dreaming of the sugar-growing capacities of the belt of rich disintegrated lava which slopes upwards from the sea to the bases of the mountains. Hitherto, sugar growing has been a very disastrous speculation, and few

of the planters at present do more than keep their heads
above water.

Were labour plentiful and the duties removed, fortunes
might be made, for the soil yields on an average about
three times as much as that of the State of Louisiana.
Two and a half tons to the acre is a common yield, five
tons a frequent one, and instances are known of the
slowly matured cane of a high altitude yielding as much
as seven tons! The magnificent climate makes it a very
easy crop to grow. There is no brief harvest time with
its rush, hurry, and frantic demand for labour, nor frost
to render necessary the hasty cutting of an immature
crop. The same number of hands is kept on all the year
round. The planters can plant pretty much when they
please, or not plant at all for two or three years, the only
difference in the latter case being that the *rattoons* which
spring up after the cutting of the former crop are smaller
in bulk. They can cut when they please, whether the
cane be tasselled or not, and they can plant, cut, and
grind at one time!

It is a beautiful crop in any stage of growth, especially
in the tasselled stage. Every part of it is useful—the
cane pre-eminently—the leaves as food for horses and
mules, and the tassels for making hats. Here and elsewhere there is a plate of cut cane always within reach, and
the children chew it incessantly. I fear you will be tired
of sugar, but I find it more interesting than the wool and
mutton of Victoria and New Zealand, and it is a most important item of the wealth of this toy kingdom, which

last year exported 16,995,402 lbs. of sugar and 192,105 gallons of molasses.*   With regard to molasses, the Government prohibits the manufacture of rum, so the planters are deprived of a fruitful source of profit.   It is really difficult to tear myself from the subject of sugar, for I see the cane waving in the sun while I write, and hear the busy hum of the crushing-mill.

I. L. B.

* In 1873 the export of sugar reached a total of upwards of 23.000.000 lbs.

LETTER IX.

THIS is such a pleasant house and household, Mrs. A. is as bright as though she were not an invalid, and her room, except at meals, is the gathering-place of the family. The four boys are bright, intelligent beings, out of doors, barefooted, all day, and with a passion for horses, of which their father possesses about thirty. The youngest, Ephy, is the brightest child for three years old that I ever saw, but absolutely crazy about horses and mules. He talks of little else, and is constantly asking me to draw horses on his slate. He is a merry, audacious little creature, but came in this evening quite subdued. The sun was setting gloriously behind the forest-covered slopes, flooding the violet distances with a haze of gold, and, in a low voice, he said, " I've seen God."

There is the usual Chinese cook, who cooks and waits and looks good-natured, and of course has his own horse, and his wife, a most minute Chinese woman, comes in and attends to the rooms and to Mrs. A., and sews and mends. She wears her native dress—a large, stiff, flat cane hat, like a tray, fastened firmly on or to her head ; a scanty loose frock of blue denim down to her knees, wide trousers of the same down to her ancles, and slippers. Her hair is knotted up ; she always wears silver arm-

lets, and would not be seen without the hat for anything. There is not a bell in this or any house on the
islands, and the bother of servants is hardly known, for
the Chinamen do their work like automatons, and disappear at sunset. In a land where there are no carpets,
no fires, no dust, no hot water needed, no windows to
open and shut—for they are always open—no further service is really required. It is a simple arcadian life, and
people live more happily than any that I have seen elsewhere. It is very cheerful to live among people whose
faces are not soured by the east wind, or wrinkled by the
worrying effort to " keep up appearances," which deceive
nobody; who have no formal visiting, but real sociability;
who regard the light manual labour of domestic life as
a pleasure, not a thing to be ashamed of; who are
contented with their circumstances, and have leisure to
be kind, cultured, and agreeable ; and who live so tastefully, though simply, that they can at any time ask a
passing stranger to occupy the simple guest chamber, or
share the simple meal, without any of the soul-harassing
preparations which often make the exercise of hospitality
a thing of terror to people in the same circumstances at
home.

People will ask you, " What is the food ? " We have
everywhere bread and biscuit made of California flour,
griddle cakes with molasses, and often cracked wheat,
butter not very good, sweet potatoes, boiled *kalo*, Irish
potatoes, and *poi*. I have not seen fish on any table
except at the Honolulu Hotel, or any meat but beef,
which is hard and dry as compared with ours. We have

China or Japan tea, and island coffee. Honolulu is the only place in which intoxicants are allowed to be sold; and I have not seen beer, wine, or spirits in any house. Bananas are an important article of diet, and sliced guavas, eaten with milk and sugar, are very good. The cooking is always done in detached cook houses, in and on American cooking-stoves.

As to clothing. I wear my flannel riding dress for both riding and walking, and a black silk at other times. The resident ladies wear prints and silks, and the gentlemen black cloth or dark tweed suits. Flannel is not required, neither are puggarees or white hats or sunshades at any season. The changes of temperature are very slight, and there is no chill when the sun goes down. The air is always like balm; the rain is tepid and does not give cold; in summer it may be three or four degrees warmer. Windows and doors stand open the whole year. A blanket is agreeable at night, but not absolutely necessary. It is a truly delightful climate and mode of living, with such an abundance of air and sunshine. My health improves daily, and I do not consider myself an invalid.

Between working, reading aloud, talking, riding, and "loafing," I have very little time for letter writing; but I must tell you of a delightful fern-hunting expedition on the margin of the forest that I took yesterday, accompanied by Mr. Thompson and the two elder boys. We rode in the *mauka* direction, outside cane ready for cutting, with silvery tassels gleaming in the sun, till we reached the verge of the forest, where an old trail was nearly obliterated by a trailing matted grass four feet high, and thousands of woody ferns, which conceal streams, holes, and pitfalls. When further riding was impossible, we tethered our horses and proceeded on foot. We were then 1,500 feet above the sea by the aneroid barometer, and the increased coolness was perceptible. The mercury is about four degrees lower for each 1,000 feet of ascent—rather more than this indeed on the windward side of the islands. The forest would be quite impenetrable were it not for the remains of wood-hauling trails, which, though grown up to the height of my shoulders, are still passable.

Underneath the green maze, invisible streams, deep down, made sweet music, sweeter even than the gentle murmur of the cool breeze among the trees. The forest on the volcano track, which I thought so tropical and wonderful a short time ago, is nothing for beauty to compare with this "garden of God." I wish I could describe it, but cannot; and as you know only our pale, small-leaved trees, with their uniform green, I cannot say that it is like this or that. The first line of a hymn, "Oh, Paradise! oh, Paradise!" rings in my brain, and the rustic exclamation we used to hear when we were children, "Well, I never!" followed by innumerable notes of admiration, seems to exhaust the whole vocabulary of wonderment. The former cutting of some trees gives atmosphere, and the tumbled nature of the ground shows everything to the best anvantage. There were openings over which huge candle-nuts, with their pea-green and silver foliage, spread their giant arms, and the light played through their branches on an infinite variety of ferns. There were groves of bananas and plantains with shiny leaves 8 feet long, like enormous hart's-tongue, the bright-leaved *noni*, the dark-leaved *koa*, the mahogany of the Pacific; the great glossy-leaved Eugenia—a forest tree as large as our largest elms; the small-leaved *ohia*, its rose-crimson flowers making a glory in the forests, and its young shoots of carmine red vying with the colouring of the New England fall; and the strange *lauhala* hung its stiff drooping plumes, which creak in the faintest breeze; and the superb breadfruit hung its untempting fruit, and from spreading guavas we shook the ripe yellow treasures, scooping out the inside, all juicy and crimson, to make drinking cups of the rind; and there were trees that had surrendered their own lives to a conquering army of vigorous parasites which had clothed their skeletons with an unapproachable and indistinguishable beauty, and over trees and parasites the tender tendrils of great mauve morning glories trailed and wreathed themselves, and the strong, strangling stems of the *ié* wound themselves round the tall *ohias*, which supported their quaint yucca-like spikes of leaves fifty feet from the ground.

There were some superb plants of the glossy tropical-looking bird's-nest fern, or *Asplenium Nidus*, which makes its home on the stems and branches of trees, and brightens the forest with its great shining fronds. I got a specimen from a *koa* tree. The plant had nine fronds, each one measuring from 4 feet 1 inch to 4 feet 7 inches in length, and from 7 to 9 inches in breadth. There were some very fine tree-ferns (*Cibotium Chamissoi?*), two

of which being accessible, we measured, and found
them seventeen and twenty feet high, their fronds
eight feet long, and their stems four feet ten inches
in circumference three feet from the ground. They
showed the most various shades of green, from the
dark tint of the mature frond, to the pale pea
green of those which were just uncurling themselves.
I managed to get up into a tree for the first time in my
life to secure specimens of two beautiful parasitic ferns
(Polypodium tamariscinum and P. Hymenophylloides ?).
I saw for the first time, too, a lygodium and the large
climbing potato-fern (Polypodium spectrum), very like
a yam in the distance, and the Vittaria elongata, whose
long grassy fronds adorn almost every tree. The beautiful Microlepia tenuifolia abounded, and there were a few
plants of the loveliest fern I ever saw (Trichomanes mei-
folium), in specimens of which I indulged sparingly,
and almost grudgingly, for it seemed unfitting that a
form of such perfect beauty should be mummied in a
herbarium. There was one fern in profusion, with from
90 to 130 pair of pinnæ on each frond; and the fronds,
though often exceeding five feet in length, were only two
inches broad (Nephrolepis pectinata). There were
many prostrate trees, which nature has entirely covered
with choice ferns, specially the rough stem of the
tree-fern. I counted seventeen varieties on one trunk,
and on the whole obtained thirty-five specimens for my
collection.

The forest soon became completely impenetrable, the
beautiful Gleichenia Hawaiiensis forming an impassable

network over all the undergrowth. And, indeed, without this it would have been risky to make further explorations, for often masses of wonderful matted vegetation sustained us temporarily over streams six or eight feet below, whose musical tinkle alone warned us of our peril. I shall never again see anything so beautiful as this fringe of the impassable timber belt. I enjoyed it more than anything I have yet seen; it was intoxicating, my eyes were "satisfied with seeing." It was a dream, a rapture, this maze of form and colour, this entangled luxuriance, this bewildering beauty, through which we caught bright glimpses of a heavenly sky above, while far away, below glade and lawn, shimmered in surpassing loveliness the cool blue of the Pacific. To me, with my hatred of reptiles and insects, it is not the least among the charms of Hawaii, that these glorious entanglements and cool damp depths of a redundant vegetation give shelter to nothing of unseemly shape and venomous proboscis or fang. Here, in cool, dreamy, sunny Onomea, there are no horrid, drumming, stabbing, mosquitos as at Honolulu, to remind me of what I forget sometimes, that I am not in Eden.

I. L. B.

NOTE.—Throughout these letters the botanical names given are only those which are current on the Islands. Those specimens of ferns which survived the rough usage which befel them, are to be seen in the Herbarium of the Botanical Garden at Oxford, and have been named and classified by my cousin, Professor Lawson.

LETTER X.

THERE is something fearful in the isolation of this valley, open at one end to the sea, and walled in on all others by *palis* or precipices, from 1,000 to 2,000 feet in height, over the easiest of which hangs the dizzy track, which after trailing over the country for sixty difficult miles, connects Waipio with the little world of Hilo. The evening is very sombre, and darkness comes on early between these high walls. I am in a native house in which not a word of English is spoken, and Deborah, among her own people, has returned with zest to the exclusive use of her own tongue. This is more solitary than solitude, and tired as I am with riding and roughing it, I must console myself with writing to you. The natives, after staring and giggling for some time, took this letter out of my hand, with many exclamations, which, Deborah tells me, are at the rapidity and minuteness of my writing. I told them the letter was to my sister, and they asked if I had your picture. They are delighted with it, and it is going round a large circle assembled without. They see very few foreign women here, and are surprised that I have not brought a foreign man with me.

There was quite a bustle of small preparations before

we left Onomea.   Deborah was much excited, and I was
not less so, for it is such a complete novelty to
take a five days' ride alone with natives.   D. is a
very nice native girl of seventeen, who speaks English
tolerably, having been brought up by Mr. and Mrs.
Austin.   She was lately married to a white man employed
on the plantation.   Mr. A. most kindly lent me a
favourite mule, but declined to state that she would not
kick, or buck, or turn obstinate, or lie down in the
water, all which performances are characteristic of mules.
She has, however, as he expected, behaved as the most
righteous of her species.   Our equipment was a matter
for some consideration, as I had no waterproof; but
eventually I wore my flannel riding dress, and carried my
plaid in front of the saddle.   My saddle-bags, which were
behind, contained besides our changes of clothes, a jar
of Liebig's essence of beef, some potted beef, a tin of
butter, a tin of biscuits, a tin of sardines, a small loaf,
and some roast yams.   Deborah looked very *piquante*
in a bloomer dress of dark blue, with masses of shining hair in natural ringlets falling over the collar,
mixing with her *lei* of red rose-buds.   She rode a
powerful horse, of which she has much need, as this
is the most severe road on horses on Hawaii, and it
takes a really good animal to come to Waipio and go
back to Hilo.

We got away at seven in bright sunshine, and D.'s
husband accompanied us the first mile to see that our
girths and gear were all right.   It was very slippery, but
my mule deftly gathered her feet under her, and slid

when she could not walk. From Onomea to the place where we expected to find the guide, we kept going up and down the steep sides of ravines, and scrambling through torrents till we reached a deep and most picturesque gulch, with a primitive school-house at the bottom, and some grass-houses clustering under palms and *papayas*, a valley scene of endless ease and perpetual afternoon. Here we found that D.'s uncle, who was to have been our guide, could not go, because his horse was not strong enough, but her cousin volunteered his escort, and went away to catch his horse, while we tethered ours and went into the school-house.

This reminded me somewhat of the very poorest schools connected with the Edinburgh Ladies' Highland School Association, but the teacher had a remarkable paucity of clothing, and he seemed to have the charge of his baby, which, much clothed, and indeed much muffled, lay on the bench beside him. For there were benches, and a desk, and even a blackboard and primers down in the deep wild gulch, where the music of living waters, and the thunderous roll of the Pacific, accompanied the children's tuneless voices as they. sang an Hawaiian hymn. I shall remember nothing of the scholars but rows of gleaming white teeth, and splendid brown eyes. I thought both teacher and children very apathetic. There were lamentably few, though the pretty rigidly enforced law, which compels all children between the ages of six and fifteen to attend school for forty weeks of the year, had probably gathered together all the children of the district. They all wore coloured

chemises and *leis* of flowers.   Outside, some natives
presented us with some ripe *papayas*.

Mounting again, we were joined by two native women,
who were travelling the greater part of the way hither,
and this made it more cheerful for D.   The elder one
had nothing on her head but her wild black hair, and
she wore a black *holuku*, a *lei* of the orange seeds of the
pandanus, orange trousers and big spurs strapped on her
bare feet.   A child of four, bundled up in a black poncho,
rode on a blanket behind the saddle, and was tied to the
woman's waist, by an orange shawl.   The younger
woman, who was very pretty, wore a sailor's hat, *leis* of
crimson *ohia* blossoms round her hat and throat, a black
holuku, a crimson poncho, and one spur, and held up a
green umbrella whenever it rained.

We were shortly joined by Kaluna, the cousin, on an
old, big, wall-eyed, bare-tailed, raw-boned horse, whose
wall-eyes contrived to express mingled suspicion and
fear, while a flabby, pendant, lower lip, conveyed the
impression of complete abjectness.   He looked like some
human beings who would be vicious if they dared, but
the vice had been beaten out of him long ago, and only
the fear remained.   He has a raw suppurating sore
under the saddle, glueing the blanket to his lean back,
and crouches when he is mounted.   Both legs on one
side look shorter than on the other, giving a crooked
look to himself and his rider, and his bare feet are worn
thin as if he had been on lava.   I rode him for a mile
yesterday, and when he attempted a convulsive canter,
with three short steps and a stumble in it, his abbreviated

off-legs made me feel as if I were rolling over on one side. Kaluna beats him the whole time with a heavy stick; but except when he strikes him most barbarously about his eyes and nose, he only cringes, without quickening his pace. When I rode him mercifully the true hound nature came out. The sufferings of this wretched animal have been the great drawback on this journey. I have now bribed Kaluna with as much as the horse is worth to give him a month's rest, and long before that time I hope the owl-hawks will be picking his bones.

The horse has come before the rider, but Kaluna is no nonentity. He is a very handsome youth of sixteen, with eyes which are remarkable, even in this land of splendid eyes, a straight nose, a very fine mouth, and beautiful teeth, a mass of wavy, almost curly hair, and a complexion not so brown as to conceal the mantling of the bright southern blood in his cheeks. His figure is lithe, athletic, and as pliable as if he were an invertebrate animal, capable of unlimited doublings up and contortions, to which his thin white shirt and blue cotton trousers are no impediment. He is almost a complete savage; his movements are impulsive and uncontrolled, and his handsome face looks as if it belonged to a half-tamed creature out of the woods. He talks loud, laughs incessantly, croons a monotonous chant, which sounds almost as heathenish as tom-toms, throws himself out of his saddle, hanging on by one foot, lingers behind to gather fruits, and then comes tearing up, beating his horse over the ears and nose, with a fearful yell and a prolonged sound like

har-r-r-ouche, striking my mule and threatening to over-
turn me as he passes me on the narrow track. He is the
most thoroughly careless and irresponsible being I ever
saw, reckless about the horses, reckless about himself,
without any manners or any obvious sense of right and
propriety. In his mouth this musical tongue becomes
as harsh as the speech of a cocatoo or parrot. His
manner is familiar. He rides up to me, pokes his head
under my hat, and says, interrogatively, "Cold!" by
which I understand that the poor boy is shivering himself.
In eating he plunges his hand into my bowl of fowl, or
snatches half my biscuit. Yet I daresay he means well,
and I am thoroughly amused with him, except when he
maltreats his horse.

It is a very strange life going about with natives, whose
ideas, as shown by their habits, are, to say the least
of it, very peculiar. Deborah speaks English fairly,
having been brought up by white people, and is a very
nice girl. But were she one of our own race I should
not suppose her to be more than eleven years old, and
she does not seem able to understand my ideas on any
subject, though I can be very much interested and amused
with hearing hers.

We had a perfect day until the middle of the afternoon.
The dimpling Pacific was never more than a mile from
us as we kept the narrow track in the long green grass,
and on our left the blunt snow-patched peaks of Mauna
Kea rose from the girdle of forest, looking so delusively
near that I fancied a two-hours' climb would take us to
his lofty summit. The track for twenty-six miles is just

in and out of gulches, from 100 to 800 feet in depth, all
opening on the sea, which sweeps into them in three booming rollers. The candle-nut or *kukui* (aleurites triloba) tree,
which on the whole predominates, has leaves of a rich deep
green when mature, which contrast beautifully with the
flaky silvery look of the younger foliage. Some of the shal-
lower gulches are filled exclusively with this tree, which
in growing up to the light to within 100 feet of the top,
presents a mass and density of leafage quite unique, giving
the gulch the appearance as if billows of green had rolled
in and solidified there. Each gulch has some specialty
of ferns and trees, and in such a distance as sixty miles
they vary considerably with the variations of soil, climate,
and temperature. But everywhere the rocks, trees, and
soil are covered and crowded' with the most exquisite
ferns and mosses, from the great tree-fern, whose bright
fronds light up the darker foliage, to the lovely maiden-
hair and graceful selaginellas which are mirrored in pools
of sparkling water. Everywhere, too, the great blue
morning glory opened to a heaven not bluer than itself.

The descent into the gulches is always solemn. You
canter along a bright breezy upland,. and are suddenly
arrested by a precipice, and from the depths of a forest
abyss a low plash or murmur rises, or a deep bass sound,
significant of water which must be crossed, and one reluctantly leaves the upper air to plunge into heavy
shadow, and each experience increases one's apprehensions
concerning the next. Though in some gulches the *kukui*
preponderates, in others the *lauhala* whose aërial roots support it in otherwise impossible positions, and in others the

sombre *ohia*, yet there were some grand clefts in which
nature has mingled her treasures impartially, and out of
cool depths of ferns rose the feathery coco-palm, the
glorious breadfruit, with its green melon-like fruit, the
large *ohia*, ideal in its beauty,—the most gorgeous flowering tree I have ever seen, with spikes of rose-crimson
blossoms borne on the old wood, blazing among its
shining many-tinted leafage,—the tall *papaya* with its
fantastic crown, the profuse gigantic plantain, and innumerable other trees, shrubs, and lianas, in the beauty
and bounteousness of an endless spring. Imagine my
surprise on seeing at the bottom of one gulch, a grove of
good-sized, dark-leaved, very handsome trees, with an
abundance of smooth round green fruit upon them, and
on reaching them finding that they were orange trees,
their great size, far exceeding that of the largest at
Valencia, having prevented me from recognizing them
earlier ! In another, some large shrubs with oval, shining,
dark leaves, much crimped at the edges, bright green
berries along the stalks, and masses of pure white flowers
lying flat, like snow on evergreens, turned out to be
coffee ! The guava with its obtuse smooth leaves, sweet
white blossoms on solitary axillary stalks, and yellow
fruit was universal. The novelty of the fruit, foliage,
and vegetation is an intense delight to me. I should
like to see how the rigid aspect of a coniferous tree, of
which there is not one indigenous to the islands, would
look by contrast. We passed through a long thicket of
sumach, an exotic from North America, which still re-
tains its old habit of shedding its leaves, and its grey,

wintry, desolate-looking branches reminded me that there
are less-favoured parts of the world, and that you are
among mist, cold, murk, slush, gales, leaflessness, and all
the dismal concomitants of an English winter.

It is wonderful that people should have thought of
crossing these gulches on anything with four legs. Formerly, that is, within the last thirty years, the precipices
could only be ascended by climbing with the utmost care,
and descended by being lowered with ropes from crag to
crag, and from tree to tree, when hanging on by the
hands became impracticable to even the most experienced
mountaineer. In this last fashion Mr. Coan and Mr.
Lyons were let down to preach the gospel to the people
of the then populous valleys. But within recent years,
narrow tracks, allowing one horse to pass another, have
been cut along the sides of these precipices, without any
windings to make them easier, and only deviating enough
from the perpendicular to allow of their descent by the
sure-footed native-born animals. Most of them are worn
by water and animals' feet, broken, rugged, jagged, with
steps of rock sometimes three feet high, produced by
breakage here and there. Up and down these the animals
slip, jump, and scramble, some of them standing still until
severely spurred, or driven by some one from behind.
Then there are softer descents, slippery with damp, and
perilous in heavy rains, down which they slide dexterously,
gathering all their legs under them. On a few of these
tracks a false step means death, but the vegetation which
clothes the *pali* below, blinds one to the risk. I don't
think anything would induce me to go up a swinging

zigzag—up a terrible *pali* opposite to me as I write, the sides of which are quite undraped.

All the gulches for the first twenty-four miles contain running water. The great Hakalau gulch we crossed early yesterday, has a river with a smooth bed as wide as the Thames at Eton. Some have only small quiet streams, which pass gently through ferny grottoes. Others have fierce strong torrents dashing between abrupt walls of rock, among immense boulders into deep abysses, and cast themselves over precipice after precipice into the ocean. Probably, many of these are the courses of fire torrents, whose jagged masses of *a-a* have since been worn smooth, and channelled into holes by the action of water. A few are crossed on narrow bridges, but the majority are forded, if that quiet conventional term can be applied to the violent flounderings by which the horses bring one through. The transparency deceives them, and however deep the water is, they always try to lift their fore feet out of it, which gives them a disagreeable rolling motion. (Mr. Brigham in his valuable monograph on the Hawaiian volcanoes quoted below,* appears as much impressed with these gulches as I am.)

* "The road from Hilo to Laupahoehoe, a distance of thirty miles, runs somewhat inland, and is one of the most remarkable in the world. Ravines, 1,800 or 2,000 feet deep, and less than a mile wide, extend far up the slopes of Mauna Kea. Streams, liable to sudden and tremendous freshets, must be traversed on a path of indescribable steepness, winding zig-zag up and down the beautifully-wooded slopes or precipices, which are ornamented with cascades of every conceivable form. Few strangers, when they come to the worst precipices, dare to ride down, but such is the nature of the rough steps, that a horse or mule will pass them with less difficulty than a man on foot who is unused to climbing. No

We lunched in one glorious valley, and Kaluna made drinking cups which held fully a pint, out of the beautiful leaves of the Arum esculentum. Towards afternoon turbid-looking clouds lowered over the sea, and by the time we reached the worst *pali* of all, the south side of Laupahoehoe, they burst on us in torrents of rain accompanied by strong wind. This terrible precipice takes one entirely by surprise. Kaluna, who rode first, disappeared so suddenly that I thought he had gone over. It is merely a dangerous broken ledge, and besides that it looks as if there were only foothold for a goat, one is dizzied by the sight of the foaming ocean immediately below, and, when we actually reached the bottom, there was only a narrow strip of shingle between the stupendous cliff and the resounding surges, which came up as if bent on destruction. The path by which we descended looked a mere thread on the side of the precipice. I don't know what the word beetling means, but if it means anything bad, I will certainly apply it to that *pali*.

A number of disastrous-looking native houses are clustered under some very tall palms in the open part of the gulch, but it is a most wretched situation; the roar of the surf is deafening, the scanty supply of water is brackish, there are rumours that leprosy is rife, and the people are said to be the poorest on Hawaii. We were warned that we could not spend a night comfortably there, so wet, tired, and stiff, we rode on other six miles to the house of a native called Bola-Bola,

less than sixty-five streams must be crossed in a distance of thirty miles."
—Brigham " On the Hawaiian Volcanoes."

where we had been instructed to remain. The rain was heavy and ceaseless, and the trail had become so slippery that our progress was much retarded. It was a most unpropitious-looking evening, and I began to feel the painful stiffness arising from prolonged fatigue in saturated clothes. I indulged in various imaginations as we rode up the long ascent leading to Bola-Bola's, but this time they certainly were not of sofas and tea, and I never aspired to anything beyond drying my clothes by a good fire, for at Hilo some people had shrugged their shoulders, and others had laughed mysteriously at the idea of our sleeping there, and some had said it was one of the worst of native houses.

A single glance was enough. It was a dilapidated frame-house, altogether forlorn, standing unsheltered on a slope of the mountain, with one or two yet more forlorn grass piggeries, which I supposed might be the cook house, and eating-house near it.

A prolonged *har-r-r-rouche* from Kaluna brought out a man with a female horde behind him, all shuffling into clothes as we approached, and we stiffly dismounted from the wet saddles in which we had sat for ten hours, and stiffly hobbled up into the littered verandah, the water dripping from our clothes, and squeezing out of our boots at every step. Inside there was one room about 18 × 14 feet, which looked as if the people had just arrived and had thrown down their goods promiscuously. There were mats on the floor not over clean, and half the room was littered and piled with mats rolled up, boxes, bamboos, saddles, blankets, lassos, cocoanuts, *kalo* roots, bananas, quilts, pans, calabashes, bundles of hard *poi* in *ti* leaves, bones, cats, fowls, clothes. A frightful old woman, looking like a relic of the old heathen days, with bristling grey hair cut short, her body tattooed all over, and no clothing but a ragged blanket huddled round her shoulders; a girl about twelve, with torrents of shining hair, and a piece of bright green calico thrown round her, and two very good-looking young women in rose-coloured chemises, one of them holding a baby, were squatting and lying on the mats, one over another, like a heap of savages.

When the man found that we were going to stay all night he bestirred himself, dragged some of the things to one side and put down a shake-down of *pulu* (the silky covering of the fronds of one species of tree-fern), with a sheet over it, and a gay quilt of orange and red cotton. There was a thin printed muslin curtain to divide off one half of the room, a usual arrangement in native houses. He then helped to unsaddle the horses, and the confusion of the room was increased by a heap of our wet saddles, blankets, and gear. All this time the women lay on the floor and stared at us.

Rheumatism seemed impending, for the air up there was chilly, and I said to Deborah that I must make some change in my dress, and she signed to Kaluna, who sprang at my soaked boots and pulled them off, and my stockings too, with a savage alacrity which left it doubtful for a moment whether he had not also pulled off my feet! I had no means of making any further change except putting on a wrapper over my wet clothes.

Meanwhile the man killed and boiled a fowl, and boiled
some sweet potato, and when these untempting viands,
and a calabash of *poi* were put before us, we sat round
them and eat; I with my knife, the others with their
fingers. There was some coffee in a dirty bowl. The
females had arranged a row of pillows on their mat, and
all lay face downwards, with their chins resting upon
them, staring at us with their great brown eyes, and
talking and laughing incessantly. They had low sensual faces, like some low order of animal. When
our meal was over, the man threw them the relics,
and they soon picked the bones clean. It surprised
me that after such a badly served meal the man brought
a bowl of water for our hands, and something intended
for a towel.

By this time it was dark, and a stone, deeply hollowed
at the top, was produced, containing beef fat and a piece
of rag for a wick, which burned with a strong flaring
light. The women gathered themselves up and sat round
a large calabash of *poi*, conveying the sour paste to their
mouths with an inimitable twist of the fingers, laying
their heads back and closing their eyes with a look of
animal satisfaction. When they had eaten they lay down
as before, with their chins on their pillows, and again
the row of great brown eyes confronted me. Deborah,
Kaluna, and the women talked incessantly in loud shrill
voices till Kaluna uttered the word *auwé* with a long
groaning intonation, apparently signifying weariness,
divested himself of his clothes and laid down on a mat
alongside our shake-down, upon which we let down the

dividing curtain and wrapped ourselves up as warmly as possible.

I was uneasy about Deborah who had had a cough for some time, and consequently took the outside place under the window which was broken, and presently a large cat jumped through the hole and down upon me, followed by another and another, till five wild cats had effected an entrance, making me a stepping-stone to ulterior proceedings. Had there been a sixth I think I could not have borne the infliction quietly. Strips of jerked beef were hanging from the rafters, and by the light which was still burning I watched the cats climb up stealthily, seize on some of these, descend, and disappear through the window, making me a stepping-stone as before, but with all their craft they let some of the strips fall, which awoke Deborah, and next I saw Kaluna's magnificent eyes peering at us under the curtain. Then the natives got up, and smoked and eat more *poi* at intervals, and talked, and Kaluna and Deborah quarrelled, jokingly, about the time of night she told me, and the moon through the rain-clouds occasionally gave us delusive hopes of dawn, and I kept moving my place to get out of the drip from the roof, and so the night passed. I was amused all the time, though I should have preferred sleep to such nocturnal diversions. It was so new, and so odd, to be the only white person among eleven natives in a lonely house, and yet to be as secure from danger and annoyance as in our own home.

At last a pale dawn did appear, but the rain was still coming down heavily, and our poor animals were standing

dismally with their heads down and their tails turned
towards the wind.   Yesterday evening I took a change of
clothes out of the damp saddle-bags, and put them into
what I hoped was a dry place, but they were soaked,
wetter even than those in which I had been sleeping, and
my boots and Deborah's were so stiff, that we gladly
availed ourselves of Kaluna's most willing services.   The
mode of washing was peculiar : he held a calabash with
about half-a-pint of water in it, while we bathed our faces
and hands, and all the natives looked on and tittered.
This was apparently his idea of politeness, for no persuasion would induce him to put the bowl down on the
mat, and Deborah evidently thought it was proper
respect.   We had a repetition of the same viands as the
night before for breakfast, and, as before, the women lay
with their chins on their pillows and stared at us.

The rain ceased almost as soon as we started, and
though it has not been a bright day, it has been very
pleasant. There are no large gulches on to-day's journey.
The track is mostly through long grass, over undulating
uplands, with park-like clumps of trees, and thickets of
guava and the exotic sumach.   Different ferns, flowers,
and vegetation, with much less luxuriance and little
water, denoted a drier climate and a different soil.
There are native churches at distances of six or seven
miles all the way from Hilo, but they seem too large and
too many for the scanty population.

We moved on in single file at a jog-trot wherever the
road admitted of it, meeting mounted natives now and
then, which led to a delay for the exchange of *nuhou;*

and twice we had to turn into the thicket to avoid what here seems to be considered a danger. There are many large herds of semi-wild bullocks on the mountains, branded cattle, as distinguished from the wild or un-branded, and when they are wanted for food, a number of experienced *vaccheros* on strong shod horses go up, and drive forty or fifty of them down. We met such a drove bound for Hilo, with one or two men in front and others at the sides and behind, uttering loud shouts. The bullocks are nearly mad with being hunted and driven, and at times rush like a living tornado, tearing up the earth with their horns. As soon as the galloping riders are seen and the crooked-horned beasts, you retire behind a screen. There must be some tradition of some one having been knocked down and hurt, for reckless as the natives are said to be, they are careful about this, and we were warned several times by travellers whom we met, that there were "bullocks ahead." The law provides that the *vaccheros* shall station one of their number at the head of a gulch to give notice when cattle are to pass through.

We jogged on again till we met a native who told us that we were quite close to our destination; but there were no signs of it, for we were still on the lofty uplands, and the only prominent objects were huge headlands confronting the sea. I got off to walk, as my mule seemed footsore, but had not gone many yards when we came suddenly to the verge of a *pali*, about 1,000 feet deep, with a narrow fertile valley below, with a yet higher *pali* on the other side, both abutting perpendicularly on the sea. I should think the valley is not more than three miles long, and it is walled in by high inaccessible mountains. It is in fact, a gulch on a vastly enlarged scale. The prospect below us was very charming, a fertile region perfectly level, protected from the sea by sandhills, watered by a winding stream, and bright with fishponds, meadow lands, *kalo* patches, orange and coffee groves, figs, breadfruit, and palms. There were a number of grass-houses, and a native church with a spire, and another up the valley testified to the energy and aggressiveness of Rome. We saw all this from the moment we reached the *pali;* and it enlarged, and the detail grew upon us with every yard of the laborious descent of broken craggy track, which is the only mode of access to the valley from the outer world. I got down on foot with difficulty; a difficulty much increased by the long rowels of my spurs, which caught on the rocks and entangled my dress, the simple expedient of taking them off not having occurred to me!

A neat frame-house, with large stones between it and the river, was our destination. It belongs to a native named Halemanu, a great man in the district, for, besides being a member of the legislature, he is deputy sheriff. He is a man of property, also; and though he cannot speak a word of English, he is well educated in Hawaiian, and writes an excellent hand. I brought a letter of introduction to him from Mr. Severance, and we were at once received with every hospitality, our horses cared for, and ourselves luxuriously lodged. We walked up the valley before dark to get a view of a cascade, and found

supper ready on our return. This is such luxury after
last night. There is a very light bright sitting-room,
with papered walls, and manilla matting on the floor, a
round centre table with books and a photographic album
upon it, two rocking-chairs, an office-desk, another table
and chairs, and a Canadian lounge. I can't imagine in
what way this furniture was brought here. Our bedroom opens from this, and it actually has a four-post
bedstead with mosquito bars, a lounge and two chairs,
and the floor is covered with native matting. The washing apparatus is rather an anomaly, for it consists of a
basin and crash towel placed in the verandah, in full view
of fifteen people. The natives all bathe in the river.

Halemanu has a cook house and native cook, and an
eating-room, where I was surprised to find everything in
foreign style—chairs, a table with a snow white cover,
and table napkins, knives, forks, and even saltcellars.
I asked him to eat with us, and he used a knife and fork
quite correctly, never, for instance, putting the knife into
his mouth. I was amused to see him afterwards, sitting
on a mat among his family and dependants, helping himself to *poi* from a calabash with his fingers. He gave us
for supper delicious river fish fried, boiled *kalo*, and Waipio
coffee with boiled milk.

It is very annoying only to be able to converse with
this man through an interpreter; and Deborah, as is
natural, is rather unwilling to be troubled to speak
English, now that she is among her own people. After
supper we sat by candlelight in the parlour, and he
showed me his photograph album. At eight he took

a large Bible, put on glasses, and read a chapter in
Hawaiian; after which he knelt and prayed with profound reverence of manner and tone.   Towards the end
I recognized the Hawaiian words for " Our Father." *
Here in Waipio there is something pathetic in the idea
of this Fatherhood, which is wider than the ties of kin
and race.   Even here not one is a stranger, an alien, a
foreigner ! And this man, so civilized and Christianized,
only now in middle life, was, he said, " a big boy when
the first teachers came," and may very likely have witnessed horrors in the *heiau*, or temple, close by, of which
little is left now.

This bedroom is thoroughly comfortable.   Kaluna
wanted to sleep on the lounge here, probably because
he is afraid of *akuas*, or spirits, but we have exiled him
to a blanket on the parlour lounge.

I. L. B.

* The Lord's Prayer in Hawaiian runs thus :—E ko mako Makua i-loko
o ka Lani, e hoanoia Kou Inoa E hiki mai Kou auhuni e malamaia Kou
Makemake ma ka-nei honua e like me ia i malamaia ma ka Lani e haawi
mai i a makau i ai no keia la e kala mai i ko makou lawehalaana me
makou e kala nei i ka poe i lawehala mai i a makou mai alakai i a makou i
ka hoowalewaleia mai ata e hookapele i a makou mai ka ino no ka mea
Nou ke Aupuni a me ka Mana a me ka hoonaniia a mau loa 'ku.   Amene.

LETTER X.—(*continued.*)

WE were thoroughly rested this morning, and very glad of a fine day for a visit to the great cascade which is rarely seen by foreigners. My mule was slightly galled with the girth, and having a strong fellow feeling with Elisha's servant, "Alas, master, for it was borrowed!" I have bought for $20 a pretty, light, half-broken bay mare, which I rode to-day and liked much.

After breakfast, which was a repetition of last night's supper, we three, with Halemanu's daughter as guide, left on horseback for the waterfall, though the natives tried to dissuade us by saying that stones came down, and it was dangerous; also that people could not go in their clothes, there was so much wading. In deference to this last opinion, D. rode without boots, and I without stockings. We rode through the beautiful valley till we reached a deep gorge turning off from it, which opens out into a nearly circular chasm with walls 2,000 feet in height, where we tethered our horses. A short time after leaving them, D. said, "She says we can't go further in our clothes," but when the natives saw me plunge boldly into the river in my riding dress, which is really not unlike a fashionable Newport bathing suit, they thought better of it. It was a thoroughly rough tramp, wading ten times through the river, which was sometimes up to our knees, and sometimes to our waists, and besides the fighting among slippery rocks in rushing water, we had to crawl and slide up and down wet, mossy masses of dislodged rock, to push with eyes shut through wet jungles of Indian shot, guava, and a thorny vine, and sometimes to climb from tree to tree at a considerable height. When, after an hour's fighting we arrived in sight of the cascade, but not of the basin into which it falls, our pretty guide declined to go further, saying that the wind was rising, and that stones would fall and kill us, but being incredulous on this point, I left them, and with great difficulty and many bruises, got up the river to its exit from the basin, and there, being unable to climb the rocks on either side, stood up to my throat in the still tepid water till the scene became real to me.

I do not care for any waterfall but Niagara, nor do I care in itself for this one, for though its first leap is 200 feet and its second 1,600, it is so frittered away and dissipated in spray, owing to the very magnitude of its descent, that there is no volume of water within sight to create mass or sound. But no words can paint the majesty of the surroundings, the caverned, precipitous walls of rock coming down in one black plunge from the blue sky above to the dark abyss of water below, the sullen shuddering sound with which pieces of rock came hurtling down among the trees, the thin tinkle of the water as it falls, the full rush of the river, the feathery growth of ferns, gigantic below, but so diminished by the height above, as only to show their presence by the green tinge upon the rocks, while in addition to the gloom produced by the stupendous height of the cliffs, there is a cool, green darkness of dense forest, and mighty trees of strange tropical forms glass themselves in the black mirror of the basin. For one moment a ray of sunshine turned the upper part of the spray into a rainbow, and never to my eyes had the bow of promise looked so heavenly as when it spanned the black, solemn, tree-shadowed abyss, whose deep, still waters only catch a sunbeam on five days of the year.

I found the natives regaling themselves on *papaya*, and on live fresh-water shrimps, which they find in great numbers in the river. I remembered that white people at home calling themselves civilized, eat live, or at least raw, oysters, but the sight of these active, squirming shrimps struggling between the white teeth of my associates was yet more repulsive.

We finished our adventurous expedition with limbs much bruised, as well as torn and scratched, and before we emerged from the chasm saw a rock dislodged, which came crashing down not far from us, carrying away an *ohia*. It is a gruesome and dowie den, but well worth a visit.

We mounted again, and rode as far as we could up the valley, fording the river in deep water several times, and coming down the other side. The coffee trees in full blossom were very beautiful, and they, as well as the oranges, have escaped the blight which has fallen upon both in other parts of the island. In addition to the usual tropical productions, there were some very fine fig trees and thickets of the castor-oil plant, a very handsome shrub, when, as here, it grows to a height of from ten to twenty-two feet. The natives, having been joined by some Waipio women, rode at full gallop over all sorts of ground, and I enjoyed the speed of my mare without any apprehension of being thrown off. We rode among most extensive *kalo* plantations, and large artificial fish-ponds, in which hundreds of gold-fish were gleaming, and came back by the sea shore, green with the maritime convolvulus, and the smooth-bottomed river, which the Waipio folk use as a road. Canoes glide along it, brown-skinned men wade down it floating bundles of *kalo* after them, and strings of laden horses and mules follow each other along its still waters. I hear that in another and nearly unapproachable valley, a river serves the same purpose. While we were riding up it, a great gust lifted off its surface in fine spray, and almost blew us from our horses. Hawaii has no hurricanes, but at some hours of the day Waipio is subject to terrific gusts, which really justify the people in their objection to visiting the cascade. Some time ago, in one of these, this house was lifted up, carried twenty feet, and deposited in its present position.

Supper was ready for us—*kalo*, yams, spatchcock, *poi*, coffee, rolls, and Oregon kippered salmon; and when I told Halemanu that the spatchcock and salmon reminded me of home, he was quite pleased, and said he would provide the same for breakfast to-morrow.

The owner of the mare, which I have named " Bessie Twinker," had willingly sold her to me, though I told him I could not pay him for her until I reached Onomea. I do not know what had caused my credit to suffer during

my absence, but D., after talking long with him this
evening, said to me, "He says he can't let you have the
horse, because when you've taken it away, he thinks you
will never send him the money." I told her indignantly
to tell him that English women never cheated people, a
broad and totally unsustainable assertion, which had the
effect of satisfying the poor fellow.

After Halemanu, Deborah, Kaluna, and a number of
natives had eaten their *poi*, Halemanu brought in a very
handsome silver candlestick, and expressed a wish that
Deborah should interpret for us. He asked a great many
sensible questions about England, specially about the
state of the poor, the extent of the franchise, and the
influence of religion. When he heard that I had spent
some years in Scotland, he said, "Do you know Mr.
Wallace?" I was quite puzzled, and tried to recall any
man of that name who I had heard of as having visited
Hawaii, when a happy flash of comprehension made me
aware of his meaning, and I replied that I had seen his
sword several times, but that he died long before I knew
Scotland, and indeed before I was born; but that the
Scotch held his memory in great veneration, and were
putting up a monument to him. But for the mistake as
to dates, he seemed to have the usual notions as to the
exploits of Wallace. He deplores most deeply the
dwindling of his people, and his manner became very sad
about it. D. said, "He's very unhappy; he says,
soon there will be no more Kanakas." He told me
that this beautiful valley was once very populous, and
even forty years ago, when Mr. Ellis visited it, there

were 1,300 people here. Now probably there are not more than 200.

Here was the *Puhonua*, or place of refuge for all this part of the island. This, and the very complete one of Honaunau, on the other side of Hawaii, were the Hawaiian "Cities of Refuge." Could any tradition of the Mosaic ordinance on this subject have travelled hither? These two sanctuaries were absolutely inviolable. The gates stood perpetually open, and though the fugitive was liable to be pursued to their very threshold, he had no sooner crossed it than he was safe from king, chief, or avenger. These gates were wide, and some faced the sea, and others the mountains. Hither the murderer, the manslayer, the *tabu*-breaker fled, repaired to the presence of the idol, and thanked it for aiding him to reach the place of security. After a certain time the fugitives were allowed to return to their families, and none dared to injure those to whom the high gods had granted their protection.

In time of war, tall spears from which white flags were unfurled, were placed at each end of the enclosure, and until the proclamation of peace invited the vanquished to enter. These flags were fixed a short distance outside the walls, and no pursuing warrior, even in the hot flush of victory, could pursue his routed foe one foot beyond. Within was the sacred pale of *pahu tabu*, and anyone attempting to strike his victim there would have been put to death by the priests and their adherents. In war time the children, old people, and many of the women of the neighbouring districts, were received within the enclosure, where they awaited the issue of the conflict in security, and were safe from violence in the event of defeat. These *puhonuas* contain pieces of stone weighing from two to three tons, raised six feet from the ground, and the walls, narrowing gradually towards the top, are fifteen feet wide at the base and twelve feet high. They are truly grand monuments of humanity in the midst of the barbarous institutions of heathenism, and it shows a considerable degree of enlightenment that even rebels in arms and fugitives from invading armies were safe, if they reached the sacred refuge, for the priests of *Keawe* knew no distinctions of party.

In dreadful contrast to this place of mercy, there were some very large *heiaus* (or temples) here, on whose hideous altars eighty human sacrifices are said to have been offered at one time. One of the legends told me concerning this lovely valley is, that King Umi, having vanquished the kings of the six divisions of Hawaii, was sacrificing captives in one of these *heiaus*, when the voice of his god, *Kuahilo*, was heard from the clouds, demanding more slaughter. Fresh human blood streamed from the altars, but the insatiable demon continued to call for more, till Umi had sacrificed all the captives and all his own men but one, whom he at first refused to give up, as he was a great favourite, but *Kuahilo* thundered from heaven, till the favourite warrior was slain, and only the king and the sacrificing priest remained.

This valley of the "vanquished waters" abounds in legends. Some of these are about a cruel monster, King Hooku, who lived here, and whose memory, so far as he is remembered, is much execrated. It is told of him that if a man were said to have a handsome head he sent some of his warriors to behead him, and then hacked and otherwise disfigured the face for a diversion. On one occasion he ordered a man's arm to be cut off and brought to him, simply because it was said to be more beautifully tattooed than his own. It is fifty-four years since the last human sacrifice was exposed on the Waipio altars, but there are several old people here who must have been at least thirty when Hawaii threw off idolatry for ever. Halemanu has again closed the evening with the simple worship of the true God.

I. L. B.

LETTER XI.

THERE is a rumour that the king is coming as the guest of Admiral Pennock in the *Benicia*. If it turns out to be true, it will turn our quiet life upside down.

We met with fearful adventures in the swollen gulches between Laupahoehoe and Onomea. It is difficult to begin my letter with the plain prose of our departure from Waipio, which we accomplished on the morning after I last wrote. On rising after a sound sleep, I found that my potted beef, which I had carefully hung from a nail the night before, had been almost carried away by small ants. These ants swarm in every house on low altitudes. They assemble in legions as if by magic, and by their orderly activity carry away all that they do not devour, of all eatables which have not been placed on tables which have rags dipped in a solution of corrosive sublimate wound round their legs.

We breakfasted by lamplight, and because I had said that some of the viands reminded me of home, our kind host had provided them at that early hour. He absolutely refused to be paid anything for the accommodation of our party, and said he should be ashamed of himself if he took anything from a lady travelling without a husband.

It was such a perfect morning. The full moon hung over the enclosing *palis*, gleaming on coffee and bread-fruit groves, and on the surface of the river, which was just quivering under a soft sea breeze. The dew was heavy, smoke curled idly from native houses, the east was flushing with the dawn, and the valley looked the picture of perfect peace. A number of natives assembled to see us start, and they all shook hands with us, ex-changing *alohas*, and presenting us with *leis* of roses and *ohias*. D. looked very pretty with a red hibiscus blossom in her shining hair. You would have been amused to see me shaking hands with men dressed only in *malos*, or in the short blue shirt reaching to the waist, much worn by them when at work.

I rode my mare with some pride of proprietorship, and our baggage for a time was packed on the mule, and we started up the tremendous *pali* at the tail of a string of twenty mules and horses laden with *kalo*. This was in the form of *paiai*, or hard food, which is composed, as I think I mentioned before, of the root baked and pounded, but without water. It is put up in bundles wrapped in *ti* leaves, of from twenty to thirty pounds each, secured with cocoanut fibre, in which state it will keep for months, and much of the large quantity raised in Waipio is exported to the plantations, the Waimea ranches, and the neighbouring districts. A square mile of *kalo*, it is estimated, would feed 15,000 Hawaiians for a year.

It was a beautiful view from the top of the *pali*. The white moon was setting, the earliest sunlight was lighting up the dewy depths of the lonely valley, reddening with a rich rose red the huge headland which forms one of its sentinels; heavy snow had fallen during the night on Mauna Kea, and his great ragged dome, snow-covered down to the forests, was blushing like an Alpine peak at the touch of the early sun. It ripened into a splendid joyous day, which redeemed the sweeping uplands of Hamakua from the dreariness which I had thought belonged to them. There was a fresh sea-breeze, and the sun, though unclouded, was not too hot. We halted for an early lunch at the clean grass-house we had stopped at before, and later in the afternoon at that of the woman with whom we had ridden from Hakalau, who received us very cordially, and regaled us with *poi* and pork.

In order to avoid the amenities of Bola Bola's we rode thirty-four miles, and towards evening descended the tremendous steep, which leads to the surf-deafened village of Laupahoehoe. Halemanu had given me a note of introduction to a widow named Honolulu, which Deborah said began thus, "As I know that you have the only clean house in L," and on presenting it we were made very welcome. Besides the widow, a very redundant beauty, there were her two brothers and two male cousins, and all bestirred themselves in our service, the men in killing and cooking the supper, and the woman in preparing the beds. It was quite a large room, with doors at the end and side, and fully a third was curtained off by a calico curtain, with a gorgeous Crétonne pattern upon it. I was delighted to see a four-post bed, with mosquito bars, and a clean *pulu* mattrass, with a linen

sheet over it, covered with a beautiful quilt with a quaint
arabesque pattern on a white ground running round it,
and a wreath of green leaves in the centre. The native
women exercise the utmost ingenuity in the patterns and
colours of these quilts. Some of them are quite works
of art. The materials, which are plain and printed
cottons, cost about $8, and a complete quilt is worth
from $18 to $50. The widow took six small pillows,
daintily covered with silk, out of a chest, the uses of
which were not obvious, as two large pillows were already
on the bed. It was astonishing to see a native house so
handsomely furnished in so poor a place. The mats on
the floor were numerous and very fine. There were two
tables, several chairs, a bureau with a swinging mirror
upon it, a basin, crash towels, a carafe and a kerosene
lamp. It is all very well to be able to rough it, and yet
better to enjoy doing so, but such luxuries add much to
one's contentment after eleven hours in the saddle.

Honolulu wore a green chemise at first, but when supper
was ready she put a Macgregor tartan *holuku* over it.
The men were very active, and cooked the fowl in about
the same time that it takes to pluck one at home. They
spread the finest mat I have seen in the centre of the
floor as a tablecloth, and put down on it bowls containing
the fowl and sweet potatoes, and the unfailing calabash of
poi. Tea, coffee and milk were not procurable, and as
the water is slimy and brackish, I offered a boy a dime
to get me a cocoanut, and presently eight great, mis-
shapen things were rolled down at the door. The outside
is a smooth buff rind, underneath which is a fibrous

covering, enormously strong and about an inch thick, which when stripped off reveals the nut as we see it, but of a very pale colour. Those we opened were quite young, and each contained nearly three tumblers of almost effervescent, very sweet, slightly acidulated, perfectly limpid water, with a strong flavour of cocoanut. It is a delicious beverage. The meat was so thin and soft that it could have been spooned out like the white of an egg if we had had any spoons. We all sat cross-legged round our meal, and all Laupahoehoe crowded into the room and verandah with the most persistent, unwinking, gimleting stare I ever saw. It was really unpleasant, not only to hear a Babel of talking, of which, judging from the constant repetition of the words *wahine haole*, I was the subject, but to have to eat under the focussed stare of twenty pair of eyes. My folding camp-knife appears an object of great interest, and it was handed round, inside and outside the house. When I retired about seven, the assemblage was still in full session.

The stars were then bright, but when I woke the next morning a strong breeze was blowing, the surf was roaring so loud as almost to drown human voices, and rolling up in gigantic surges, and to judge from appearances, the rain which was falling in torrents had been falling for some hours. There was much buzzing among the natives regarding our prospects for the day. I shall always think from their tone and manner, and the frequent repetition of the names of the three worst gulches, that the older men tried to dissuade us from going; but Deborah, who was very anxious to be at home by Sunday, said that

the verdict was that if we started at once for our ride of
twenty-three miles we might reach Onomea before the
freshet came on.   This might have been the case had it
not been for Kaluna. Not only was his horse worn out, but
nothing would induce him to lead the mule, and she went
off on foraging expeditions continually, which further
detained us. Kaluna had grown quite polite in his savage
way.   He always insisted on putting on and taking off
my boots, carried me once through the Waipio river,
helped me to pack the saddle-bags, and even offered to
brush my hair! He frequently brought me guavas on
the road, saying, "eat," and often rode up, saying interrogatively, "tired?" "cold?"   D. told me that he was
very tired, and I was very sorry for him, for he was so
thinly and poorly dressed, and the natives are not strong
enough to bear exposure to cold as we can, and a temperature at 68° is cold to them.   But he was quite incor-
rigible, and thrashed his horse to the last.

We breakfasted on fowl, *poi*, and cocoanut milk, in
presence of even a larger number of spectators than the
night before, one of them a very old man looking savagely
picturesque, with a red blanket tied round his waist,
leaving his lean chest and arms, which were elaborately
tattooed, completely exposed.

The mule had been slightly chafed by the gear, and in
my anxiety about a borrowed animal, of which Mr. Austin
makes a great joke, I put my saddle-bags on my own
mare, in an evil hour, and not only these, but some fine
cocoanuts, tied up in a waterproof which had long ago
proved its worthlessness.   It was a grotesquely miserable

picture. The house is not far from the beach, and the surf, beyond which a heavy mist hung, was coming in with such a tremendous sound that we had to shout at the top of our voices in order to be heard. The sides of the great gulch rose like prison walls, cascades which had no existence the previous night hurled themselves from the summit of the cliffs directly into the sea, the rain, which fell in sheets, not drops, covered the ground to the depth of two or three inches, and dripped from the wretched, shivering horses, which stood huddled together with their tails between their legs. My thin flannel suit was wet through even before we mounted. I dispensed with stockings, as I was told that wearing them in rain chills and stiffens the limbs. D., about whom I was anxious, as well as about the mule, had a really water-proof cloak, and I am glad to say has quite lost the cough from which she suffered before our expedition. She does not care about rain any more than I do.

We soon reached the top of the worst and dizziest of all the *palis*, and then splashed on mile after mile, down sliding banks, and along rocky tracks, from which the soil had been completely carried, the rain falling all the time. In some places several feet of soil had been carried away, and we passed through water-rents, the sides of which were as high as our horses' heads, where the ground had been level a few days before. By noon the aspect of things became so bad that I wished we had a white man with us, as I was uneasy about some of the deepest gulches. When four hours' journey from Onomea, Kaluna's horse broke down, and he left us to get another, and we rode a mile out of our way to visit Deborah's grandparents.

Her uncle carried us across some water to their cook-house, where, happily, a *kalo* baking had just been accomplished in a hole in the ground, lined with stones, among which the embers were still warm. In this very small hut, in which a man could hardly stand upright, there were five men only dressed in *malos*, four women, two of them very old, much tattooed, and huddled up in blankets, two children, five pertinaciously sociable dogs, two cats, and heaps of things of different kinds. They are a most gregarious people, always visiting each other, and living in each other's houses, and so hospitable that no Hawaiian, however poor, will refuse to share his last mouthful of *poi* with a stranger of his own race. These people looked very poor, but probably were not really so, as they had a nice grass-house, with very fine mats, within a few yards.

A man went out, cut off the head of a fowl, singed it in the flame, cut it into pieces, put it into a pot to boil, and before our feet were warm the bird was cooked, and we ate it out of the pot with some baked *kalo*. D. took me out to see some mango trees, and a pond filled with gold fish, which she said had been hers when she was a child. She seemed very fond of her relatives, among whom she looked like a fairy princess; and I think they admired her very much, and treated her with some deference. The object of our visit was to procure a *lé* of birds' feathers which they had been making for her, and for which I am sure 800 birds must have been sacrificed. It was a very

beautiful as well as costly ornament,* and most ingeniously
packed for travelling by being laid at full length within a
slender cylinder of bamboo.

We rode on again, somewhat unwillingly on my part,
for though I thought my apprehensions might be cowardly
and ignorant, yet D. was but a child, and had the
attractive wilfulness of childhood, and she was, I saw,
determined to get back to her husband, and the devotion
and affection of the young wife were so pleasant to see,
that I had not the heart to offer serious opposition to her
wishes, especially as I knew that I might be exaggerating
the possible peril. I gathered, however, from what she
said, that her people wanted us to remain until Monday,
especially as none of them could go with us, their horses
being at some distance. I thought it a sign of difficulties
ahead, that on one of the most frequented tracks in
Hawaii, we had not met a single traveller, though it was
Saturday, a special travelling day.

We crossed one gulch in which the water was strong,
and up to our horses' bodies, and came upon the incor-
rigible Kaluna, who, instead of catching his horse, was
recounting his adventures to a circle of natives, but

---

* A small bird, Melithreptes Pacifica, inhabits the mountainous regions
of Hawaii, and has under each wing a single feather, one inch long, of a
bright canary yellow. The birds are caught by means of a viscid substance
smeared on poles. Formerly they were strictly *tabu*. It is of these feathers
that the *mamo* or war-cloak of Kamehameha I., now used on state occasions
by the Hawaiian kings, is composed. This priceless mantle is four feet long,
eleven and a half feet wide at the bottom, and its formation occupied nine
successive reigns. It is one of the costliest of royal ornaments, if the
labour spent upon it is estimated, and the feathers of which it is made
have been valued at a dollar and a half for five.

promised to follow us soon.   D. then said that the next
gulch was rather a bad one, and that we must not wait
for Kaluna, but ride fast, and try to get through it.   When
we reached the *pali* above it, we heard the roaring of a
torrent, and when we descended to its brink it looked
truly bad, but D. rode in, and I waited on the margin.
She got safely across, but when she was near the opposite
side her large horse plunged, slipped, and scrambled in
a most unpleasant way, and she screamed something to
me which I could not hear.   Then I went in, and

> " At the first plunge the horse sank low,
>   And the water broke o'er the saddle bow :"

but the brave animal struggled through, with the water
up to the top of her back, till she reached the place where
D.'s horse had looked so insecure.   In another moment
she and I rolled backwards into deep water, as if she had
slipped from a submerged rock.   I saw her fore feet paw-
ing the air, and then only her head was above water.   I
struck her hard with my spurs, she snorted, clawed, made
a desperate struggle, regained her footing, got into shallow water, and landed safely.   It was a small but not an
agreeable adventure.

We went on again, the track now really dangerous from
denudation and slipperiness.   The rain came down, if
possible, yet more heavily, and coursed fiercely down each
pali track.   Hundreds of cascades leapt from the cliffs,
bringing down stones with a sharp rattling sound.   We
crossed a bridge over one gulch, where the water was
thundering down in such volume that it seemed as if it

must rend the hard basalt of the *palis*.   Then we reached
the lofty top of the great Hakalau gulch, the largest of
all, with the double river, and the ocean close to the ford.
Mingling with the deep reverberations of the surf, I heard
the sharp crisp rush of a river, and of "a river that has
no bridge."

The dense foliage, and the exigencies of the steep track,
which had become very difficult, owing to the washing
away of the soil, prevented me from seeing anything till I
got down.   I found Deborah speaking to a native, who
was gesticulating very emphatically, and pointing up the
river.   The roar was deafening, and the sight terrific.
Where there were two shallow streams a week ago, with a
house and good-sized piece of ground above their confluence, there was now one spinning, rushing, chafing,
foaming river, twice as wide as the Clyde at Glasgow, the
land was submerged, and, if I remember correctly, the
house only stood above the flood.   And, most fearful to
look upon, the ocean, in three huge breakers, had come
quite in, and its mountains of white surge looked fearfully
near the only possible crossing.   I entreated D. not to go
on.   She said we could not go back, that the last gulch
was already impassable, that between the two there was
no house in which we could sleep, that the river had a
good bottom, that the man thought if our horses were
strong we could cross now, but not later, &c.   In short,
she overbore all opposition, and plunged in, calling to me,
"spur, spur, all the time."

Just as I went in, I took my knife and cut open the
cloak which contained the cocoanuts, one only remaining.

Deborah's horse I knew was strong, and shod, but my
unshod and untried mare, what of her? My soul and
senses literally reeled among the dizzy horrors of the
wide, wild tide, but with an effort I regained sense and
self-possession, for we were in, and there was no turning.
D., ahead, screeched to me what I could not hear; she
said afterwards it was "spur, spur, and keep up the river;"
the native was shrieking in Hawaiian from the hinder
shore, and waving to the right, but the torrents of rain,
the crash of the breakers, and the rush and hurry of the
river confused both sight and hearing. I saw D.'s great
horse carried off his legs, my mare, too, was swimming,
and shortly afterwards, between swimming, struggling,
and floundering, we reached what had been the junction
of the two rivers, where there was foothold, and the water
was only up to the seat of the saddles.

Remember, we were both sitting nearly up to our waists
in water, and it was only by screaming that our voices
were heard above the din, and to return or go on seemed
equally perilous. Under these critical circumstances the
following colloquy took place, on my side, with teeth
chattering, and on hers, with a sudden forgetfulness of
English produced by her first sense of the imminent
danger we were in.

Self.—" My mare is so tired, and so heavily weighted,
we shall be drowned, or I shall."

Deborah (with more reason on her side).—" But can't
go back, we no stay here, water higher all minutes, spur
horse, think we come through."

Self.—" But if we go on there is broader, deeper water

between us and the shore; your husband would not like you to run such a risk."

Deborah.—" Think we get through, if horses give out, we let go; I swim and save you."

Even under these circumstances a gleam of the ludicrous shot through me at the idea of this small fragile being bearing up my weight among the breakers. I attempted to shift my saddle-bags upon her powerful horse, but being full of water and under water, the attempt failed, and as we spoke both our horses were carried off their vantage ground into deep water.

With wilder fury the river rushed by, its waters whirled dizzily, and, in spite of spurring and lifting with the rein, the horses were swept seawards. It was a very fearful sight. I saw Deborah's horse spin round, and thought woefully of the possible fate of the bright young wife, almost a bride; only the horses' heads and our own heads and shoulders were above water; the surf was thundering on our left, and we were drifting towards it " broadside on." When I saw the young girl's face of horror I felt increased presence of mind, and raising my voice to a shriek, and telling her to do as I did, I lifted and turned my mare with the rein, so that her chest and not her side should receive the force of the river, and the brave animal, as if seeing what she should do, struck out desperately. It was a horrible suspense. Were we stemming the torrent, or was it sweeping us back that very short distance which lay between us and the mountainous breakers? I constantly spurred my mare, guiding her slightly to the left, the side grew nearer, and after exhausting struggles, Deborah's horse touched ground, and her voice came faintly towards me like a voice in a dream, still calling "Spur, spur." My mare touched ground twice, and was carried off again before she fairly got to land some yards nearer the sea than the bridle track.

When our tired horses were taking breath I felt as if my heart stopped, and I trembled all over, for we had narrowly escaped death. I then put our saddle-bags on Deborah's horse. It was one of the worst and steepest of the *palis* that we had to ascend; but I can't remember anything about the road except that we had to leap some place which we could not cross otherwise. Deborah, then thoroughly alive to a sense of risk, said that there was only one more bad gulch to cross before we reached Onomea, but it was the most dangerous of all, and we could not get across, she feared, but we might go and look at it. I only remember the extreme solitude of the region, and scrambling and sliding down a most precipitous *pali*, hearing a roar like cataract upon cataract, and coming suddenly down upon a sublime and picturesque scene, with only standing room, and that knee-deep in water, between a savage torrent and the cliff. This gulch, called the Scotchman's gulch, I am told, because a Scotchman was drowned there, must be at its crossing three-quarters of a mile inland, and three hundred feet above the sea. In going to Waipio, on noticing the deep holes and enormous boulders, some of them higher than a man on horseback, I had thought what a fearful place it would be if it were ever full; but my imagination had not reached the reality. One huge compressed impetuous torrent, leaping in creamy foam, boiling in creamy eddies, rioting in deep black chasms, roared and thundered over the whole in rapids of the most tempestuous kind, leaping down to the ocean in three grand broad cataracts, the nearest of them not more than forty feet from the crossing. Imagine the Moriston at the Falls, four times as wide and fifty times as furious, walled in by precipices, and with a miniature Niagara above and below, and you have a feeble illustration of it.

Portions of two or three rocks only could be seen, and on one of these, about twelve feet from the shore, a nude native, beautifully tattooed, with a lasso in his hands, was standing nearly up to his knees in foam; and about a third of the way from the other side, another native in deeper water, steadying himself by a pole. A young woman on horseback, whose near relative was dangerously ill at Hilo, was jammed under the cliff, and the men were going to get her across. Deborah, to my dismay, said that if she got safely over we would go too, as these natives were very skilful. I asked if she thought her husband would let her cross, and she said "No." I asked her if she were frightened, and she said "Yes;" but she wished so to get home, and her face was as pale as a brown face can be. I only hope the man will prove worthy of her affectionate devotion.

Here, though people say it is a most perilous gulch, I was not afraid for her life or mine, with the amphibious natives to help us; but I was sorely afraid of being bruised, and scarred, and of breaking the horses' legs, and I said I

would not cross, but would sleep among the trees; but
the tumult drowned our voices, though the Hawaiians by
screeching could make themselves understood.   The
nearest man then approached the shore, put the lasso
round the nose of the woman's horse, and dragged it into
the torrent; and it was exciting to see a horse creeping
from rock to rock in a cataract with alarming possibilities
in every direction.   But beasts may well be bold, as they
have not " the foreknowledge of death."   When the
nearest native had got the horse as far as he could, he
threw the lasso to the man who was steadying himself
with the pole, and urged the horse on.   There was a deep
chasm between the two into which the animal fell, as he
tried to leap from one rock to another.   I saw for a
moment only a woman's head and shoulders, a horse's
head, a commotion of foam, a native tugging at the lasso,
and then a violent scramble on to a rock, and a plunging
and floundering through deep water to shore.

Then Deborah said she would go, that her horse was a
better and stronger one; and the same process was
repeated with the same slip into the chasm, only with the
variation that for a second she went out of sight altogether.
It was a terribly interesting and exciting spectacle with
sublime accompaniments.   Though I had no fear of
absolute danger, yet my mare was tired, and I had made
up my mind to remain on that side till the flood abated;
but I could not make the natives understand that I wished
to turn, and while I was screaming " No, no," and trying
to withdraw my stiffened limbs from the stirrups, the noose
was put round the mare's nose, and she went in.   It was

horrible to know that into the chasm as the others went I too must go, and in the mare went with a blind plunge. With violent plunging and struggling she got her fore feet on the rock, but just as she was jumping up to it altogether she slipped back snorting into the hole, and the water went over my eyes. I struck her with my spurs, the men screeched and shouted, the hinder man jumped in, they both tugged at the lasso, and slipping and struggling, the animal gained the rock, and plunged through deep water to shore, the water covering that rock with a rush of foam, being fully two feet deep.

Kaluna came up just after we had crossed, undressed, made his clothes into a bundle, and got over amphibiously, leaping, swimming, and diving, looking like a water-god, with the horse and mule after him. His dexterity was a beautiful sight; but on looking back I wondered how human beings ever devised to cross such a flood. We got over just in time. Some travellers who reached Laupahoehoe shortly after we left, more experienced than we were, suffered a two days' detention rather than incur a similar risk. Several mules and horses, they say, have had their legs broken in crossing this gulch by getting them fast between the rocks.

Shortly after this, Deborah uttered a delighted exclamation, and her pretty face lighted up, and I saw her husband spurring along the top of the next *pali*, and he presently joined us, and I exchanged my tired mare for his fresh, powerful horse. He knew that a freshet was imminent, and believing that we should never leave Laupahoehoe, he was setting off, provided with tackle for getting himself across, intending to join us, and remain with us till the rivers fell. The presence of a responsible white man seemed a rest at once. We had several more gulches to cross, but none of them were dangerous; and we rode the last seven miles at a great pace, though the mire and water were often up to the horses' knees, and came up to Onomea at full gallop, with spirit and strength enough for riding other twenty miles. Dry clothing, hot baths, and good tea followed delightfully upon our drowning ride. I remained over Sunday at Onomea, and yesterday rode here with a native in heavy rain, and received a warm welcome. Our adventures are a nine days' wonder, and every one says that if we had had a white man or an experienced native with us, we should never have been allowed to attempt the perilous ride. I feel very thankful that we are living to tell of it, and that Deborah is not only not worse but considerably better. E——— will expect some reflections; but none were suggested at the time, and I will not now invent what I ought to have thought and felt.

Due honour must be given to the Mexican saddle. Had I been on a side-saddle, and encumbered with a riding-habit, I should have been drowned. I feel able now to ride anywhere and any distance upon it, while Miss Karpe, who began by being much stronger than I was, has never recovered from the volcano ride, and seems quite ill.

Last night Kilauea must have been tremendously active. At ten P.M., from the upper verandah, we saw the whole western sky fitfully illuminated, and the glare reddened the snow which is lying on Mauna Loa, an effect of fire on ice which can rarely be seen.

I. L. B.

LETTER XII.

HILO,
February 22.

MY sojourn here is very pleasant, owing to the kindness
and sociability of the people. I think that so much
culture and such a variety of refined tastes can seldom
be found in so small a community. There have been
pleasant little gatherings for sewing, while some gentlemen
read aloud, fern-printing in the verandah, microscopic
and musical evenings, little social luncheons, and on
Sunday evenings what is colloquially termed, " a sing,"
at this most social house. One of the things I have
specially enjoyed has been spending an afternoon at the
Rev. Titus Coan's. He is not only one of the most
venerable of the remaining missionaries, but such an
authority on the Hawaiian volcanoes as to entitle him to
be designated "the high-priest of Pélé!" In his modest
quiet way he told thrilling stories of the old missionary
days.

As you know, the islands cast off idolatry in 1819, but
it was not till 1835 that Mr. and Mrs. Coan arrived in
Hilo, where Mr. and Mrs. Lyman had been toiling for
some time, and had produced a marked change on the
social condition of the people. Mr. C. was a fervid
speaker, and physically very robust, and when he had
mastered the language, he undertook much of the

travelling and touring, and Mr. Lyman took charge of the home mission station, and the boarding and industrial school which he still indefatigably superintends. There were 15,000 natives then in the district, and its extremes were 100 miles apart. Portions of it could only be reached with peril to limbs and even life. Horses were only regarded as wild animals in those days, and Mr. C. traversed on foot the district I have just returned from, not lazily riding down the gulch sides, but climbing, or being let down by ropes from tree to tree, and from crag to crag. In times of rain like last week, when it was impossible to ford the rivers, he sometimes swam across, with a rope to prevent him from being carried away, through others he rode on the broad shoulders of a willing native, while a company of strong men locked hands and stretched themselves across the torrent, between him and the cataract, to prevent him from being carried over in case his bearer should fall. This experience was often repeated three or four times a day. His smallest weekly number of sermons was six or seven, and the largest from twenty-five to thirty. He often travelled in drowning rain, crossed dangerous streams, climbed slippery precipices, and frequently preached in wind and rain with all his garments saturated. On every occasion he received aid from the natives, who were so kind and friendly, that when he used to sleep in the woods at night, he hung his watch on a tree, knowing that it was perfectly safe from pilfering or curious touch. Indeed the Christian teachers seem to have been regarded as *tabu*.

Before the end of that year, Mr. Coan had made the circuit of Hawaii, a foot and canoe trip of 300 miles, in which he nearly suffered canoe-wreck twice. In all, he has admitted into the Christian church by baptism, 12,000 persons, besides 4000 infants. He gave a most interesting account of one great baptism. The greatest care was previously taken in selecting, teaching, watching, and examining the candidates. Those from the distant villages came and spent several months here for preliminary instruction. Many of these were converts of two years' standing, a larger class had been on the list for more than a year, and a smaller one for a lesser period. The accepted candidates were announced by name several weeks previously, and friends and enemies everywhere were called upon to testify all that they knew about them. On the first Sunday in July, 1838, 1705 persons, formerly heathens, were baptised. They were seated close together on the earth-floor in rows, with just space between for one to walk, and Mr. Lyman and Mr. Coan passing through them, sprinkled every bowed head, after which Mr. C. admitted the weeping hundreds into the fellowship of the Universal Church by pronouncing the words, "I baptise you all in the Name of the Father, and of the Son, and of the Holy Ghost." After this, 2400 converts received the Holy Communion. I give Mr. C.'s own words concerning those who partook of it, " who truly and earnestly repented of their sins, and steadfastly purposed to lead new lives." " The old and decrepit, the lame, the blind, the maimed, the withered, the paralytic, and those afflicted with divers diseases and

torments; those with eyes, noses, lips, and limbs consumed; with features distorted, and figures depraved and
loathsome: these came hobbling upon their staves, or led
and borne by others to the table of the Lord. Among
the throng you would have seen the hoary priest of idolatry, with hands but recently washed from the blood of
human victims, together with thieves, adulterers, highway
robbers, murderers, and mothers whose hands reeked with
the blood of their own children. It seemed like one of
the crowds the Saviour gathered, and over which He pronounced the words of healing."

Though the people cast off idolatry in 1819, before the
arrival of the missionaries, they were very indifferent to
Christian teaching until 1837, the year before the great
baptism, when a great religious stir began, and for four
years affected all the islands. I wish you could have
heard Mr. C. and Mrs. Lyman tell of that stirring time,
when nearly all the large population of the Hilo and Puna
districts turned out to hear the Gospel, and how the
young people went up into the mountains and carried the
news of the love of God and the good life to come to the
sick and old, who were afterwards baptized, when often
the only water which could be obtained for the rite was
that which dripped sparingly from the roofs of caves. The
Hawaiian notions of a future state, where any existed, were
peculiarly vague and dismal, and Mr. Ellis says that the
greater part of the people seemed to regard the tidings of
ora loa ia Jesu (endless life by Jesus) as the most joyful
news they had ever heard, "breaking upon them," to use
their own phrase, "like light in the morning." "Will

my spirit never die, and can this poor weak body live
again ? " an old chiefess exclaimed, and this delighted surprise seemed the general feeling of the natives. From
less difficult distances the sick and lame were brought on
litters and on the backs of men, and the infirm often
crawled to the trail by which the missionary was to pass,
that they might hear of this good news which had come
to Hawaii-nei.

There were but these two preachers for the 15,000
people scattered for 100 miles, who were all ravenous to
hear, and could not wait for the tardy modes of evangeli-
zation. " If we die," said they, " let us die in the light."
So this strange thing fell out, that whole villages from
miles away gathered to the mission station. Two-thirds
of the population of the district came in, and within the
radius of a mile the grass and banana houses clustered as
thick as they could stand. Beautiful Hilo in a short time
swelled from a population of 1000 to 10,000 ; and at any
hour of the day or night the sound of the conch shell
brought together from 3000 to 6000 worshippers. It
was a vast camp-meeting which continued for two years,
but there was no disorder, and a decent quiet ruled
throughout the strangely extemporized city. A new
morality, a new social order, new notions on nearly all
subjects, had to be inculcated as well as a new religion.
Mrs. C. and Mrs. L. daily assembled the women and children, and taught them the habits and industries of civilization, to attend to their persons, to braid hats, and to
wear and make clothes.

During this time, on November 7, 1837, one of the

striking phenomena which make the islands remarkable
occurred. The crescent sand-beach, said to be the most
beautiful in the Pacific, the fringe of palms, the far-reach-
ing groves behind, and the great ocean, slept in summer
calm, as they sleep to-day. Four sermons, as usual, had
been preached to audiences of 6000 people. There had
been a funeral, the natives say, though Mr. C. does not
remember it, and his text had been " Be ye also ready,"
and larger throngs than usual had followed the preachers
to their homes. The fatiguing day was over, the natives
were singing hymns in the still evening air, and Mr. C.
" had gathered his family for prayers " in the very room in
which he told me this story, when they were startled by
" a sound as if a heavy mountain had fallen on the beach."
There was at once a fearful cry, wailing, and indescribable
confusion. The quiet ocean had risen in a moment in a
gigantic wave, which, rushing in with the speed of a race-
horse, and uplifting itself over the shore, swept everything
into promiscuous ruin ; men, women, children, dogs,
houses, food, canoes, clothing, floated wildly on the flood,
and hundreds of people were struggling among the billows
in the midst of their earthly all. Some were dashed on
the shore, some were saved by friends who hurried to
their aid, some were carried out to sea by the retiring
water, and some stout swimmers sank exhausted ; yet the
loss of life was not nearly so great as it would have been
among a less amphibious people. Mr. C. described the
roaring of the ocean, the cries of distress, the shrieks of
the perishing, the frantic rush of hundreds to the shore,
and the desolation of the whole neighbourhood of the

beach, as forming a scene of the most thrilling and awful interest.

You will remember that I wrote from Kilauea regarding the terror which the Goddess of the Crater inspired, and her high-priest was necessarily a very awful personage. The particular high-priest of whom Mr. Coan told me was six feet five inches in height, and his sister, who was co-ordinate with him in authority, had a scarcely inferior altitude. His chief business was to keep Pélé appeased. He lived on the shore, but often went up to Kilauea with sacrifices. If a human victim were needed, he had only to point to a native, and the unfortunate wretch was at once strangled. He was not only the embodiment of heathen piety, but of heathen crime. Robbery was his pastime. His temper was so fierce and so uncurbed that no native dared even to tread on his shadow. More than once he had killed a man for the sake of food and clothes not worth fifty cents. He was a thoroughly wicked savage. Curiosity attracted him into one of the Hilo meetings, and the bad giant fell under the resistless, mysterious influence which was metamorphosing thousands of Hawaiians. " I have been deceived," he said, " I have deceived others, I have lived in darkness, and did not know the true God. I worshipped what was no God. I renounce it all. The true God has come. He speaks. I bow down to Him. I wish to be His son." The priestess, his sister, came soon afterwards, and they remained here several months for instruction. They were then about seventy years old, but they imbibed the New Testament spirit so thoroughly that they became as

gentle, loving, and quiet as little children. After a long
probationary period they were baptized, and after several
years of pious and lowly living, they passed gently and
trustfully away.

The old church which was the scene of these earlier
assemblages, came down with a crash after a night of
heavy rain, the large timbers, which were planted in the
moist earth after the fashion of the country to support
the framework, having become too rotten to support the
weight of the saturated thatch. Without a day's loss of
time the people began a new church. All were volunteers,
some to remove from the wreck of the old building such
timbers as might still be of service; some to quarry stone
for a foundation, an extravagance never before dreamed
of by an islander; some to bring sand in gourd-shells
upon their heads, or laboriously gathered in the folds of
bark-cloth aprons; some to bring lime from the coral
reefs twenty feet under water; whilst the majority hurried
to the forest belt, miles away on the mountain side, to
fell the straightest and tallest trees. Then 50 or 100
men, (for in that day horses and oxen were known only as
wild beasts of the wilderness,) attached hawsers to the
butt ends of logs, and dragged them away through bush
and brake, through broken ground and river beds, till
they deposited them on the site of the new church. The
wild, monotonous chant, as the men hauled in the timber,
lives in the memories of the missionaries' children, who
say that it seemed to them as if the preparations for
Solomon's temple could not have exceeded the accumu-
lations of the islanders!

I think that the greater number of the converts of those four years must have died ere this. In 1867 the old church at Hilo was divided into seven congregations, six of them with native pastors. To meet the wants of the widely-scattered people, fifteen churches have been built, holding from 500 up to 1000. The present Hilo church, a very pretty wooden one, cost about $14,000. All these have been erected mainly by native money and labour. Probably the native Christians on Hawaii are not much better or worse than Christian communities elsewhere, but they do seem a singularly generous people. Besides liberally sustaining their own clergy, the Hilo Christians have contributed altogether $100,000 for religious purposes. Mr. Coan's native congregation, sorely dwindled as it is, raises over $1200 annually for foreign missions; and twelve of its members have gone as missionaries to the islands of Southern Polynesia.

Poor people! It would be unfair to judge of them as we may legitimately be judged of, who inherit the influences of ten centuries of Christianity. They have only just emerged from a bloody and sensual heathenism, and to the instincts and volatility of these dark Polynesian races, the restraining influences of the Gospel are far more severe than to our cold, unimpulsive northern natures. The greatest of their disadvantages has been that some of the vilest of the whites who roamed the Pacific had settled on the islands before the arrival of the Christian teachers, dragging the people down to even lower depths of depravity than those of heathenism, and that there are still resident foreigners who corrupt and destroy them.

184 HAWAII. [LETTER XII.

I must tell you a story which the venerable Mrs. Lyman told me yesterday. In 1825, five years after the first missionaries landed, Kapiolani, a female *alii* of high rank, while living at Kaiwaaloa (where Captain Cook was murdered), became a Christian. Grieving for her people, most of whom still feared to anger Pélé, she announced that it was her intention to visit Kilauea, and dare the fearful goddess to do her worst. Her husband and many others tried to dissuade her, but she was resolute, and taking with her a large retinue, she took a journey of one hundred miles, mostly on foot, over the rugged lava, till she arrived near the crater. There a priestess of Pélé met her, threatened her with the displeasure of the goddess if she persisted in her hostile errand, and prophesied that she and her followers would perish miserably. Then, as now, *ohelo* berries grew profusely round the terminal wall of Kilauea, and there, as elsewhere, were sacred to Pélé, no one daring to eat of them till he had first offered some of them to the divinity. It was usual on arriving at the crater to break a branch covered with berries, and turning the face to the pit of fire, to throw half the branch over the precipice, saying, " Pélé, here are your *ohelos*. I offer some to you, some I also eat," after which the natives partook of them freely. Kapiolani gathered and eat them without this formula, after which she and her company of eighty persons descended to the black edge of Hale-mau-mau. There, in full view of the fiery pit, she thus addressed her followers :—" *Jehovah is my God. He kindled these fires. I fear not Pélé. If I perish by the anger of Pélé, then you may fear the power of Pélé ; but if I trust in Jehovah, and he should save me from the wrath of Pélé, when I break through her tabus, then you must fear and serve the Lord Jehovah. All the Gods of Hawaii are vain! Great is Jehovah's goodness in sending teachers to turn us from these vanities to the living God and the way of righteousness!"* Then they sang a hymn. I can fancy the strange procession winding its backward way over the cracked, hot, lava sea, the robust belief of the princess hardly sustaining the limping faith of her followers, whose fears would not be laid to rest until they reached the crater's rim without any signs of the pursuit of an avenging deity. It was more sublime than Elijah's appeal on the soft, green slopes of Carmel, but the popular belief in the Goddess of the Volcano survived this flagrant instance of her incapacity, and only died out many years afterwards.

Besides these interesting reminiscences, I have been hearing most thrilling stories from Mrs. Lyman and Mr. Coan of volcanoes, earthquakes, and tidal waves. Told by eye-witnesses, and on the very spot where the incidents occurred, they make a profound, and, I fear, an incommunicable impression. I look on these venerable people as I should on people who had seen the Deluge, or the burial of Pompeii, and wonder that they eat and dress and live like other mortals! For they have felt the perpetual shudder of earthquakes, and their eyes, which look so calm and kind, have seen the inflowing of huge tidal waves, the dull red glow of lava streams, and the leaping of fire cataracts into deep-lying pools, burning them dry in a night time. There were years in which there was no day in which the smoke of underground furnaces was out of their sight, or night which was not lurid with flames. Once they traced a river of lava burrowing its way 1500 feet below the surface, and saw it emerge, break over a precipice, and fall hissing into the ocean. Once from their highest mountain a pillar of fire 200 feet in diameter lifted itself for three weeks 1000 feet into the air, making night day, for a hundred miles round, and leaving as its monument a cone a mile in circumference. We see a clothed and finished earth; they see the building of an island, layer on layer, hill on hill, the naked and deformed product of the melting, forging, and welding, which go on perpetually in the crater of Kilauea.

I could fill many sheets with what I have heard, but must content myself with telling you very little. In 1855 the fourth recorded eruption of Mauna Loa occurred. The lava flowed directly Hilo-wards, and for several months, spreading through the dense forests which belt the mountain, crept slowly shorewards, threatening this beautiful portion of Hawaii with the fate of the Cities of the Plain. Mr. C. made several visits to the eruption, and on each return the simple people asked him how much longer it would last. For five months they watched the inundation, which came a little nearer every day. Should they fly or not? Would their beautiful homes become a waste of jagged lava and black sand, like the neighbouring district of Puna, once as fair as Hilo?" Such questions suggested themselves as they nightly watched the nearing glare, till the fiery waves met with obstacles which piled them up in hillocks, eight miles from Hilo, and the suspense was over. Only gigantic causes can account for the gigantic phenomena of this lava-flow. The eruption travelled forty miles in a straight line, or sixty, including sinuosities. It was from one to three miles broad, and from five to two hundred feet deep, according to the contours of the mountain slopes over which it flowed. It lasted for thirteen months, pouring out a torrent of lava which covered nearly 300 square miles of land, and whose volume was estimated at thirty-eight thousand millions of cubic feet! In 1859 lava fountains 400 feet in height, and with a nearly equal diameter, played on the summit of Mauna Loa. This eruption ran fifty miles to the sea in eight days, but the flow lasted much longer, and added a new promontory to Hawaii.

These magnificent overflows, however threatening, had done little damage to cultivated regions, and none to human life ; and people began to think that the volcano was reformed. But in 1868 terrors occurred which are without precedent in island history. While Mrs. L. was giving me the narrative in her graphic but simple way, and the sweet wind rustled through the palms, and brought the rich scent of the ginger plant into the shaded room, she seemed to be telling me some weird tale of another world. On March 27, five years ago, a series of earthquakes began, and became more startling from day to day, until their succession became so rapid that "the island quivered like the lid of a boiling pot nearly all the time between the heavier shocks. The trembling was like that of a ship struck by a heavy wave." Then the terminal crater of Mauna Loa (Mokuaweoweo) sent up columns of smoke, steam, and red light, and it was shortly seen that the southern slope of its dome had been rent, and that four separate rivers of molten stone were pouring out of as many rents, and were flowing down the mountain sides in diverging lines. Suddenly the rivers were arrested, and the blue mountain dome appeared against the still blue sky without an indication of fire, steam, or smoke. Hilo was much agitated by the sudden lull. No one was deceived into security, for it was certain that the strangely pent-up fires must make themselves felt.

The earthquakes became nearly continuous; scarcely an appreciable interval occurred between them; "the throbbing, jerking, and quivering motions grew more positive, intense, and sharp; they were vertical, rotary, lateral, and undulating," producing nausea, vertigo, and vomiting. Late in the afternoon of a lovely day, April 2, the climax came. "The crust of the earth rose and sank like the sea in a storm." Rocks were rent, mountains fell, buildings and their contents were shattered, trees swayed like reeds, animals were scared, and ran about demented; men thought the judgment had come. The earth opened in thousands of places, the roads in Hilo cracked open, horses and their riders, and people afoot, were thrown violently to the ground; "it seemed as if the rocky ribs of the mountains, and the granite walls and pillars of the earth were breaking up."

At Kilauea the shocks were as frequent as the ticking of a watch. In Kau, south of Hilo, they counted 300 shocks on this direful day; and Mrs. L.'s son, who was in that district at the time, says that the earth swayed to and fro, north and south, then east and west, then round and round, up and down, in every imaginable direction, everything crashing about them, " and the trees thrashing as if torn by a strong rushing wind." He and others sat on the ground bracing themselves with hands and feet to avoid being rolled over. They saw an avalanche of red earth, which they supposed to be lava, burst from the mountain side, throwing rocks high into the air, swallowing up houses, trees, men, and animals; and travelling three miles in as many minutes, burying a hamlet, with thirty-one inhabitants and 500 head of cattle. The people of the valleys fled to the mountains, which themselves were splitting in all directions, and collecting on an elevated spot, with the earth reeling under them, they spent the night of April 2 in prayer and singing. Looking towards the shore, they saw it sink, and at the same moment a wave, whose height was estimated at from forty to sixty feet, hurled itself upon the coast, and receded five times, destroying whole villages, and even strong stone houses, with a touch, and engulfing for ever forty-six people who had lingered too near the shore.

Still the earthquakes continued, and still the volcano gave no sign. The nerves of many people gave way in these fearful days. Some tried to get away to Honolulu, others kept horses saddled on which to fly, they knew not whither. The hourly question was, "What of the volcano?" People put their ears to the quivering ground, and heard, or thought they heard, the surgings of the imprisoned lava sea rending its way among the ribs of the earth.

Five days after the destructive earthquake of April 2, the ground south of Hilo burst open with a crash and roar which at once answered all questions concerning the volcano. The molten river, after travelling underground for twenty miles, emerged through a fissure two miles in length with a tremendous force and volume. It was in a pleasant pastoral region, supposed to be at rest for ever, at the top of a grass-covered plateau sprinkled with native and foreign houses, and rich in herds of cattle. Four huge fountains boiled up with terrific fury, throwing crimson lava, and rocks weighing many tons, to a height of from 500 to 1000 feet. Mr. Whitney, of Honolulu, who was near the spot, says:—"From these great fountains to the sea flowed a rapid stream of red lava, rolling, rushing, and tumbling, like a swollen river, bearing along in its current large rocks that made the lava foam as it dashed down the precipice and through the valley into the sea, surging and roaring throughout its length like a cataract, with a power and fury perfectly indescribable. It was nothing else than a *river of fire* from 200 to 800 feet wide and twenty deep, with a *speed varying from ten to twenty-five miles an hour!*" This same intelligent observer noticed as a peculiarity of the spouting that the lava was ejected by a *rotary motion*, and in the air both lava and stones always

rotated *towards the south*.   At Kilauea I noticed that the
lava was ejected in a southerly direction.   From the
scene of these fire fountains, whose united length was
about a mile, the river in its rush to the sea divided
itself into four streams, between which it shut up men
and beasts.   One stream hurried to the sea in four
hours, but the others took two days to travel ten miles.
The aggregate width was a mile and a half.   Where it
entered the sea it extended the coast-line half a mile,
but this worthless accession to Hawaiian acreage was
dearly purchased by the loss, for ages at least, of 4000
acres of valuable pasture land, and a much larger quantity
of magnificent forest.   The whole south-east shore of
Hawaii sank from four to six feet, which involved the
destruction of several hamlets and the beautiful fringe of
cocoa-nut trees.   Though the region was very thinly
peopled, 200 houses and 100 lives were sacrificed in this
week of horrors, and from the reeling mountains, the
uplifted ocean, and the fiery inundation, the terrified
survivors fled into Hilo, each with a tale of woe and loss.
The number of shocks of earthquake counted was 2000 in
two weeks, an average of 140 a day; but on the other
side of the island the number was incalculable.

I. L. B.

LETTER XIII.

THE quiet, dreamy, afternoon existence of Hilo is disturbed. Two days ago an official intimation was received that the American Government had placed the U. S. ironclad "Benicia" at the disposal of King Lunalilo for a cruise round Hawaii, and that he would arrive here the following morning with Admiral Pennock and the U. S. generals Scholfield and Alexander.

Now this monarchy is no longer an old-time chieftaincy, made up of calabashes and *poi*, feather-cloaks, *kahilis*, and a little fuss, but has a civilized constitutional king, the equal of Queen Victoria, a civil list, &c., and though Lunalilo comes here trying to be a private individual and to rest from *Hookupus*, state entertainments, and privy councils, he brings with him a royal chamberlain and an adjutant-general in attendance. So the good people of Hilo have been decorating their houses anew with ferns and flowers, furbishing up their clothes, and holding mysterious consultations regarding etiquette and entertainments, just as if royalty were about to drop down in similar fashion on Bude or Tobermory. There were amusing attempts to bring about a practical reconciliation between the free-and easiness of Republican notions and the respect due to a sovereign who reigns by " the

THE MOUNTAIN MAUNA KEA FROM HILO.

[*Page* 193.

will of the people" as well as by "the grace of God,"
but eventually the tact of the king made everything go
smoothly.

At eight yesterday morning the " Benicia " anchored
inside the reef, and Hilo blossomed into a most striking
display of bunting ; the Hawaiian colours, eight blue, red
and white stripes, with the English union in the corner,
and the flaunting flag of America being predominant.
My heart warmed towards our own flag as the soft breeze
lifted its rich folds among the glories of the tropical trees.
Indeed, bunting to my mind never looked so well as when
floating and fainting among cocoa-nut palms and all the
shining greenery of Hilo, in the sunshine of a radiant
morning.   It was bright and warm, but the cool bulk of
Mauna Kea, literally covered with snow, looked down
as winter upon summer.   Natives galloped in from all
quarters, brightly dressed, wreathed, and garlanded, delighted in their hearts at the attention paid to their
sovereign by a great foreign power, though they had been
very averse to this journey, from a strange but prevalent
idea that once on board a U. S. ship the king would be
kidnapped and conveyed to America.

Lieut.-Governor Lyman and Mr. Severance, the sheriff,
went out to the " Benicia," and the king landed at ten
o'clock, being "graciously pleased" to accept the Governor's house as his residence during his visit.   The
American officers, naval and military, were received by
the same loud, hospitable old whaling captain who entertained the Duke of Edinburgh some years ago here, and
to judge from the hilarious sounds which came down the

road from his house, they had what they would call "a good time." I had seen Lunalilo in state at Honolulu, but it was much more interesting to see him here, and this royalty is interesting in itself, as a thing on sufferance, standing between this helpless nationality and its absorption by America. The king is a very fine-looking man of thirty-eight, tall, well formed, broad-chested, with his head well set on his shoulders, and his feet and hands small. His appearance is decidedly commanding and aristocratic : he is certainly handsome even according to our notions. He has a fine open brow, significant at once of brains and straightforwardness, a straight proportionate nose, and a good mouth. The slight tendency to Polynesian overfulness about his lips is concealed by a well-shaped moustache. He wears whiskers cut in the English fashion. His eyes are large, dark-brown of course, and equally of course, he has a superb set of teeth. Owing to a slight fulness of the lower eyelid, which Queen Emma also has, his eyes have a singularly melancholy expression, very alien, I believe, to his character. He is remarkably gentlemanly looking, and has the grace of movement which seems usual with Hawaiians. When he landed he wore a dark morning suit and a black felt hat.

As soon as he stepped on shore, the natives, who were in crowds on the beach, cheered, yelled, and waved their hats and handkerchiefs, and then a procession was formed, or rather formed itself, to escort him to the governor's house. A rabble of children ran in front, then came the king, over whom the natives had thrown some beautiful garlands of *ohia* and *mailé* (Alyxia olivæformis), with the governor on one side and the sheriff on the other, the chamberlain and adjutant-general walking behind. Then a native staggering under the weight of an enormous Hawaiian flag, the Hilo band, with my friend Upa beating the big drum, and an irregular rabble (*i.e.* unorganised crowd) of men, women, and children, going at a trot to keep up with the king's rapid strides. The crowd was unwilling to disperse even when he entered the house, and he came out and made a short speech, the gist of which was that he was delighted to see his native subjects, and would hold a reception for them on the ensuing Monday, when we shall see a most interesting sight, a native crowd gathered from all Southern Hawaii for a *hookupu*, an old custom, signifying the bringing of gift-offerings to a king or chief.

In the afternoon Dr. Wetmore and I rode to the beautiful Puna woods on a botanising excursion. We were galloping down to the beach round a sharp corner, when we had to pull our horses almost on their haunches to avoid knocking over the king, the American admiral, the captain of the "Benicia," nine of their officers, and the two generals. When I saw the politely veiled stare of the white men it occurred to me that probably it was the first time that they had seen a white woman riding cavalier fashion! We had a delicious gallop over the sands to the Waiakea river, which we crossed, and came upon one of the vast lava-flows of ages since, over which we had to ride carefully, as the *pahoehoe* lies in rivers, coils, tortuosities, and holes partially concealed by a luxuriant growth of ferns and convolvuli. The country is thickly

sprinkled with cocoa-nuts and bread-fruit trees, which
merge into the dense, dark, glorious forest, which tenderly
hides out of sight hideous broken lava, on which one
cannot venture six feet from the track without the risk of
breaking one's limbs. All these tropical forests are absolutely impenetrable, except to axe and billhook, and after
a trail has been laboriously opened, it needs to be cut
once or twice a year, so rapid is the growth of vegetation.
This one, through the Puna woods, only admits of one
person at a time. It was really rapturously lovely.
Through the trees we saw the soft steel-blue of the
summer sky : not a leaf stirred, not a bird sang, a hush
had fallen on insect life, the quiet was perfect, even the
ring of our horses' hoofs on the lava was a discord.
There was a slight coolness in the air and a fresh mossy
smell. It only required some suggestion of decay, and
the rustle of a fallen leaf now and then, to make it an
exact reproduction of a fine day in our English October.
The forest was enlivened by many natives bound for
Hilo, driving horses loaded with cocoa-nuts, bread-fruit,
live fowls, *poi* and *kalo*, while others with difficulty urged
garlanded pigs in the same direction, all as presents for
the king. We brought back some very scarce parasitic
ferns.

HILO, February 24.

I rode over by myself to Onomea on Saturday to get
a little rest from the excitements of Hilo. A gentleman
lent me a strong showy mare to go out on, telling me
that she was frisky and must be held while I mounted ;

but before my feet were fairly in the stirrups, she shook herself from the Chinaman who held her, and danced away. I rode her five miles before she quieted down. She pranced, jumped, danced, and fretted on the edge of precipices, was furious at the scow and fords, and seemed demented with good spirits. Onomea looked glorious, and its serenity was most refreshing. I rode into Hilo the next day in time for morning service, and the mare, after a good gallop, subsided into a staidness of demeanour befitting the day. Just as I was leaving, they asked me to take the news to the sheriff that a man had been killed a few hours before. He was riding into Hilo with a child behind him, and they went over by no means one of the worst of the *palis*. The man and horse were killed, but the child was unhurt, and his wailing among the deep ferns attracted the attention of passers-by to the disaster. The natives ride over these dangerous *palis* so carelessly, and on such tired, starved horses, that accidents are not infrequent. Hilo had never looked so lovely to me as in the pure bright calm of this Sunday morning.

The verandahs of all the native houses were crowded with strangers, who had come in to share in the jubilations attending the king's visit. At the risk of emulating " Jenkins," or the " Court Newsman," I must tell you that Lunalilo, who is by no means an habitual church-goer, attended Mr. Coan's native church in the morning, and the foreign church at night, when the choir sang a very fine anthem. I don't wish to write about his faults, which have doubtless been rumoured in the English papers.

It is hoped that his new responsibilities will assist him to conquer them, else I fear he may go the way of several of the Hawaiian kings. He has begun his reign with marked good sense in selecting as his advisers confessedly the best men in his kingdom, and all his public actions since his election have shown both tact and good feeling. If sons, as is often asserted, take their intellects from their mothers, he should be decidedly superior, for his mother, Kekauluohi, a chieftainess of the highest rank, and one of the queens of Kamehameha II., who died in London, was in 1839 chosen for her abilities by Kamehameha III. as his *kuhina nui*, or premier, an officer recognised under the old system of Hawaiian government as second only in authority to the king, and without whose signature even his act was not legal. As Kaahumanu II. she continued to hold this important position until her death in 1845.

But the present king does not come of the direct line of the Hawaiian kings, but of a far older family. His father is a commoner, but Hawaiian rank is inherited through the mother. He received a good English education at the school which the missionaries established for the sons of chiefs, and was noted as a very bright scholar, with an early developed taste for literature and poetry. His disposition is said to be most amiable and genial, and his affability endeared him especially to his own countrymen, by whom he was called *alii lokomaikai,* "the kind chief." In spite of his high rank, which gave him precedence of all others on the islands, he was ignored by two previous governments, and often com-

plained that he was never allowed any opportunity of
becoming acquainted with public affairs, or of learning
whether he possessed any capacity for business. Thus,
without experience, but with noble and liberal instincts,
and the highest and most patriotic aspirations for the
welfare and improvement of his " weak little kingdom,"
he was unexpectedly called to the throne about three
months ago, amidst such an enthusiasm as had never
before been witnessed on Hawaii-nei, as the unanimous
choice of the people. He called on Mr. Coan the day of
his arrival; and when the flute band of Mr. Lyman's
school serenaded him, he made the youths a kind address,
in which he said he had been taught as they were, and
hoped hereafter to profit by the instruction he had
received.

This has been a great day in Hilo. The old native
custom of *hookupu* was revived, and it has been a most
interesting spectacle. I don't think I ever enjoyed sight-
seeing so much. The weather has been splendid, which
was most fortunate, for many of the natives came in from
distances of from sixty to eighty miles. From early
daylight they trooped in on their half broken steeds, and
by ten o'clock there were fully a thousand horses tethered
on the grass by the sea. Almost every house displayed
flags, and the court-house, where the reception was to
take place, was most tastefully decorated. It is a very
pretty two-storied frame building, with deep double
verandahs, and stands on a large lawn of fine *manienie*
grass,* with roads on three sides. Long before ten,

* Cynodon Dactylon (?)

crowds had gathered outside the low walls of the lawn,
natives and foreigners galloped in all directions, boats
and canoes enlivened the bay, bands played, and the
foreigners, on this occasion rather a disregarded minority,
assembled in holiday dress in the upper verandah of the
court-house. Hawaiian flags on tall bamboos decorated
the little gateways which gave admission to the lawn,
an enormous standard on the government flagstaff could
be seen for miles, and the stars and stripes waved from
the neighbouring plantations and from several houses in
Hilo. At ten punctually, Lunalilo, Governor Lyman,
the sheriff of Hawaii, the royal chamberlain, and the
adjutant-general, walked up to the court-house, and the
king took his place, standing in the lower verandah with
his suite about him. All the foreigners were either on
the upper balcony, or on the stairs leading to it, on which,
to get the best possible view of the spectacle, I stood for
three mortal hours. The attendant gentlemen were well
dressed, but wore "shocking bad hats;" and the king
wore a sort of shooting suit, a short brown cut-away
coat, an ash-coloured waistcoat and ash-coloured trousers
with a blue stripe. He stood bareheaded. He dressed
in this style in order that the natives might attend the
reception in every-day dress, and not run the risk of
spoiling their best clothes by Hilo torrents. The dress
of the king and his attendants was almost concealed by
wreaths of *ohia* blossoms and festoons of *mailé*, some of
them two yards long, which had been thrown over them,
and which bestowed a fantastic glamour on the otherwise
prosaic inelegance of their European dress. But indeed

the spectacle, as a whole, was altogether poetical, as it was an ebullition of natural, national, human feeling, in which the heart had the first place. I very soon ceased to notice the incongruous elements, which were supplied chiefly by the Americans present. There were Republicans by birth and nature, destitute of traditions of loyalty or reverence for aught on earth ; who bore on their faces not only republicanism, but that quintessence of puritan republicanism which hails from New England ; and these were subjects of a foreign king, nay, several of them office-holders who had taken the oath of allegiance, and from whose lips " His Majesty, Your Majesty," flowed far more copiously than from ours which are " to the manner born."

On the king's appearance, the cheering was tremendous, —regular British cheering, well led, succeeded by that which is not British, " three cheers and a tiger," but it was " Hi, hi, hi, hullah ! " Every hat was off, every handkerchief in air, tears in many eyes, enthusiasm universal, for the people were come to welcome the king of their choice ; the prospective restorer of the Constitution " trampled upon " by Kamehameha V., " the kind chief," who was making them welcome to his presence after the fashion of their old feudal lords. When the cheering had subsided, the eighty boys of Missionary Lyman's School, who, dressed in white linen with crimson *leis*, were grouped in a hollow square round the flagstaff, sang the Hawaiian national anthem, the music of which is the same as ours. More cheering and enthusiasm, and then the natives came through the gate across

the lawn, and up to the verandah where the king stood,
in one continuous procession, till 2400 Hawaiians had
enjoyed one moment of infinite and ever to be remembered satisfaction in the royal presence. Every now and
then the white, pale-eyed, unpicturesque face of a foreigner
passed by, but these were few, and the foreign school
children were received by themselves after Mr. Lyman's
boys.   The Americans have introduced the villanous
custom of shaking hands at these receptions, borrowing
it, I suppose, from a presidential reception at Washington;
and after the king had gone through this ceremony with
each native, the present was deposited in front of the
verandah, and the gratified giver took his place on the
grass.   Not a man, woman, or child came empty handed.
Every face beamed with pride, wonder, and complacency,
for here was a sovereign for whom cannon roared, and
yards were manned, of their own colour, who called
them his brethren.

The variety of costume was infinite. All the women
wore the native dress, the sack or *holuku*, many of which
were black, blue, green, or bright rose colour, some were
bright yellow, a few were pure white, and others were a
mixture of orange and scarlet. Some wore very pretty
hats made from cane-tops, and trimmed with hibiscus
blossoms or passion-flowers ; others wore bright-coloured
handkerchiefs, knotted lightly round their flowing hair,
or wreaths of the Microlepia tenuifolia. Many had
tied bandanas in a graceful knot over the left shoulder.
All wore two, three, four, or even six beautiful *leis*,
besides long festoons of the fragrant *mailé*. *Leis* of the

crimson *ohia* blossoms were universal; but besides these there were *leis* of small red and white double roses, *pohas*,* yellow amaranth, sugar cane tassels like frosted silver, the orange pandanus, the delicious gardenia, and a very few of orange blossoms, and the great granadilla or passion-flower. Few if any of the women wore shoes, and none of the children had anything on their heads.

A string of 200 Chinamen passed by, "plantation hands," with boyish faces, and cunning, almond-shaped eyes. They were dressed in loose blue denim trousers with shirts of the same, fastening at the side over them, their front hair closely shaven, and the rest gathered into pigtails, which were wound several times round their heads. These all deposited money in the adjutant-general's hand. The dress of the Hawaiian men was more varied and singular than that of the women, every kind of dress and undress, with *leis* of *ohia* and garlands of *mailé* covering all deficiencies. The poor things came up with pathetic innocence, many of them with nothing on but an old shirt, and cotton trousers rolled up to the knees. Some had red shirts and blue trousers, others considered that a shirt was an effective outer garment. Some wore highly ornamental, dandified shirts, and trousers tucked into high, rusty, mud-covered boots. A few young men were in white straw hats, white shirts, and white trousers, with crimson *leis* round their hats and throats. Some had diggers' scarves round their waists; but the most

* Physalis Peruviana.

effective costume was sported by a few old men, who had
tied crash towels over their shoulders.

It was often amusing and pathetic at once to see them
come up. Obviously, when the critical moment arrived,
they were as anxious to do the right thing as a *débutante*
is to back her train successfully out of the royal presence
at St. James's. Some were so agitated at last as to
require much coaching from the governor as to how to
present their gifts and shake hands. Some half dropped
down on their knees, others passionately and with tears
kissed the king's hand, or grasped it convulsively in both
their own; while a few were so embarrassed by the
presents they were carrying that they had no hands at
all to shake, and the sovereign good-naturedly clapped
them on the shoulders. Some of them, in shaking hands,
adroitly slipped coins into the king's palm, so as to make
sure that he received their loving tribute. There had
been a *hui*, or native meeting, which had passed resolu-
tions, afterwards presented to Lunalilo, setting forth that
whereas he received a great deal of money in revenue
from the *haoles*, they, his native people, would feel that
he did not love them if he would not receive from their
own hands contributions in silver for his support. So,
in order not to wound their feelings, he accepted these
rather troublesome cash donations.

One woman, sorely afflicted with quaking palsy, dragged
herself slowly along. One hand hung by her side helpless, and the other grasped a live fowl so tightly that she
could not loosen it to shake hands, whereupon the king
raised the helpless arm, which called forth much cheering.

There was one poor cripple who had only the use of his arms. His knees were doubled under him, and he trailed his body along the ground. He had dragged himself two miles "to lie for a moment at the king's feet," and even his poor arms carried a gift. He looked hardly like a human shape, as his desire was realised ; and, I doubt not, would have been content then and there to die. There were ancient men, tattooed all over, who had passed their first youth when the idols were cast away, and who remembered the old days of tyranny when it was an offence, punishable with death, for a man to let his shadow fall on the king ; and when none of "the swinish multitude" had any rights which they could sustain against their chiefs. These came up bewildered, trembling, almost falling on their knees, hardly daring to raise their eyes to the king's kind, encouraging face, and bathed his hand with tears while they kissed it. Numbers of little children were led up by their parents; there were babies in arms, and younglings carried on parents' backs, and the king stooped and shook hands with all, and even pulled out the babies' hands from under their mufflings, and the old people wept, and cheers rent the air.

Next in interest to this procession of beaming faces, and the blaze of colour, was the sight of the presents, and the ungrudging generosity with which they were brought. Many of the women presented live fowls tied by the legs, which were deposited, one upon another, till they formed a fainting, palpitating heap under the hot sun. Some of the men brought decorated hogs tied by one leg, which squealed so persistently in the presence of royalty, that they were removed to the rear. Hundreds carried nets of sweet potatoes, eggs, and *kalo*, artistically arranged. Men staggered along in couples with bamboos between them, supporting clusters of bananas weighing nearly a hundredweight. Others brought yams, cocoa-nuts, oranges, onions, pumpkins, early pineapples, and even the great delicious granadilla, the fruit of the large passion-flower. A few maidens presented the king with bouquets of choice flowers, and costly *leis* of the yellow feathers of the Melithreptes Pacifica. There were fully two tons of *kalo* and sweet potatoes in front of the court house, hundreds of fowls, and piles of bananas, eggs, and cocoa-nuts. The *hookupu* was a beautiful sight, all the more so that not one of that radiant, loving, gift-offering throng came in quest of office, or for any other thing that he could obtain. It was just the old-time spirit of reverence for the man who typifies rule, blended with the extreme of personal devotion to the prince whom a united people had placed upon the throne. The feeling was genuine and pathetic in its intensity. It is said that the natives like their king better, because he was truly, "above all," the last of a proud and imperious house, which, in virtue of a pedigree of centuries, looked down upon the nobility of the Kamehamehas.

When the last gift was deposited, the lawn in front of the court-house was one densely-packed, variegated mass of excited, buzzing Hawaiians. While the king was taking a short rest, two ancient and hideous females, who looked like heathen priestesses, chanted a monotonous and heathenish-sounding chant or *mêlé*, in eulogy of some ancient idolater. It just served to remind me that this attractive crowd was but one generation removed from slaughter-loving gods and human sacrifices.

The king and his suite re-appeared in the upper balcony, where all the foreigners were assembled, including the two venerable missionaries and a French priest of benign aspect, and his appearance was the signal for a fresh outburst of enthusiasm. Advancing to the front, he made an extemporaneous speech, of which the following is a literal translation :—

" To all present I tender my warmest *aloha*. This day, on which you are gathered to pay your respects to me, I will remember to the day of my death. (Cheers.) I am filled with love for you all, fellow-citizens (*makaainana*), who have come here on this occasion, and for all the people, because by your unanimous choice I have been made your King, a young sovereign, to reign over you, and to fill the very distinguished office which I now occupy. (Cheers.) You are parents to me, and I will be your Father. (Tremendous cheering.) Formerly, in the days of our departed ancestors, you were not permitted to approach them ; they and you were kept apart ; but now we meet and associate together. (Cheers.) I urge you all to persevere in the right, to forsake the ignorant ways of the olden time. There is but one God, whom it is our duty to obey. Let us forsake every kind of idolatry.

" In the year 1820 Rev. Messrs. Bingham, Thurston, and others came to these Islands and proclaimed the Word of God. It is their teachings which have enabled you to be what you are to-day. Now they have all gone to that spirit land, and only Mrs. Thurston remains. We are greatly indebted to them. (Cheers.) There are also among us here (alluding to Revs. Coan and Lyman) old and grey-haired fathers, whose examples we should endeavour to imitate, and obey their teachings.

" I am very glad to see the young men of the present time so well instructed in knowledge—perhaps some of them are your children. You must persevere in your search of wisdom and in habits of morality. Do not be indolent. (Cheers.) Those who have striven hard after knowledge

and good character, are the ones who deserve and shall receive places of
trust hereafter under the government.

"At the present time I have four foreigners as my ministerial advisers.
But if, among these young men now standing before me, and under this
flag, there are any who shall qualify themselves to fill these positions, then
I will select them to fill their places.   (Loud cheers.)   *Aloha* to you all."

His manner as a speaker was extremely good, with
sufficient gesticulation for the emphasis of particular
points.   The address was frequently interrupted by ap-
plause, and when at its conclusion he bowed gracefully
to the crowd and said, " My *aloha* to you all," the
cheering and enthusiasm were absolutely unbounded.
And so the great *hookupu* ended, and the assemblage
broke up into knots to discuss the royal speech and the
day's doings.

I. L. B.

LETTER XIV.

The king "signified his intention to honour Mr. and Mrs. Severance with his company" on the evening of the day after the reception, and this involved a regular party and supper. You can hardly imagine the difficulties connected with "refreshments," where few, if any, of the materials which we consider necessary for dishes suitable for such occasions can be procured at the stores, and even milk and butter are scarce commodities. I had won a reputation as a cook by making a much appreciated Bengal curry, and an English "roly-poly" pudding, and when I offered my services, Mrs. S. kindly accepted them, and she and I, with the Chinese cook and a Chinese prisoner to assist us, have been cooking for a day and a half. I wanted to make a gigantic trifle, a dish not known here, and we hunted every store, hoping to find almonds and raspberry jam among the "assorted notions," but in vain; however, grated cocoa-nut supplied the place of the first, and a kind friend sent a pot of the last. The Chinamen were very diverting. The cook looked on, and laughed constantly, and perhaps was a little jealous: at all events when he thought we had spoilt some cakes in the oven, he capered into Mrs. S.'s room, gesticulating, and exclaiming satirically, "Lu, Lu! cakes so good, cakes so fine!'' No intoxicants were to be used on the occasion, Hilo notions being rigid on this subject; but I hope it was not a crime that I clandestinely used two glasses of sherry, without which my trifle would have been a failure. We worked hard, and made trifle, sponge cake, pound cake, spiced cake, dozens of cocoa-nut cakes and drops, custards, and sandwiches of potted meat, and enjoyed our preparations so much that we found it hard to exchange kitchen for social duties, and go to ''Father Lyman,'' who entertained the king and a number of Hilo folk in the evening.

Their rooms, not very large, were quite full. When the king entered, the company received him standing, and the flute band in the verandah played the national anthem, and afterwards at intervals during the evening sang some Hawaiian songs of the king's composition. I was presented to him, and as he is very courteous to strangers, he talked to me a good deal. He is a very gentlemanly, courteous, unassuming man, hardly assuming enough in fact, and apparently very intelligent and well read. I was exceedingly pleased with him. He spoke a good deal of Queen Emma's reception in England, and of her raptures with Venice, and some other cities of the continent. He said he had the greatest desire to visit some parts of Europe, Great Britain specially, because he thought that by coming in contact with some of our leading statesmen, he might gain a more accurate knowledge than he possessed of the principles of constitutional government. He said he hoped that in two years Hawaii-nei would be so settled as to allow of his travelling, and that in the meantime he was studying French with a view to enjoying the continent.

He asked a great many questions regarding things at home, especially concerning the limitation of the power of the Crown. He cannot reconcile the theoretical right of the sovereign to choose his advisers with his practically submitting to receive them from a Parliamentary majority. He seemed to find a difficulty in understanding that the sovereign's right to refuse his assent to a Bill which had passed both Houses was by no means the same thing in practice as the possession of a veto. He said that in his reading of our constitutional history, the power of the sovereign seemed almost absolute, while if he understood facts rightly, the throne was more of an "ornament," or "figure-head," than a power at all. He asked me if it was true that Republican feeling was spreading very much in England, and if I thought that the monarchy would survive the present sovereign, on whose prudence and exalted virtues he seemed to think it rested. He said he thought his little kingdom had aped the style of the great monarchies too much, and that he should like to abolish a good many high sounding titles, sinecure offices, the household troops, and some of the "imitation pomp" of his court. He said he had never enjoyed anything so much since his accession as the *hookupu* of the morning, and asked me what I thought of it. I was glad to be able to answer truthfully that I had never seen a state pageant or ceremonial that I had enjoyed half so much, or that had impressed me so favourably.

He has a very musical voice, and a natural nobility and
refinement of manner, with an obvious tact and good
feeling, rather, I should think, the result of amiable and
gentlemanly instincts than of training or consideration,
all which combine to make him interesting, altogether
apart from his position as a Polynesian sovereign.

Where there are no servants, a party involves the hosts
and their friends in the bustle of personal preparation,
but all worked with a will, and by sunset the decorations
were completed. All the Chinese lamps in Hilo were
hung in the front verandah, and seats were placed in the
front and side verandahs, on which the drawing-room
opens by four doors, so there was plenty of room, though
there were thirty people. The side verandah was
enclosed by a drapery of flags, and the whole was tastefully decorated with festoons and wreaths of ferns. The
king arrived early with his attendants, and was received
by the host and hostess, and like a perfectly civilized
guest, he handed Mrs. S. into the room. The great
wish of the genial entertainers was to prevent stiffness
and give the king a really social evening, so the "chair
game," magical music, and a refined kind of blind man's
buff, better suited to the occasion, but less "jolly" than
the old riotous game, were shortly introduced. Lunalilo
only looked on at first, and then entered into the games
with a heartiness and zest which showed that he at least
enjoyed the evening. Supper was served at nine.
Several nests of Japanese tables had been borrowed, and
these, dispersed about the room and verandah, broke up
the guests into little social knots. Three Hilo ladies

and I were the waitresses, and I was pleased to see that the good things were thoroughly appreciated, and that the trifle was universally popular. After supper there was a little dancing, and as few of the Hilo people knew any dance correctly, it was very amusing for the on-lookers. There was a great deal of promenading in the verandah, and a great deal of talking and merriment, which were enjoyed by a crowd of natives who stood the whole evening outside the garden fence. I don't think that any of the Hilo people are so unhappy as to possess an evening dress, and the pretty morning dresses of the ladies, and the thick boots, easy morning coats, and black ties of the gentlemen, gave a jolly " break-down " look to the affair, which would have been deemed inadmissible in less civilized society.

Some of my photographs of some of our eminent literary and scientific men were lying on the table, and the king in looking at them showed a surprising amount of knowledge of what they had written or done, quite entitling him to unite in Stanley's "Communion of Educated Men." I had previously asked him for his signature for my autograph collection, and he said he had composed a stanza for me which he thought I might like to have in addition. He called with it on the following afternoon, apologising for his dress, a short jacket and blue trowsers, stuffed into boots plastered with mud up to the knees. I was surprised when he asked me if the lines were correctly spelt, for he speaks English remarkably well. They are simply a kind wish, unaffectedly expressed.

HILO. HAWAII, Feb. 26.

" Wheresoe'er thou may'st roam,
 Wheresoe'er thou mak'st thy home,
 May God thy footsteps guide,
 Watch o'er thee and provide.
 This is my earnest prayer for thee,
 Welcome, stranger, from over the sea."

LUNALILO R.

It startles one sometimes to hear American vulgarisms uttered in his harmonious tones. The American admiral and generals had just arrived from the volcano, stiff, sore, bruised, jaded, "done," and the king said, "I guess the Admiral's about used up." He is really remarkably attractive, but I am sorry to observe a look of irresolution about his mouth, indicative of a facility of disposition capable of being turned to the worst account. I think from what I have heard that the Hawaiian kings have fallen victims rather to unscrupulous foreigners, than to their own bad instincts.

My last day has been taken up with farewell visits, and I finish this on board the "Kilauea." Miss Karpe and I had to ride two miles, to a point at which it was possible to embark without risk, a heavy surf having for three weeks rendered it impossible for loaded boats to communicate with the shore at Hilo. My clothes were soaked when we reached the rocks, and Upa, very wet, carried us into a wet whale-boat, with water up to our ancles, which brought us over a heavy sickening swell into this steamer, which is dirty as well as wet. I told Upa to lead my mare, and ride his own horse, but the

last I saw of him was on the mare's back, racing a troop
of natives along the beach.*

I. L. B.

* This was almost his last exploit. A few days later the sheriff ha
the painful duty of committing him as a leper to the leper settlement on
Molokai.   He was a leading spirit among the Hilo natives, and his joyous
nature will be missed by everyone.   He has left a wife and some beautiful
children, who, it is feared, will eventually share his fate.

LETTER XV.

WAIMEA. HAWAII.

THERE is no limit to the oddities of the steam-ship
" Kilauea." She lay rolling on the Hilo swell for two
hours, and two hours after we sailed her machinery broke
down, and we lay-to for five hours, in what they here call
a heavy gale and sea. It was a miserable night. No
privacy : the saloon both hot and wet, almost every one
sick. I lay in my berth in my soaked clothes watching
the proceedings of a gigantic cockroach, and listening,
not without amusement, to the awful groans of a Chinaman, and a " rough customer" from California, who
occupied the next berths.

In the middle of the night the water came in great
dashes through the skylight upon the table, and soon the
saloon was afloat to the depth of from four to six inches.
When the " Kilauea" rolled, and the water splashed in
simultaneously, we were treated to vigorous " douches " in
our berths, which soon saturated the pillows, mattresses,
and our clothing. One sea put out the lamp, and a ship's
lantern, making " darkness visible," was swung in its
stead. In an English ship there would have been a great
fuss and a great flying about of stewards, or pretence of
mending matters, but when the passengers shouted for
our good steward, the serene creature came in with a

melancholy smile on his face, said nothing, but quietly
sat down on the transom, with his bare feet in the water,
contemplating it with a comic air of helplessness. Breakfast, of course, could not be served, but a plate was put
at one end of the table for the silent old Scotch captain,
who tucked up his feet and sat with his oilskins and
sou'-wester on, while the charming steward, with trousers
rolled up to his knees, waded about, pacifying us by
bringing us excellent curry as we sat on the edges of our
berths, and putting on a sweetly apologetic manner, as if
penitent for the gross misbehaviour of the ship. Such a
man would reconcile me to far greater discomfort than that
of the " Kilauea." I wonder if he is ever unamiable, or
tired, or perturbed?

The next day was fine, and we were all much on deck
to dry our clothes in the sun. The southern and leeward coasts of Hawaii as far as Kawaaloa are not much
more attractive than coal-fields. Contrasted with the
shining shores of Hilo, they are as dust and ashes;
long reaches of black lava and miles of clinkers marking
the courses of lava-flows, whose black desolation and de-
formity nature, as yet, has done almost nothing to clothe.
Cocoa-nut trees usually, however, fringe the shore, but
were it not for the wonderful colour of the ocean, like
liquid transparent turquoise, revealing the coral forests
shelving down into purple depths, and the exciting proximity of sharks, it would have been wearisome. After
leaving the bay where Captain Cook met his death, we
passed through a fleet of twenty-seven canoes, each one
hollowed out of the trunk of a single tree, from fifteen to

twenty-five feet long, about twenty inches deep, hardly wide enough for a fat man, and high and pointed at both ends. On one side there is an outrigger formed of two long bent sticks, to the outer ends of which is bound a curved beam of light wood, which skims along the surface of the water, rendering the canoe secure from an upset on that side, while the weight of the outrigger makes an upset on the other very unlikely. In calms they are paddled, and shoot over the water with great rapidity, but whenever there is any breeze a small sprit-sail is used. They are said to be able to stand very rough water, but they are singularly precarious and irresponsible looking contrivances, and for these, as well as for all other seas, I should much prefer a staunch whale-boat. We sailed for some hours along a lava coast, streamless, rainless, verdureless, blazing under the fierce light of a tropical sun, and some time after noon anchored in the scorching bay of Kawaihae.

A foreign store, a number of native houses, a great *heiau*, or heathen temple on a height, a fringe of cocoanut palms, and a background of blazing hills, flaring with varieties of red, hardly toned down by any attempt at vegetation, a crystalline atmosphere palpitating with heat, deep, rippleless, clear water, with coral groves below, and a view of the three great Hawaiian mountains, are the salient features of this outlet of Hawaiian commerce. But ah! how soft and mild a blue the sky was, looking inland, where, for the first time, I saw far aloft, above solid masses of white cloud, sky hung, strangely uplifted, the great volcanic domes of Mauna Kea, Mauna Loa, and

Hualalai, looking as if they had all passed into an endless repose.

This bay, which affords excellent holding ground, and
is screened by highlands from the sudden and violent
gusts of wind, called " *mumuku*," which sweep down
between the mountains with almost irresistible fury, used
to be a great place of call for whalers, who purchased
large quantities of " recruits " here; yams in the earlier
days, and more lately Irish potatoes, which flourish in
the thirsty soil.   But whaling in the North Pacific seems
to be nearly " played out," and the arrival of a whaler is
not a common occurrence.

Shortly before we arrived I found that the sailing of
the San Francisco steamer is put off for a week, so I took
advantage of a kind invitation I received some time ago
to visit Waimea, and go from thence to Waimanu, a
wonderful valley beyond Waipio, very little visited by
foreigners.   A gentleman and lady rode up here with me,
and I got a horse on the beach with a native bullock
saddle on him, an uncouth contrivance of wood not
covered with hide, and a strong lassoing horn.   The
great wooden stirrups could not be shortened, but I soon
found myself able, in true savage fashion, to gallop up
and down hill without any.

The chief object of interest on this ride is the great
heiau, which stands on a bare steep hill above the sea,
not easy of access.   It was the last heathen temple built
on Hawaii.   On entering the huge pile, which stood gaunt
and desolate in the thin red air, the story of the old
bloody heathenism of the islands flashed upon my

memory. The entrance is by a narrow passage between
two high walls, and it was by this that the sacrificing
priests dragged the human victims into the presence of
Tairi, a hideous wooden idol, crowned with a helmet, and
covered with red feathers, the favourite war-god of Kamehameha the Great, by whom this temple was built, before
he proceeded to the conquest of Oahu.

The shape is an irregular parallelogram, 224 feet long,
and 100 wide. At each end, and on the *mauka* side,
the walls, which are very solid and compact, though built
of lava stones without mortar, are twenty feet high, and
twelve feet wide at the bottom, but narrow gradually towards the top, where they are finished with a course of
smooth stones six feet broad. On the sea side, the wall,
which has been partly thrown down, was not more than
six or seven feet high, and there were paved platforms for
the accommodation of the *alii*, or chiefs, and the people
in their orders. The upper terrace is spacious, and
paved with flat smooth stones which were brought from a
considerable distance, the greater part of the population
of the island having been employed on the building. At
the south end there was an inner court, where the principal idol stood, surrounded by a number of inferior
deities, for the Hawaiians had "gods many, and lords
many." Here also was the *anu*, a lofty frame of
wickerwork, shaped like an obelisk, hollow, and five feet
square at its base. Within this, the priest, who was the
oracle of the god, stood, and of him the king used to
inquire concerning war or peace, or any affair of national
importance. It appears that the tones of the oracular

voice were more distinct than the meaning of the utterances. However, the supposed answers were generally acted upon.

On the outside of this inner court was the *lélé*, or altar, on which human and other sacrifices were offered. On the day of the dedication of the temple to' Tairi, vast offerings of fruit, dogs, and hogs were presented, and eleven human beings were immolated on the altar. These victims were taken from among captives, or those who had broken *Tabu*, or had rendered themselves obnoxious to the chiefs, and were often blind, maimed, or crippled persons. Sometimes they were dispatched at a distance with a stone or club, and their bodies were dragged along the narrow passage up which I walked shuddering; but oftener they were bound and taken alive into the *heiau* to be slain in the outer court. The priests, in slaying these sacrifices, were careful to mangle the bodies as little as possible. From two to twenty were offered at once. They were laid in a row with their faces downwards on the altar before the idol, to whom they were presented in a kind of prayer by the priest, and, if offerings of hogs were presented at the same time, these were piled upon them, and the whole mass was left to putrify.

The only dwellings within the *heiau* were those of the priests, and the " sacred house " of the king, in which he resided during the seasons of strict *Tabu*. A doleful place this *heiau* is, haunted not only by the memories of almost unimaginable terrors, but by the sore thought that generations of Hawaiians lived and died in the unutterable darkness of this ignorant worship, passing in long procession from these grim rites into the presence of the Father whose infinite compassions they had never known.

Every hundred feet of ascent from the rainless, fervid beach of Kawaihae increased the freshness of the temperature, and rendered exercise more delightful. From the fringe of palms along the coast to the damp hills north of Waimea, a distance of ten miles, there is not a tree or stream, though the scorched earth is deeply scored by the rush of fierce temporary torrents. Hitherto, I have only travelled over the green coast which faces the trade winds, where clouds gather and shed their rains, and this desert, which occupies a great part of leeward Hawaii, displeases me. It lies burning in the fierce splendours of a zone, which, until now, I had forgotten was the torrid zone, unwatered and unfruitful, red and desolate under the sun. The island is here only twenty-two miles wide, and strong winds sweep across it, whirling up its surface in great brown clouds, so that the uplands in part appear a smoking plain, backed by naked volcanic cones. No water, no grass, no ferns. Some thornless thistles, a little brush of sapless-looking indigo, and some species of compositæ struggle for a doleful existence. There is nothing tropical about it but the intense heat. The red soil becomes suffused with a green tinge ten miles from the beach, and at the summit of the ascent the desert blends with this beautiful Waimea plain, one of the most marked features of Hawaii. The air became damp and cool; miles of fine smooth green grass stretched out before us; high hills, broken, pinnacled, wooded, and cleft with deep ravines, rose on our left; we heard the dash and music of falling water : to the north it was like the Munster Thal, to the south altogether volcanic. The tropics had vanished. There were frame houses sheltered from the winds by artificial screens of mulberry trees, and from the incursions of cattle by rough walls of lava stones five feet high ; a mission and court house, a native church, much too large for the shrunken population, and other indications of an inhabited region. Except for the woods which clothe the hills, the characteristic of the scenery is baldness.

On clambering over the wall which surrounds my host's kraal of dwellings, I heard in the dusk strange sweet voices crying rudely and emphatically, " Who are you ? What do you want ?" and was relieved to find that the somewhat inhospitable interrogation only proceeded from two Australian magpies. Mr. S—— is a Tasmanian, married to a young half-white lady : and her native mother and seven or eight dark girls are here, besides a number of natives and Chinese, and half Chinese, who are employed about the place. Sheep are the source of my host's wealth. He has 25,000 at three stations on Mauna Kea, and, at an altitude of 6000 feet they flourish, and are free from some of the maladies to which they are liable elsewhere. Though there are only three or four sheep owners on the islands, they exported 288,526 lbs. of wool last year.* Mr. S.—— has also 1000 head of cattle and 50 horses.

* In 1873 the export of wool had increased to 329,507 lbs.

The industry of Waimea is cattle raising, and some
feeble attempts are being made to improve the degenerate
island breed by the importation of a few short-horn cows
from New Zealand. These plains afford magnificent
pasturage as well as galloping ground. They are a very
great thoroughfare. The island, which is an equilateral
triangle, about 300 miles in " circuit," can only be
crossed here. Elsewhere, an impenetrable forest belt,
and an impassable volcanic wilderness, compel travellers
to take the burning track of adamant which snakes round
the southern coast, when they are minded to go from one
side of Hawaii to the other. Waimea also has the
singular distinction of a road from the beach, which is
traversed on great occasions by two or three oxen and
mule teams, and very rarely by a more ambitious conveyance. There are few hours of day or night in which the
tremulous *thud* of shoeless horses galloping on grass is
not heard in Waimea.

The altitude of this great table-land is 2500 feet, and
the air is never too hot, the temperature averaging 64°
Fahrenheit. There is mist or rain on most days of the
year for a short time, and the mornings and evenings are
clear and cool. The long sweeping curves of the three
great Hawaiian mountains spring from this level. The
huge bulk of Mauna Kea without shoulders or spurs, rises
directly from the Waimea level on the south to the altitude of 14,000 feet, and his base is thickly clustered
with tufa-cones of a bright red colour, from 300 to 1000
feet in height. Considerably further back, indeed forty
miles away, the smooth dome of Mauna Loa appears very

serene now, but only thirteen years ago the light was so
brilliant, from one of its tremendous eruptions, that here
it was possible to read a newspaper by it, and during its
height candles were unnecessary in the evenings! Nearer
the coast, and about thirty miles from here, is the less
conspicuous dome of the dead volcano of Hualalai. If
all Hawaii, south of Waimea, were submerged to a depth
of 8000 feet, three nearly equi-distant, dome-shaped
volcanic islands would remain, the highest of which
would have an altitude of 6000 feet. To the south of
these plains violent volcanic action is everywhere apparent, not only in tufa cones, but in tracts of ashes,
scoriæ, and volcanic sand. Near the centre there are
some very curious caves, possibly "lava bubbles," which
were used by the natives as places of sepulture. The
Kohala hills, picturesque, wooded, and abrupt, bound
Waimea on the north, with their exquisite grassy slopes,
and bring down an abundance of water to the plain, but
owing to the lightness of the soil and the evaporation
produced by the tremendous winds, the moisture dis-
appears within two miles of the hills, and an area of rich
soil, ten miles by twelve, which, if irrigated, would be
invaluable, is nothing but a worthless dusty desert, perpetually encroaching on the grass. As soon as the plains
slope towards the east, the vegetation of the tropics re-
appears, and the face of the country is densely covered
with a swampy and impenetrable bush hardly at all explored, which shades the sources of the streams which fall
into the Waipio and Waimanu Valleys, and is supposed

to contain water enough to irrigate the Saharas of leeward Hawaii.

The climate of the plain is most invigorating. If there
were waggon roads and obtainable comforts, Waimea, with
its cool equable temperature, might become the great
health resort of invalids from the Pacific coast. But
Hawaii is not a place for the sick or old; for, if people
cannot ride on horseback, they can have neither society
nor change. Mr. Lyons, one of the most famous of the
early missionaries, still clings to this place, where he has
worked for forty years. He is an Hawaiian poet; and,
besides translating some of our best hymns, has composed enough to make up the greater part of a bulky
volume, which is said to be of great merit. He says that
the language lends itself very readily to rhythmical expression. He was indefatigable in his youth, and was
four times let down the *pali* by ropes to preach in the
Waimanu Valley. Neither he nor his wife can mount a
horse now, and it is very dreary for them, as the population has receded and dwindled from about them. Their
house is made lively, however, by some bright little native
girls, who board with them, and receive an English and
industrial education.

The moral atmosphere of Waimea has never been a
wholesome one. The region was very early settled by a
class of what may be truly termed " mean whites," the
" beach-combers " and riff-raff of the Pacific. They
lived infamous lives, and added their own to the indigenous vices of the islands, turning the district into a
perfect sink of iniquity, in which they were known by

such befitting *aliases* as "Jake the Devil," &c.   The
coming of the missionaries, and the settlement of moral,
orderly whites on Hawaii, have slowly created a public
opinion averse to flagrant immorality, and the outrageous
license of former years would now meet with legal penal-
ties.   Many of the old settlers are dead, and others have
drifted to regions beyond restraining influences, but still
"the Waimea crowd" is not considered up to the mark.
Most of the present set of foreigners are Englishmen who
have married native women.   It was in such quarters as
this that the great antagonistic influence to the complete
Christianization of the natives was created, and it is from
such suspicious sources that the aspersions on missionary
work are usually derived.

Waimea has its own beauty—the grand breezy plain, the
gigantic sweep of the mountain curves, the incessant
changes of colour, and the morning view of Mauna Kea,
with the pure snow on its ragged dome, rose-flushed in
the early sunlight.   I don't agree with Disraeli that
"happiness is atmosphere;" yet constant sunshine, and a
climate which never threatens one with discomfort or ills,
certainly conduce to equable cheerfulness.

I am quite interested with a native lady here, the first
I have met with who has been able to express her ideas
in English.   She is extremely shrewd and intelligent,
very satirical, and a great mimic.   She very cleverly
burlesques the way in which white people express their
admiration of scenery, and, in fact, ridicules admiration
of scenery for itself.   She evidently thinks us a sour,
morose, worrying, forlorn race.   "We," she said, "are

always happy; we never grieve long about anything;
when any one dies we break our hearts for some days,
and then we are happy again.   We are happy all day
long, not like white people, happy one moment, gloomy
another : we've no cares, the days are too short.   What
are *haoles* always unhappy about?"   Perhaps she expresses the general feeling of her careless, pleasure-loving,
mirth-loving people, who, whatever commands they dis-
obey, fulfil the one, " Take no thought for the morrow."
The fabrication of the beautiful quilts I before wrote of
is a favourite occupation of native women, and they make
all their own and their husbands' clothes ; but making
leis, going into the woods to collect materials for them,
talking, riding, bathing, visiting, and otherwise amusing
themselves, take up the greater part of their time.
Perhaps if we white women always wore *holukus* of one
shape, we should have fewer gloomy moments !

I. L. B.

ORDINARY FEMALE COSTUME.   [*Page* 229.

LETTER XVI.

I AM sitting at the door of a grass lodge, at the end of all things, for no one can pass further by land than this huge lonely cleft. About thirty natives are sitting about me, all staring, laughing, and chattering, and I am the only white person in the region. We have all had a meal, sitting round a large calabash of *poi* and a fowl, which was killed in my honour, and roasted in one of their stone ovens. I have forgotten my knife, and have had to help myself after the primitive fashion of aborigines, not without some fear, for some of them I am sure are in an advanced stage of leprosy. The brown tattooed limbs of one man are stretched across the mat, the others are sitting cross-legged, making *lauhala leis*. One man is making fishing-lines of a beautifully white and marvellously tenacious fibre, obtained from an Hawaiian "flax" plant (possibly *Urtica argentea*), very different from the New Zealand *Phormium tenax*. Nearly all the people of the valley are outside, having come to see the *wahine haole*: only one white woman, and she a resident of Hawaii, having been seen in Waimanu before. I am really alone, miles of mountain and gulch lie between me and the nearest whites. This is a wonderful place : a ravine about three miles long and

three-quarters of a mile wide, without an obvious means
of ingress, being walled in by precipices from 2000
to 4000 feet high. Five cascades dive from the
palis at its head, and unite to form a placid river about
up to a horse's body here, and deep enough for a horse to
swim in a little below. Dense forests of various shades
of green fill up the greater part of the valley,
concealing the basins into which the cascades leap,
and the grey basalt of the *palis* is mostly hidden by
greenery. At the open end, two bald bluffs, one of them
2000 feet in height, confront the Pacific, and its loud
booming surf comes up to within one hundred yards of
the house where I am writing, but is banked off by a
heaped-up barrier of colossal shingle.

Hot and silent, a sunset world of an endless afternoon,
it seems a palpable and living dream. And a few of
these people, I understand, have dreamed away their lives
here, never having been beyond their valley, at least by
land. But it is a dream of ceaseless speech and rippling
laughter. They are the merriest people I have yet seen,
and doubtless their isolated life is dear to them.

I wish I could sketch this most picturesque scene. In
the verandah, which is formed of mats, two handsome
youths, and five women in green, red, and orange chemises,
all with *leis* of ferns round their hair, are reclining on the
ground. Outside of this there is a pavement of large
lava stones, and groups in all colours, wreathed and
garlanded, including some much disfigured old people,
crouching in red and yellow blankets, are sitting and lying
there. Some are fondling small dogs; and a number of

large ones, with a whole tribe of amicable cats, are picking bones. Surf-boards, paddles, saddles, lassos, spurs, gear, and bundles of *ti* leaves are lying about. Thirteen horses are tethered outside, some of which brought the riders who escorted me triumphantly from the head of the valley. The foreheads of the precipices opposite are reddening in the sunset, and between them and me horses and children are constantly swimming across the broad, still stream which divides the village into two parts; and now and then a man in a *malo*, and children who have come up the river swimming, with their clothes in one hand, increase the assemblage.

All are intently watching me, but are as kind and good-natured as possible; and my guide from Waipio is discoursing to them about me. He knows a little abrupt, disjointed, almost unintelligible English, and comes up every now and then with an interrogation in his manner, "Father? mother? married? watch? How came?" "You" appears beyond his efforts. "*Kilauea? Lunalilo?*" Then he goes back and orates rapidly, gesticulating emphatically. A very handsome, pleasant-looking man, with a red sash round his waist, who, I understand from signs, is the schoolmaster, emerged from the throng, and sat down beside me; but his English appears limited to these words, "How old?" When I told him by counting on my fingers he laughed heartily, and said "Too old," and he told the others, and they all laughed. I have photographs of Queen Victoria and Mr. Coan in my writing-book, and when I exhibited them they crowded round me clapping their hands, and screaming with

delight when they recognized Mr. Coan. The king's
handwriting was then handed round amidst reverent
" ahs " and " ohs," or what sounded like them. This
letter was also passed round and examined lengthwise,
sidewise, and upside down. They shrieked with satirical
laughter when I pressed some fragile ferns in my blotting-
book. The natives think it quite idiotic in us to attach
any value to withered leaves. My inkstand with its double-
spring lids has been a great amusement. Each one opened
both, and shut them again, and a chorus of "*maikai, maikai*,"
(good) ran round the circle. They seem so simple and
good that at last I have trusted them with my watch, which
excites unbounded admiration, probably because of its
small size. It is now on its travels; but I am not the
least anxious about it. A man pointed to a hut some
distance on the other side of the river, and appeared
interrogative, and on my replying affirmatively, he mounted
a horse and carried off the watch in the direction indicated.
Mr. Ellis came to this valley in a canoe, and he mentions
that when he preached, the natives, who seemed to be very
indifferent to the general truths of Christianity, became
very deeply interested when they heard of *Ora loa ia Jesu*
(endless life by Jesus). While I was up the valley the
poor people made a wonderful bed of seven fine mats, one
over the other, on one side of the house, and screened it
off with a flaring muslin curtain; but on the other side
there are ten pillows in a row, so that I wonder how many
are to occupy the den during the night. I am now writing
inside the house, with a hollowed stone, with some beef
fat and a wick in it, for a light, and two youths seem

delegated to attend upon me. One holds my ink, and if I look up, the other rushes for something that I am supposed to want. They insist on thinking that I am cold because my clothes are wet, and have thrown over me several folds of *tapa*, made from the inner bark of the *wauti* or cloth plant (*Broussonetia papyrifera*). They brought me a *kalo* leaf containing a number of living freshwater shrimps, and were quite surprised when I did not eat them.

WAIPIO, *March 5th.*

It seems fully a week since I left Waimea yesterday morning, so many new experiences have been crowded into the time. I will try to sketch my expedition while my old friend Halemanu is preparing dinner. The morning opened gloriously. The broad Waimea plains were flooded with red and gold, and the snowy crest of Mauna Kea was cloudless. We breakfasted by lamp light (the days of course are short in this latitude), and were away before six. My host kindly provided me with a very fine horse and some provisions in a leather wallet, and with another white man and a native accompanied me as far as this valley, where they had some business. The morning deepened into gorgeousness. A blue mist hung in heavy folds round the violet bases of the mountains, which rose white and sharp into the rose-flushed sky; the dew lay blue and sparkling on the short crisp grass ; the air was absolutely pure, and with a suspicion of frost in it. It was all very fair, and the horses enjoyed the morning freshness, and danced and champed their bits

as though they disliked being reined in. We rode over
level grass-covered ground, till we reached the Hamakua
bush, fringed with dead trees, and full of *ohias* and immense
fern trees, some of them with a double tier of fronds, far
larger and finer than any that I saw in New Zealand.
There are herds of wild goats, cattle, and pigs on the
island, and they roam throughout this region, trampling,
grubbing, and rending, grinding the bark of the old
trees and eating up the young ones. This ravaging is
threatening at no distant date to destroy the beauty and
alter the climate of the mountainous region of Hawaii.
The cattle are a hideous breed—all bones, hide, and
horns.

We were at the top of the Waipio *pali* at eight, and our
barefooted horses, used to the soft pastures of Waimea,
refused to carry us down its rocky steep, so we had to
walk. I admired this lonely valley far more than before.
It was full of infinite depths of blue—blue smoke in lazy
spirals curled upwards; it was eloquent in a morning
silence that I felt reluctant to break. Against its dewy
greenness the beach shone like coarse gold, and its slow
silver river lingered lovingly, as though loth to leave it, and
be merged in the reckless loud-tongued Pacific. Across
the valley, the track I was to take climbed up in thready
zigzags, and disappeared round a bold headland. It was
worth a second visit just to get a glimpse of such a vision
of peace.

Halemanu, with hospitable alacrity, soon made breakfast ready, after which Mr. S., having arranged for my
further journey, left me here, and for the first time I

found myself alone among natives ignorant of English.
For the Waimanu trip it is essential to have a horse bred
in the Waimanu Valley and used to its dizzy *palis*, and
such a horse was procured, and a handsome native,
called Hananui, as guide. We were away by ten, and
galloped across the valley till we came to the nearly
perpendicular *pali* on the other side. The sight of this
air-hung trail from Halemanu's house has turned back
several travellers who were bent on the trip, but I had
been told that it was quite safe on a Waimanu horse;
and keeping under my fears as best I could, I let
Hananui precede me, and began the ascent, which is
visible from here for an hour.   The *pali* is as nearly
perpendicular as can be.   Not a bush or fern, hardly
a tuft of any green thing, clothes its bare, scathed sides.
It terminates precipitously on the sea at a height of
2000 feet. Up this shelving wall, something like a
sheep track, from thirty to forty-six inches broad, goes
in great swinging zigzags, sometimes as broken steps
of rock breast high, at others as a smooth ledge with
hardly foothold, in three places carried away by heavy
rains—altogether the most frightful track that imagination can conceive.*   It was most unpleasant to see the
guide's horse straining and scrambling, looking every
now and then as if about to fall over backwards. My
horse went up wisely and nobly, but slipping, jumping,
scrambling, and sending stones over the ledge, now and
then hanging for a second by his fore feet.   The higher

---

* The Inspector of Schools has since told me that there is a track as
bad, if not worse, in the Hana district on Maui.

we went the narrower and worse it grew. The girth was loose, so as not to impede the horse's respiration, the broad cinch which usually passes under the body having been fastened round his chest, and yet it was once or twice necessary to run the risk of losing my balance by taking my left foot out of the stirrup to press it against the horse's neck to prevent it from being crushed, while my right hung over the precipice. We came to a place where the path had been carried away, leaving a declivity of loose sand and gravel. You can hardly realize how difficult it was to dismount, when there was no margin outside the horse. I somehow slid under him, being careful not to turn the saddle, and getting hold of his hind leg, screwed myself round carefully behind him. It was alarming to see these sure-footed creatures struggle and slide in the deep gravel as though they must go over, and not less so to find myself sliding, though I was grasping my horse's tail.

Between the summit and Waimanu, a distance of ten miles, there are nine gulches, two of them about 900 feet deep, all very beautiful, owing to the broken ground, the luxuriant vegetation, and the bright streams, but the *kona*, or south wind, was blowing, bringing up the hot breath of the equatorial belt, and the sun was perfectly unclouded, so that the heat of the gorges was intense. They succeed each other occasionally with very great rapidity. Between two of the deepest and steepest there is a ridge not more than fifty yards wide.

Soon after noon we simultaneously stopped our horses. The Waimanu Valley lay 2500 feet (it is said) below us,

and the trail struck off into space. It was a scene of
loneliness to which Waipio seems the world. In a
second the eye took in the twenty grass lodges of its
inhabitants, the five cascades which dive into the dense
forests of its upper end, its river like a silver ribbon,
and its meadows of living green. In ten seconds a
bird could have spanned the ravine and feasted on its
loveliness, but we could only tip over the dizzy ridge
that overhangs the valley, and laboriously descend into
its heat and silence. The track is as steep and broken
as that which goes up from hence, but not nearly so
narrow, and without its elements of terror, for *kukuis,*
lauhalas, ohias, and *ti* trees, with a lavish growth of ferns
and trailers, grow luxuriantly in every damp rift of rock,
and screen from view the precipices of the *pali.* The
valley looks as if it could only be reached in a long
day's travel, so very far it is below, but the steepness
of the track makes it accessible in an hour from the
summit. As we descended, houses and a church which
had looked like toys at first, dilated on our sight, the
silver ribbon became a stream, the specks on the meadows
turned into horses, the white wavy line on the Pacific
beach turned into a curling wave, and lower still, I saw
people, who had seen us coming down, hastily shuffling
into clothes.

There were four houses huddled between the *pali* and
the river, and six or eight, with a church and school-
house on the other side; and between these and the
ocean a steep narrow beach, composed of large stones
worn as round and smooth as cannon balls, on which

the surf roars the whole year round. The *pali* which walls in the valley on the other side is inaccessible. The school children and a great part of the population had assembled in front of the house which I described before. There was a sort of dyke of rough lava stones round it, difficult to climb, but the natives, though they are very kind, did not, on this or any similar occasion, offer me any help, which neglect, I suppose, arises from the fact that the native women never need help, as they are as strong, fearless, and active as the men, and rival them in swimming and other athletic sports. An old man, clothed only with his dark skin, was pounding baked *kalo* for *poi*, in front of the house; a woman with flowers in her hair, but apparently not otherwise clothed, was wading up to her waist in the river, pushing before·her a light trumpet-shaped basket used for catching shrimps, and the other women wore the usual bright-coloured chemises.

I wanted to make the most of the six hours of daylight left, and we remounted our horses and rode for some distance up the river, which is the highway of the valley, all the children swimming on our right and left, each holding up a bundle of clothes with one hand, and two canoes paddled behind us. The river is still and clear, with a smooth bottom, but comes halfway up a horse's body, and riders take their feet out of the stirrups, bring them to a level with the saddle, lean slightly back, and hold them against the horse's neck. Equestrians following this fashion, canoes gliding, children and dogs swimming, were a most amusing picture. Several of the children swim to and from school every day. I was anxious to get rid of this voluntary escort, and we took a gallop over the soft springy grass till we reached some very pretty grass houses, under the shade of the most magnificent bread-fruit trees on Hawaii, loaded with fruit. There were orange trees in blossom, and coffee trees with masses of sweet white flowers lying among their flaky branches like snow, and the unfailing cocoa-nut rising out of banana groves, and clusters of gardenia smothering the red hibiscus. Here Hananui adopted a showman's air; he made me feel as if I were one of Barnum's placarded monsters. I had nothing to do but sit on my horse and be stared at. I felt that my bleached face was unpleasing, that my eyes and hair were faded, and that I had a great deal to answer for in the way of colour and attire. From the way in which he asked me unintelligible questions, I gathered that the people were catechizing him about me, and that he was romancing largely at my expense. They brought me some bananas and cocoa-nut milk, which were most refreshing.

Beyond the houses the valley became a jungle of Indian shot (*Canna indica*), eight or nine feet high, guavas and *ohias*, with an entangled undergrowth of ferns rather difficult to penetrate, and soon Hananui, whose soul was hankering after the delights of society, stopped, saying, " *Lios* (horses) no go." " We'll try," I replied, and rode on first. He sat on his horse laughing immoderately, and then followed me. I see that in travelling with natives it is essential to have a definite plan of action in one's own mind, and to verge on self-assertion in carrying it

out. We fought our way a little further, and then he
went out of sight altogether in the jungle, his horse having
floundered up to his girths in soft ground, on which we
dismounted and tethered the horses. H. had never been
any further, and as I failed to make him understand that
I desired to visit the home of the five cascades, I had to
reverse our positions and act as guide. We crept along
the side of a torrent among exquisite trees, moss, and
ferns, till we came to a place where it divided. There
were three horses tethered there, some wearing apparel
lying on the rocks, and some human footprints along one
of the streams, which decided me in favour of the other.
H. remonstrated by signs, as doubtless he espied an
opportunity for much gossip in the other direction, but
on my appearing persistent, he again laughed and
followed me.

From this point it was one perfect, rapturous, intoxicating, supreme vision of beauty, and I felt, as I now believe,
that at last I had reached a scene on which foreign eyes
had never looked. The glories of the tropical forest
closed us in with their depth, colour, and redundancy.
Here the operations of nature are rapid and decisive.
A rainfall of eleven feet in a year and a hothouse temperature force every plant into ceaseless activity, and
make short work of decay. Leafage, blossom, fruitage,
are simultaneous and perennial. The river, about as
broad as the Cam at Cambridge, leaped along, clear like
amber, pausing to rest awhile in deep bright pools, where
fish were sporting above the golden sand, a laughing,
sparkling, rushing, terrorless stream, " without mysteries

or agonies," broken by rocks, green with mosses and
fragile ferns, and in whose unchilled waters, not more
than three feet deep, wading was both safe and pleasant.
It was not possible to creep along its margin, the forest
was so dense and tangled, so we waded the whole way,
and wherever the water ran fiercely my unshod guide
helped me. One varied, glorious maze of vegetation came
down to it, and every green thing leant lovingly towards it,
or stooped to touch it, and over its whole magic length was
arched and interlaced the magnificent large-leaved *ohia*,
whose millions of spikes of rose-crimson blossoms lit up
the whole arcade, and the light of the afternoon sun
slanted and trickled through them, dancing in the mirthful water, turning its far-down sands to gold, and bright-
ening the many-shaded greens of candlenut and breadfruit.
It shone on majestic fern-trees, on the fragile *Polypodium
tamariscinum*, which clung tremblingly to the branches of
the *ohia*, on the beautiful lygodium, which adorned the
uncouth trunk of the breadfruit; on shining banana
leaves and glossy trailing yams; on gigantic lianas,
which, climbing to the tops of the largest trees, descended
in vast festoons, passing from tree to tree, and interlacing
the forest with a living network; and on lycopodiums
of every kind, from those which wrapped the rocks
in feathery green to others hardly distinguishable
from ferns. But there were twilight depths too, where
no sunlight penetrated the leafy gloom, damp and cool:
dreamy shades, in which the music of the water was all
too sweet, and the loveliness too entrancing, creating
that sadness, hardly " akin to pain," which is latent in

all intense enjoyment.   Here and there a tree had fallen
across the river, from which grew upwards and trailed
downwards, fairy-like, semi-transparent mosses and ferns,
all glittering with moisture and sunshine, and now and
then a scarlet tropic bird heightened the effect by the
flash of his plumage.

After an hour of wading we emerged into broad sunny
daylight at the home of the five cascades, which fall from
a semicircular precipice into three basins.   It is not,
however, possible to pass from one to the other.   This
great gulf is a grand sight, with its dark deep basin from
which it seemed so far to look up to the heavenly blue,
and the water falling calmly and unhurriedly, amidst innumerable rainbows, from a height of 3000 feet.   The sides
were draped with ferns flourishing under the spray, and
at the base the rock was very deeply caverned.   I enjoyed
a delicious bath, relying on sun and wind to dry my
clothes, and then reluctantly waded down the river.   At
its confluence with another stream, still arched by *ohias*,
a man and two women appeared rising out of the water,
like a vision of the elder world in the days of Fauns, and
Naiads, and Hamadryads.   The water was up to their
waists, and *leis* of *ohia* blossoms and ferns, and masses
of unbound hair fantastically wreathed with moss, fell
over their faultless forms, and their rich brown skin
gleamed in the slant sunshine.   They were catching
shrimps with trumpet-shaped baskets, perhaps rather
a prosaic occupation.   They joined us, and we waded
down together to the place where they had left their
horses.   The women slipped into their *holukus*, and the

man insisted on my riding his barebacked horse to the
place where we had left our own, and then we all galloped
over the soft grass.

Waimanu had turned out to meet us about thirty
people on horseback, all of whom shook hands with me,
and some of them threw over me garlands of *ohia*, pandanus, and hibiscus. Where our cavalcade entered the
river, a number of children and dogs and three canoes
awaited us, and thus escorted I returned triumphantly
to the house. The procession on the river of paddling
canoes, swimming children, and dogs, and more than
thirty riders, with their feet tucked up round their horses'
necks, all escorting a " pale face," was grotesque and
enchanting, and I revelled in this lapse into savagery,
and enjoyed heartily the kindliness and goodwill of this
unsophisticated people.

When darkness spread over the valley, clear voices
ascended in a weird recitative, the room filled up with
people, pipes circulated freely, *poi* was again produced,
and calabashes of cocoa-nut milk. The *mélés* were long,
and I crept within my curtain and lay down, but the
drowsiness which legitimately came over me after riding
thirty miles and wading two, was broken in upon by two
monstrous cockroaches really as large as mice, with fierce-
looking antennæ and prominent eyes, both of which
mounted guard on my pillow. On rising to drive them
away, I found to my dismay that they were but the leaders
of a host, which only made a temporary retreat, rustling
over the mat and dried grass with the crisp tread of mice,
and scaring away sleep for some hours. Worse than

these were the mosquitoes, also an imported nuisance, which stabbed and stung without any preliminary droning; and the heat was worse still, for thirteen human beings were lying on the floor and the door was shut. Had I known that two of these were lepers, I should have felt far from comfortable. As it was, I got up soon after midnight, and cautiously stepping among the sleeping forms, went out of doors. Everything favoured reflection, but I think the topics to which my mind most frequently reverted were my own absolute security—a lone white woman among "savages," and the civilizing influence which Christianity has exercised, so that even in this isolated valley, gouged out of a mountainous coast, there was nothing disagreeable or improper to be seen. The night was very still, but the sea was moaning; the river rippled very gently as it brushed past the reeds; there was a hardly perceptible vibration in the atmosphere, which suggested falling water and quivering leaves; and the air was full of a heavy, drowsy fragrance, the breath of orange flowers, perhaps, and of the night-blowing Cereus, which had opened its ivory urn to the moon. I should have liked to stay out all night in the vague, delicious moonlight, but the dew was heavy, and moreover I had not any boots on, so I reluctantly returned to the grass house, which was stifling with heat and smells of cocoa-nut oil, tobacco, and the rancid smoke from beef fat.

Before sunrise this morning my horse was saddled, and a number of natives had assembled. Hananui had disappeared, but the man who lent me his bare-backed horse yesterday was ready to act as guide. My boots could not then be found, so I adopted the native fashion of riding with bare feet. We again rode up the river in that slow and solemn fashion in which horses walk in water, galloped over a stretch of grass, crossed a bright stream several times, and then entered a dense jungle of Indian shot, plantains, and sadlerias, with breadfruit, *kukui*, and *ohia* rising out of it. There were thousands of plantains, a fruit resembling the banana, but that it requires cooking. The Indian shot, the yellow-blossomed variety, was of a gigantic size. Its hard, black seeds put into a bladder furnish the *chic-chac*, which in many places is used as an accompaniment to the utterly abominable and heathenish tom-tom. Here guavas as large as oranges and as yellow as lemons ripened and fell unheeded. Sometimes deep down we heard the rush of water, and Paalau got down and groped for it on his hands and knees; sometimes we heard a noise as of hippopotami, but nothing could be seen but the tips of ears, as a herd of happy, unbroken horses, scared by our approach, crashed away through the jungle. Clear rapid streams, fern-fringed, sometimes offered us a few yards of highway, but the jungle ever grew more dense, the forest trees larger, the lianas more tangled, the streams more sunk and rocky, and though the horses shut their eyes and boldly pushed through the tangle, we were fairly foiled when within half a mile from the head of the valley. I thoroughly appreciated the unsightly leather guards which are here used to cover the stirrups and feet, as without them I could not have ridden ten yards. We were so hemmed in that it was difficult to dismount, but I bound some wild *kalo* leaves round my feet, and managed to get over some broken rock to a knoll, from which I obtained a superb view of the wonderful cleft. *Palis* 3000 feet in height walled in its head with a complete inaccessibility. It lay in cool dewy shadow till the sudden sun flushed its precipices with pink, and a broad bar of light revealed the great chasm in which it terminates, while far off its portals opened upon the red eastern sky. This little lonely world had become so very dear to me, that I found it hard to leave it.

There was some stir near the sea, for a man was about to build a grass house, and they were preparing a stone pavement for it. Thirty people sat on the ground in a line from the beach, and passed stones from hand to hand, as men pass buckets at a fire. It seemed a very attractive occupation, and I could hardly get Hananui to leave it. The natives are most gregarious and social in their habits. They assemble together for everything that has to be made or done, and their occupations and amusements are shared by both sexes. In old days it is said that a king of Hawaii assembled most of the adults of the then populous island, and formed a human chain three miles long to pass up stones for the building of the great *Heiau* in Kona. It is said that this valley had 2000 inhabitants forty years ago, but they have dwindled to 117. The former estimate is probably not an excessive one, for nearly the whole valley is suitable for the culture of *kalo*, and a square mile of *kalo* will feed 15,000 natives for a·year.

Two women were shrimping in the river, the children were swimming to school, blue smoke curled up into the still air, *kalo* was baking among the stones, and a group of women sat sewing and making *leis* on the ground. The Waimanu day had begun; and it was odd to think that through the long summer years days dawned like this, and that the people of the valley grew grey and old in shrimping and sewing and *kalo* baking. All Waimanu shook hands with me, the kindly "*Aloha*" filled the air, and the women threw garlands over us both. I could hardly induce my host to accept a dollar and a half for my entertainment. From the dizzy summit of the *pali*, where the sun was high and hot, I looked my last on the dark, cool valley, slumbering in an endless calm, the deepest, greenest, quaintest cleft on all the island.

The sun was fierce and bright, the ocean had a metallic glint, the hot breath of the *kona* was scorching. My hands, swollen from mosquito bites, could not be stuffed into my gloves, and inflamed under the sun, and my wet boots baked and stiffened on my feet. Hananui plaited a crown of leaves for my hot head, which I found a great relief. I was still minded to linger, for one side of each glorious gulch was cool with shadow and dripping with dew. The blue morning glories were yet unwilted, rivulets dropped down into ferny grottoes and lingered there, rose *ohia* blossoms lighted shady places, orange flowers gleamed like stars amidst the dense leafage, and the crimped-leaved coffee shrubs were white with their mimic snow. It was my last tropical dream, and I was rudely roused by finding myself on the unsightly verge of the

great bluff on the north side of this valley, which plunges
to the sea with an uncompromising perpendicular dip of
2000 feet, and carries on its dizzy brow a shelving trail
not more than two feet wide !

I felt that I must go back and live and die in Waimanu
rather than descend that scathed steep, and being stupid
with terror flung myself from my horse, forgetting that it
was much safer to trust to his four feet than to my two,
and to an animal without " nerves," dizziness, or "the
fore-knowledge of death," than to my palsied, cowardly
self.   I had intended to go into details of the horrible
descent, but the "*pilikia*" is over now, and Halemanu
claps me on the shoulder with an approving smile, ejacu-
lating, " *Maikai, maikai*" (good).   Besides, my returning
senses inform me that I have not tasted food since yesterday, and some delicious river fishes are smoking on the
table. .   .   .   .   .

I. L. B.

LETTER XVII.

. . . I HAVE been spending the day at Lahaina on
Maui, on my way from Kawaihae to Honolulu. Lahaina
is thoroughly beautiful and tropical looking, with its white
latticed houses peeping out from under coco palms,
breadfruit, candlenut, tamarinds, mangoes, bananas, and
oranges, with the brilliant green of a narrow strip of
sugar-cane for a background, and above, the flushed
mountains of Eeka, riven here and there by cool green
chasms, rise to a height of 6000 feet. Beautiful Lahaina!
It is an oasis in a dazzling desert, straggling for nearly
two miles along the shore, but compressed into a width of
half a mile. It was a great missionary centre, as well as
a great whaling station, but the whalers have deserted it,
and missions are represented now only by the seminary
of Lahainaluna on the hillside. An old palace, the remains of a fort, a custom-house, and a native church are
the most conspicuous buildings. The stores and dwellings of the foreign residents are scattered along the shore,
and the light frame house, with its green verandah, buried
amid gorgeous exotics and shaded by candlenut and
breadfruit, looks as seemly and in keeping as in far-off
Massachusetts, under hickory and elm. The grass houses

of the natives cluster along the waters' edge, or in lanes dark with mangoes and bananas, and fragrant with gardenia fringing the cane-fields. These, with adobe houses and walls, the flush of the soil, the gaudy dresses of the natives, the masses of brilliant exotics, the intense blue of the sea, and the dry blaze of the tropical heat, give a decided individuality to the capital of Maui. The heat of Lahaina is a dry, robust, bracing, joyous heat. The mercury stood at 80°, the usual temperature of the "flare" or sea level on the leeward side of the islands; but I strolled through the cane-fields and along the glaring beach without suffering the least incopvenience from the sun, and found the unusual precaution of a white umbrella perfectly needless.

The beach is formed of pure white broken coral; the sea is blue with the calm, pure blue of turquoise, but crystalline in its purity, and breaks for ever over the environing coral reef with a low deep music. Blue water stretched to the far horizon, the sky was blazing blue, the leafage was almost dazzling to the eye, the mountainous island of Molokai floated like a great blue morning glory on the yet bluer sea; a sweet, soft breeze rustled through the palms, lazy ripples plashed lightly on the sand; humanity basked, flower-clad, in sunny indolence; everything was redundant, fervid, beautiful. How can I make you realize the glorious, bountiful, sun-steeped tropics under our cold grey skies, and amidst our pale, monotonous, lustreless greens?

Yet Molokai is only enchanting in the distance, for its blue petals enfold 400 lepers doomed to endless isolation,

and 300 more are shortly to be weeded out and sent
thither. In to-day's paper appeared the painful notice,
"All lepers are required to report themselves to the
Government health officer within fourteen days from this
date for inspection, and final banishment to Molokai."
It is hoped that leprosy may be "stamped out" by these
stringent measures, but the leprous taint must be strong
in many families, and the social, gregarious natives
smoke each other's pipes and wear each other's clothes,
and either from fatalism or ignorance have disregarded all
precautions regarding this woful disease ; and now that
measures are being taken for the isolation of lepers, they
are concealing them under mats and in caves and woods.
This forlorn malady, called here Chinese leprosy, in the
cases that I have seen, confers nothing of the white, scaly
look attributed to Syrian leprosy; but the face is red,
puffed, bloated, and shining, and the eyes glazed, and I
am told that in its advanced stage the swollen limbs
decay and drop off. It is a fresh item of the infinite
curse which has come upon this race, and with Molokai
in sight the Hesperides vanished, and I ceased to believe
that the Fortunate Islands exist here or elsewhere on
this weary earth.

My destination was the industrial training and boarding
school for girls, taught and superintended by two English
ladies of Miss Sellon's sisterhood, Sisters Mary Clara and
Phœbe ; and I found it buried under the shade of the
finest candlenut trees I have yet seen. A rude wooden
cross in front is a touching and fitting emblem of the
Saviour, for whom these pious women have sacrificed

friends, sympathy, and the social intercourse and amenities which are within daily reach of our workers at home.
The large house, which is either plastered stone or
adobe, contains the dormitories, visitors' room, and
oratory, and three houses at the back, all densely shaded,
are used as schoolroom, cook-house, laundry, and refectory. There is a playground under some fine tamarind
trees, and an adobe wall encloses, without secluding, the
whole. The visitors' room is about twelve feet by
eight feet, very bare, with a deal table and three chairs
in it, but it was vacant, and I crossed to the large, shady,
airy schoolroom, where I found the senior sister engaged
in teaching, while the junior was busy in the cook-house.
These ladies in eight years have never left Lahaina.
Other people may think it necessary to leave its broiling
heat and seek health and recreation on the mountains,
but their work has left them no leisure, and their zeal no
desire, for a holiday. A very solid, careful English education is given here, as well as a thorough training in all
housewifely arts, and in the more important matters of
modest dress and deportment, and propriety in language.
There are thirty-seven boarders, native and half-native,
and mixed native and Chinese, between the ages of four
and eighteen. They provide their own clothes, beds,
and bedding, and I think pay forty dollars a year. The
capitation grant from Government for two years was
2325 dollars. Sister Phœbe was my cicerone, and I
owe her one of the pleasantest days I have spent on
the islands. The elder Sister is in middle life, but
though fragile-looking, has a pure complexion and a

lovely countenance; the younger is scarcely middle-aged, one of the brightest, bonniest, sweetest-looking women I ever saw, with fun dancing in her eyes and round the corners of her mouth; yet the regnant expression on both faces was serenity, as though they had attained to " the love which looketh kindly, and the wisdom which looketh soberly on all things."

I never saw such a mirthful-looking set of girls. Some were cooking the dinner, some ironing, others reading English aloud; but each occupation seemed a pastime, and whenever they spoke to the Sisters they clung about them as if they were their mothers. I heard them read the Bible and an historical lesson, as well as play on a piano and sing, and they wrote some very difficult passages from dictation without any errors, and in a flowing, legible handwriting that I am disposed to envy. Their accent and intonation were pleasing, and there was a briskness and emulation about their style of answering questions, rarely found in country schools with us, significant of intelligence and good teaching. All but the younger girls spoke English as fluently as Hawaiian. I cannot convey a notion of the blitheness and independence of manner of these children. To say that they were free and easy would be wrong; it was rather the manner of very frolicsome daughters to very indulgent mothers or aunts. It was a family manner rather than a school manner, and the rule is obviously one of love. The Sisters are very wise in adapting their discipline to the native character and circumstances. The rigidity which is customary in similar institutions

at home would be out of place, as well as fatal here, and
would ultimately lead to a rebound of a most injurious
description. Strict obedience is of course required, but the
rules are few and lenient, and there is no more pressure
of discipline than in a well-ordered family. The native
amusements generally are objectionable, but Hawaiians
are a dancing people, and will dance, or else indulge in
less innocent pastimes ; so the Sisters have taught them
various English dances, and I never saw anything
prettier or more graceful than their style of dancing.
There is no uniform dress. The girls wear pretty print
frocks, made in the English style, and several of them
wore the hibiscus in their shining hair. Some of the
older girls were beautiful in face as well as graceful in
figure, but there was a snaky undulation about their
movements which I never saw among Europeans. All
looked bubbling over with fun and frolic, and there was
a refinement and intelligence about their expression
which contrasted favourably with that of the ordinary
female face on the islands.

There are two dormitories, excellently ventilated, with
a four-post bed, with mosquito-bars, for each girl, and
the beds were covered with those brilliant-coloured quilts
in which the natives delight, and in which they exercise
considerable ingenuity as well as individuality of taste.
One Sister sleeps in each dormitory, and these highly-
educated and refined women have no place of retirement
except a very plain oratory ; and having taken the vow of
poverty, they have of course no possessions, none of the
books, pictures, and knick-knacks wherewith others adorn

their surroundings. Their whole lives, with the exception of the time passed in the oratory, are spent with the girls, and in visiting the afflicted at their homes, and this through eight blazing years, with the mercury always at 80°!

The Hawaiian women have no notions of virtue as we understand it, and if there is to be any future for this race it must come through a higher morality. Consequently the removal of these girls from evil and impure surroundings, the placing them under the happiest influences in favour of purity and goodness, the forming and fostering of industrious and housewifely habits, and the raising them in their occupations and amusements above those which are natural to their race, are in themselves a noble, and in some degree, a hopeful work, but it admits of neither pause nor relaxation. Those who carry it on are truly " the lowest in the meanest task," for they have undertaken not only the superintendence of menial work (so called), but the work itself, in teaching by example and instruction the womanly industries of home. They have no society, until lately no regular Liturgical worship, and of necessity a very infrequent celebration of the Holy Communion; and they have undergone the trial which arose very naturally out of the ecclesiastical relations of the American missionaries, of being regarded as enemies, or at least dangerous interlopers, by the excellent men who had long resided on the islands as Christian teachers, and with whose views on such matters as dress and recreation their own are somewhat at variance. In the first instance, the habit they wore, their designations, the presence of Miss Sellon, the fame of whose Ritualistic tendencies had reached the islands, and their manifest connection with a section of the English Church which is regarded here with peculiar disfavour, roused a strongly antagonistic feeling regarding their work and the drift of their religious teaching. They are not connected with what is known at home as the " Honolulu Mission." *

I. L. B.

* It gives me pleasure to add that the Sisters have lived down this very natural distrust, and that in a subsequent residence of five months on the islands, I never heard but one opinion, and that of the most favourable kind, regarding the Lahaina School, and the excellence and wisdom of the manner in which it is conducted. I have been told by many who on most points are quite out of sympathy with the Sisters, not only that their work is recognized as a most valuable agency, but that their influence has come to be regarded as among the chiefest of the blessings of Lahaina.

LETTER XVIII.

OAHU, with its grey pinnacles, its deep valleys, its cool chasms, its ruddy headlands, and volcanic cones, all clothed in green by the recent rains, looked unspeakably lovely as we landed by sunrise in a rose-flushed atmosphere, and Honolulu, shady, dew-bathed, and brilliant with flowers, deserved its name, "The Paradise of the Pacific." The hotel is pleasant, and Mrs. D.'s presence makes it sweet and homelike; but in a very few days I have lost much of the health I gained on Hawaii, and the "Rolling Moses" and the Rocky Mountains can hardly come too soon. For Honolulu is truly a metropolis, gay, hospitable, and restless, and this hotel centralizes the restlessness. Visiting begins at breakfast time, when it ends I know not, and receiving and making visits, court festivities, entertainments given by the commissioners of the great powers, riding parties, picnics, verandah parties, "sociables," and luncheon and evening parties on board the ships of war, succeed each other with frightful rapidity. This is all on the surface, but beneath and better than this is a kindness which leaves no stranger to a sense of loneliness, no want uncared for, and no sorrow unalleviated. This, more

than its beauty and its glorious climate, makes Honolulu
"Paradise" for the many who arrive here sick and
friendless. I notice that the people are very intimate
with each other, and generally address each other by
their Christian names. Very many are the descendants of the clerical and secular members of the mission,
and these, besides being naturally intimate, are further
drawn and held together by a society called "The
Cousins' Society," the objects of which are admirable.
The people take an intense interest in each other, and
love each other unusually. Possibly they may hate each
other as cordially when occasion offers. It is a charming
town, and the society is delightful. I wish I were well
enough to enjoy it.

For people in the early stages of consumption this
climate is perfect, owing to its equability, as also for
bronchial affections. Unlike the health resorts of the
Mediterranean, Algeria, Madeira, and Florida, where
great summer heats or an unhealthy season compel half-
cured invalids to depart in the spring, to return the next
winter with fresh colds to begin the half-cure process
again, people can live here until they are completely
cured, as the climate is never unhealthy, and never too
hot. Though the regular trades, which blow for nine
months of the year, have not yet set in, and the mercury
stands at 80°, there is no sultriness: a tremulous sea-
breeze and a mountain breeze fan the town, and the
purple nights, when the stars hang out like lamps, and
the moon gives a light which is almost golden, are cool
and delicious. Roughly computed, the annual mean

temperature is 75° 55', with a divergence in either direction of only 7° 55'. As a general rule the temperature is cooler by four degrees for every thousand feet of altitude, so that people can choose their climate to suit themselves without leaving the islands.

I am gradually learning a little of the topography of this island and of Honolulu, but the last is very intricate. The appearance of Oahu from the sea is deceptive. It looks hardly larger than Arran, but it is really forty-six miles long by twenty-five broad, and is 530 square miles in extent. Diamond Hill, or Leahi, is the most pro-minent object south of the town, beyond the palm groves of Waikiki. It is red and arid, except when, as now, it is verdure-tinged by recent rains. Its height is 760 feet, and its crater nearly as deep, but its cone is rapidly diminishing. Some years ago, when the enormous quantity of thirty-six inches of rain fell in one week, the degradation of both exterior and interior was something incredible, and the same process is being carried on slowly or rapidly at all times. The Punchbowl, imme-diately behind Honolulu, is a crater of the same kind, but of yet more brilliant colouring: so red is it indeed, that one might suppose that its fires had but just died out. In 1786 an observer noted it as being composed of' high peaks; but atmospheric influences have reduced it to the appearance of a single wasting tufa cone, similar to those which stud the northern slopes of Mauna Kea. There are a number of shore craters on the island, and six groups of tufa cones, but from the disintegration of the lava, and the great depth of the soil in many places, it is supposed that volcanic action ceased earlier than on Maui or Hawaii. The shores are mostly fringed with coral reefs, often half a mile in width, composed of cemented coral fragments, shells, sand, and a growing species of zoophyte. The ancient reefs are elevated thirty, forty, and even 100 feet in some places, forming barriers which have changed lagoons into solid ground. Honolulu was a bay or lagoon, protected from the sea by a coral reef a mile wide; but the elevation of this reef twenty-five feet has furnished a site for the capital, by converting the bay into a low but beautifully situated plain.

The mountainous range behind is a rocky wall with outlying ridges, valleys of great size cutting the mountain to its core on either side, until the culminating peaks of Waiolani and Konahuanui, 4000 feet above the sea, seem as if rent in twain to form the Nuuanu Valley. The windward side of this range is fertile, and is dotted over with rice and sugar plantations, but the leeward side has not a trace of the redundancy of the tropics, and this very barrenness gives a unique charm to the exotic beauty of Honolulu.

To me it is daily a fresh pleasure to stroll along the shady streets and revel among palms and bananas, to see clusters of the granadilla and night-blowing cereus mixed with the double blue pea, tumbling over walls and fences, while the vermilion flowers of the *Erythrina umbrosa*, like spikes of red coral, and the flaring magenta Bougainvillea (which is not a flower at all, but an audacious freak of terminal leaves) light up the shade, and the purple-leaved Dracæna which we grow in pots for dinner-table ornament, is as common as a weed.

Besides this hotel, and the handsome but exaggerated and inappropriate Government buildings not yet finished, there are few "imposing edifices" here. The tasteful but temporary English Cathedral, the Kaiwaiaho Church, diminished once to suit a dwindled population, but already too large again; the prison, a clean, roomy building, empty in the daytime, because the convicts are sent out to labour on roads and public works; the Queen's Hospital for Curables, for which Queen Emma and her husband became mendicants in Honolulu; the Court House, a staring, unshaded building; and the Iolani Palace, almost exhaust the category. Of this last, little can be said, except that it is appropriate and proportioned to a kingdom of 56,000 souls, which is more than can be said of the income of the king, the salaries of the ministers, and some other things. It stands in pleasure-grounds of about an acre in extent, with a fine avenue running through them, and is approached by a flight of steps which leads to a tolerably spacious hall, decorated in the European style. Portraits of Louis Philippe and his queen, presented by themselves, and of the late Admiral Thomas, adorn the walls. The Hawaiians have a profound respect for this officer's memory, as it was through him that the sovereignty of the islands was promptly restored to the native rulers, after the infamous affair of its cession to England, as represented by Lord George Paulet. There are also some ornamental vases and miniature copies of some of Thorwaldsen's works.

The throne-room takes up the left wing of the palace. This unfortunately resembles a rather dreary drawing-room in London or New York, and has no distinctive features except a decorated chair, which is the Hawaiian throne. There is an Hawaiian crown also, neither grand nor costly, but this I have not seen. At present the palace is only used for state receptions and entertainments, for the king is living at his private residence of Haemoeipio, not far off.

Miss W. kindly introduced me to Queen Emma, or Kaleleonalani, the widowed queen of Kamehameha IV., whom you will remember as having visited England a few years ago, when she received great attention. She has one-fourth of English blood in her veins, but her complexion is fully as dark as if she were of unmixed Hawaiian descent, and her features, though refined by education and circumstances, are also Hawaiian; but she is a very pretty, as well as a very graceful woman. She was brought up by Dr. Rooke, an English physician here, and though educated at the American school for the children of chiefs, is very English in her leanings and sympathies, an attached member of the English Church, and an ardent supporter of the "Honolulu Mission." Socially she is very popular, and her exceeding kindness and benevolence, with her strongly national feeling as an Hawaiian, make her much beloved by the natives.

The winter palace, as her town house is called, is a large shady abode, like an old-fashioned New England house externally, but with two deep verandahs, and the

entrance is on the upper one. The lower floor seemed
given up to attendants and offices, and a native woman
was ironing clothes under a tree. Upstairs, the house is
like a tasteful English country house, with a pleasant
English look, as if its furniture and ornaments had been
gradually accumulating during a series of years, and
possessed individual histories and reminiscences, rather
than as if they had been ordered together as "plenish-
ings" from stores. Indeed, it is the most English-looking
house I have seen since I left home, except Bishops-
court at Melbourne. If there were a bell I did not see it;
and we did not ring, for the queen received us at the door
of the drawing-room, which was open. I had seen her
before in European dress, driving a pair of showy black
horses in a stylish English phaeton; but on this occasion
she was not receiving visitors formally, and was indulging
in wearing the native *holuku*, and her black wavy hair
was left to its own devices. She is rather below the
middle height, very young-looking for her age, which is
thirty-seven, and very graceful in her movements. Her
manner is indeed very fascinating from a combination
of unconscious dignity with ladylike simplicity. Her
expression is sweet and gentle, with the same look of
sadness about her eyes that the king has, but she has a
brightness and archness of expression which give a great
charm to her appearance. She has sorrowed much: first,
for the death, at the age of four, of her only child, the
Prince of Hawaii, who when dying was baptized into the
English Church by the name of Albert Edward, Queen
Victoria and the Prince of Wales being his sponsors; and

secondly, for the premature death of her husband, to
whom she was much attached. She speaks English
beautifully, only hesitating now and then for the most
correct form of expression. She spoke a good deal and
with great pleasure of England; and described Venice
and the emotions it excited in her so admirably, that I
should like to have heard her describe all Europe.

A few days afterwards I went to a garden party at her
house. It was a very pretty sight, and the "everybody" of Honolulu was there to the number of 250.
I must describe it for the benefit of ——, who persists
in thinking that coloured royalty must necessarily be
grotesque. People arrived shortly before sunset, and
were received by Queen Emma, who sat on the lawn,
with her attendants about her, very simply dressed in
black silk. The king, at whose entrance the band played
the national anthem, stood on another lawn, where
presentations were made by the chamberlain; and those
who were already acquainted with him had an opportunity for a few minutes' conversation. He was dressed
in a very well-made black morning suit, and wore the
ribbon and star of the Austrian order of Francis Joseph.
His simplicity was atoned for by the superlative splendour of his suite; the governor of Oahu, and the high
chief Kalakaua, who was a rival candidate for the throne,
being conspicuously resplendent. The basis of the
costume appeared to be the Windsor uniform, but it
was smothered with epaulettes, cordons, and lace; and
each dignitary has a uniform peculiar to his office, so
that the display of gold lace was prodigious. The chiefs

A HAWAIIAN LADY.   [*Page* 265.

are so raised above the common people in height, size, and general nobility of aspect, that many have supposed them to be of a different race; and the *alii* who represented the dwindled order that night were certainly superb enough in appearance to justify the supposition. Beside their splendour and stateliness, the forty officers of the English and American war-ships, though all in full-dress uniform, looked decidedly insignificant; and I doubt not that the natives who were assembled outside the garden railings in crowds were not behind me in making invidious comparisons.

Chairs and benches were placed under the beautiful trees, and people grouped themselves on these, and promenaded, flirted, talked politics and gossip, or listened to the royal band, which played at intervals, and played well. The dress of the ladies, whether white or coloured, was both pretty and appropriate. Most of the younger women were in white, and wore natural flowers in their hair; and many of the elder ladies wore black or coloured silks, with lace and trains. There were several beautiful *leis* of the gardenia, which filled all the garden with their delicious odour. Tea and ices were handed round on Sèvres china by footmen and pages in appropriate liveries. What a wonderful leap from calabashes and *poi, malos* and *paus*, to this correct and tasteful civilization! As soon as the brief amber twilight of the tropics was over, the garden was suddenly illuminated by myriads of Chinese lanterns, and the effect was bewitching. The upper suite of rooms was thrown open for those who preferred dancing under cover; but I think that the greater part of the assem-

blage chose the shady walks and purple night. Supper
was served at eleven, and the party broke up soon afterwards; but I must confess that, charming as it was, I
left before eight, for society makes heavier demands on
my strength than the rough open-air life of Hawaii.

The dwindling of the race is a most pathetic subject.
Here is a sovereign chosen amidst an outburst of popular
enthusiasm, with a cabinet, a legislature, and a costly
and elaborate governing machinery, sufficient in Yankee
phrase to "run" an empire of several millions, and here
are only 49,000 native Hawaiians; and if the decrease
be not arrested, in a quarter of a century there will not
be an Hawaiian to govern. The chiefs, or *alii*, are a
nearly extinct order; and, with a few exceptions, those
who remain are childless. In riding through Hawaii I
came everywhere upon traces of a once numerous population, where the hill slopes are now only a wilderness
of guava scrub, and upon churches and school-houses all
too large, while in some hamlets the voices of young
children were altogether wanting. This nation, with its
elaborate governmental machinery, its churches and
institutions, has to me the mournful aspect of a shrivelled
and wizened old man dressed in clothing much too big,
the garments of his once athletic and vigorous youth.
Nor can I divest myself of the idea that the laughing,
flower-clad hordes of riders who make the town gay with
their presence, are but like butterflies fluttering out their
short lives in the sunshine,

"   .   .   . a wreck and residue,
Whose only business is to perish."

The statistics on this subject are perfectly appalling. If we reduce Captain Cook's estimate of the native population by one-fourth, it was 300,000 in 1779. In 1872 it was only 49,000. The first official census was in 1832, when the native population was 130,000. This makes the decrease 80,000 in forty years, or at the rate of 2000 a year, and fixes the period for the final extinction of the race in 1897, if that rate were to continue. It is a pity, for many reasons, that it is dying out. It has shown a singular aptitude for politics and civilization, and it would have been interesting to watch the development of a strictly Polynesian monarchy starting under passably fair conditions. Whites have conveyed to these shores slow but infallible destruction on the one hand, and on the other the knowledge of the life that is to come; and the rival influences of blessing and cursing have now been fifty years at work, producing results with which most reading people are familiar.

I have not heard the subject spoken of, but I should think that the decrease in the population must cause the burden of taxation to press heavily on that which remains. Kings, cabinet ministers, an army, a police, a national debt, a supreme court, and common schools, are costly luxuries or necessaries. The civil list is ludicrously out of proportion to the resources of the islands, and the heads of the four departments—Foreign Relations, Interior, Finance, and Law (Attorney-General) —receive $5,000 a year each! Expenses and salaries have been increasing for the last thirty years. For schools alone every man between twenty-one and sixty pays a

tax of two dollars annually, and there is an additional
general tax for the same purpose. I suppose that there
is not a better educated country in the world. Education is compulsory; and besides the primary schools,
there are a number of academies, all under Government
supervision, and there are 324 teachers, or one for
every twenty-seven children. There is a Board of Education, and Kamakau, its president, reported to the
last biennial session of the legislature that out of
8931 children between the ages of six and fifteen,
8287 were actually attending school! Among other
direct taxes, every quadruped that can be called a
horse, above two years old, pays a dollar a year, and
every dog a dollar and a half. Does not all this sound
painfully civilized? If the influence of the tropics has
betrayed me into rhapsody and ecstacy in earlier letters,
these dry details will turn the scale in favour of prosaic
sobriety!

I have said little about Honolulu, except of its tropical
beauty. It does not look as if it had " seen better days."
Its wharves are well cared for, and its streets and roads
are very clean. The retail stores are generally to be
found in two long streets which run inland, and in a
splay street which crosses both. The upper storekeepers,
with a few exceptions, are Americans, but one street is
nearly given up to Chinamen's stores, and one of the
wealthiest and most honourable merchants in the town is
a Chinaman. There is an ice factory, and icecream is
included in the daily bill of fare here, and iced water is
supplied without limit, but lately the machinery has only

worked in spasms, and the absence of ice is regarded as a local calamity, though the water supplied from the water-works is both cool and pure. There are two good photo-graphers and two booksellers. I don't think that plateglass fronts are yet to be seen. Many of the storekeepers em-ploy native "assistants;" but the natives show little aptitude for mercantile affairs, or indeed for the "splendid science" of money-making generally, and in this respect contrast with the Chinamen, who, having come here as Coolies, have contrived to secure a large share of the small traffic of the islands. Most things are expensive, but they are good. I have seen little of such decided rubbish as is to be found in the cheap stores of London and Edinburgh, except in tawdry artificial flowers. Good black silks are to be bought, and are as essential to the equipment of a lady as at home. Saddles are to be had at most of the stores, from the elaborate Mexican and Californian saddle, worth from 30 to 50 dollars, to a worthless imitation of the English saddle, dear at five. Boots and shoes, perhaps because in this climate they are a mere luxury, are frightfully dear, and so are books, writing paper, and stationery generally; a sheet of Bristol board, which we buy at home for 6d., being half a dollar here. But it is quite a pleasure to make purchases in the stores. There is so much cordiality and courtesy that, as at this hotel, the bill recedes into the background, and the purchaser feels the indebted party.

The money is extremely puzzling. These islands, like California, have repudiated greenbacks, and the only paper currency is a small number of treasury notes for large amounts. The coin in circulation is gold and silver, but gold is scarce, which is an inconvenience to people who have to carry a large amount of money about with them. The coinage is nominally that of the United States, but the dollars are Mexican, or French 5 franc pieces, and people speak of " rials," which have no existence here, and of " bits," a Californian slang term for $12\frac{1}{2}$ cents, a coin which to my knowledge does not exist anywhere. A dime, or 10 cents, is the lowest coin I have seen, and copper is not in circulation. An envelope, a penny bottle of ink, a pencil, a spool of thread, cost 10 cents each; postage-stamps cost 2 cents each for inter-island postage, but one must buy five of them, and dimes slip away quickly and imperceptibly. There is a loss on English money, as half-a-crown only passes for a half-dollar, sixpence for a dime, and so forth; indeed, the average loss seems to be about twopence in the shilling.

There are four newspapers : the *Honolulu Gazette*, the *Pacific Commercial Advertiser*, *Ka Nupepa Kuokoa* (the "Independent Press"), and a lately started spasmodic sheet, partly in English and partly in Hawaiian, the *Nuhou* (News).* The two first are moral and respectable, but indulge in the American sins of personalities and mutual vituperation. The *Nuhou* is scurrilous and diverting, and appears " run " with a special object, which I have not as yet succeeded in unravelling from its pungent but not always intelligible pages. I think perhaps the writing in each paper has something of the American

* The *Nuhou* has since expired.

tendency to hysteria and convulsions, though these maladies are mild as compared with the " real thing" in the
Alta California, which is largely taken here.   Besides
these there are monthly sheets called *The Friend*, the
oldest paper in the Pacific, edited by good. " Father
Damon," and the *Church Messenger*, edited by Bishop
Willis, partly devotional and partly devoted to the Honolulu Mission.   All our popular American and English
literature is read here, and I have hardly seen a table
without " Scribner's" or " Harper's Monthly," or " Good
Words."

I have lived far too much in America to feel myself a
stranger where, as here, American influence and customs
are dominant ; but the English who are in Honolulu just
now, *in transitu* from New Zealand, complain bitterly of
its "Yankeeism," and are very far from being at home,
and I doubt not that Mr. M——, whom you will see, will
not confirm my favourable description.   It is quite true
that the islands are Americanized, and with the exception
of the Finance Minister, who is a Scotchman, Americans
" run" the Government and fill the Chief Justiceship
and other high offices of State.   It is, however, perfectly fair, for Americans have civilized and Christianized Hawaii-nei, and we have done little except
make an unjust and afterwards disavowed seizure of
the islands.

On looking over this letter I find it an *olla podrida* of
tropical glories, royal festivities, finance matters, and
odds and ends in general.   I dare say you will find it
dull after my letters from Hawaii, but there are others

who will prefer its prosaic details to Kilauea and Waimanu; and I confess that, amidst the general lusciousness of tropical life, I myself enjoy the dryness and tartness of statistics, and hard uncoloured facts.

I. L. B.

LETTER XIX.

MY latest news of you is five months old, and though I have not the slightest expectation that I shall hear from you, I go up to the roof to look out for the "Rolling Moses" with more impatience and anxiety than those whose business journeys are being delayed by her non-arrival. If such an unlikely thing were to happen as that she were to bring a letter, I should be much tempted to stay five months longer on the islands rather than try the climate of Colorado, for I have come to feel at home, people are so very genial, and suggest so many plans for my future enjoyment, the islands in their physical and social aspects are so novel and interesting, and the climate is unrivalled and restorative.

Honolulu has not yet lost the charm of novelty for me. I am never satiated with its exotic beauties, and the sight of a kaleidoscopic whirl of native riders is always fascinating. The passion for riding, in a people who only learned equitation in the last generation, is most curious. It is very curious, too, to see women incessantly enjoying and amusing themselves in riding, swimming, and making leis. They have few home ties in the shape of children, and I fear make them fewer still by neglecting them for the

sake of riding and frolic, and man seems rather the help-
meet than the " oppressor" of woman; though I believe
that the women have abandoned that right of choosing
their husbands, which, it is said, that they exercised in
the old days.   Used to the down-trodden look and har-
rassed care-worn faces of the over-worked women of the
same class at home and in the colonies, the laughing,
careless faces of the Hawaiian women have the effect upon
me of a perpetual marvel.   But the expression generally
has little of the courteousness, innocence, and childishness
of the negro physiognomy.   The Hawaiians are a handsome people, scornful and sarcastic-looking even with
their mirthfulness; and those who know them say that
they are always quizzing and mimicking the *haoles*, and
that they give everyone a nickname, founded on some
personal peculiarity.

The women are free from our tasteless perversity as to
colour and ornament, and have an instinct of the becoming.   At first the *holuku*, which is only a full, yoke
nightgown, is not attractive, but I admire it heartily now,
and the sagacity of those who devised it.   It conceals
awkwardness, and befits grace of movement; it is fit for
the climate, is equally adapted for walking and riding,
and has that general appropriateness which is desirable
in costume.   The women have a most peculiar walk, with
a swinging motion from the hip at each step, in which
the shoulder sympathises.   I never saw anything at all
like it.   It has neither the delicate shuffle of the French-
woman, the robust, decided jerk of the Englishwoman,
the stately glide of the Spaniard, or the stealthiness of

NATIVES OF HONOLULU.   [*Page* 274.

the squaw; and I should know a Hawaiian woman by it in any part of the world. A majestic *wahine* with small, bare feet, a grand, swinging, deliberate gait, hibiscus blossoms in her flowing hair, and a *lē* of yellow flowers falling over her *holuku*, marching through these streets, has a tragic grandeur of appearance, which makes the diminutive, fair-skinned *haole*, tottering along hesitatingly in high-heeled shoes, look grotesque by comparison.

On Saturday, our kind host took Mrs. D. and myself to the market, where we saw the natives in all their glory. The women, in squads of a dozen at a time, their Pa-ús streaming behind them, were cantering up and down the streets, and men and women were thronging into the market-place; a brilliant, laughing, joking crowd, their jaunty hats trimmed with fresh flowers, and *leis* of the crimson *ohia* and orange *lauhala* falling over their costumes, which were white, green, black, scarlet, blue, and every other colour that can be dyed or imagined. The market is a straggling, open space, with a number of shabby stalls partially surrounding it, but really we could not see the place for the people. There must have been 2000 there.

Some of the stalls were piled up with wonderful fish, crimson, green, rose, blue, opaline—fish that have spent their lives in coral groves under the warm, bright water. Some of them had wonderful shapes too, and there was one that riveted my attention and fascinated me. It was, I thought at first, a heap, composed of a dog fish, some limpets, and a multitude of water snakes, and other abominable forms; but my eyes slowly informed me of

the fact, which I took in reluctantly and with extreme
disgust, that the whole formed one living monster, a
revolting compound of a large paunch with eyes, and a
multitude of nervy, snaky, out-reaching, twining, grasping, tentacular arms, several feet in length, I should think,
if extended, but then lying in a crowded undulating
heap; the creature was dying, and the iridescence was
passing over what seemed to be its body in waves of
colour, such as glorify the last hour of the dolphin. But
not the colours of the rainbow could glorify this hideous,
abominable form, which ought to be left to riot in ocean
depths, with its loathsome kindred. You have read
" *Les Travailleurs du Mer*," and can imagine with what
feelings I looked upon a living Devil-fish! The monster
is much esteemed by the natives as an article of food,
and indeed is generally relished. I have seen it on
foreign tables, salted, under the name of squid.*

We passed on to beautiful creatures, the *kihi-kihi*, or
sea-cock, with alternate black and yellow transverse
bands on his body; the *hinalea*, like a glorified mullet,
with bright green, longitudinal bands on a dark shining
head, a purple body of different shades, and a blue spotted
tail with a yellow tip. The *Ohua* too, a pink scaled fish,
shaped like a trout; the *opukai*, beautifully striped and
mottled; the mullet and flying fish as common here as
mackerel at home; the *hala*, a fine pink-fleshed fish, the

* This monster is a cephalopod of the order *Dibranchiata*, and has eight
flexible arms, each crowded with 120 pair of suckers, and two longer
feelers about six feet in length, differing considerably from the others in
form.

albicore, the bonita, the *manini* striped black and white, and many others. There was an abundance of *opilu* or limpets, also the *pipi*, a small oyster found among the coral; the *ula*, as large as a clawless lobster, but more beautiful and variegated; and turtles which were cheap and plentiful. Then there were purple-spiked sea urchins, black-spiked sea eggs or *wana*, and *ina* or eggs without spikes, and many other curiosities of the bright Pacific. It was odd to see the pearly teeth of a native meeting in some bright-coloured fish, while the tail hung out of his mouth, for they eat fish raw, and some of them were obviously at the height of epicurean enjoyment. Seaweed and fresh-water weed are much relished by Hawaiians, and there were four or five kinds for sale, all included in the term *limu*. Some of this was baked, and put up in balls weighing one pound each. There were packages of baked fish, and dried fish, and of many other things which looked uncleanly and disgusting; but no matter what the package was, the leaf of the *Ti* tree was invariably the wrapping, tied round with sennet, the coarse fibre obtained from the husk of the cocoa-nut. Fish, here, averages about ten cents per pound, and is dearer than meat; but in many parts of the islands it is cheap and abundant.

There is a ferment going on in this kingdom, mainly got up by the sugar planters and the interests dependent on them, and two political lectures have lately been given in the large hall of the hotel in advocacy of their views; one, on annexation, by Mr. Phillips, who has something of the oratorical gift of his cousin, Wendell Phillips; and

the other, on a reciprocity treaty, by Mr. Carter. Both
were crowded by ladies and gentlemen, and the first was
most enthusiastically received. Mrs. D. and I usually
spend our evenings in writing and working in the verandah, or in each other's rooms; but I have become so
interested in the affairs of this little state, that in spite
of the mosquitos, I attended both lectures, but was not
warmed into sympathy with the views of either speaker.

I daresay that some of my friends here would quarrel
with my conclusions, but I will briefly give the *data* on
which they are based. The census of 1872 gives the native
population at 49,044 souls; of whom, 700 are lepers;
and it is *decreasing* at the rate of from 1,200 to 2,000 a
year, while the excess of native males over females on the
islands is 3,216. The foreign population is 5,366, and it
is *increasing* at the rate of 200 a year; and the number
of half-castes of all nations has *increased* at the rate of
140 a year. The Chinese, who came here originally as
plantation coolies, outnumber all the other nationalities
together, excluding the Americans; but the Americans
constitute the ruling and the monied class. Sugar is
the reigning interest on the islands, and it is almost
entirely in American hands. It is burdened here by the
difficulty of procuring labour, and at San Francisco by
a heavy import duty. There are thirty-five plantations
on the islands, and there is room for fifty more. The
profit, as it is, is hardly worth mentioning, and few of
the planters do more than keep their heads above water.
Plantations which cost $50,000 have been sold for
$15,000; and others, which cost $150,000 have been

sold for $40,000.   If the islands were annexed, and the
duty taken off, many of these struggling planters would
clear $50,000 a year and upwards.   So, no wonder that
Mr. Phillips's lecture was received with enthusiastic
plaudits.   It focussed all the clamour I have heard on
Hawaii and elsewhere, exalted the "almighty dollar,"
and was savoury with the odour of coming prosperity.
But he went far, very far; he has aroused a cry among
the natives "*Hawaii for the Hawaiians*," which, very
likely, may breed mischief; for I am very sure that this
brief civilization has not quenched the "red fire" of race;
and his hint regarding the judicious disposal of the king
in the event of annexation, was felt by many of the more
sober whites to be highly impolitic.

The reciprocity treaty, very lucidly advocated by Mr.
Carter, and which means the cession of a lagoon with
a portion of circumjacent territory on this island, to the
United States, for a Pacific naval station, meets with
more general favour as a safer measure; but the natives
are indisposed to bribe the great Republic to remit the
sugar duties by the surrender of a square inch of
Hawaiian soil; and, from a British point of view, I
heartily sympathise with them.   Foreign, *i.e.* American,
feeling is running high upon the subject.   People say
that things are so bad that something must be done, and
it remains to be seen whether natives or foreigners can
exercise the strongest pressure on the king.   I was un-
favourably impressed in both lectures by the way in which
the natives and their interests were quietly ignored, or
as quietly subordinated to the sugar interest.

It is never safe to forecast destiny; yet it seems most probable that sooner or later in this century, the closing catastrophe must come. The more thoughtful among the natives acquiesce helplessly and patiently in their advancing fate; but the less intelligent, as I had some opportunity of hearing at Hilo, are becoming restive and irritable, and may drift into something worse if the knowledge of the annexationist views of the foreigners is diffused among them. Things are preparing for change, and I think that the Americans will be wise in their generation if they let them ripen for many years to come. Lunalilo has a broken constitution, and probably will not live long. Kalakaua will probably succeed him, and "after him the deluge," unless he leaves a suitable successor, for there are no more chiefs with pre-eminent claims to the throne. The feeling among the people is changing, the feudal instinct is disappearing, the old despotic line of the Kamehamehas is extinct; and king-making by paper ballots, introduced a few months ago, is an approximation to president-making, with the canvassing, stumping, and wrangling, incidental to such a contested election. Annexation, or peaceful absorption, is the "manifest destiny" of the islands, with the probable result lately most wittily prophesied by Mark Twain in the *New York Tribune*, but it is impious and impolitic to hasten it. Much as I like America, I shrink from the day when her universal political corruption and her unrivalled political immorality shall be naturalised on Hawaii nei. . . . Sunday evening. The "Rolling Moses" is in, and Sabbatic quiet has given place to

general excitement.   People thought they heard her
steaming in at 4 a.m., and got up in great agitation.
Her guns fired during morning service, and I doubt
whether I or any other person heard another word of the
sermon.   The first batch of letters for the hotel came,
but none for me; the second, none for me; and I had
gone to my room in cold despair, when some one tossed
a large package in at my verandah door, and to my infinite joy I found that one of my benign fellow-passengers
in the *Nevada*, had taken the responsibility of getting my
letters at San Francisco and forwarding them here.   I
don't know how to be grateful enough to the good man.
With such late and good news, everything seems bright;
and I have at once decided to take the first schooner for
the leeward group, and remain four months longer on the
islands.

I. L. B.

LETTER XX.

I AM spending a few days on some quaint old mission premises, and the "guest house," where I am lodged, is a dobe house, with walls two feet thick, and a very thick grass roof comes down six feet all round to shade the windows. It is itself shaded by date palms and algarobas, and is surrounded by hibiscus, oleanders, and the *datura arborea(?)*, which at night fill the air with sweetness. I am the only guest, and the solitude of the guest house in which I am writing is most refreshing to tired nerves. There is not a sound but the rustling of trees.

The first event to record is that the trade winds have set in, and though they may yet yield once or twice to the *kona*, they will soon be firmly established for nine months. They are not soft airs as I supposed, but riotous, rollicking breezes, which keep up a constant clamour, blowing the trees about, slamming doors, taking liberties with papers, making themselves heard and felt everywhere, flecking the blue Pacific with foam, lowering the mercury three degrees, bringing new health and vigour with them, —wholesome, cheery, frolicsome north-easters. They brought me here from Oahu in eighteen hours, for which I thank them heartily.

You will think me a Sybarite for howling about those eighteen hours of running to leeward, when the residents of Kauai, if they have to go to Honolulu in the intervals between the quarterly trips of the *Kilauea,* have to spend from three to nine days in beating to windward. These inter-island voyages of extreme detention, rolling on a lazy swell in tropical heat, or beating for days against the strong trades without shelter from the sun, and without anything that could be called accommodation, were among the inevitable hardships to which the missionaries' wives and children were exposed in every migration for nearly forty years.

When I reached the wharf at Honolulu the sight of the *Jenny,* the small sixty-ton schooner by which I was to travel, nearly made me give up this pleasant plan, so small she looked, and so cumbered with natives and their accompaniments of mats, dogs, and calabashes of *poi.* But she is clean, and as sweet as a boat can be which carries through the tropics cattle, hides, sugar, and molasses. She is very low in the water, her deck is the real "fisherman's walk, two steps and overboard;" and on this occasion was occupied solely by natives. The Attorney General and Mrs. Judd were to have been my fellow voyagers, but my disappointment at their non-appearance was considerably mitigated by the fact that there was not stowage room for more than one white passenger! Mrs. Dexter pitied me heartily, for it made her quite ill to look down the cabin hatch; but I convinced her that no inconveniences are legitimate subjects for sympathy which are endured in the pursuit of pleasure. There was just room

on deck for me to sit on a box, and the obliging, gentlemanly master, who, with his son and myself, were the
only whites on board, sat on the taffrail.

The *Jenny* spread her white duck sails, glided gracefully away from the wharf, and bounded through the coral
reef; the red sunlight faded, the stars came out, the
Honolulu light went down in the distance, and in two
hours the little craft was out of sight of land on the broad,
crisp Pacific. It was so chilly, that after admiring as long
as I could, I dived into the cabin, a mere den, with a
table, and a berth on each side, in one of which I lay down,
and the other was alternately occupied by the captain and
his son. But limited as I thought it, boards have been
placed across on some occasions, and eleven whites have
been packed into a space six feet by eight! The heat
and suffocation were nearly intolerable, the black flies
swarming, the mosquitos countless and vicious, the fleas
agile beyond anything, and the cockroaches gigantic.
Some of the finer cargo was in the cabin, and large rats,
only too visible by the light of a swinging lamp, were
assailing it, and one with a portentous tail ran over my
berth more than once, producing a *stampede* among the
cockroaches each time. I have seldom spent a more
miserable night, though there was the extreme satisfaction of knowing that every inch of canvas was drawing.

Towards morning the short jerking motion of a ship
close hauled, made me know that we were standing in
for the land, and at daylight we anchored in Koloa Roads.
The view is a pleasant one. The rains have been
abundant, and the land, which here rises rather gradually

from the sea, is dotted with houses, abounds in signs of cultivation, and then spreads up into a rolling country between precipitous ranges of mountains. The hills look something like those of Oahu, but their wonderful greenness denotes a cooler climate and more copious rains, also their slopes and valleys are densely wooded, and Kauai obviously has its characteristic features, one of which must certainly be a superabundance of that most unsightly cactus, the prickly pear, to which the motto *nemo me impune lacessit* most literally applies.

I had not time to tell you before that this trip to Kauai was hastily arranged for me by several of my Honolulu friends, some of whom gave me letters of introduction, while others wrote forewarning their friends of my arrival. I am often reminded of Hazael's question, " Is thy servant a dog that he should do this thing ? " There is no inn or boarding house on the island, and I had hitherto believed that I could not be concussed into following the usual custom whereby a traveller throws himself on the hospitality of the residents. Yet, under the influence of Honolulu persuasions, I am doing this very thing, but with an amount of *mauvaise honte* and trepidation, which I will not voluntarily undergo again.

My first introduction was to Mrs. Smith, wife of a secular member of the Mission, and it requested her to find means of forwarding me a distance of twenty-three miles. Her son was at the landing with a buggy, a most unpleasant index of the existence of carriage roads, and brought me here ; and Mrs. Smith most courteously met me at the door. When I presented my

letter I felt like a thief detected in a first offence, but I
was at once made welcome, and my kind hosts insist on
my remaining with them for some days. Their house is
a pretty old-fashioned looking tropical dwelling, much
shaded by exotics, and the parlour is homelike with new
books. There are two sons and two daughters at home,
all, as well as their parents, interesting themselves
assiduously in the welfare of the natives. Six bright-
looking native girls are receiving an industrial training in
the house. Yesterday being Sunday, the young people
taught a Sunday school twice, besides attending the
native church, an act of respect to Divine service in
Hawaiian which always has an influence on the native
attendance.

We have had some beautiful rides in the neighbourhood.
It is a wild, lonely, picturesque coast, and the Pacific
moans along it, casting itself on it in heavy surges, with a
singularly dreary sound. There are some very fine specimens
of the phenomena called "blow-holes" on the shore, not
like the "spouting cave" at Iona, however. We spent a
long time in watching the action of one, though not the
finest. At half tide this "spouting horn" throws up a
column of water over sixty feet in height from a very
small orifice, and the effect of the compressed air rushing
through a crevice near it, sometimes with groans and
shrieks, and at others with a hollow roar like the warning
fog-horn on a coast, is magnificent, when, as to-day, there
is a heavy swell on the coast.

Kauai is much out of the island world, owing to the infrequent visits of the *Kilauea*, but really it is only twelve

hours by steam from the capital. Strangers visit it seldom, as it has no active volcano like Hawaii, or colossal crater like Maui, or anything sensational of any kind. It is called the " Garden Island," and has no great wastes of black lava and red ash like its neighbours. It is queerly shaped, almost circular, with a diameter of from twenty-eight to thirty miles, and its area is about 500 square miles. Waialeale, its highest mountain, is 4,800 feet high, but little is known of it, for it is swampy and dangerous, and a part of it is a forest-covered and little explored table-land, terminating on the sea in a range of perpendicular precipices 2,000 feet in depth, so steep it is said, that a wild cat could not get round them. Owing to these, and the virtual inaccessibility of a large region behind them, no one can travel round the island by land, and small as it is, very little seems to be known of portions of its area.

Kauai has apparently two centres of formation, and its mountains are thickly dotted with craters. The age and density of the vegetation within and without those in this Koloa district, indicate a very long cessation from volcanic action. It is truly an oddly contrived island. An elevated rolling region, park-like, liberally ornamented with clumps of *ohia, lauhala, hau,* (hibiscus) and *koa,* and intersected with gullies full of large eugenias, lies outside the mountain spurs behind Koloa. It is only the tropical trees, specially the *lauhala* or " screw pine," the whimsical shapes of outlying ridges, which now and then lie like the leaves in a book, and the strange forms of extinct craters, which distinguish it from some of our most beauti-

ful park scenery, such as Windsor Great Park or Belvoir.
It is a soft tranquil beauty, and a tolerable road which
owes little enough to art, increases the likeness to the
sweet home scenery of England. In this part of the
island the ground seems devoid of stones, and the grass is
as fine and smooth as a race course.

The latest traces of volcanic action are found here.
From the Koloa Ridge to, and into the sea, a barren
uneven surface of *pahoehoe* extends, often bulged up in
immense bubbles, some of which have partially burst,
leaving caverns, one of which, near the shore, is paved
with the ancient coral reef!

The valleys of Kauai are long, and widen to the sea,
and their dark rich soil is often ten feet deep. On
the windward side the rivers are very numerous and
picturesque. Between the strong winds and the lightness of the soil, I should think that like some parts of
the Highlands, "it would take a shower every day."
The leeward side, quite close to the sea, is flushed and
nearly barren, but there is very little of this desert
region. Kauai is less legible in its formation than
the other islands. Its mountains, from their impenetrable forests, dangerous breaks, and swampiness,
are difficult of access, and its ridges are said to be more
utterly irregular, its lavas more decomposed, and its
natural sections more completely smothered under a
profuse vegetation than those of any other island in the
tropical Pacific. Geologists suppose, from the degradation of its ridges, and the absence of any recent volcanic
products, that it is the oldest of the group, but so far as

I have read, none of them venture to conjecture how
many ages it has taken to convert its hard basalt into the
rich soil which now sustains trees of enormous size.
If this theory be correct, the volcanoes must have gone on
dying out from west to east, from north to south, till only
Kilauea remains, and its energies appear to be declining.
The central mountain of this island is built of a heavy
ferruginous basalt, but the shore ridges contain less iron,
are more porous, and vary in their structure from a
compact phonolite, to a ponderous basalt.

The population of Kauai is a widely scattered one of
4,900, and as it is an out of the world region the people
are probably better, and less sophisticated. They are
accounted rustics, or " pagans," in the classical sense,
elsewhere. Horses are good and very cheap, and the
natives of both sexes are most expert riders. Among
their feats, are picking up small coins from the ground
while going at full gallop, or while riding at the same
speed wringing off the heads of unfortunate fowls, whose
bodies are buried in the earth.

There are very few foreigners, and they appear on
the whole a good set, and very friendly among each
other. Many of them are actively interested in promoting
the improvement of the natives, but it is uphill work, and
ill-rewarded, at least on earth. The four sugar plantations employ a good deal of Chinese labour, and I fear
that the Chinamen are stealthily tempting the Hawaiians
to smoke opium.

All the world over, however far behind aborigines are
in the useful arts, they exercise a singular ingenuity in

devising means for intoxicating and stupifying themselves. On these islands distillation is illegal, and a
foreigner is liable to conviction and punishment for
giving spirits to a native Hawaiian, yet the natives
contrive to distil very intoxicating drinks, specially from
the root of the *ti* tree, and as the spirit is unrectified it is
both fiery and unwholesome. Licences to sell spirits are
confined to the capital. In spite of the notoriously bad
effect of alcohol in the tropics, people drink hard, and
the number of deaths which can be distinctly traced to
spirit drinking is quite startling.

The prohibition on selling liquor to natives is the
subject of incessant discussions and "interpellations" in
the national legislature. Probably all the natives agree in
regarding it as a badge of the "inferiority of colour;"
but I have been told generally that the most intelligent
and thoughtful among them are in favour of its continuance,
on the ground that if additional facilities for drinking
were afforded, the decrease in the population would be
accelerated. In the printed "Parliamentary Proceedings,"
I see that petitions are constantly presented praying
that the distillation of spirits may be declared free,
while a few are in favour of "total prohibition."
Another prayer is "that Hawaiians may have the same
privileges as white people in buying and drinking
spirituous liquors."

A bill to repeal the invidious distinction was brought
into the legislature not long since; but the influence of
the descendants of the missionaries and of an influential
part of the white community is so strongly against spirit

drinking, as well as against the sale of drink to the natives, that the law remains on the Statute-book.

The tone in which it was discussed is well indicated by the language of Kalakaua, the present king's rival: "The restrictions imposed by this law do the people no good, but rather harm; for instead of inculcating the principles of honour, they teach them to steal behind the bar, the stable, and the closet, where they may be sheltered from the eyes of the law. The heavy licence imposed on the liquor dealers, and the prohibition against selling to the natives are an infringement of our civil rights, binding not only the purchaser but the dealer against acquiring and possessing property. Then, Mr. President, I ask, where lies virtue, where lies justice? Not in those that bind the liberty of this people, by refusing them the privilege that they now crave, of drinking spirituous liquors without restriction. Will you by persisting that this law remain in force make us a nation of hypocrites? or will you repeal it, that honour and virtue may for once be yours, O Hawaii." A committee of the Assembly, in reporting on the question of the prohibition of the sale of intoxicants to anybody, through its chairman, Mr. Carter, stated, "Experience teaches that such prohibition could not be enforced without a strong public sentiment to indorse it, and such a sentiment does not prevail in this community, as is evidenced by the fact that the sale of intoxicating drinks to natives is largely practised in defiance of law and the executive, and that the manufacture of intoxicating drinks, though prohibited, is carried on in every district of the kingdom." So the question which is rising in every country ruled or colonised by Anglo-Saxons, is also agitated here with very strong feeling on both sides.

I was led to this digression by seeing, for the first time, some very fine plants of the *Piper methysticum*. This is *awa*, truly a "plant of renown" throughout Polynesia. Strange tales are told of it. It is said to produce profound sleep, with visions more enchanting than those of opium or hasheesh, and that its repetition, instead of being deleterious, is harmless and even wholesome. Its sale is prohibited, except on the production of evidence that it has been prescribed as a drug. Nevertheless no law on the islands is so grossly violated. It is easy to *give* it, and easy to grow it, or dig it up in the woods, so that, in spite of the legal restrictions, it is used to an enormous extent. It was proposed absolutely to prohibit the sale of it, though the sum paid for the licence is no inconsiderable item in the revenue of a kingdom, which, like many others, is experiencing the difficulty of "making both ends meet;" but the committee which sat upon the subject reported "that such prohibition is not practicable, unless its growth and cultivation are prevented. So long as public sentiment permits the open violation of the existing laws regulating its sale without rebuke, so long will it be of little use to attempt prohibition." One cannot be a day on the islands without hearing wonderful stories about *awa;* and its use is defended by some who are strongly opposed to the use as well as abuse of intoxicants. People who like "The Earl and the Doctor" delight themselves in the strongly sensuous element which pervades Polynesian life, delight themselves too, in contemplating the preparation and results of the *awa* beverage ; but both are to me extremely disgusting, and I cannot believe that a drink, which stupifies the senses, and deprives a human being of the power to exercise reason and will, is anything but hurtful to the moral nature.

While passing the Navigator group, one of my fellow-passengers, who had been for some time in Tutuila, described the preparation of *awa* poetically, the root "being masticated by the pearly teeth of dusky flower-clad maidens ;" but I was an accidental witness of a nocturnal "*awa* drinking" on Hawaii, and saw nothing but very plain prose. I feel as if I must approach the subject mysteriously. I had no time to tell you of the circumstance when it occurred, when also I was completely ignorant that it was an illegal affair; and now with a sort of "guilty knowledge" I tremble to relate what I saw, and to divulge that though I could not touch the beverage, I tasted the root, which has an acrid pungent taste, something like horse-radish, with an aromatic flavour in addition, and I can imagine that the acquired taste for it must, like other acquired tastes, be perfectly irresistible, even without the additional gratification of the results which follow its exercise.

In the particular instance which I saw, two girls who were not beautiful, and an old man who would have been hideous but for a set of sound regular teeth, were sitting on the ground masticating the *awa* root, the process being contemplated with extreme interest by a number of adults.

When, by careful chewing, they had reduced the root to a pulpy consistence, they tossed it into a large calabash, and relieved their mouths of superfluous saliva before preparing a fresh mouthful. This went on till a considerable quantity was provided, and then water was added, and the mass was kneaded and stirred with the hands till it looked like soap suds. It was then strained; and after more water had been added it was poured into cocoa-nut calabashes, and handed round. Its appearance eventually was like weak, frothy coffee and milk. The appearance of purely animal gratification on the faces of those who drank it, instead of being poetic, was of the low gross earth. Heads thrown back, lips parted with a feeble sensual smile, eyes hazy and unfocussed, arms folded on the breast, and the mental faculties numbed and sliding out of reach.

Those who drink it pass through the stage of idiocy into a deep sleep, which it is said can be reproduced once without an extra dose, by bathing in cold water. Confirmed *awa* drinkers might be mistaken for lepers, for they are covered with whitish scales, and have inflamed eyes and a leathery skin, for the epidermis is thickened and whitened, and eventually peels off. The habit has been adopted by not a few whites, specially on Hawaii, though, of course, to a certain extent clandestinely. *Awa* is taken also as a medicine, and was supposed to be a certain cure for corpulence.

The root and base of the stem are the parts used, and it is best when these are fresh. It seems to exercise a powerful fascination, and to be loved and glorified as

whisky is in Scotland, and wine in southern Europe.   In
some of the other islands of Polynesia, on festive occasions,
when the chewed root is placed in the calabash, and the
water is poured on, the whole assemblage sings appropriate songs in its praise; and this is kept up until the
decoction has been strained to its dregs.   But here, as the
using it as a beverage is an illicit process, a great mystery
attends it.   It is said that *awa* drinking is again on the
increase, and with the illicit distillation of unwholesome
spirits, and the illicit sale of imported spirits and the
opium smoking, the consumption of stimulants and
narcotics on the islands is very considerable.*

To turn from drink to climate.   It is strange that with
such a heavy rainfall, dwellings built on the ground and
never dried by fires should be so perfectly free from damp
as they are.   On seeing the houses here and in Honolulu,
buried away in dense foliage, my first thought was, "how
lovely in summer, but how unendurably damp in winter,"
forgetting that I arrived in the nominal winter, and that
it is really summer all the year.   Lest you should think
that I am perversely exaggerating the charms of the
climate, I copy a sentence from a speech made by Kamehameha IV., at the opening of an Hawaiian agricultural
society :—

"Who ever heard of winter on our shores?   Where
among us shall we find the numberless drawbacks which,
in less favoured countries, the labourer has to contend

* According to the revenue returns for the biennial period ending March
31, 1874, the revenue derived from *awa* was over $9000, and that from
opium over $46,000.

with ?   They have no place in our beautiful group, which
rests like a water lily on the swelling bosom of the Pacific.
The heaven is tranquil above our heads, and the sun
keeps his jealous eye upon us every day, while his rays
are so tempered that they never wither prematurely what
they have warmed into life."*   The kindness of my hosts
is quite overwhelming.   They will not hear of my buying
a horse, but insist on my taking away with me the one
which I have been riding since I came, the best I have
ridden on the islands, surefooted, fast, easy, and ambitious.
I have complete sympathy with the passion which the
natives have for riding.   Horses are abundant and cheap
on Kauai: a fairly good one can be bought for $20.   I
think every child possesses one.   Indeed the horses seem
to outnumber the people.

The eight native girls who are being trained and educated
here as a " family school " have their horses, and go out
to ride as English children go for a romp into a play-ground.
Yesterday Mrs. S. said, "Now, girls, get the horses,"
and soon two little creatures of eight and ten came gal-

---

* The following paragraph from Dr. Rupert Anderson's sober-minded
book on the Sandwich Islands fully bears out the king's remarks : "The
islands all lie within the range of the trade winds, which blow with great
regularity nine months of the year, and on the leeward side, where their
course is obstructed by mountains, there are regular land and sea breezes.
The weather at all seasons is delightful, the sky usually cloudless, the
atmosphere clear and bracing.   Nothing can exceed the soft brilliancy of
the moonlight nights.   Thunderstorms are rare and light in their nature.
Hurricanes are unknown.   The general temperature is the nearest in the
world to that point regarded by physiologists as most conducive to health
and longevity.   By ascending the mountains any desirable degree of
temperature may be obtained."

loping up on two spirited animals. They had not only caught and bridled them, but had put on the complicated Mexican saddles as securely as if men had done it; and I got a lesson from them in making the Mexican knot with the thong which secures the cinch, which will make me independent henceforward.

These children can all speak English, and their remarks are most original and amusing. They have not a particle of respect of manner, as we understand it, but seem very docile. They are naïve and fascinating in their manners, and the most joyous children I ever saw. When they are not at their lessons, or household occupations, they are dancing on stilts, acting plays of their own invention, riding or bathing, and they laugh all day long. Mrs. S. has trained nearly seventy since she has been here. If there were nothing else they see family life in a pure and happy form, which must in itself be a moral training, and by dint of untiring watchfulness they are kept aloof from the corrupt native associations. Indeed they are not allowed to have any intercourse with natives, for, according to one of the missionaries who has spent many years on the islands: " None know or can conceive without personal observation the nameless taint that pervades the whole garrulous talk and gregarious life of all heathen peoples, and above which our poor Hawaiian friends have not yet risen." Of this universal impurity of speech every one speaks in the strongest terms, and careful white parents not only seclude their children in early years from unrestrained intercourse with the natives, but prevent them from acquiring the Hawaiian tongue. In this respect the training of native girls involves a degree of patient watchfulness which must at times press heavily on those who undertake it, as the carefulness of years might fail of its result, if it were intermitted for one afternoon.

I. L. B.

LETTER XXI.

AFTER my letters from Hawaii, and their narratives
of volcanoes, freshets, and out of the world valleys, you
will think my present letters dull, so I must begin this
one pleasantly, by telling you that though I have no
stirring adventures to relate, I am enjoying myself and
improving again in health, and that the people are hospitable, genial, and cultivated, and that Kauai, though
altogether different from Hawaii, has an extreme beauty
altogether its own, which wins one's love, though it
does not startle one into admiration like that of the
Hawaiian gulches. Is it because that, though the magic
of novelty is over it, there is a perpetual undercurrent
of home resemblance? The dash of its musical waters
might be in Cumberland; its swelling uplands, with
their clumps of trees, might be in Kent; and then again,
steep, broken, wooded ridges, with glades of grass, suggest the Val Moutiers; and broader sweeps of mountain
outline, the finest scenery of the Alleghanies.

But yet the very things which have a certain tenderness of familiarity, are in a foreign setting. The great
expanse of restful sea, so faintly blue all day, and so
faintly red in the late afternoon, is like no other ocean

in its unutterable peace ; and this joyous, riotous trade-
wind, which rustles the trees all day, and falls asleep
at night, and cools the air, seems to come from some
widely different laboratory than that in which our vicious
east winds, and damp west winds, and piercing north
winds, and suffocating south winds are concocted.   Here
one cannot ride "into the teeth of a north-easter," for
such the trade-wind really is, without feeling at once
invigorated, and wrapped in an atmosphere of balm.   It
is not here so tropical looking as in Hawaii, and though
there are not the frightful volcanic wildernesses which
make a thirsty solitude in the centre of that island,
neither are there those bursts of tropical luxuriance
which make every gulch an epitome of Paradise: I
really cannot define the difference, for here, as there,
palms glass themselves in still waters, bananas flourish,
and the forests are green with ferns.

We took three days for our journey of twenty-three
miles from Koloa, the we, consisting of Mrs. ——, the
widow of an early missionary teacher, venerable in years
and character, a native boy of ten years old, her squire,
a second Kaluna, without Kaluna's good qualities, and
myself.   Mrs. —— is not a bold horsewoman, and preferred to keep to a foot's pace, which fretted my ambitious
animal, whose innocent antics alarmed her in turn.   We
only rode seven miles the first day, through a park-
like region, very like Western Wisconsin, and just like
what I expected and failed to find in New Zealand.
Grass-land much tumbled about, the turf very fine and
green, dotted over with clumps and single trees, with

picturesque, rocky hills, deeply cleft by water-courses
were on our right, and on our left the green slopes
blended with the flushed, stony soil near the sea, on
which indigo and various compositæ are the chief vegetation.   It was hot, but among the hills on our right, cool
clouds were coming down in frequent showers, and the
white foam of cascades gleamed among the *ohias*, whose
dark foliage at a distance has almost the look of pine
woods.

Our first halting place was one of the prettiest places I
ever saw, a buff frame-house, with a deep verandah
festooned with passion flowers, two or three guest houses
also bright with trailers, scattered about under the trees
near it, a pretty garden, a background of grey rocky hills
cool with woods and ravines, and over all the vicinity,
that air of exquisite trimness which is artificially produced
in England, but is natural here.

Kaluna the Second soon showed symptoms of being
troublesome.   The native servants were away, and he
was dull, and for that I pitied him.   He asked leave to
go back to Koloa for a "sleeping tapa," which was
refused, and either out of spite or carelessness, instead
of fastening the horses into the pasture, he let them go,
and the following morning when we were ready for our
journey they were lost.   Then he borrowed a horse, and
late in the afternoon returned with the four animals, who
were all white with foam and dust, and this escapade
detained us another night.   Subsequently, after disobey-
ing orders, he lost his horse, which was a borrowed one,
deserted his mistress, and absconded !

The slopes over which we travelled were red, hot, and stony, cleft in one place however, by a green, fertile valley, full of rice and *kalo* patches, and native houses, with a broad river, the Hanapépé, flowing quietly down the middle, which we forded near the sea, where it was half-way up my horse's sides. After plodding all day over stony soil in the changeless sunshine, as the shadows lengthened, we turned directly up towards the mountains and began a two hours ascent. It was delicious. They were so cool, so green, so varied, their grey pinnacles so splintered, their precipices so abrupt, their ravines so dark and deep, and their lower slopes covered with the greenest and finest grass; then dark *ohias* rose singly, then in twos and threes, and finally mixed in dense forest masses, with the pea-green of the *kukui*.

It became yet lovelier as the track wound through deep wooded ravines, or snaked along the narrow tops of spine-like ridges; the air became cooler, damper, and more like elixir, till at a height of 1500 feet we came upon Makaueli, ideally situated upon an unequalled natural plateau, a house of patriarchal size for the islands, with a verandah festooned with roses, fuchsias, the water lemon, and other passion flowers, and with a large guest-house attached. It stands on a natural lawn, with abrupt slopes, sprinkled with orange trees burdened with fruit, *ohias*, and hibiscus. From the back verandah the forest-covered mountains rise, and in front a deep ravine widens to the grassy slopes below and the lonely Pacific,—as I write, a golden sea, on which the island of Niihau, eighteen miles distant, floats like an amethyst.

The solitude is perfect. Except the "quarters" at the back, I think there is not a house, native or foreign, within six miles, though there are several hundred natives on the property. Birds sing in the morning, and the trees rustle throughout the day; but in the cool evenings the air is perfectly still, and the trickle of a stream is the only sound.

The house has the striking novelty of a chimney, and there is a fire all day long in the dining-room.

I must now say a little about my hosts and try to give you some idea of them. I heard their history from Mr. Damon, and thought it too strange to be altogether true until it was confirmed by themselves.* The venerable lady at the head of the house emigrated from Scotland to New Zealand many years ago, where her husband was unfortunately drowned, and she being left to bring up a large family, and manage a large property, was equally successful with both. Her great ambition was to keep her family together, something on the old patriarchal system; and when her children grew up, and it seemed as if even their very extensive New Zealand property was not large enough for them, she sold it, and embarking her family and moveable possessions on board a clipper-ship, owned and commanded by one of her sons-in-law, they sailed through the Pacific in search of a home where they could remain together.

They were strongly tempted by Tahiti, but some

* These circumstances are well-known throughout the islands, and with the omission of some personal details, there is nothing which may not be known by a larger public.

reasons having decided them against it, they sailed northwards and put into Honolulu. Mr. Damon, who was
seaman's chaplain, on going down to the wharf one day,
was surprised to find their trim barque, with this immense
family party on board, with a beautiful and brilliant old
lady at its head, books, pictures, work, and all that could
add refinement to a floating home, about them, and cattle
and sheep of valuable breeds in pens on deck. They
then sailed for British Columbia, but were much disappointed with it, and in three months they re-appeared
at Honolulu, much at a loss regarding their future
prospects.

The island of Niihau was then for sale, and in a very
short time they purchased it of Kamehameha V. for a
ridiculously low price, and taking their wooden houses with
them, established themselves for seven years. It is truly
isolated, both by a heavy surf and a disagreeable sea-
passage, and they afterwards bought this beautiful and
extensive property, made a road, and built the house.
Only the second son and his wife live now on Niihau,
where they are the only white residents among 350
natives. It has an area of 70,000 acres, and could
sustain a far larger number of sheep than the 20,000 now
upon it. It is said that the transfer of the island involved some hardships, owing to a number of the natives
having neglected to legalise their claims to their *kuleanas*,
but the present possessors have made themselves
thoroughly acquainted with the language, and take the
warmest interest in the island population. Niihau is
famous for its very fine mats, and for necklaces of shells

six yards long, as well as for the extreme beauty and variety of the shells which are found there.

The household here consists first and foremost of its head, Mrs. ——, a lady of the old Scotch type, very talented, bright, humorous, charming, with a definite character which impresses its force upon everybody; beautiful in her old age, disdaining that servile conformity to prevailing fashion which makes many old people at once ugly and contemptible: speaking English with a slight, old-fashioned, refined Scotch accent, which gives naïveté to everything she says, up to the latest novelty in theology and politics: devoted to her children and grandchildren, the life of the family, and though upwards of seventy, the first to rise, and the last to retire in the house. She was away when I came, but some days afterwards rode up on horseback, in a large drawn silk bonnet, which she rarely lays aside, as light in her figure and step as a young girl, looking as if she had walked out of an old picture, or one of Dean Ramsay's books.

Then there are her eldest son, a bachelor, two widowed daughters with six children between them, three of whom are grown up young men, and a tutor, a young Prussian officer, who was on Maximilian's staff up to the time of the Queretaro disaster, and is still suffering from Mexican barbarities. The remaining daughter is married to a Norwegian gentleman, who owns and resides on the next property. So the family is together, and the property is large enough to give scope to the grandchildren as they require it.

They are thoroughly Hawaiianised. The young people

all speak Hawaiian as easily as English, and the three
young men, who are superb young fellows, about six feet
high, not only emulate the natives in feats of horsemanship, such as throwing the lasso, and picking up a coin
while going at full gallop, but are surf-board riders, an
art which it has been said to be impossible for foreigners
to acquire.

The natives on Niihau and in this part of Kauai, call
Mrs. —— " Mama." Their rent seems to consist in
giving one or more days' service in a month, so it is a
revival of the old feudality. In order to patronise native
labour, my hosts dispense with a Chinese, and employ a
native cook, and native women come in and profess to
do some of the housework, but it is a very troublesome
arrangement, and ends in the ladies doing all the finer
cooking, and superintending the coarser, setting the table,
trimming the lamps, cutting out and "fixing" all the
needlework, besides planning the indoor and outdoor
work which the natives are supposed to do. Having
related their proficiency in domestic duties, I must add
that they are splendid horsewomen, one of them an
excellent shot, and the other has enough practical knowledge of seamanship, as well as navigation, to enable her
to take a ship round the world ! It is a busy life, owing
to the large number of natives daily employed, and the
necessity of looking after the native *lunas*, or overseers.
Dr. Smith at Koloa, twenty-two miles off, is the only
doctor on the island, and the natives resort to this house
in great numbers for advice and medicine in their many
ailments. It is much such a life as people lead at

Raasay, Applecross, or some other remote Highland
place, only that people who come to visit here, unless
they ride twenty-two miles, must come to the coast in
the *Jenny* instead of being conveyed by one of David
Hutcheson's luxurious steamers.   If the *Clansman* were
" put on," probably the great house would not contain
the strangers who would arrive !

We were sitting in the library one morning when Mr.
M., of Timaru, N.Z., rode up with an introduction, and
was of course cordially welcomed.   He goes on to England, where you will doubtless cross-question him concerning my statements.   During his visit a large party of
us made a delightful expedition to the Hanapépé Falls,
one of the " lions " of Kauai.   It is often considered too
"rough " for ladies, and when Mrs. —— and I said we
were going, I saw Mr. M. look as if he thought we should
be a dependent nuisance ; I was amused afterwards with
his surprise at Mrs. ——'s courageous horsemanship, and
at his obvious confusion as to whether he should help
us, which question he wisely decided in the negative.

If "happiness is atmosphere," we were surely happy.
The day was brilliant, and as cool as early June at home,
but the sweet, joyous trade-wind could not be brewed
elsewhere than on the Pacific.   The scenery was glorious,
and mountains, trees, frolicsome water, and scarlet birds,
all rioted as if in conscious happiness.   Existence was a
luxury, and reckless riding a mere outcome of the animal
spirits of horses and riders, and the *thud* of the shoeless
feet as the horses galloped over the soft grass was sweeter
than music.   I could hardly hold my horse at all, and

down hills as steep as the east side of Arthur's Seat, over
knife-like ridges too narrow for two to ride abreast, and
along side-tracks only a foot wide, we rode at full gallop,
till we pulled up at the top of a descent of 2,000 feet
with a broad, rapid river at its feet, emerging from
between colossal walls of rock to girdle a natural lawn of
the bright *manienie* grass. There had been a "drive"
of horses, and numbers of these, with their picturesque
saddles, were picketed there, while their yet more picturesque, scarlet-shirted riders lounged in the sun.

It was a difficult two hours' ride from thence to the
Falls, worthy of Hawaii, and since my adventures in the
Hilo gulches I cannot cross running water without feeling
an amount of nervousness which I can conceal, but cannot reason myself out of. In going and returning, we
forded the broad, rugged river twenty-six times, always
in water up to my horse's girths, and the bottom was so
rocky and full of holes, and the torrent so impetuous,
that the animals floundered badly and evidently disliked
the whole affair. Once it had been possible to ride along
the edge, but the river had torn away what there was of
margin in a freshet, so that we had to cross perpetually,
to attain the rough, boulder-strewn strips which lay
between the cliffs and itself. Sometimes we rode over
roundish boulders like those on the top of Ben Cruachan,
or like those of the landing at Iona, and most of
those under the rush of the bright foaming water were
covered with a silky green weed, on which the horses
slipped alarmingly. My companions always took the
lead, and by the time that each of their horses had

struggled, slipped, and floundered in and out of holes, and breasted and leapt up steep banks, I was ready to echo Mr. M.'s exclamation regarding Mrs. ——, " I never saw such riding; I never saw ladies with such nerve." I certainly never saw people encounter such difficulties for the sake of scenery. Generally, a fall would be regarded as practically inaccessible which could only be approached in such a way.

I will not inflict another description of similar scenery upon you, but this, though perhaps exceeding all others in beauty, is not only a type, perhaps the finest type, of a species of *cañon* very common on these islands, but is also so interesting geologically that you must tolerate a very few words upon it.

The valley for two or three miles from the sea is nearly level, very fertile, and walled in by *palis* 250 feet high, much grooved vertically, and presenting fine layers of conglomerate and grey basalt ; and the Hanapépé winds quietly through the region which it fertilises, a stream several hundred feet wide, with a soft, smooth bottom. But four miles inland the bed becomes rugged and declivitous, and the mountain walls close in, forming a most magnificent *cañon* from 1,000 to 2,500 feet deep. Other *cañons* of nearly equal beauty descend to swell the Hanapépé with their clear, cool, tributaries, and there are " meetings of the waters " worthier of verse than those of Avoca. The walls are broken and highly fantastic, narrowing here, receding there, their strangely-arched recesses festooned with the feathery trichomanes, their clustering columns and broken buttresses suggesting

some old-world minster, and their stately tiers of
columnar basalt rising one above another in barren grey
into the far-off blue sky. The river in carving out the
gorge so grandly has most energetically removed all rubbish, and even the tributaries of the lateral *cañons* do
not accumulate any " wash " in the main bed. The walls
as a rule rise clear from the stream, which, besides its
lateral tributaries, receives other contributions in the
form of waterfalls, which hurl themselves into it from
the cliffs in one leap.

After ascending it for four miles all further progress was
barred by a *pali* which curves round from the right, and
closes the chasm with a perpendicular wall, over which
the Hanapépé precipitates itself from a height of 326
feet, forming the Koula Falls. At the summit is a very
fine entablature of curved columnar basalt, resembling
the clam shell cave at Staffa, and two high, sharp, and
impending peaks on the other side form a stately gateway
for a stream which enters from another and broader
valley; but it is but one among many small cascades,
which round the arc of the falls flash out in foam among
the dark foliage, and contribute their tiny warble to the
diapason of the waterfall. It rewards one well for pene-
trating the deep gash which has been made into the
earth. It seemed so very far away from all buzzing,
frivolous, or vexing things, in the cool, dark abyss into
which only the noon-day sun penetrates. All beautiful
things which love damp ; all exquisite, tender ferns and
mosses ; all shade-loving parasites flourish there in
perennial beauty. And high above in the sunshine, the

pea-green candle-nut struggles with the dark *ohia* for precarious roothold on rocky ledges, and dense masses of Eugenia, aflame with crimson flowers, and bananas, and all the leafy wealth born of heat and damp fill up the clefts which fissure the *pali.* Every now and then some scarlet tropic bird flashed across the shadow, but it was a very lifeless and a very silent scene. The arches, buttresses, and columns suggest a temple, and the deep tone of the fall is as organ music. It is all beauty, solemnity, and worship.

It was sad to leave it and to think how very few eyes can ever feast themselves on its beauty. We came back again into gladness and sunshine, and to the vulgar necessity of eating, which the natives ministered to by presenting us with a substantial meal of stewed fowls and sweet potatoes at the nearest shanty. There must have been something intoxicating in the air, for we rode wildly and recklessly, galloping down steep hills (which on principle I object to), and putting our horses to their utmost speed. Mine ran off with me several times, and once nearly upset Mr. M.'s horse, as he probably will tell you.

The natives annoy me everywhere by their inhumanity to their horses. To-day I became an object of derision to them for hunting for sow-thistles, and bringing back a large bundle of them to my excellent animal. They starve their horses from mere carelessness or laziness, spur them mercilessly, when the jaded, famished things almost drop from exhaustion, ride them with great sores under the saddles, and with their bodies deeply cut with the rough girths; and though horses are not regarded as more essential in any part of the world, they neglect and maltreat them in every way, and laugh scornfully if one shows any consideration for them. Except for short shopping distances in Honolulu, I have never seen a native man or woman walking. They think walking a degradation, and I have seen men take the trouble to mount horses to go 100 yards.

I have no time to tell you of a three days' expedition which five of us made into the heart of the nearer mountainous district, attended by some mounted natives. Mr. K., from whose house we started, has the finest mango grove on the islands. It is a fine foliaged tree, but is everywhere covered with a black blight, which gives the groves the appearance of being in mourning, as the tough, glutinous film covers all the older leaves. The mango is an exotic fruit; and people think a great deal of it, and send boxes of mangoes as presents to their friends. It is yellow, with a reddish bloom, something like a magnum bonum plum, three times magnified. The only way of eating it in comfort is to have a tub of water beside you. It should be eaten in private by any one who wants to retain the admiration of his friends. It has an immense stone, and a disproportionately small pulp. I think it tastes strongly of turpentine at first, but this is a heresy.

Beyond Waielva and its mango groves there is a very curious sand bank about 60 feet high, formed by wind and currents, and of a steep, uniform angle from top to bottom. It is very coarse sand, composed of shells, coral, and lava. When two handfuls are slapped together, a sound like the barking of a dog ensues, hence its name, the Barking Sands. It is a common amusement with strangers to slide their horses down the steep incline, which produces a sound like subterranean thunder, which terrifies unaccustomed animals. Besides this phenomenon, the mirage is often seen on the dry, hot soil, and so perfectly, too, that strangers have been known to attempt to ride round the large lake which they saw before them.

Pleasant as our mountain trip was, both in itself, and as a specimen of the way in which foreigners recreate themselves on the islands, I was glad to get back to the broad Waimea, on which long shadows of palms reposed themselves in the slant sunshine, and in the short red twilight to arrive at this breezy height, and be welcomed by a blazing fire.

Mrs. ——, in speaking of the mode of living here, was telling me that on a recent visit to England she felt depressed the whole time by what appeared to her "the scarcity" in the country. I never knew the meaning of the Old Testament blessing of "plenty" and "bread to the full" till I was in abundant Victoria, and it is much the same here. At home we know nothing of this, which was one of the chiefest of the blessings promised in the Old Testament. Its *genialising* effect is very obvious. A man feels more practically independent, I think, when he can say to all his friends, "Drop in to dinner whenever you like," than if he possessed the franchise six times over ; and people can indulge in hospitality and exercise the franchise, too, here, for meat is only twopence a pound, and bananas can be got for the gathering. The ever-increasing cost of food with us makes free-hearted hospitality an impossibility, and withers up all those kindly instincts which find expression in housing and feeding both friends and strangers.

I. L. B.

LETTER XXII.

I RODE from Makaueli to Dr. Smith's, at Koloa, with two native attendants, a *luna* to sustain my dignity, and an inferior native to carry my carpet-bag. Horses are ridden with curb-bits here, and I had only brought a light snaffle, and my horse ran away with me again on the road, and when he stopped at last, these men rode alongside of me, mimicking me, throwing themselves back with their feet forwards, tugging at their bridles, and shrieking with laughter, exclaiming *Maikai! Maikai!* (good).

I remained several days at Koloa, and would gladly have accepted the hospitable invitation to stay as many weeks, but for a cowardly objection to " beating to windward" in the *Jenny*. The scenery in the Koloa woods is exquisitely beautiful. Such supreme beauty produces on me some of the effects which fine music has upon those who have an exquisite sense of it. It speaks in a language of its own, like music, and is equally untranslatable.

One day, the girls asked me to go with them to the forests and return by moonlight, but they only spoke of them as the haunts of ferns, because they supposed that I should

think nothing of them after the forests of Australia and
New Zealand! They were not like the tropical woods of
Hawaii, and owe more to the exceeding picturesqueness
of the natural scenery. Hawaii is all domes and humps,
Kauai all peaks and sierras. There were deep ravines,
along which bright fern-shrouded streams brawled among
wild bananas, overarched by Eugenias, with their gory
blossoms : walls of peaks, and broken precipices, grey
ridges rising out of the blue forest gloom, high mountains with mists wreathing their spiky summits, for a
background: gleams of a distant silver sea: and the nearer
many-tinted woods were not matted together in jungle
fashion, but festooned and adorned with numberless
lianas, and even the prostrate trunks of fallen trees took
on new beauty from the exquisite ferns which covered
them. Long cathedral aisles stretched away in far-off
vistas, and so perfect at times was the Gothic illusion,
that I found myself listening for anthems and the roll of
organs. So cool and moist it was, and triumphantly
redundant in vagaries of form and greenery, it was a forest
of forests, and it became a necessity to return the next
day, and the next; and I think if I had remained at
Koloa I should have been returning still.

This place is outside the beauty, among cane-fields,
and is much swept by the trade winds. Mr. Rice, my
host, is the son of an esteemed missionary, and he and
his wife take a deep interest in the natives. When he
brought her here as a bride a few months ago, the natives
were so delighted that he had married an island lady who
could speak Hawaiian, that they gave them an *ahaaina*,

A FOREST STREAM IN KAUAI. [*Page* 316.

or native feast, on a grand scale. The food was cooked
in Polynesian style, by being wrapped up in greens called
luau, and baked underground. There were two bullocks,
nineteen hogs, a hundred fowls, any quantity of *poi* and
fruit, and innumerable native dishes. Five hundred
natives, profusely decorated with *leis* of flowers and
mailé, were there, and each brought a gift for the bride.
After the feast they chaunted *mélés* in praise of Mr. Rice,
and Mrs. Rice played to them on her piano, an instru-
ment which they had not seen before, and sang songs to
them in Hawaiian. Mr. and Mrs. R. teach in and
superintend a native Sunday-school, and have enlisted
twenty native teachers, and in order to keep up the
interest and promote cordial feeling, they and the other
teachers meet once a month for a regular teachers'
meeting, taking the houses in rotation. Refreshments
are served afterwards, and they say that nothing can be
more agreeable than the good feeling at the meetings,
and the tact and graceful hospitality which prevail at
the subsequent entertainments.

The Hawaiians are a most pleasant people to foreigners,
but many of their ways are altogether aggravating.
Unlike the Chinamen, they seldom do a thing right
twice. In my experience, they have almost never saddled
and bridled my horse quite correctly. Either a strap
has been left unbuckled, or the blanket has been wrinkled
under the saddle. They are too easy to care much about
anything. If any serious loss arises to themselves or
others through their carelessness, they shrug their
shoulders, and say, " What does it matter ? " Any
trouble is just a *pilikia*. They can't help it. If they

lose your horse from neglecting to tether it, they only
laugh when they find you are wanting to proceed on your
journey. Time, they think, is nothing to any one.
"What's the use of being in a hurry?" Their neglect
of their children, a cause from which a large proportion
of the few born perish, is a part of this universal carelessness. The crime of infanticide, which formerly
prevailed to a horrible extent, has long been extinct;
but the love of pleasure and the dislike of trouble which
partially actuated it, are apparently still stronger among
the women than the maternal instinct, and they do not
take the trouble necessary to rear their infants. They
give their children away, too, to a great extent, and I
have heard of instances in which children have been so
passed from hand to hand, that they are quite ignorant
of their real parents. It is an odd caprice in some cases,
that women who have given away their own children are
passionately attached to those whom they have received as presents, but I have nowhere seen such tenderness lavished upon infants as upon the pet dogs that
the women carry about with them. Though they are so
deficient in adhesiveness to family ties, that wives seek
other husbands, and even children desert their parents
for adoptive homes, the tie of race is intensely strong,
and they are remarkably affectionate to each other,
sharing with each other food, clothing, and all that they
possess. There are no paupers among them but the
lunatics and the lepers, and vagrancy is unknown.
Happily on these sunny shores no man or woman can be
tempted into sin by want.

With all their faults, and their intolerable carelessness,

all the foreigners like them, partly from the absolute security which they enjoy among them. They are so thoroughly good-natured, mirthful, and friendly, and so ready to enter heart and soul into all *haole* diversions, that the islands would be dreary indeed if the dwindling race became extinct.

Among the many misfortunes of the islands, it has been a fortunate thing that the missionaries' families have turned out so well, and that there is no ground for the common reproach that good men's sons turn out reprobates.

The Americans show their usual practical sagacity in missionary matters. In 1853, when these islands were nominally Christianised, and a native ministry consisting of fifty-six pastors had been established, the American Board of Missions, which had expended during thirty-five years nine hundred and three thousand dollars in Christianising the group, and had sent out 149 male and female missionaries, resolved that it should not receive any further aid either in men or money.

In the early days, the King and chiefs had bestowed lands upon the Mission, on which substantial mission premises had been erected, and on withdrawing from the islands, the Board wisely made over these lands to the Mission families as freehold property. The result has been that, instead of a universal migration of the young people to America, numbers of them have been attached to Hawaiian soil. The establishment at an early date of Punahou College, at which for a small sum both boys and girls receive a first-class English education, also

contributed to retain them on the islands, and numbers
of the young men entered into sugar-growing, cattle-
raising, storekeeping, and other businesses here.   At
Honolulu and Hilo a large proportion of the residents of
the upper class are missionaries' children ; most of the
respectable foreigners on Kauai are either belonging to,
or intimately connected with, the Mission families ; and
they are profusely scattered through Maui and Hawaii in
various capacities, and are bound to each other by ties of
extreme intimacy and friendliness, as well as by marriage
and affinity.   This "clan" has given society what it
much wants—a sound moral core, and in spite of all
disadvantageous influences, has successfully upheld a
public opinion in favour of religion and virtue.   The
members of it possess the moral backbone of New
England, and its solid good qualities, a thorough knowledge of the language and habits of the natives, a hereditary interest in them, a solid education, and in many
cases much general culture.

In former letters I have mentioned Mr. Coan and Mr.
Lyons as missionaries.   I must correct this, as there
have been no actual missionaries on the islands for
twenty years.   When the Board withdrew its support,
many of the missionaries returned to America ; some,
especially the secular members, went into other positions
on the group, while the two first-mentioned and two or
three besides, remained as pastors of native congregations.

I venture to think that the Board has been premature
in transferring the islands to a native pastorate at such

a very early stage of their Christianity. Such a pastorate must be too feeble to uphold a robust Christian standard. As an adjunct it would be essential to the stability of native Christianity, but it is not possible that it can be trusted as the sole depository of doctrine and discipline, and even were it all it ought to be, it would lack the power to repress the lax morality which is ruining the nation. Probably each year will render the overhaste of this course more apparent, and it is likely that some other mode of upholding pure Christianity will have to be adopted, when the venerable men who now sustain and guide the native pastors by their influence shall have been gathered to their rest.

I. L. B.

LETTER XXIII.

BEFORE leaving Kauai I must tell you of a solitary expedition I have just made to the lovely valley of Hana- lei. It was only a three days' "frolic," but an essentially "good time." Mr. Rice provided me with a horse and a very pleasing native guide. I did not leave till two in the afternoon, as I only intended to ride fifteen miles, and, as the custom is, ask for a night's lodging at a settler's house. However, as I drew near Mr. B.'s ranch, I felt my false courage oozing out of the tips of my fingers, and as I rode up to the door, certain obnoxious colonial words, such as "sundowners," and "bummers," occurred to me, and I felt myself a "sundowner" when the host came out and asked me to dismount. He said he was sorry his wife was away, but he would do his best for me in her absence, and took me down to a room where a very rough-looking man was tenderly nursing a baby a year old, which was badly burned or scalded, and which began to cry violently at my entrance, and required the united efforts of the two bereaved men to pacify it. They had the charge of it between them. I took it while they went to make some tea, and it kicked, roared, and fought until they came back. By that time I had prepared a neat little speech, saying that I was not the least tired, and would only

trouble them for a glass of water; and, having covered
my cowardice successfully, I went on, having been urged
by the hospitable ranchman to be sure to stay for the
night at his father-in-law's house, a few miles further on.
I saw that the wishes of the native went in the same
direction, but after my one experience I assured myself
that I had not the necessary nerve for this species of
mendicancy, and went on as fast as the horse could gallop
wherever the ground admitted of it, the scenery becoming
more magnificent as the dark, frowning mountains of
Hanalei loomed through the gathering twilight.

But they were fifteen miles off, and on the way we
came to a broad, beautiful ravine, through which a broad,
deep river glided into the breakers. I had received some
warnings about this, but it was supposed that we could
cross in a ferry scow, of which, however, I only found the
bones. The guide and the people at the ferryman's house
talked long without result, but eventually, by many signs,
I contrived to get them to take me over in a crazy punt,
half full of water, and the horses swam across. Before
we reached the top of the ravine, the last redness of twilight had died from off the melancholy ocean, the black
forms of mountains looked huge in the darkness, and the
wind sighed so eerily through the creaking *lauhalas*, as
to add much to the effect. It became so very dark that
I could only just see my horse's ears, and we found ourselves occasionally in odd predicaments, such as getting
into crevices, or dipping off from steep banks; and it was
in dense darkness that we arrived above what appeared to
be a valley with twinkling lights, lying at the foot of a

precipice, and walled in on all sides but one by lofty
mountains. It was rather queer, diving over the wooded
pali on a narrow track, with nothing in sight but the
white jacket of the native, who had already indicated that
he was at the end of his resources regarding the way, but
just as a river gleamed alarmingly through the gloom, a
horseman on a powerful horse brushed through the wood,
and on being challenged in Hawaiian replied in educated
English, and very politely turned with me, and escorted
me over a disagreeable ferry in a scow without rails, and
to my destination, two miles beyond.

Yesterday, when I left, the morning was brilliant, and
after ascending the *pali*, I stayed for some time on an
eminence which commands the valley, presented by Mr.
Wyllie to Lady Franklin, in compliment to her admiration
of its loveliness. Hanalei has been likened by some to
Paradise, and by others to the Vale of Caschmir. Everyone who sees it raves about it. " See Hanalei and die,"
is the feeling of the islanders, and certainly I was not
disappointed, nor should I be with Paradise itself were it
even a shade less fair ! It has every element of beauty,
and in the bright sunshine, with the dark shadows on the
mountains, the waterfalls streaking their wooded sides,
the river rushing under *kukuis* and *ohias*, and then lingering lovingly amidst living greenery, it looked as if the
curse had never lighted there.

Its mouth, where it opens on the Pacific, is from two
to three miles wide, but the boundary mountains gradually
approach each other, so that five miles from the sea a narrow gorge of wonderful beauty alone remains. The crystal

Hanalei flows placidly to the sea for the last three or four miles, tired by its impetuous rush from the mountains, and mirrors on its breast hundreds of acres of cane, growing on a plantation formerly belonging to Mr. Wyllie, an enterprising Ayrshire man, and one of the ablest and most disinterested foreigners who ever administered Hawaiian affairs. Westward of the valley there is a region of mountains, slashed by deep ravines. The upper ridges are densely timbered, and many of the *ohias* have a circumference of twenty-five feet, three feet from the ground. It was sad to turn away for ever from the loveliness of Hanalei, even though by taking another route, which involved a ride of forty miles, I passed through and in view of, most entrancing picturesqueness. Indeed, for mere loveliness, I think that part of Kauai exceeds anything that I have seen.

The atmosphere and scenery were so glorious that it was possible to think of nothing all day, but just allow oneself passively to drink in sensations of exquisite pleasure. I wish all the hard-worked people at home, who lead joyless lives in sunless alleys, could just have one such day, and enjoy it as I did, that they might know how fair God's earth is, and how far fairer His Paradise must be, if even from this we cannot conceive " of the things which He hath prepared for them that love Him." I never before felt so sad for those whose lives are passed amidst unpropitious surroundings, or so thankful for my own capacity of enjoying nature.

Just as we were coming up out of a deep river, a native riding about six feet from me was caught in a quicksand.

He jumped off, but the horse sank half way up its body. I wanted to stay and see it extricated, for its struggles only sank it deeper, but the natives shrugged their shoulders, and said in Hawaiian, "only a horse," and something they always say when anything happens, equivalent to "What's the odds?" It was a joyously-exciting day, and I was galloping down a grass hill at a pace which I should not have assumed had white people been with me, when a native rode up to me and said twice over, "*maikai! paniola*," and laughed heartily. When my native came up, he pointed to me and again said "*paniola*;" and afterwards we were joined by two women, to whom my guide spoke of me as *paniola*; and on coming to the top of a hill they put their horses into a gallop, and we all rode down at a tremendous, and, as I should once have thought, a break-neck speed, when one of the women patted me on the shoulder, exclaiming, "*maikai! maikai! paniola.*" I thought they said "*spaniola*," taking me for a Spaniard, but on reaching Lihue, and asking the meaning of the word, Mrs. Rice said, "Oh, lassoing cattle, and all that kind of thing." I was disposed to accept the inference as a compliment; but when I told Mrs. R. that the word had been applied to myself, she laughed very much, and said she would have toned down its meaning had she known that!

We rode through forests lighted up by crimson flowers, through mountain valleys greener than Alpine meadows, descended steep *palis*, and forded deep, strong rivers, pausing at the beautiful Wailua Falls, which leap in a broad sheet of foam and a heavy body of water into a dark

basin, walled in by cliffs so hard that even the ferns and
mosses which revel in damp, fail to find roothold in the
naked rock.   Both above and below, this river passes
through a majestic *cañon*, and its neighbourhood abounds
in small cones, some with crateriform cavities at the top,
some broken down, and others, apparently of great age,
wooded to their summits.   A singular ridge, called
Mauna Kalalea, runs along this part of the island, picturesque beyond anything, and, from its abruptness and
peculiar formation, it deceives the eye into judging it to
be as high as the gigantic domes of Hawaii.   Its peaks
are needle-like, or else blunt projections of columnar
basalt, rising ofttimes as terraces.   At a beautiful village
called Anahola the ridge terminates abruptly, and its
highest portion is so thin that a large patch of sky can be
seen through a hole which has been worn in it.

I reached Lihue by daylight, having established my
reputation as a *paniola* by riding forty miles in 7½ hours,
"very good time" for the islands.   I hope to return
here in August, as my hospitable friends will not allow
me to leave on any other condition.   The kindness I
have received on Kauai is quite overwhelming, and I shall
remember its refined and virtuous homes as long as its
loveliness and delicious climate.

HAWAIIAN HOTEL.   HONOLULU.   April 23rd.

I have nothing new to add.   Mr. Dexter is so far
recovered that I fear I shall not find my friends here
on my return.   People are in the usual fever about the
mail, and I must close this.   I. L. B.

LETTER XXIV.

IT is three weeks since I left the Hawaiian Hotel and its green mist of algarobas, but my pleasant visits in this island do not furnish much that will interest you. There was great excitement on the wharf at Honolulu the evening I left. It was crowded with natives, the king's band was playing, old hags were chanting *melés*, and several of the royal family, and of the "upper ten thousand" were there, taking leave of the Governess of Hawaii, the Princess Keelikolani, the late king's half-sister. The throng and excitement were so great, that we were outside the reef before I got a good view of this lady, the largest and the richest woman on the islands. Her size and appearance are most unfortunate, but she is said to be good and kind. She was dressed in a very common black *holuku*, with a red bandana round her throat, round which she wore a *lé* of immense oleanders, as well as round her hair, which was cut short. She had a large retinue, and her female attendants all wore *leis* of oleander. They spread very fine mats on the deck, under *pulu* beds, covered with gorgeous quilts, on which the Princess and her suite slept, and in the morning the beds were removed, breakfast was spread on the mats, and she, some of her attendants, and two or three white men who received invitations, sat on the deck round it.   It was a far less attractive meal than that which the serene steward served below.   The calabashes, which contained the pale pink *poi*, were of highly polished *kou* wood, but there were no foreign refinements.   The other dishes were several kinds of raw fish, dried devil-fish, boiled *kalo*, sweet potatoes, bananas, and cocoa-nut milk.

I had a very uncomfortable night on a mattress on the deck, which was overcrowded with natives, and some of the native women and two foreigners had got a whiskey bottle, and behaved disgracefully.   We went round by the Leper Island.

I landed at Maaleia, on the leeward side of the sandy isthmus which unites East and West Maui, got a good horse, and, with Mr. G——, rode across to the residence of "Father Alexander," at Wailuku, a flourishing district of sugar plantations.   Mr. and Mrs. Alexander were among the early missionaries, and still live on the mission premises.   Several of their sons are settled on the island in the sugar business, and it was to the Heiku plantation, fifteen miles off, of which Mr. S. Alexander is manager, that I went on the following day, still escorted by Mr. G——.   Here we heard that captains of schooners which had arrived from Hawaii, report that a light is visible on the terminal crater of Mauna Loa, 14,000 feet above the sea, that Kilauea, the flank crater, is unusually active, and that several severe shocks of earthquake have been felt. This is exciting news.

Behind Wailuku is the Iao valley, up which I rode with two island friends, and spent a day of supreme, satisfied admiration. At Iao people may throw away pen and pencil in equal despair. The trail leads down a gorge dark with forest trees, and then opens out into an amphitheatre, walled in by precipices, from three to six thousand feet high, misty with a thousand waterfalls, plumed with *kukuis*, and feathery with ferns. A green-clad needle of stone, one thousand feet in height, the last refuge of an army routed when the Wailuku (waters of destruction) ran red with blood, keeps guard over the valley. Other needles there are ; and mimic ruins of bastions and ramparts and towers came and passed mysteriously: and the shining fronts of turrets gleamed through trailing mists, changing into drifting visions of things that came and went, in sunshine and shadow, mountains raising battered peaks into a cloudless sky, green crags moist with ferns, and mists of water that could not fall, but frittered themselves away on slopes of maiden-hair, and depths of forest and ferns through which bright streams warble through the summer years. Clouds boiling up from below drifted at times across the mountain fronts, or lay like snow masses in the unsunned chasms : and over the grey crags and piled up pinnacles, and glorified green of the marvellous vision, lay a veil of thin blue haze, steeping the whole in a serenity which seemed hardly to belong to earth.

The track from Wailuku to Heiku is over a Sahara in miniature, a dreary expanse of sand and shifting sand-hills, with a dismal growth in some places of thornless thistles and indigo, and a tremendous surf thunders on the margin. Trackless, glaring, choking, a guide is absolutely necessary to a stranger, for the footprints or wheel-marks of one moment are obliterated the next. I crossed the isthmus three times, and the third time was quite as incapable of shaping my course across it as the first, and though I had recklessly declined a guide, was only too thankful for the one who was forced upon me. It is a hateful ride, yet anything so hideous and aggressively odious is a salutary experience in a land of so much beauty. Sand, sand, sand! Sand-hills, smooth and red; sand plains, rippled, white, and glaring; sand drifts shifting; sand clouds whirling; sand in your eyes, nose, and mouth; sand stinging your face like pin points; sand hiding even your horse's ears; sand rippling like waves, hissing like spin-drift, malignant, venomous! You can only open one eye at a time for a wink at where you are going. Looking down upon it from Heiku, you can see nothing all day but the dense brown clouds of a perpetual sand-storm.

My charming hostess and her husband made Heiku so fascinating, that I only quitted it hoping to return. The object which usually attracts strangers to Maui is the great dead volcano of Haleakala, "The house of the sun," and I was fortunate in all the circumstances of my ascent. My host at Heiku provided me with a horse and native attendant, and I rode over the evening before to the house of his brother, Mr. J. Alexander, who accompanied me, and his intelligent and cultured society was one of the pleasures of the day.

People usually go up in the afternoon, camp near the summit, light a fire, are devoured by fleas, roast and

freeze alternately till morning, and get up to see the grand
spectacle of the sunrise, but I think our plan pre-
ferable, of leaving at two in the morning. The moon
had set. It was densely dark, and it was raining on
one side of the road, though quite fine on the other. By
the lamplight which streamed from our early breakfast
table, I only saw wet mules and horses, laden with gear
for a mountain ascent, a trim little Japanese, who darted
about helping, my native, who was picturesquely dressed
in a Mexican poncho, Mr. Alexander, who wore something which made him unrecognisable ; and myself, a
tatterdemalion figure, wearing a much-worn green top-
coat of his over my riding suit, and a tartan shawl
arranged so as to fall nearly to my feet. Then we went
forth into the darkness. The road soon degenerated into
a wood road, then into a bridle track, then into a mere
trail ascending all the way ; and at dawn, when the rain
was over, we found ourselves more than half-way up the
mountain, amidst rocks, scoriæ, tussocks, *ohelos*, a few
common compositæ, and a few coarse ferns and woody
plants, which became coarser and scantier the higher we
went up, but never wholly ceased ; for, at the very summit, 10,200 feet high, there are some tufts of grass, and
stunted specimens of a common asplenium in clefts.
Many people suffer from mountain sickness on this ascent, but I suffered from nothing but the excruciating
cold, which benumbed my limbs and penetrated to my
bones ; and though I dismounted several times and tried
to walk, uphill exercise was impossible in the rarefied
air. The atmosphere was but one degree below the

freezing-point, but at that height, a brisk breeze on soaked clothes was scarcely bearable.

The sunrise turned the densely packed clouds below into great rosy masses, which broke now and then, showing a vivid blue sea, and patches of velvety green. At seven, after toiling over a last steep bit, among scoriæ, and some very scanty and unlovely vegetation, we reached what was said to be the summit, where a ragged wall of rock shut out the forward view. Dismounting on some cinders, we stepped into a gap, and from thence looked down into the most gigantic crater on the earth. I confess that with the living fires of Kilauea in my memory, I was at first disappointed with the deadness of a volcano of whose activity there are no traditions extant. Though during the hours which followed, its majesty and wonderment grew upon me, yet a careful study of the admirable map of the crater, a comparison of the heights of the very considerable cones which are buried within it, and the attempt to realize the figures which represent its circumference, area, and depth, not only give a far better idea of it than any verbal description, but impress its singular sublimity and magnitude upon one far more forcibly than a single visit to the actual crater.

I mentioned in one of my first letters that East Maui, that part of the island which lies east of the isthmus of perpetual dust-storms, consists of a mountain dome 10,000 feet in height, with a monstrous base. Its slopes are very regular, varying from eight to ten degrees. Its lava-beds differ from those of Kauai and Oahu in being lighter in colour, less cellular, and more impervious to water. The windward side of the mountain is gashed and slashed by streams, which in their violence have excavated large pot-holes, which serve as reservoirs, and it is covered to a height of over 2000 feet by a luxuriant growth of timber. On the leeward side, several black and very fresh-looking streams of lava run into the sea, and the whole coast for some height above the shore shows most vigorous volcanic action. Elsewhere the rock is red and broken, and lateral cones abound near the base.

The ascent from Makawao, though it is over rather a desolate tract of land, has in its lower stages such a dismal growth of pining *koa* and spurious sandal-wood, and in its upper ones so much *ohelo* scrub, with grass and common aspleniums quite up to the top, that as one sits lazily on one's sure-footed horse, the fact that one is ascending a huge volcano is not forced upon one by any overmastering sterility and nakedness. Somehow, one expects to pass through some ulterior stage of blackness up to the summit. It is no such thing; and the great surprise of Haleakala to me was, that when according to calculation there should have been a summit, an abyss of vast dimensions opened below. The mountain top has been in fact blown off, and one is totally powerless to imagine what the forces must have been which rent it asunder.

The crater was clear of fog and clouds, and lighted in every part by the risen sun. The whole, with its contents, can be seen at a single glance, though its girdling precipices are nineteen miles in extent. Its huge, irregular floor is 2000 feet below; New York might be hidden away within it, with abundant room to spare; and more than one of the numerous subsidiary cones which uplift themselves solitary or in clusters through the area, attain the height of Arthur's Seat at Edinburgh. On the north and east are the Koolau and Kaupo Gaps, as deep as the crater, through which oceans of lava found their way to the sea. It looks as if the volcanic forces, content with rending the mountain top in twain, had then passed into an endless repose.

The crater appears to be composed of a hard grey clinkstone, much fissured; but lower down the mountain, the rock is softer, and has a bluish tinge. The internal cones are of very regular shape, and most of them look as if their fires had only just gone out, with their sides fiercely red, and their central cavities lined with layers of black ash. They are all composed of cinders of light specific gravity, and much of the ash is tinged with the hydrated oxide of iron. Very few of the usual volcanic products are present.* Small quantities of sulphur, in a very impure form, exist here and there, but there are no sulphur or steam-cracks, or hot springs on any part of the mountain. With its cold ashes and dead force, it is a most tremendous spectacle of the power of fire.

Some previous travellers had generously left some faggots on the summit, and we made a large fire for

* According to Mr. Brigham, the products of the Hawaiian volcanos are: native sulphur, pyrites, salt, sal ammoniac, hydrochloric acid, hæmatite, sulphurous acid, sulphuric acid, quartz, crystals, palagonite, feldspar, chrysolite, Thompsonite, gypsum, solfatarite, copperas, nitre, arragonite, Labradorite, limonite.

warmth, and I rolled my blanket round me, and sat with
my feet among the hot embers, but all to no purpose.
The wind was strong and keen, and the fierce splendour
of the tropic sun conveyed no heat. Mr. A. went away
investigating, the native rolled himself in his poncho and
fell asleep by the fire, and I divided the time between
glimpses into the awful desolation of the crater, snatched
between the icy gusts of wind, and the enjoyment of the
wonderful cloud scenery which to everybody is a great
charm of the view from Haleakala. The day was perfect; for first we had an inimitable view of the crater
and all that could be seen from the mountain-top, and
then an equally inimitable view of Cloudland. There
was the gaunt, hideous, desolate abyss, with its fiery
cones, its rivers and surges of black lava and grey ash,
crossing and mingling all over the area, mixed with
splotches of colour and coils of satin rock, its walls dark
and frowning, everywhere riven and splintered, and clouds
perpetually drifting in through the great gaps, and filling
up the whole crater with white swirling masses, which
in a few minutes melted away in the sunshine, leaving it
all as sharply definite as before. Before noon clouds
surrounded the whole mountain, not in the vague floccu-
lent, meaningless masses one usually sees, but in Arctic
oceans, where lofty icebergs, floes and pack, lay piled on
each other, glistening with the frost of a Polar winter;
then alps on alps, and peaks of well remembered ranges
gleaming above glaciers, and the semblance of forests in
deep ravines loaded with new fallen snow. Snow-drifts,
avalanches, oceans held in bondage of eternal ice, and all

this massed together, shifting, breaking, glistering, filling up the broad channel which divides Maui from Hawaii, and far away above the lonely masses, rose, in turquoise blue, like distant islands, the lofty Hawaiian domes of Mauna Kea and Mauna Loa, with snow on Mauna Kea yet more dazzling than the clouds. There never was a stranger contrast than between the hideous desolation of the crater below, and those blue and jewelled summits rising above the shifting clouds.

After some time the scene shifted, and through glacial rifts appeared as in a dream the Eeka mountains which enfold the Iao valley, broad fields of cane 8000 feet below, the flushed palm-fringed coast, and the deep blue sea sleeping in perpetual calm. But according to the well-known fraud which isolated altitudes perpetrate upon the eye, it appeared as if we were looking *up* at our landscape, not down ; and no effort of the eye or imagination would put things at their proper levels.

But gradually the clouds massed themselves, the familiar earth disappeared, and we were " pinnacled in mid-heaven " in unutterable isolation, blank forgotten units, in a white, wonderful, illuminated world, without permanence or solidity. Our voices sounded thin in the upper air. The keen, incisive wind that swept the summit, had no kinship with the soft breezes which were rustling the tasselled cane in the green fields of earth which had lately gleamed through the drift. It was a new world and without sympathy, a solitude which could be felt. Was it nearer God, I wonder, because so far from man and his little works and ways ? At least they

seemed little there, in presence of the tokens of a
catastrophe which had not only blown off a mountain
top, and scattered it over the island, but had disem-
bowelled the mountain itself to a depth of 2000 feet.

Soon after noon we began to descend; and in a hollow
of the mountain, not far from the ragged edge of the
crater, then filled up with billows of cloud, we came upon
what we were searching for; not, however, one or two,
but thousands of silverswords, their cold, frosted silver
gleam making the hill-side look like winter or moonlight.
They can be preserved in their beauty by putting them
under a glass shade, but it must be of monstrous dimensions, as the finer plants measure 2 ft. by 18 in. without
the flower stalk. They exactly resemble the finest work
in frosted silver, the curve of their globular mass of
leaves is perfect, and one thinks of them rather as the
base of an *épergne* for an imperial table, or as a prize at
Ascot or Goodwood, than as anything organic. A particular altitude and temperature appear essential to them,
and they are not found straggling above or below a given
line.

We reached Makawao very tired, soon after dark, to be
heartily congratulated on our successful ascent, and bearing no .worse traces of it than lobster-coloured faces,
badly blistered.

After accepting sundry hospitalities I rode over here,
skirting the mountain at a height of 2000 feet, a most
tedious ride, only enlivened by the blaze of nasturtiums
in some of the shallow gulches. It is very pretty here,
and I wish all invalids could revel in the sweet changeless

air. The name signifies " ripe bread-fruit of the
gods." The plantation is 2000 feet above the sea, and
is one of the finest on the islands; and owing to the
slow maturity of the cane at so great a height, the yield
is from five to six tons an acre. Water is very scarce;
all that is used in the boiling-house and elsewhere has
been carefully led into concrete tanks for storage, and
even the walks in the proprietor's beautiful garden are
laid with cement for the same purpose. He has planted
many thousand Australian eucalyptus trees on the hill-
side in the hope of procuring a larger rainfall, so that
the neighbourhood has quite an exotic appearance.

The coast is black and volcanic-looking below, jutting
into the sea in naked lava promontories, which nature
has done nothing to drape. Concerning a river of
specially black lava, which runs into the sea to the south
of this house, the following legend is told :—

" A withered old woman stopped to ask food and
hospitality at the house of a dweller on this promontory,
noted for his penuriousness. His *kalo* patches flourished,
cocoa-nuts and bananas shaded his hut, nature was lavish
of her wealth all round him. But the withered hag was
sent away unfed, and as she turned her back on the man
she said, ' I will return to-morrow.'

" This was Pélé, the goddess of the volcano, and she
kept her word, and came back the next day in earthquakes and thunderings, rent the mountain, and blotted
out every trace of the man and his dwelling with a flood
of fire."

Maui is very "foreign" and civilised, and although it has a native population of over 12,000, the natives are much crowded on plantations, and one encounters little of native life. There is a large society composed of planters' and merchants' families, and the residents are profuse in their hospitality. It is not infrequently taken undue advantage of, and I have heard of planters compelled to feign excuses for leaving their houses, in order to get rid of unintroduced and obnoxious visitors, who have quartered themselves on them for weeks at a time. It is wonderful that their patient hospitality is not worn out, even though, as they say, they sometimes "entertain angels unawares."

                                                    I. L. B.

LETTER XXV.

My departure from Ulupalakua illustrates some of the uncertainties of island travelling. On Monday night my things were packed, and my trunk sent off to the landing; but at five on Tuesday, Mr. Whipple came to my door to say that the *Kilauea* was not in Lahaina roads, and was probably laid up for repairs. I was much disappointed, for the mild climate had disagreed with me, and I was longing for the roystering winds and unconventional life of windward Hawaii, and there was not another steamer for three weeks.

However, some time afterwards, I was unpacking, and in the midst of a floor littered with ferns, photographs, books, and clothes, when Mrs. W. rushed in to say that the steamer was just reaching the landing below, and that there was scarcely the barest hope of catching her. Hopeless as the case seemed, we crushed most of my things promiscuously into a carpet bag, Mr. W. rode off with it, a horse was imperfectly saddled for me, and I mounted him, with my bag, straps, spurs, and a package of ferns in one hand, and my plaid over the saddle, while Mrs. W. stuffed the rest of my possessions into a clothes bag, and the Chinaman ran away frantically to catch a horse on which to ride down with them.

I galloped off after Mr. W., though people called to me that I could not catch the boat, and that my horse would fall on the steep broken descent. My saddle slipped over his neck, but he still sped down the hill with the rapid "racking" movement of a Narraganset pacer. First a new veil blew away, next my plaid was missing, then I passed my trunk on the ox-cart which should have been at the landing; but still though the heat was fierce, and the glare from the black lava blinding, I dashed heedlessly down, and in twenty minutes had ridden three miles down a descent of 2,000 feet, to find the *Kilauea* puffing and smoking with her anchor up; but I was in time, for her friendly clerk, knowing that I was coming, detained the scow. You will not wonder at my desperation when I tell you that half-way down, a person called to me, "Mauna Loa is in action!"

While I was slipping off the saddle and bridle, Mr. W. arrived with the carpet-bag, yet more over-heated and shaking with exertion than I was, then the Chinaman with a bag of oddments, next a native who had picked up my plaid and ferns on the road, and another with my trunk, which he had rescued from the ox-cart; so I only lost my veil and two brushes, which are irreplaceable here.

The quiet of the nine hours' trip in the *Kilauea* restored my equanimity, and prepared me to enjoy the delicious evening which followed. The silver waters of Kawaihae Bay reflected the full moon, the three great mountains of Hawaii were cloudless as I had not before seen them, all the asperity of the leeward shore was

softened into beauty, and the long shadows of bending
palms were as still and perfect as the palms themselves.
But there was a new sight above the silver water, for the
huge dome of Mauna Loa, forty miles away, was burning
red and fitfully. A horse and servant awaited me, and
we were soon clattering over the hard sand by the
shining sea, and up the ascent which leads to the windy
table-lands of Waimea. The air was like new life. At a
height of 500 feet we met the first whiff of the trades,
the atmosphere grew cooler and cooler, the night-wind
fresher, the moonlight whiter; wider the sweeping
uplands, redder the light of the burning mountain, till I
wrapped my plaid about me, but still was chilled to the
bone, and when the four hours' ride was over, soon after
midnight, my limbs were stiff with tropical cold. And
this, within 20° of the equator, and only 2,500 feet above
the fiery sea-shore, with its temperature of 80°, where
Sydney Smith would certainly have desired to " take off
his flesh, and sit in his bones ! "

I delight in Hawaii more than ever, with its unconventional life, great upland sweeps, unexplored forests,
riotous breezes, and general atmosphere of freedom,
airiness, and expansion. As I find that a lady can travel
alone with perfect safety, I have many projects in view,
but whatever I do or plan to do, I find my eyes always
turning to the light on the top of Mauna Loa. I know
that the ascent is not feasible for me, and that so far as I
am concerned the mystery must remain unsolved; but that
glory, nearly 14,000 feet aloft, rising, falling, " a pillar
of cloud by day and a pillar of fire by night," uplifted in

its awful loneliness above all human interests, has an intolerable fascination. As the twilight deepens, the light intensifies, and often as I watch it in the night, it seems to flare up and take the form of a fiery palm-tree. No one has ascended the mountain since the activity began a month ago; but the fire is believed to be in "the old traditional crater of Mokuaweoweo, in a region rarely visited by man."

A few days ago I was so fortunate as to make the acquaintance of Mr. W. L. Green (now Minister of The Interior), an English resident in Honolulu, a gentleman of wide scientific and literary culture, one of whose objects in visiting Hawaii is the investigation of certain volcanic phenomena. He asked me to make the ascent of Mauna Kea with him, and we have satisfactorily accomplished it to-day.

The interior of the island, in which we have spent the last two days, is totally different, not only from the luxuriant windward slopes, but from the fiery leeward margin. The altitude of the central plateau is from 5,000 to 6,000 feet, there is not a single native dwelling on it, or even a trail across it, it is totally destitute of water, and sustains only a miserable scrub of *mamané*, stunted *ohias*, *pukeawe*, *ohelos*, a few compositæ, and some of the hardiest ferns. The transient residents of this sheep station, and those of another on Hualalai, thirty miles off, are the only human inhabitants of a region as large as Kent. Wild goats, wild geese (Bernicla sandvicensis), and the Melithreptes Pacifica, constitute its chief population. These geese are web-footed, though water does not exist.   They build their nests in the grass, and lay two or three white eggs.

Our track from Waimea lay for the first few miles over light soil, destitute of any vegetation, across dry glaring rocky beds of streams, and round the bases of numerous tufa cones, from 200 to 1500 feet in height, with steep smooth sides, composed of a very red ash. We crossed a flank of Mauna Kea at a height of 6000 feet, and a short descent brought us out upon this vast tableland, which lies between the bulbous domes of Mauna Kea, Mauna Loa, and Hualalai, the loneliest, saddest, dreariest expanse I ever saw.

The air was clear and the sun bright, yet nothing softened into beauty this formless desert of volcanic sand, stones, and lava, on which tufts of grass and a harsh scrub war with wind and drought for a loveless existence.   Yet, such is the effect of atmosphere, that Mauna Loa, utterly destitute of vegetation, and with his sides scored and stained by the black lava-flows of ages, looked like a sapphire streaked with lapis lazuli.   Nearly blinded by scuds of sand, we rode for hours through the volcanic wilderness; always the same rigid *mamané*, (Sophora Chrysophylla ?) the same withered grass, and the same thornless thistles, through which the strong wind swept with a desolate screech.

The trail, which dips 1000 feet, again ascends, the country becomes very wild, there are ancient craters of great height densely wooded, wooded ravines, the great bulk of Mauna Kea with his ragged crest towers above tumbled rocky regions, which look as if nature, dis-

gusted with her work, had broken it to pieces in a
passion ; there are living and dead trees, a steep
elevation, and below, a broad river of most jagged and
uneven *a-a*. The afternoon fog, which serves instead of rain, rolled up in dense masses, through
which we heard the plaintive bleating of sheep, and
among blasted trees and distorted rocks we came upon
Kalaieha.

I have described the "foreign residences" elsewhere.
Here is one of another type, in which a wealthy sheep-
owner's son, married to a very pretty native woman, leads
for some months in the year from choice, a life so rough,
that most people would think it a hardship to lead it
from necessity. There are two apartments, a loft and a
"lean-to." The hospitable owners gave me their sleep-
ing-room, which was divided from the "living-room" by
a canvass partition. This last has a rude stone chimney
split by an earthquake, holding fire enough to roast an
ox. Round it the floor is paved with great rough stones.
A fire of logs, fully three feet high, was burning, but
there was a faulty draught, and it emitted a stinging
smoke. I looked for something to sit upon, but there
was nothing but a high bench, or chopping-block, and a
fixed seat in the corner of the wall. The rest of the
furniture consisted of a small table, some pots, a frying-
pan, a tin dish and plates, a dipper, and some tin
pannikins. Four or five rifles and "shot-guns," and a
piece of raw meat, were hanging against the wall. A tin
bowl was brought to me for washing, which served the
same purpose for every one. The oil was exhausted, so

recourse was had to the native expedient of a jar of beef fat with a wick in it.

We were most hospitably received, but the native wife, as is usually the case, was too shy to eat with us or even to appear at all. Our host is a superb young man, very frank and prepossessing looking, a thorough mountaineer, most expert with the lasso and in hunting wild cattle. The "station" consists of a wool shed, a low grass hut, a hut with one side gone, a bell-tent, and the more substantial cabin in which we are lodged. Several saddled horses were tethered outside, and some natives were shearing sheep, but the fog shut out whatever else there might be of an outer world. Every now and then a native came in and sat on the floor to warm himself, but there were no mats as in native houses. It was intolerably cold. I singed my clothes by sitting in the chimney, but could not warm myself. A fowl was stewed native fashion, and some rice was boiled, and we had sheep's milk and some ice cold water, the drip, I think, from a neighbouring cave, as running and standing water are unknown.

There are 9000 sheep here, but they require hardly any attendance except at shearing time, and dogs are not used in herding them. Indeed, labour is much dispensed with, as the sheep are shorn unwashed, a great contrast to the elaborate washings of the flocks of the Australian Riverina. They come down at night of their own sagacity, in close converging columns, sleep on the gravel about the station, and in the early morning betake themselves to their feeding grounds on the mountain.

Mauna Kea, and the forests which skirt his base, are
the resort of thousands of wild cattle, and there are
many men nearly as wild, who live half savage lives
in the woods, gaining their living by lassoing and
shooting these animals for their skins. Wild black swine
also abound.

The mist as usual disappeared at night, leaving a sky
wonderful with stars, which burned blue and pale against
the furnace glare on the top of Mauna Loa, to which we
are comparatively near. I woke at three from the hopeless cold, and before five went out with Mr. Green to
explore the adjacent lava. The atmosphere was perfectly pure, and suffused with rose-colour, not a cloud-
fleece hung round the mountain tops, hoar-frost whitened
the ground, the pure white smoke of the volcano rose
into the reddening sky, and the air was elixir. It has
been said and written that there are no steam-cracks or
similar traces of volcanic action on Mauna Kea, but in
several fissures I noticed ferns growing belonging to an
altitude 4000 feet lower, and on putting my arm down,
found a heat which compelled me to withdraw it, and as
the sun rose these cracks steamed in all directions.
There are caves full of ferns, lava bubbles in reality,
crust over crust, each from twelve to eighteen inches thick,
rolls of lava cooled in coils, and hideous *a-a* streams on
which it is impossible to walk two yards without the risk
of breaking one's limbs or cutting one's boots to pieces.

While we breakfasted a young man in rags, without
shoes or stockings, but with the accent and address of a
gentleman, came in, a man of good family and education

in England, but who had "gone to the bad out here," and had joined a gang of bullock-catchers. Why do people persist in sending "ne'er-do-weels" to such regions without a definite occupation? It is certain ruin.

I will not weary you with the details of our mountain ascent. Our host provided ourselves and the native servant with three strong bullock-horses, and accompanied us himself. The first climb is through deep volcanic sand slashed by deep clefts, showing bands of red and black ash. We saw no birds, but twice started a rout of wild black hogs, and once came upon a wild bull of large size with some cows and a calf, all so tired with tramping over the lava that they only managed to keep just out of our way. They usually keep near the mountain top in the daytime for fear of the hunters, and come down at night to feed. About 11,000 were shot and lassoed last year. Mr. S—— says that they don't need any water but that of the dew-drenched grass, and that horses reared on the mountains refuse to drink, and are scared by the sight of pools or running streams. Unlike horses I saw at Waikiki, which shut their eyes and plunged their heads into water up to their ears, in search of a saltish weed which grows in the lagoons.

The actual forest, which is principally *koa*, ceases at a height of about 6000 feet, but a deplorable vegetation beginning with *mamané* scrub, and ending with withered wormwood and tufts of coarse grass, straggles up 3000 feet higher, and a scaly orange lichen is found in rare patches at a height of 11,000 feet.

The side of Mauna Kea towards Waimea is precipitous and inaccessible, but to our powerful mountain horses the ascent from Kalaieha presented no difficulty.

We rode on hour after hour in intense cold, till we reached a height where the last stain of lichen disappeared, and the desolation was complete and oppressive. This area of tufa cones, dark and grey basalt, clinkers, scoriæ, fine ash, and ferruginous basalt, is something gigantic. We were three hours in ascending through it, and the eye could at no time take in its limit, for the mountain which from any point of view below appears as a well defined dome with a ragged top, has at the summit the aspect of a ridge, or rather a number of ridges, with between 20 and 30 definite peaks, varying in height from 900 to 1400 feet. Among these cones are large plains of clinkers and fine gravel, but no lava-streams, and at a height of 12,000 feet the sides of some of the valleys are filled up with snow, of a purity so immaculate and a brilliancy so intense as the fierce light of the tropical sun beat upon it, that I feared snow-blindness. We ascended one of the smaller cones which was about 900 feet high, and found it contained a crater of nearly the same depth, with a very even slope, and lined entirely with red ash, which at the bottom became so bright and fiery-looking that it looked as if the fires, which have not burned for ages, had only died out that morning.

After riding steadily for six hours, our horses, snorting and panting, and plunging up to their knees in fine vol-canic ash, and halting, trembling and exhausted, every few feet, carried us up the great tufa cone which crowns

the summit of this vast fire-flushed, fire-created mountain, and we dismounted in deep snow on the crest of the
highest peak in the Pacific, 13,953 feet above the sea.
This summit is a group of six red tufa cones, with very
little apparent difference in their altitude, and with deep
valleys filled with red ash between them. The terminal
cone on which we were has no cavity, but most of
those forming the group, as well as the thirty which I
counted around and below us, are truncated cones with
craters within, and with outer slopes, whose estimated
angle is about 30°. On these slopes the snow lay heavily.
In coming up we had had a superb view of Mauna Loa,
but before we reached the top, the clouds had congre-
gated, and lay in glistening masses all round the mountain about half-way up, shutting out the smiling earth,
and leaving us alone with the view of the sublime desolation of the volcano.

We only remained an hour on the top, and came down
by a very circuitous route, which took us round numerous
cones, and over miles of clinkers varying in size from a
ton to a few ounces, and past a lake the edges of which
were frozen, and which in itself is a curiosity, as no other
part of the mountain "holds water." Not far off is a
cave, a lava-bubble, in which the natives used to live
when they came up here to quarry a very hard adjacent
phonolite for their axes and other tools. While the
others poked about, I was glad to make it a refuge from
the piercing wind. Hundreds of unfinished axes lie
round the cave entrance, and there is quite a large mound
of unfinished chips.

This is a very interesting spot to Hawaiian antiquaries. They argue, from the amount of the chippings, that this mass of phonolite was quarried for ages by countless generations of men, and that the mountain top must have been upheaved, and the island inhabited, in a very remote past. The stones have not been worked since Captain Cook's day; yet there is not a weather-stain upon them, and the air is so dry and rarified that meat will keep fresh for three months. I found a mass of crystals of the greenish volcanic glass, called olivine, imbedded in a piece of phonolite which looked as blue and fresh as if only quarried yesterday.

We travelled for miles through ashes and scoriæ, and then descended into a dense afternoon fog; but Mr. S. is a practised mountaineer, and never faltered for a moment, and our horses made such good speed that late in the afternoon we were able to warm ourselves by a gallop, which brought us in here ravenous for supper before dark, having ridden for thirteen hours. I hope I have made it clear that the top of this dead volcano, whether cones or ravines, is deep soft ashes and sand.

To-morrow morning I intend to ride the thirty miles to Waimea with two native women, and the next day to go off on my adventurous expedition to Hilo, for which I have bought for $45 a big, strong, heavy horse, which I have named Kahélé. He has the poking head and un-mistakable gait of a bullock horse, but is said to be "a good traveller."

I. L. B.

LETTER XXVI.

THIS is the height of enjoyment in travelling. I have just encamped under a *lauhala* tree, with my saddle inverted for a pillow, my horse tied by a long lariat to a guava bush, my gear, saddle-bags, and rations for two days lying about, and my saddle blanket drying in the sun. Overhead the sun blazes, and casts no shadow; a few fleecy clouds hover near him, and far below, the great expanse of the Pacific gleams in a deeper blue than the sky. Far above, towers the rugged and snow-patched, but no longer mysterious dome of Mauna Loa; while every-where, ravines, woods, waterfalls, and stretches of lawn-like grass delight the eye. All green that I have ever seen, of English lawns in June, or Alpine valleys, seems poor and colourless as compared with the dazzling green of this sixty-five miles. It is a joyous green, a glory. Whenever I look up from my writing, I ask, Was there ever such green? Was there ever such sunshine? Was there ever such an atmosphere? Was there ever such an adventure? And Nature—for I have no other companion, and wish for none—answers, "No." The novelty is that I am alone, my conveyance my own horse; no luggage to look after, for it is all in my saddle-bags; no guide to bother, hurry, or hinder me; and with know-

ledge enough of the country to stop when and where I
please. A native guide, besides being a considerable expense, is a great nuisance; and as the trail is easy to find,
and the rivers are low, I resolved for once to taste the
delights of perfect independence ! This is a blessed
country, for a lady can travel everywhere in absolute security.

My goal is the volcano of Kilauea, with various diverging expeditions, involving a ride of about 350 miles ; but
my health has so wonderfully improved, that it is easier
to me now to ride forty miles in a day than ten some
months ago.

You have no idea of the preparations required for such
a ride, and the importance which " littles " assume. Food
for two days had to be taken, and all superfluous weight
to be discarded, as every pound tells on a horse on a
hard journey. My saddle-bags contain, besides " Sunday
clothes," dress for any " gaieties " which Hilo may offer;
but I circumscribed my stock of clothes as much as possible, having fallen into the rough-and-ready practice
of washing them at night, and putting them on un-
ironed in the morning. I carry besides, a canvas bag on
the horn of my saddle, containing two days' provender,
and a knife, horse-shoe nails, glycerine, thread, twine,
leather thongs, with other little et ceteras, the lack of which
might prove troublesome, a thermometer and aneroid
in a leather case, and a plaid. I have discarded, owing
to their weight, all the well-meant luxuries which were
bestowed upon me, such as drinking cups, flasks, etnas,
sandwich cases, knife cases, spoons, pocket mirrors, &c.

The inside of a watchcase makes a sufficient mirror, and I make a cup from a *kalo* leaf. All cases are a mistake, —at least I think so, as I contemplate my light equipment with complacency.

Yesterday's dawn was the reddest I have seen on the mountains, and the day was all the dawn promised. A three-mile gallop down the dewy grass, and slackened speed through the bush, brought me once again to the breezy slopes of Hamakua, and the trail I travelled in February, with Deborah and Kaluna. Though as green then as now, it was the rainy season, a carnival of rain and mud. Somehow the summer does make a difference, even in a land without a winter. The temperature was perfect. It was dreamily lovely. No song of birds, or busy hum of insects, accompanied the rustle of the *lauhala* leaves and the low murmur of the surf. But there is no hot sleep of noon here—the delicious trades keep the air always wakeful.

When the gentleman who guided me through the bush left me on the side of a *pali*, I discovered that Kahélé, though strong, gentle, and sure-footed, possesses the odious fault known as balking, and expressed his aversion to ascend the other side in a most unmistakable manner. He swung round, put his head down, and no amount of spurring could get him to do anything but turn round and round, till the gentleman, who had left me, returned, beat him with a stick, and threw stones at him, till he got him started again.

I have tried coaxing him, but without result, and have had prolonged fights with him in nearly every gulch, and

on the worst *pali* of all he refused for some time to breast
a step, scrambled round and round in a most dangerous
place, and slipped his hind legs quite over the edge before
I could get him on.

His sociability too is ridiculously annoying. Whenever he sees natives in the distance, he neighs, points his
ears, holds up his heavy head, quickens his pace, and as
soon as we meet them, swings round and joins them,
and can only be extricated after a pitched battle. On a
narrow bridge I met Kaluna on a good horse, improved
in manners, appearance, and English, and at first he
must have thought that I was singularly pleased to see
him, by my turning round and joining him at once; but
presently, seeing the true state of the case, he belaboured
Kahélé with a heavy stick. The animal is very gentle
and companionable, and I dislike to spur him; besides,
he seems insensible to it; so the last time I tried Rarey's
plan, and bringing his head quite round, twisted the
bridle round the horn of the saddle, so that he had to
turn round and round for my pleasure, rather than to
indulge his own temper, a process which will, I hope,
conquer him mercifully.

But in consequence of these battles, and a halt which I
made, as now, for no other purpose than to enjoy my
felicitous circumstances, the sun was sinking in a mist of
gold behind Mauna Loa long before I reached the end of my
day's journey. It was extremely lovely. A heavy dew
was falling, odours of Eden rose from the earth, colours
glowed in the sky, and the dewiest and richest green was
all round. It was eerie, but delightful. There were

several gulches to cross after the sun had set, and a
silence, which was almost audible, reigned in their leafy
solitudes. It was quite dark when I reached the trail
which dips over the great *pali* of Laupahoehoe, 700 feet
in height; but I found myself riding carelessly down
what I hardly dared to go up, carefully and in company,
four months before. But whatever improvement time
has made in my health and nerves, it has made none in
this wretched zoophyte village.

Leading Kahélé, I groped about till I found the house
of the widow Honolulu, with whom I had lodged before,
and presently all the natives assembled to stare at me.
After rubbing my horse and feeding him on a large bundle
of *ti* leaves that I had secured on the road, I took my
own meal as a spectacle. Two old crones seized on my
ankles, murmuring *lomi, lomi,* and subjected them to the
native process of shampooing. They had unrestrained
curiosity as to the beginning and end of my journey. I
said "*Waimea, Hamakua,*" when they all chorused,
"*Maikai;*" for a ride of forty miles was not bad for a
wahine haole. I said, "*Wai, lio,*" (water for the horse),
when they signified that there was only some brackish
stuff unfit for drinking.

In spite of the garrulous assemblage, I was asleep
before eight, and never woke till I found myself in a
blaze of sunshine this morning, and in perfect solitude.
I got myself some breakfast, and then looked about the
village for some inhabitants, but found none, except an
unhappy Portuguese with one leg, and an old man who
looked like a leper, to whom I said, "*Ko*" (cane) "*lio*"

(horse), exhibiting a rial at the same time, on which he cut me a large bundle, and I sat on a stone and watched Kahélé as he munched it for an hour and a half.

It was very hot and serene down there between those *palis* 700 and 800 feet high. The huts of the village were all shut, and not a creature stirred. The palms above my head looked as if they had always been old, and there was no movement among their golden plumes. The sea itself rolled shorewards more silently and lazily than usual. An old dog slept in the sunshine, and whenever I moved, by a great effort, opened one eye. The man who cut the cane fell asleep on the grass. Kahéle ate as slowly as if he had resolved to try my patience, and be revenged on me for my conquest of him yesterday, and his heavy munching was the only vital sound. I got up and walked about to assure myself that I was awake, saddled and bridled the horse, and mounted the great southward *pali*, thankful to reach the breeze and the upper air in full possession of my faculties, after the torpor and paralysis of the valley below.

Never were waters so bright or stretches of upland lawns so joyous as to-day, or the forest entanglements so entrancing. The beautiful *Eugenia malaccensis* is now in full blossom, and its stems and branches are blazing in all the gulches, with bunches of rose-crimson stamens borne on short spikelets.

Hilo. Hawaii, *May 24th.*

Once more I am in dear beautiful Hilo. Death entered my Hawaiian " home " lately, and took " Baby Bell "

away, and I miss her sweet angel-presence at every turn;
but otherwise there are no changes, and I am very happy
to be under the roof of these dear friends again, and indeed each tree, flower, and fern in Hilo is a friend. I
would not even wish the straggling Pride of India, and
over-abundant lantana, away from this fairest of the island
Edens. I wish I could transport you here this moment
from our sour easterly skies to this endless summer and
endless sunshine, and shimmer of a peaceful sea, and an
atmosphere whose influences are all cheering. Though
from 13 to 16 feet of rain fall here in the year the air is
not damp. Wet clothes hung up in the verandah even
during rain, dry rapidly, and a substance so sensitive to
damp as botanical paper does not mildew.

I met Deborah on horseback near Onomea, and she
told me that the Austins were expecting me, and so I
spent three days very pleasantly with them on my way
here.

I. L. B.

That old *Kilauea* has just come in, and has brought
the English mail, and a United States mail, an event which
sets Hilo agog.   Then for a few hours its still, drowsy
life becomes galvanized, and people really persuade themselves that they have something to do, and all the foreigners
write letters hastily, or add postscripts to those already
written, and lose the mail, and rush down frantically to
the beach to send their late letters by favour of the obliging purser.   The mail to-day was an event to me, as it
has brought your long-looked-for letters.

LETTER XXVII.

MR. and Mrs. Severance and I have just retured from a three-days' expedition to Puna in the south of Hawaii, and I preferred their agreeable company even to solitude ! My sociable Kahélé was also pleased, and consequently behaved very well. We were compelled to ride for twenty-three miles in single file, owing to the extreme narrowness of the lava track, which has been literally hammered down in some places to make it passable even for shod horses. We were a party of four, and a very fat policeman on a very fat horse brought up the rear.

At some distance from Hilo there is a glorious burst of tropical forest, and then the track passes into green grass dotted over with clumps of the pandanus and the beautiful eugenia. In that hot dry district the fruit was already ripe, and we quenched our thirst with it. The " native apple," as it is called, is of such a brilliant crimson colour as to be hardly less beautiful than the flowers. The rind is very thin, and the inside is white, juicy, and very slightly acidulated. We were always near the sea, and the surf kept bursting up behind the trees in great snowy drifts, and every opening gave us a glimpse of deep blue water. The coast the whole way is composed of great blocks of very hard black lava, more or less elevated, upon which the surges break in perpetual thunder.

Suddenly the verdure ceased, and we emerged upon a hideous scene, one of the many lava flows from Kilauea, an irregular branching stream, about a mile broad. It is suggestive of fearful work on the part of nature, for here the volcano has not created but destroyed. The black tumbled sea mocked the bright sunshine, all tossed, jagged, spiked, twirled, thrown heap on heap, broken, rifted, upheaved in great masses, burrowing in ravines of its own making, full of broken bubble caves, and torn by a-a streams. Close to the track crystals of olivine lie in great profusion, and in a few of the crevices there are young plants of a fern which everywhere has the audacity to act as the herald of vegetation.

Beyond this desert the country is different in its features from the rest of the island, a green smiling land of Beulah, varied by lines of craters covered within and without with vegetation. For thirty miles the track passes under the deep shade of coco palms, of which Puna is the true home; and from under their feathery shadow, and from amidst the dark leafage of the bread-fruit, gleamed the rose-crimson apples of the eugenia, and the golden balls of the guava. I have not before seen this exquisite palm to advantage, for those which fringe the coast have, as compared with these, a look of tattered, sombre, harassed antiquity. Here they stood in thousands, young as well as old, their fronds gigantic, their stems curving every way, and the golden light, which is peculiar to them, toned into a golden green. They were loaded with fruit in all stages, indeed it is produced in such abundance that thousands of nuts lie unheeded on

the ground. Animals, including dogs and cats, revel in
the meat, and in the scarcity of good water the milk is a
useful substitute.

Late in the afternoon we reached our destination, a
comfortable frame house, on one of those fine natural
lawns in which Hawaii abounds. A shower at seven each
morning keeps Puna always green. Our kind host, a
German, married to a native woman, served our meals in
a house made of grass and bamboo; but the wife and
children, as is usual in these cases, never appeared at
table, and contented themselves with contemplating us
at a great distance.

The next afternoon we rode to one of the natural
curiosities of Puna, which gave me intense pleasure. It
lies at the base of a cone crowned with a *heiau* and a
clump of coco palms. Passing among bread-fruit and
guavas into a palm grove of exquisite beauty, we came
suddenly upon a lofty wooded cliff of hard basaltic rock,
with ferns growing out of every crevice in its ragged but
perpendicular sides. At its feet is a cleft about 60 feet
long, 16 wide, and 18 deep, full of water at a temperature of 90°. This has an absolute transparency of a
singular kind, and perpetrates wonderful optical illusions.
Every thing put into it is transformed. The rocks,
broken timber, and old cocoa nuts which lie below it,
are a frosted blue; the dusky skins of natives are changed
to alabaster; and as my companion, in a light print
holuku, swam to and fro, her feet and hands became like
polished marble tinged with blue, and her dress floated
through the water as if woven of blue light. Everything

about this spring is far more striking and beautiful than
the colour in the blue grotto of Capri.   It is heaven in
the water, a jewelled floor of marvels, "a sea of glass,"
"like unto sapphire," a type, perhaps, of that on which
the blessed stand before the throne of God.   Above, the
feathery palms rose into the crystalline blue, and made an
amber light below, and all fair and lovely things were
mirrored in the wonderful waters.   The specific gravity
must be much greater than that of ordinary water, for it
did not seem possible to sink, or even be thoroughly im-
mersed in it.   The mercury in the air was 79°, but on
coming out of the water we felt quite chilly.

I like Puna.   It is like nothing else, but something
about it made us feel as if we were dwelling in a castle of
indolence.   I developed a capacity for doing nothing,
which horrified me, and except when we energised ourselves to go to the hot spring, my companions and I
were content to dream in the verandah, and watch the
lengthening shadows, and drink cocoa-nut milk, till the
abrupt exit of the sun startled us, and we saw the young
moon carrying the old one tenderly, and a fitful glare
60 miles away, where the solemn fires of Mauna Loa are
burning at a height of nearly 14,000 feet.

HILO.

There are many "littles," but few "mickles" here.
It is among the last that two foreign gentlemen have successfully accomplished the ascent of Mauna Loa, and the
mystery of its fires is solved.   I write "successfully," as
they went up and down in safety, but they were involved

in a series of *pilikias :* girths, stirrup-leathers, and crup-
pers slipping and breaking, and their sufferings on the
summit from cold and mountain sickness appear to have
been nearly incapacitating. Although much excited,
they are collected enough to pronounce it "the most
sublime sight ever seen." They, as well as several natives
who have passed by Kilauea, report it as in full activity,
which bears against the assertion that the flank crater becomes quiet when the summit crater is active.

Another and sadder "mickle " has been the departure
of ten lepers for Molokai. The *Kilauea,* with the Marshal,
and Mr. Wilder who embodies the Board of Health, has
just left the bay, taking away forty lepers on this cruise ;
and the relations of those who have been taken from
Hilo are still howling on the beach. When one hears
the wailing, and sees the temporary agony of the separated
relatives, one longs for " the days of the Son of Man,"
and that his healing touch, as of old in Galilee, might
cleanse these unfortunates. Nine of the lepers were sent
on board from the temporary pest-house, but their case,
though deeply commiserated, has been overshadowed by
that of the talented half-white, " Bill Ragsdale," whom
I mentioned in one of my earlier letters, and who is
certainly the most "notorious " man in Hilo. He
has a remarkable gift of eloquence, both in English and
Hawaiian : a combination of pathos, invective, and sar-
casm ; and his manner, though theatrical, is considered
perfect by his native admirers. His moral character,
however, has been very low, which makes the outburst of
feeling at his fate the more remarkable.

Yesterday, he wrote a letter to Sheriff Severance, giving himself up as a leper to be dealt with by the law, expressing himself as ready to be expatriated to-day, but requesting that he might not be put into the leper-house, and that he might go on board the steamer alone. The fact of his giving himself up excited much sympathy, as, in his case, the signs of the malady are hardly apparent, and he might have escaped suspicion for some time.

He was riding about all this morning, taking leave of people, and of the pleasant Hilo lanes, which he will never see again, and just as the steamer was weighing anchor, walked down to the shore as carefully dressed as usual, decorated with *leis* of *ohia* and gardenia, and escorted by nearly the whole native population. On my first landing here, the glee club, singing and flower-clad, went out to meet him ;—now tears and sobs accompanied him, and his countrymen and women clung to him, kissing him, to the last moment, whilst all the foreigners shook hands as they offered him their good wishes. He made a short speech in native, urging quiet submission to the stringent measures which government is taking in order to stamp out leprosy, and then said a few words in English. His last words, as he stepped into the boat, were to all : " *Aloha*, may God bless you, my brothers," and then the whale boat took him the first stage towards his living grave. He took a horse, a Bible, and some legal books with him ; and, doubtless, in consideration of the prominent positions he has filled, specially that of interpreter to the Legislature, unusual indulgence will be granted to him.

At the weekly prayer meeting held this evening in the
foreign church, the medical officer gave a very pathetic
account of his interview with him this morning, in which
he had feelingly requested the prayers of the church. It
was with unusual fervour afterwards that prayer was
offered, not for him only, but for " all those who, living,
have this day been consigned to the oblivion of the grave,
and for the five hundred of our fellow-subjects now suffering on Molokai." A noble instance.of devotion has just
been given by Father Damiens, a Belgian priest, who has
gone to spend his life amidst the hideous scenes, and the
sickness and death of the ghastly valley of Kalawao.

I. L. B.

A CHAPTER ON THE LEPER SETTLEMENT ON MOLKAI.

IN 1865, the Hawaiian Legislature, recognizing the
disastrous fact that leprosy is at once contagious and in-
curable, passed an act to prevent its spread, and eventually the Board of Health established a leper settlement
on the island of Molokai for the isolation of lepers. In
carrying out the painful task of weeding out and exiling
the sufferers, the officials employed met with unusual
difficulties ; and the general foreign community was not
itself aware of the importance of making an attempt to
" stamp out" the disease, until the beginning of Lunalilo's
reign, when the apparently rapid spread of leprosy, and
sundry rumours that others than natives were affected
by it, excited general alarm, and not unreasonably, for

medical science, after protracted investigation, knows less
of leprosy than of cholera.   Nor are medical men wholly
agreed as to the manner in which infection is communi-
cated ; and, as the white residents on the islands associate
very freely and intimately with the natives, eating *poi* out of
their calabashes, and sleeping in their houses and on their
mats, there was just cause for uneasiness.

The natives themselves have been, and still are, perfectly reckless about the risk of contagion, and although
the family instinct among them is singularly weak, the
gregarious or social instinct is singularly strong, and it
has been found impossible to induce them to give up
smoking the pipes, wearing the clothes, and sleeping on
the mats of lepers, which three things are universally regarded by medical men as undoubted sources of infection.
At the beginning of 1873, it was estimated that nearly
400 lepers were scattered up and down the islands,
living among their families and friends, and the healthy
associated with them in complete apathy or fatalism.
However bloated the face and glazed the eyes, or however
swollen or decayed the limbs were, the persons so afflicted
appeared neither to scare nor disgust their friends, and,
therefore, Hawaii has absolutely needed the coercive
segregation of these living *foci* of disease.   When the
search for lepers was made, the natives hid their friends
away under mats, and in forests and caves, till the peril of
separation was over, and if they sought medical advice,
they rejected foreign educated aid in favour of the highly
paid services of Chinese and native quacks, who professed
to work a cure by means of loathsome ointments and

decoctions, and abominable broths worthy of the witches' cauldron.

However, as the year passed on, lepers were "informed against," and it became the painful duty of the sheriffs of the islands, on the statement of a doctor that any individual was truly a leper, to commit him for life to Molokai. Some, whose swollen faces and glassy goggle eyes left no room for hope of escape, gave themselves up ; and a few, who, like Mr. Ragsdale, might have remained among their fellows almost without suspicion, surrendered themselves in a way which reflects much credit upon them. Mr. Park, the Marshal, and Mr. Wilder, of the Board of Health, went round the islands repeatedly in the *Kilauea,* and performed the painful duty of collecting the victims, with true sympathy and kindness. The woe of those who were taken, the dismal wailings of those who were left, and the agonised partings, when friends and relatives clung to the swollen limbs and kissed the glistering bloated faces of those who were exiled from them for ever, I shall never forget.

There were no individual distinctions made among the sufferers. Queen Emma's cousin, a man of property, and Mr. Ragsdale, the most influential lawyer among the half-whites, shared the same doom as poor Upa, the volcano guide, and stricken Chinamen and labourers from the plantations. Before the search slackened, between three and four hundred men, women, and children were gathered out from among their families, and placed on Molokai.

Between 1866 and April 1874, eleven hundred and forty-five lepers, five hundred and sixty of whom were sent from Kahili in the spring of 1872, have arrived on Molokai, of which number four hundred and forty-two have died, the majority of the deaths having occurred since the beginning of Lunalilo's reign, when the work of segregation was undertaken in earnest. At the present time the number on the island is 703, including 22 children. These unfortunates are necessarily pauperised, and the small Hawaiian kingdom finds itself much burdened by their support. The strain on the national resources is very great, and it is not surprising that officials called upon to meet such a sad emergency should be assailed in all quarters of the globe by sentimental criticism and misstatements regarding the provision made for the lepers on Molokai. Most of these are unfounded, and the members of the Board of Health deserve great credit both for their humanity and for their prompt and careful attention to the complaints made by the sufferers.

At present the two obvious blots on the system are, the insufficient house accommodation, involving a herding together which is repulsive to foreign, though not to native, ideas ; and the absence of a resident physician to prescribe for the ailments from which leprosy is no exemption. Molokai, the island of exile, is *Molokai aina pali,* "the land of precipices," in the old native *mélés,* and its walls of rock rise perpendicularly from the sea to a height varying from 1000 to 2500 feet, in extreme grandeur and picturesqueness, and are slashed, as on Hawaii, by gulches opening out on natural lawns on the sea level. The place chosen for the centralization and

segregation of leprosy is a most singular plain of about
20,000 acres, hemmed in between the sea and a precipice
2000 feet high, passable only where a zigzag bridle track
swings over its face, so narrow and difficult that it has
been found impossible to. get cattle down over it, so that
the leper settlement below has depended for its supplies
of fresh meat upon vessels.   The settlement is accessible
also by a very difficult landing at Kalaupapa on the windward side of Molokai.

   Three miles inland from Kalaupapa is the leper village
of Kalawao, which may safely be pronounced one of the
most horrible spots on all the earth; a home of hideous
disease and slow coming death, with which science in
despair has ceased to grapple; a community of doomed
beings, socially dead, "whose only business is to perish;"
wifeless husbands, husbandless wives, children without
parents, and parents without children; men and women
who have "no more a portion for ever in anything that is
done under the sun," condemned to watch the repulsive
steps by which each of their doomed fellows passes down
to a loathsome death, knowing that by the same they too
must pass.

   A small stone church near the landing, and another at
Kalawao, tell of the extraordinary devotion of a Catholic
priest, who, with every prospect of advancement in his
Church, and with youth, culture, and refinement to hold
him back from the sacrifice, is in this hideous valley, a
self exiled man, for Christ's sake.   It was singular to
hear the burst of spontaneous admiration which his act
elicited.   No unworthy motives were suggested, all

envious speech was hushed; it was almost forgotten by
the most rigid Protestants that Father Damiens, who
has literally followed the example of Christ by "laying
down his life for the brethren," is a Romish priest, and
an intuition, higher than all reasoning, hastened to
number him with "the noble army of martyrs."

In Kalawao are placed not only the greater number of
the lepers, but the hospital buildings. Most of the
victims are of the poorer classes and live in brown huts;
but two of rank, Mrs. Napela and the Hon. P. Y. Kaeo,
Queen Emma's cousin, have neat wooden cottages on the
way from the landing, with every comfort which their
means can provide for them. The hospital buildings are
about twelve in number, well and airily situated on a
height; they are built of wood thoroughly whitewashed,
and are enclosed by a fence. Although it is hoped that
a leper hospital is not to be a permanent institution of
the kingdom, the soft green grass of the enclosure has been
liberally planted with algaroba trees, which in a year or
two will form a goodly shade, and water has been brought
in from a distance at considerable expense, so that an
abundant supply is always at hand. The lepers are dying
fast, and the number of advanced cases in the hospital
averages forty. In the centre of the hospital square there
are the office buildings, including the dispensary, which is
well supplied with medicines, so that in the absence of a
doctor, common ailments may be treated by an intelligent
English leper. The superintendent's office, where the
accounts and statistics of the settlement are kept, and
where the leper governor holds his leper court, and the

post-office, are also within the enclosure; but the true
governor and law-giver is Death.

When Mr. Ragsdale left Hilo as a leper, the course he
was likely to take on Molokai could not be accurately
forecasted; and it was felt that the presence in the leper
community of a man of his gift of eloquence and influence might either be an invaluable assistance to the
government, or else a serious embarrassment. In every
position he had hitherto occupied, he had acquired and
retained a remarkable notoriety; and no stranger could
visit the islands without hearing of poor " Bill Ragsdale's " gifts, and the grievous failings by which they
were accompanied.

Hitherto the hopes of his well wishers have been
fulfilled, and the government has found in him a most
energetic as well as prudent agent. " It is better to be
first in Britain than second in Rome;" and probably
this unfortunate man, superintendent of the leper settlement, and popularly known as " Governor Ragsdale,"
has found a nobler scope for his ambition among his
doomed brethren than in any previous position. His
remarkable power of influencing his countrymen is at
present used for their well being; and though his
authority is practically almost absolute, owing to the
isolation of the community, and its position almost outside the operation of law, he has hitherto used it with
good faith and moderation. He is nominally assisted in
his duties by a committee of twenty chosen from among
the lepers themselves; but from his superior education

and native mental ascendancy, all immediate matters in the settlement are decided by his judgment alone.

The rations of food are ample and of good quality, and notwithstanding the increase in the number of lepers, and the difficulty of communication, there has not been any authenticated case of want. Each leper receives weekly 21 lbs. of *paiai*, and from 5 to 6 of beef, and when these fail to be landed, 9 lbs. of rice, 1 lb. of sugar, and 4 lbs. of salmon. Soap and clothing are also supplied; but, for all beyond these necessaries, the lepers are dependent on their own industry, if they are able to exercise it, and the kindness of their friends. Coffee, tobacco, pipes, extra clothing, knives, toys, books, pictures, working implements and materials, have all been possessed by them in happier days; and though packages of such things have been sent by the charitable for distribution by Father Damiens, it is not possible for island benevolence fully to meet an emergency and needs so disproportionate to the population and resources of the kingdom. Besides the two Catholic churches, there are a Protestant chapel, with a pastor, himself a leper, who is a regularly ordained minister of the Hawaiian Board, and two school-houses, where the twenty-two children of the settlement receive instruction in Hawaiian from a leper teacher. There is a store, too, where those who are assisted by their friends can purchase small luxuries, which are sold at just such an advance on cost as is sufficient to clear the expense of freight. The taste for ornament has not died out in either sex, and women are to be seen in Kalawao, hideous and bloated beyond description, decorated with *leis* of flowers, and looking for admiration out of their glazed and goggle eyes.

King Kalakaua and Queen Kapiolani have paid a visit to the settlement, and were received with hearty *alohas*, and the music of a leper band. The king made a short address to the lepers, the substance of which was "that his heart was grieved with the necessity which had separated these, his subjects, from their homes and families, a necessity which they themselves recognised and acquiesced in, and it should be the earnest desire of himself and his government to render their condition in exile as comfortable as possible." While he spoke, though it is supposed that a merciful apathy attends upon leprosy, his hideous audience showed signs of deep feeling, and many shed tears at his thoughtfulness in coming to visit those, who, to use their own touching expression, were "already in the grave."

The account which follows is from the pen of a gentleman who accompanied the king, and visited the hospital on the same occasion, in company with two members of the Board of Health.

"As our party stepped on shore, we found the lepers assembled to the number of two or three hundred—there are 697 all told in the settlement—for they had heard in advance of our coming, and our ears were greeted with the sound of lively music. This proceeded from the 'band,' consisting of a drum, a fife, and two flutes, rather skilfully played upon by four young lads, whose visages were horribly marked and disfigured with leprosy. The

sprightly airs with which these poor creatures welcomed
the arrival of the party, sounded strangely incongruous
and out of place, and grated harshly upon our feelings.
And then as we proceeded up the beach, and the crowd
gathered about us, eager and anxious for a recognition
or a kind word of greeting—oh, the repulsive and sickening libels and distorted caricatures of the human face
divine upon which we looked! And as they evidently
read the ill-concealed aversion in our countenances, they
withdrew the half-proffered hand, and slunk back with
hanging heads. They felt again that they were *lepers*,
the outcasts of society, and must not contaminate us with
their touch. A few cheerful words of inquiry from the
physician, Dr. Trousseau, addressed to individuals as to
their particular cases, broke the embarrassment of this
first meeting, and soon the crowd were chatting and
laughing just like any other crowd of thoughtless
Hawaiians, and with but few exceptions, these unfortunate exiles showed no signs of the settled melancholy
that would naturally be looked for from people so hopelessly situated. Very happy were they when spoken to,
and quite ready to answer any questions. We saw
numbers whom we had known in years past, and who,
having disappeared, we had thought dead. One we had
known as a Representative, and a very intelligent one,
too, in the Legislature of 1868. On greeting him as an
old-time acquaintance, he observed, ' Yes, we meet again
—in this living grave!' He is a man of no little consideration among the people, being entrusted by the
Board of Health with the care of the store which is kept

here for the sale of such goods as the people require. All
do not appear to be lepers who are leprous. We saw
numbers who might pass along our streets any day without being suspected of the taint. They had it, however,
in one way or another. Sometimes on the extremities
only, eating away the flesh and rotting the bones of the
hands or feet; and sometimes only appearing in black
and indurated spots on the skin, noticed only on a somewhat close examination. This last sort is said to be the
worst, as being most surely fatal and easiest transmitted.
We saw women who had the disease in this stage, walking about, whom it was difficult to believe were lepers.

" If our sensibilities were shocked at the sight of the
crowd of lepers we had met at the beach, walking about
in physical strength and activity, how shall we describe
our sensations in looking upon these loathsome creatures
in the hospital, in whom it was indeed hard to recognise
anything human? The rooms were cleanly kept and
well ventilated, but the atmosphere within was pervaded
with the sickening odour of the grave. At each end,
squatted or lying prone on their respective mats or mattresses, were the yet breathing corpses of lepers in the
last stages of various forms of the disease, who glanced
inquisitively at us for a moment out of their ghoul-like
eyes—those who were not already beyond seeing—and
then withdrew within their dreadful selves. Was there
ever a more pitiful sight?

" In one room we saw a sight that will ever remain
fixed indelibly on the tablets of memory. A little blue-
eyed, flaxen haired child, apparently three or four years

old, a half-caste, that looked up at us with an expression of timorous longing to be caressed and loved; but alas, in its glassy eyes and transparent cheeks were the unmistakable signs of the curse—the sin of the parents visited upon the child!

"In another room was one—a mass of rotting flesh, with but little semblance of humanity remaining—who was dying, and whose breath came hurried and obstructed. A few hours at most, and his troubles would be over, and his happy release arrive. There had been fourteen deaths in the settlement during the previous fortnight. On the day of our visit there were fifty-eight inmates of the hospital."

Though the lifting of the veil of mystery which hangs over the death valley of Molokai discloses some of the most woeful features of the curse, it is a relief to know the worst, and that the poor leprous outcasts in their "living grave" are not outside the pale of humanity and a judicious philanthropy. All that can be done for them is to encourage their remaining capacities for industry, and to smooth, as far as is possible, the journey of death. The Hawaiian Government is doing its best to "stamp out" the disease, and to provide for the comfort of those who are isolated; and, with the limited means at its disposal, has acted with an efficiency and humanity worthy of the foremost of civilised countries.

LETTER XXVIII.

OFTEN since I finished my last letter has Hazael's reply to Elisha occurred to me, " Is thy servant a dog, that he should do this thing ? " For in answer to people who have said, " I hope nothing will induce you to attempt the ascent of Mauna Loa," I always said, " Oh, dear, no ! I should never dream of it;" or, "Nothing would persuade me to think of it ! "

This morning early, Mr. Green came in, on his way to Kilauea, to which I was to accompany him, and on my casually remarking that I envied him his further journey, he at once asked me to join him, and I joyfully accepted the invitation ! For, indeed, my heart has been secretly set on going, and I have had to repeat to myself fifty times a day, " no, I must not think of it, for it is *impossible*."

Mr. Green is going up well equipped with a tent, horses, a baggage mule, and a servant, and is confident of being able to get a guide and additional mules fifty miles from Hilo. I had to go to the Union School examination where the Hilo world was gathered, but I could think of nothing but the future; and I can hardly write sense, the prospect of the next week is so exciting, and the time for making preparations is so short. It is an adventurous trip anyhow, and the sufferings which our predecessors have undergone, from Commodore Wilkes downwards, make me anxious not to omit any precaution. The distance which has to be travelled through an uninhabited region, the height and total isolation of the summit, the uncertainty as to the state of the crater, and the duration of its activity, with the possibility of total failure owing to fog or strong wind, combine to make our ascent an experimental trip.

The news of the project soon spread through the village, and as the ascent has only once been performed by a woman, the kindly people are profuse in offers of assistance, and in interest in the journey, and every one is congratulating me on my good fortune in having Mr. Green for my travelling companion. I have hunted all the beach stores through for such essentials as will pack into small compass, and every one said "So you are going to 'the mountain;' I hope you'll have a good time;" or, "I hope you'll have the luck to get up."

Among the friends of my hosts all sorts of useful articles were produced, a camp kettle, a camping blanket, a huge Mexican poncho, a cardigan, capacious saddlebags, &c. Nor was Kahélé forgotten, for the last contribution was a bag of oats! The greatest difficulty was about warm clothing, for in this perfect climate, woollen underclothing is not necessary as in many tropical countries, but it is absolutely essential on yonder mountain, and till late in the afternoon the best intentions and the most energetic rummaging in old trunks failed to produce it. At last Mrs. ——, wife of an old Scotch settler, bestowed upon me the invaluable loan of a stout flannel shirt, and a pair of venerable worsted stockings, much darned, knitted in Fifeshire a quarter of a century ago. When she brought them, the excellent lady exclaimed, "Oh, what some people will do!" with an obvious personal reference.

She tells us that her husband, who owns the ranch on the mountain at which we are to stay the last night, has been obliged to forbid any of his natives going up as guides, and that she fears we shall not get a guide, as the native who went up with Mr. Whyte suffered so dreadfully from mountain sickness, that they were obliged to help him down, and he declares that he will not go up again. Mr. Whyte tells us that he suffered himself from vomiting and vertigo for fourteen hours, and severely from thirst also, as the water froze in their canteens; but I am almost well now, and as my capacity for "roughing it" has been severely tested, I hope to "get on" much better. A party made the ascent nine months ago, and the members of it also suffered severely, but I see no reason why cautious people, who look well to their gear and clothing, and are prudent with regard to taking exercise at the top, should suffer anything worse than the inconveniences which are inseparable from nocturnal cold at a high elevation.

My preparations are completed to-night, the last good wishes have been spoken, and we intend to leave early to-morrow morning.

I. L. B.

LETTER XXIX.*

CRATER HOUSE, KILAUEA.
June 4th.

ONCE more I write with the splendours of the quench-less fires in sight, and the usual world seems twilight and commonplace by the fierce glare of Halemaumau, and the fitful glare of the other and loftier flame, which is burning ten thousand feet higher in lonely Mokua-weo-weo.

Mr. Green and I left Hilo soon after daylight this morning, and made about " the worst time " ever made on the route. We jogged on slowly and silently for thirty miles in Indian file, through bursts of tropical beauty, over an ocean of fern-clad *pahoehoe*, the air hot and stagnant, the horses lazy and indifferent, till I was awoke from the kind of cautious doze into which one falls on a sure-footed horse, by a decided coolness in the atmo-sphere, and Kahélé breaking into a lumbering gallop, which he kept up till we reached this house, where, in spite of the exercise, we are glad to get close to a large wood fire. Although we are shivering, the mercury is 57°, but in this warm and equable climate, one's sensa-

---

* I venture to present this journal letter just as it was written, trusting that the interest which attaches to volcanic regions, will carry the reader through the minuteness and multiplicity of the details.

tions are not significant of the height of the thermo-
meter.

It is very fascinating to be here on the crater's edge,
and to look across its deep three miles of blackness to the
clouds of red light which Halemaumau is sending up,
but altogether exciting to watch the lofty curve of Mauna
Loa upheave itself against the moon, while far and faint,
we see, or think we see, that solemn light, which ever
since my landing at Kawaihae has been so mysteriously
attractive. It is three days off yet. Perhaps its spasmodic
fires will die out, and we shall find only blackness.
Perhaps anything, except our seeing it as it ought to be
seen!   The practical difficulty about a guide increases,
and Mr. Gilman cannot help us to solve it.   And if it be
so cold at 4000 feet, what will it be at 14,000?

KILAUEA. *June 5th.*

I have no room in my thoughts for anything but
volcanoes, and it will be so for some days to come.   We
have been all day in the crater, in fact, I left Mr. Green
and his native there, and came up with the guide, sore,
stiff, bruised, cut, singed, grimy, with my thick gloves
shrivelled off by the touch of sulphurous acid, and my
boots nearly burned off.   But what are cuts, bruises,
fatigue, and singed eyelashes, in comparison with the
awful sublimities I have witnessed to-day?   The activity
of Kilauea on Jan. 31 was as child's play to its activity
to-day: as a display of fireworks compared to the conflagration of a metropolis.   *Then*, the sense of awe gave
way speedily to that of admiration of the dancing fire

fountains of a fiery lake; *now*, it was all terror, horror, and sublimity, blackness, suffocating gases, scorching heat, crashings, surgings, detonations; half seen fires, hideous, tortured, wallowing waves. I feel as if the terrors of Kilauea would haunt me all my life, and be the Nemesis of weak and tired hours.

We left early, and descended the terminal wall, still as before, green with ferns, *ohias*, and sandalwood, and bright with clusters of turquoise berries, and the red fruit and waxy blossoms of the *ohelo*. The lowest depression of the crater, which I described before as a level fissured sea of iridescent lava, has been apparently partially flooded by a recent overflow from Halemaumau, and the same agency has filled up the larger rifts with great shining rolls of black lava, obnoxiously like boa-constrictors in a state of repletion. In crossing this central area for the second time, with a mind less distracted by the novelty of the surroundings, I observed considerable deposits of remarkably impure sulphur, as well as sulphates of lime and alum in the larger fissures. The presence of moisture was always apparent in connexion with these formations. The solidified surges and convolutions in which the lava lies, the latter sometimes so beautifully formed as to look like coils of wire rope, are truly wonderful. Within the cracks there are extraordinary coloured growths, orange, grey, buff, like mineral lichens, but very hard and brittle.

The recent lava flow by which Halemaumau has considerably heightened its walls, has raised the hill by which you ascend to the brink of the pit to a height of fully five hundred feet from the basin, and this elevation is at present much more fiery and precarious than the former one.   It is dead, but not cold, lets one through into cracks hot with corrosive acid, rings hollow everywhere, and its steep acclivities lie in waves, streams, coils, twists, and tortuosities of all kinds, the surface glazed and smoothish, and with a metallic lustre.

Somehow, I expected to find Kilauea as I had left it in January, though the volumes of dense white smoke which are now rolling up from it might have indicated a change ; but after the toilsome, breathless climbing of the awful lava hill, with the crust becoming more brittle, and the footing hotter at each step, instead of laughing fire fountains tossing themselves in gory splendour above the rim, there was a hot, sulphurous, mephitic chaos, covering, who knows what, of horror ?

So far as we could judge, the level of the lake had sunk to about 80 feet below the margin, and the lately formed precipice was overhanging it considerably. About seven feet back from the edge of the ledge, there was a fissure about eighteen inches wide, emitting heavy fumes of sulphurous acid gas.   Our visit seemed in vain, for on the risky verge of this crack we could only get momentary glimpses of wallowing fire, glaring lurid through dense masses of furious smoke which were rolling themselves round in the abyss as if driven by a hurricane.

After failing to get a better standpoint, we suffered so much from the gases, that we coasted the north, till we reached the south lake, one with the other on my former visit, but now separated by a solid lava barrier about

three hundred feet broad, and eighty high.   Here there
was comparatively little smoke, and the whole mass of
contained lava was ebullient and incandescent, its level
marked the whole way round by a shelf or rim of molten
lava, which adhered to the side, as ice often adheres to
the margin of rapids, when the rest of the water is

HALEMAUMAU, JAN. 31.

liberated and in motion.   There was very little centripetal action apparent.   Though the mass was violently
agitated it always took a southerly direction, and dashed
itself with fearful violence against some lofty, under-
mined cliffs which formed its southern limit.   The whole
region vibrated with the shock of the fiery surges.   To

stand there was "to snatch a fearful joy," out of a pain
and terror which were unendurable. For two or three
minutes we kept going to the edge, seeing the spectacle
as with a flash, through half closed eyes, and going back
again; but a few trials, in which throats, nostrils, and
eyes were irritated to torture by the acid gases, convinced
us that it was unsafe to attempt to remain by the lake, as
the pain and gasping for breath which followed each in-
halation, threatened serious consequences.

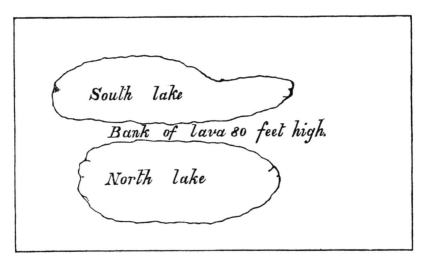

OUTLINE OF HALEMAUMAU, JUNE 4.

With regard to the north lake we were more fortunate,
and more persevering, and I regard the three hours we
spent by it as containing some of the most solemn, as well
as most fascinating, experiences of my life. The aspect
of the volcano had altogether changed within four months.
At present there are two lakes surrounded by precipices
about eighty feet high. Owing to the smoke and confusion,

it is most difficult to estimate their size even approximately, but I think that the diameter of the two cannot be less than a fifth of a mile.

Within the pit or lake by which we spent the morning, there were no fiery fountains, or regular plashings of fiery waves playing in indescribable beauty in a faint blue atmosphere, but lurid, gory, molten, raging, sulphurous, tormented masses of matter, half seen through masses as restless, of lurid smoke. Here, the violent action appeared centripetal, but with a southward tendency. Apparently, huge bulging masses of a lurid-coloured lava were wallowing the whole time one over another in a central whirlpool, which occasionally flung up a wave of fire thirty or forty feet. The greatest intensity of action was always preceded by a dull throbbing roar, as if the imprisoned gases were seeking the vent which was afforded them by the upward bulging of the wave and its bursting into spray. The colour of the lava which appeared to be thrown upwards from great depths, was more fiery and less gory than that nearer the surface. Now and then, through rifts in the smoke we saw a convergence of the whole molten mass into the centre, which rose wallowing and convulsed to a considerable height. The awful sublimity of what we did see, was enhanced by the knowledge that it was only a thousandth part of what we did not see, mere momentary glimpses of a terror and fearfulness which otherwise could not have been borne.

A ledge, only three or four feet wide, hung over the lake, and between that and the comparative *terra firma* of the older lava, there was a fissure of unknown depth, emitting hot blasts of pernicious gases. The guide would not venture on the outside ledge, but Mr. Green, in his scientific zeal, crossed the crack, telling me not to follow him, but presently, in his absorption with what he saw, called to me to come, and I jumped across, and this remained our perilous standpoint.*

Burned, singed, stifled, blinded, only able to stand on one foot at a time, jumping back across the fissure every two or three minutes to escape an unendurable whiff of heat and sulphurous stench, or when splitting sounds below threatened the disruption of the ledge : lured as often back by the fascination of the horrors below ; so we spent three hours.

There was every circumstance of awfulness to make the impression of the sight indelible. Sometimes dense volumes of smoke hid everything, and yet, upwards, from out " their sulphurous canopy " fearful sounds rose, crashings, thunderings, detonations, and we never knew then whether the spray of some hugely uplifted wave might not dash up to where we stood. At other times the smoke partially lifting, but still swirling in strong eddies, revealed a central whirlpool of fire, wallowing at unknown depths, to which the lava, from all parts of the lake, slid centrewards and downwards as into a vortex, where it mingled its waves with indescribable noise and fury, and then, breaking upwards, dashed itself to a great

* Since then, the Austins of Onomea were standing on a similar ledge, when a sound as of a surge striking below, made them jump back hastily, and in another moment the projection split off, and was engulfed in the fiery lake.

height in fierce, gory, gouts and clots, while hell itself
seemed opening at our feet.   At times, again, bits of the
lake skinned over with a skin of a wonderful silvery,
satiny sheen, to be immediately devoured; and as the
lurid billows broke, they were mingled with misplaced
patches as if of bright moonlight.   Always changing,
always suggesting force which nothing could repel, agony
indescribable, mystery inscrutable, terror unutterable,, a
thing of eternal dread, revealed only in glimpses!

It is natural to think that St. John the Evangelist, in
some Patmos vision, was transported to the brink of this
"bottomless pit," and found in its blackness and turbulence
of agony the fittest emblems of those tortures of remorse
and memory, which we may well believe are the quench-
less flames of the region of self-chosen exile from goodness
and from God.   As natural, too, that all Scripture phrases
which typify the place of woe should recur to one with
the force of a new interpretation, " Who can dwell with
the everlasting burnings?"   "The smoke of their
torment goeth up for ever and ever," "The place of hell,"
"The bottomless pit," "The vengeance of eternal fire,"
"A lake of fire burning with brimstone."   No sight can
be so fearful as this glimpse into the interior of the earth,
where fires are for ever wallowing with purposeless
force and aimless agony.

Beyond the lake there is a horrible region in which
dense volumes of smoke proceed from the upper ground,
with loud bellowings and detonations, and we took our
perilous way in that direction, over very hot lava which
gave way constantly.   It is near this that the steady fires

are situated which are visible from this house at night.
We came first upon a solitary "blowing cone," beyond
which there was a group of three or four, but it is not
from these that the smoke proceeds, but from the extensive area beyond them, covered with smoke and steam
cracks, and smoking banks, which are probably formed of
sulphur deposits.   I only visited the solitary cone, for the
footing was so precarious, the sight so fearful, and the
ebullitions of gases so dangerous, that I did not dare to
go near the others, and never wish to look upon their
like again.

The one I saw was of beehive shape, about twelve feet
high, hollow inside, and its walls were about two feet thick.
A part of its imperfect top was blown off, and a piece of its
side blown out, and the side rent gave one a frightful view
of its interior, with the risk of having lava spat at one at
intervals.   The name " Blowing Cone " is an apt one, if
the theory of their construction be correct.   It is supposed
that when the surface of the lava cools rapidly owing to
enfeebled action below, the gases force their way upwards
through small vents, which then serve as "blow holes"
for the imprisoned fluid beneath.   This, rapidly cooling
as it is ejected, forms a ring on the surface of the crust,
which, growing upwards by accretion, forms a chimney,
eventually nearly or quite closed at the top, so as to form
a cone.   In this case the cone is about eighty feet above
the present level of the lake, and fully one hundred yards
distant from its present verge.

The whole of the inside was red and molten, full of
knobs, and great fiery stalactites.   Jets of lava at a white

heat were thrown up constantly, and frequently the rent in the side spat out lava in clots, which cooled rapidly, and looked like drops of bottle green glass.   The glimpses I got of the interior were necessarily brief and intermittent. The blast or roar which came up from below was more than deafening; it was stunning: and accompanied with heavy subterranean rumblings and detonations.   The chimney, so far as I could see, opened out gradually downwards to a great width, and appeared to be about forty feet deep; and at its base there was an abyss of lashing, tumbling, restless fire, emitting an ominous surging sound, and breaking upwards with a fury which threatened to blow the cone and the crust on which it stands, into the air.

The heat was intense, and the stinging sulphurous gases which were given forth in large quantities, most poisonous. The group of cones west of this one, was visited by Mr. Green; but he found it impossible to make any further explorations.   He has seen nearly all the recent volcanic phenomena, but says that these cones present the most "infernal" appearance he has ever witnessed.   We returned for a last look at Halemaumau, but the smoke was so dense, and the sulphur fumes so stifling, that, as in a fearful dream, we only heard the thunder of its hidden surges.   I write thunder, and one speaks of the lashing of its waves; but these are words pertaining to the familiar earth, and have no place in connection with Kilauea.   The breaking lava has a voice all its own, full of compressed fury.   Its sound, motion, and aspect are all infernal. Hellish, is the only fitting term.

We are dwelling on a cooled crust all over Southern Hawaii, the whole region is recent lava, and between this and the sea there are several distinct lines of craters thirty miles long, all of which at some time or other have vomited forth the innumerable lava streams which streak the whole country in the districts of Kau, Puna, and Hilo. In fact, Hawaii is a great slag. There is something very solemn in the position of this crater-house : with smoke and steam coming out of every pore of the ground, and in front the huge crater, which to-night lights all the sky. My second visit has produced a far deeper impression even than the first, and one of awe and terror solely.

Kilauea is altogether different from the European volcanoes which send lava and stones into the air in fierce sudden spasms, and then subside into harmlessness. Ever changing, never resting, the force which stirs it never weakening, raging for ever with tossing and strength like the ocean : its labours unfinished and possibly never to be finished, its very unexpectedness adds to its sublimity and terror, for until you reach the terminal wall of the crater, it looks by daylight but a smoking pit in the midst of a dreary stretch of waste land.

Last night I thought the Southern Cross out of place ; to-night it seems essential, as Calvary over against Sinai. For Halemaumau involuntarily typifies the wrath which shall consume all evil : and the constellation, pale against its lurid light, the great love and yearning of the Father, "who spared not His own Son but delivered Him up for us all," that, "as in Adam all die, even so in Christ shall all be made alive."

AINEPO, HAWAII, *June 5th.*

WE had a great fright last evening. We had been engaging mules, and talking over our plans with our half-Indian host, when he opened the door and exclaimed, " There's no light on Mauna Loa ; the fire's gone out." We rushed out, and though the night was clear and frosty, the mountain curve rose against the sky without the accustomed wavering glow upon it, " I'm afraid you'll have your trouble for nothing," Mr. Gilman unsympathisingly remarked; " anyhow, its awfully cold up there," and rubbing his hands, reseated himself at the fire. Mr. G. and I stayed out till we were half-frozen, and I persuaded myself and him that there was a redder tinge than the moonlight above the summit, but the mountain has given no sign all day, so that I fear that I " evolved " the light out of my " inner consciousness."

Mr. Gilman was eloquent on the misfortunes of our predecessors, lent me a pair of woollen socks to put on over my gloves, told me privately that if anyone could succeed in getting a guide it would be Mr. Green, and dispatched us at eight this morning with a lurking smile at our " fool's errand," thinly veiled by warm wishes for our success. Mr. Reid has two ranches on the mountain, seven miles distant from each other, and was expected every hour at the crater-house on his way to Hilo, but it was not known from which he was coming, and as it appeared that our last hope of getting a guide lay in securing his good will, Mr. G., his servant, and pack-mule took the lower trail, and I, with a native, a string of mules, and a pack-horse, the upper. Our plans for intercepting the good man were well laid and successful, but turned out resultless.

This has been an irresistibly comical day, and it is just as well to have something amusing interjected between the sublimities of Kilauea, and whatever to-morrow may bring forth. When our cavalcades separated, I followed the guide on a blind trail into the little-known regions on the skirts of Mauna Loa. We only travelled two miles an hour, and the mules kept getting up rows, kicking, and entangling their legs in the lariats, and one peculiarly malign animal dealt poor Kahélé a gratuitous kick on his nose, making it bleed.

It is strange, unique country, without any beauty. The seaward view is over a great stretch of apparent table-land, spotted with craters, and split by cracks emitting smoke or steam. The whole region is black with streams of spiked and jagged lava, meandering over it, with charred stumps of trees rising out of them.

The trail, if such it could be called, wound among *koa* and sandalwood trees occasionally, but habitually we picked our way over waves, coils, and hummocks of pahoehoe surrounded by volcanic sand, and with only a few tufts of grass, abortive *ohelos*, and vigorous sow thistles (much relished by Kahélé) growing in their crevices. Horrid cracks, 50 or 60 feet wide, probably made by earthquakes, abounded, and a black chasm of most infernal aspect dogged us on the left. It was all scrambling up and down. Sometimes there was long, ugly grass, a brownish green, coarse and tufty, for a mile or more. Sometimes clumps of wintry-looking, dead trees, sometimes clumps of attenuated living ones; but nothing to please the eye. We saw neither man nor beast the whole way, except a wild bull, which, tearing down the mountain side, crossed the trail just in front of us, causing a stampede among the mules, and it was fully an hour before they were all caught again.

The only other incident was an earthquake, the most severe, the men here tell me, that has been experienced for two years. One is prepared for any caprices on the part of the earth here, yet when there was a fearful internal throbbing and rumbling, and the trees and grass swayed rapidly, and great rocks and masses of soil were dislodged, and bounded down the hillside, and the earth reeled, and my poor horse staggered and stopped short; far from rising to the magnitude of the occasion, I thought I was attacked with vertigo, and grasped the horn of my saddle to save myself from falling. After a moment of profound stillness, there was again a subterranean sound like a train in a tunnel, and the earth reeled again with such violence that I felt as if the horse and myself had gone over. Poor K. was nervous for some time afterwards. The motion was as violent as that of a large ship in a mid-Atlantic storm. There were four minor shocks within half an hour afterwards.

After crawling along for seven hours, and for the last two in a dripping fog, so dense that I had to keep within kicking range of the mules for fear of being lost, we heard the lowing of domestic cattle, and came to a place where felled trêes, very difficult for the horses to cross, were lying. Then a rude boundary wall appeared, inside

of which was a small, poor-looking grass house, consisting of one partially-divided room, with a small, ruinous-
looking cook-house, a shed, and an unfinished frame
house. It looked, and is, a disconsolate conclusion of a
wet day's ride. I rode into the corral, and found two or
three very rough-looking whites and half-whites standing,
and addressing one of them, I found he was Mr. Reid's
manager there. I asked if they could give me a night's
lodging, which seemed a diverting notion to them; and
they said they could give me the rough accommodation
they had, but it was hard even for them, till the new
house was put up. They brought me into this very rough
shelter, a draughty grass room, with a bench, table, and
one chair in it. Two men came in, but not the native
wife and family, and sat down to a calabash of *poi* and
some strips of dried beef, food so coarse, that they apolo-
gised for not offering it to me. They said they had sent
to the lower ranch for some flour, and in the meantime
they gave me some milk in a broken bowl, their " nearest
approach to a tumbler," they said. I was almost starving,
for all our food was on the pack-mule. This is the place
where we had been told that we could obtain tea, flour,
beef, and fowls !

By some fatality my pen, ink, and knitting were on the
pack-mule; it was very cold, the afternoon fog closed us
in, and darkness came on prematurely, so that I felt a
most absurd sense of *ennui*, and went over to the cook
house, where I found Gandle cooking, and his native wife
with a heap of children and dogs lying round the stove.
I joined them till my clothes were dry, on which the man,

who in spite of his rough exterior, was really friendly and hospitable, remarked that he saw I was "one of the sort who knew how to take people as I found them."

This regular afternoon mist which sets in at a certain altitude, blotting out the sun and sky, and bringing the horizon within a few yards, makes me certain after all that the mists of rainless Eden were a phenomenon, the loss of which is not to be regretted.

Still the afternoon hung on, and I went back to the house feeling that the most desirable event which the future could produce would be—a meal. Now and then the men came in and talked for a while, and as the darkness and cold intensified, they brought in an arrangement extemporised out of what looked like a battered tin bath, half full of earth, with some lighted faggots at the top, which gave out a little warmth and much stinging smoke. Actual, undoubted, night came on without Mr. Green, of whose failure I felt certain, and without food, and being blinded by the smoke, I rolled myself in a blanket and fell asleep on the bench, only to wake in a great fright, believing that the volcano house was burning over my head, and that a venerable missionary was taking advantage of the confusion to rob my saddle-bags, which in truth one of the men was moving out of harm's way, having piled up the fire two feet high.

Presently a number of voices outside shouted *Haole!* and Mr. Green came in shaking the water from his waterproof, with the welcome words, "Everything's settled for to-morrow." Mr. Reid threw cold water on the ascent, and could give no help ; and Mr. G. being thus left to

himself, after a great deal of trouble, has engaged as
guide an active young goat-hunter, who, though he has
never been to the top of the mountain, knows other parts
of it so well that he is sure he can take us up. Mr. G.
also brings an additional mule and pack-horse, so that
our equipment is complete, except in the matter of crup-
pers, which we have been obliged to make for ourselves
out of goats' hair rope, and old stockings. If Mr. G.
has an eye for the picturesque, he must have been gratified as he came in from the fog and darkness into the
grass room, with the flaring fire in the middle, the rifles
gleaming on the wall, the two men in very rough
clothing, and myself huddled up in a blanket sitting on
the floor, where my friend was very glad to join us.

Mr. Green has brought nothing but tea from Kapapala,
but Gandle has made some excellent rolls, besides feast-
ing us on stewed fowl, dough nuts, and milk! Little
comfort is promised for to-night, as Gandle says with a
twinkle of kindly malice in his eye, that we shall not
"get a wink of sleep, for the place swarms with fleas."
They are a great pest of the colder regions of the islands,
and like all other nuisances, are said to have been imported!   Gandle and the other man have entertained us
with the misfortunes of our predecessors, on which they
seem to gloat with ill-omened satisfaction.

I. L. B.

LETTER XXIX.—*Continued.*

THE fleas at Ainepo quite fulfilled Mr. Gandle's prognostications, and I was glad when the cold stars went out one by one, and a red, cloudless dawn broke over the mountain, accompanied by a heavy dew and a morning mist, which soon rolled itself up into rosy folds and disappeared, and there was a legitimate excuse for getting up. Our host provided us with flour, sugar, and dough nuts, and a hot breakfast, and our expedition, comprising two natives who knew not a word of English, Mr. G. who does not know very much more Hawaiian than I do, and myself, started at seven. We had four superb mules, and two good pack-horses, a large tent, and a plentiful supply of camping blankets. I put on all my own warm clothes, as well as most of those which had been lent to me, which gave me the squat, padded, look of a puffin or Esquimaux, but all, and more were needed long before we reached the top. The mules were beyond all praise. They went up the most severe ascent I have ever seen, climbing steadily for nine hours, without a touch of the spur, and after twenty-four hours of cold, thirst, and hunger, came down again as actively as cats. The pack-horses too were very good, but from the comparative clumsiness with which they move their feet they were very severely cut.

We went off, as usual, in single file, the guide first, and Mr. G. last. The track was passably legible for some time, and wound through long grass, and small *koa* trees, mixed with stunted *ohias* and a few common ferns. Half these *koa* trees are dead, and all, both living and dead, have their branches covered with a long hairy lichen, nearly white, making the dead forest in the slight mist look like a wood in England when covered with rime on a fine winter morning. The *koa* tree has a peculiarity of bearing two distinct species of leaves on the same twig, one like a curved willow leaf, the other that of an acacia.

After two hours ascent we camped on the verge of the timber line, and fed our animals, while the two natives hewed firewood, and loaded the spare pack-horse with it. The sky was by that time cloudless, and the atmosphere brilliant, and both remained so until we reached the same place twenty-eight hours later, so that the weather favoured us in every respect, for there is "weather" on the mountain, rains, fogs, and wind storms. The grass only grows sparsely in tufts above this place, and though vegetation exists up to a height of 10,000 feet on this side, it consists, for the most part, of grey lichens, a little withered grass, and a hardy asplenium.

At this spot the real business of the ascent begins, and we tightened our girths, distributed the baggage as fairly as possible, and made all secure before remounting.

We soon entered on vast uplands of *pahoehoe* which

ground away the animals' feet, a horrid waste, extending upwards for 7000 feet. For miles and miles, above and around, great billowy masses, tossed and twisted into an infinity of fantastic shapes, arrest and weary the eye, lava in all its forms, from a compact phonolite, to the lightest pumice stone, the mere froth of the volcano, exceeding in wildness and confusion the most extravagant nightmare ever inflicted on man. Recollect the vastness of this mountain. The whole south of this large island, down to, and below the water's edge, is composed of its slopes. Its height is nearly three miles, its base is 180 miles in circumference, so that Wales might be packed away within it, leaving room to spare. Yet its whole huge bulk, above a height of about 8000 feet, is one frightful desert, at once the creation and the prey of the mightiest force on earth.

Struggling, slipping, tumbling, jumping, ledge after ledge was surmounted, but still, upheaved against the glittering sky, rose new difficulties to be overcome. Immense bubbles have risen from the confused masses, and bursting, have yawned apart. Swift-running streams of more recent lava have cleft straight furrows through the older congealed surface. Massive flows have fallen in, exposing caverned depths of jagged outlines. Earthquakes have riven the mountain, splitting its sides and opening deep *crevasses*, which must be leapt or circumvented. Horrid streams of *a-a* have to be cautiously skirted, which after rushing remorselessly over the kindlier lava have heaped rugged pinnacles of brown scoriæ into impassable walls. Winding round the bases

of tossed up, fissured hummocks of *pahoehoe*, leaping
from one broken hummock to another, clambering up
acclivities so steep that the pack-horse rolled backwards
once, and my cat-like mule fell twice, moving cautiously
over crusts which rang hollow to the tread; stepping
over deep cracks, which, perhaps, led down to the burning fathomless sea, traversing hilly lakes ruptured by
earthquakes, and split in cooling into a thousand fissures,
painfully toiling up the sides of mounds of scoriæ frothed
with pumice-stone, and again for miles surmounting
rolling surfaces of billowy ropy lava—so passed the long
day, under the tropic sun, and the deep blue sky.

Towards afternoon, clouds heaped themselves in brilliant snowy masses, all radiance and beauty to us, all fog
and gloom below, girdling the whole mountain, and inter-
posing their glittering screen between us and the dark
timber belt, the black smoking shores of Kau, and the blue
shimmer of the Pacific. From that time, for twenty-four
hours, the lower world, and "works and ways of busy
men" were entirely shut out, and we were alone with this
trackless and inanimate region of horror.

For the first time our guide hesitated as to the right
track, for the faint suspicion of white smoke, which had
kept alive our hope that the fire was still burning, had
ceased to be visible. We called a halt while he recon-
noitred, tried to eat some food, found that our pulses
were beating 100 a minute, bathed our heads, specially
our temples, with snow, as we had been advised to do by the
oldest mountaineer on Hawaii, and heaped on yet more
clothing. In fact, I tied a double woollen scarf over all

my face but my eyes, and put on a French soldier's
overcoat, with cape and hood, which Mr. Green had
brought in case of emergency. The cold had become
intense. We had not wasted words at any time, and on
remounting, preserved as profound a silence as if we were
on a forlorn hope, even the natives intermitting their
ceaseless gabble.

Upwards still, in the cold bright air, coasting the
edges of deep cracks, climbing endless terraces, the
mules panting heavily, our breath coming as if from
excoriated lungs,—so we surmounted the highest ledge.
But on reaching the apparent summit we were to all
appearance as far from the faint smoke as ever, for this
magnificent dome, whose base is sixty miles in diameter,
is crowned by a ghastly volcanic table land, creviced,
riven, and ashy, twenty-four miles in circumference. A
table-land, indeed, of dark grey lava, blotched by outbursts, and torn by streams of brown *a-a*, full of hideous
crevasses and fearful shapes, as if a hundred waves of
lava had rolled themselves one on another, and had congealed in confused heaps, and been tortured in all directions by the mighty power which had upheaved the whole.

Our guide took us a little wrong once, but soon recovered himself with much sagacity. "Wrong" on
Mauna Loa means being arrested by an impassable *a-a*
stream, and our last predecessors had nearly been stopped
by getting into one in which they suffered severely.

These *a-a* streams are very deep, and when in a state
of fusion move along in a mass 20 feet high some-

times, with very solid walls. Professor Alexander, of
Honolulu, supposes them to be from the beginning less
fluid than *pahoehoe*, and that they advance very slowly,
being full of solid points, or centres of cooling: that *a-a*,
in fact, *grains* like sugar. Its hardness is indescribable.
It is an aggregate of upright, rugged, adamantine points,
and at a distance, a river of it looks like a dark brown
Mer de Glace.

At half-past four we reached the edge of an *a-a* stream,
about as wide as the Ouse at Huntingdon Bridge, and it
was obvious that somehow or other we must cross it:
indeed, I know not if it be possible to reach the crater
without passing through one or another of these obstacles. I should have liked to have left the animals
there, but it was represented as impossible to proceed on
foot, and though this was a decided misrepresentation,
Mr. Green plunged in. I had resolved that he should
never have any bother in consequence of his kindness in
taking me with him, and, indeed, everyone had enough
to do in taking care of himself and his own beast, but
I never found it harder to repress a cry for help. Not
that I was in the least danger, but there was every risk
of the beautiful mule being much hurt, or breaking her
legs. The fear shown by the animals was pathetic; they
shrank back, cowered, trembled, breathed hard and
heavily, and stumbled and plunged painfully. It was
sickening to see their terror and suffering, the struggling
and slipping into cracks, the blood and torture. The
mules with their small legs and wonderful agility were
more frightened than hurt, but the horses were splashed

with blood up to their knees, and their poor eyes looked piteous.

We were then, as we knew, close to the edge of the crater, but the faint smoke wreath had disappeared, and there was nothing but the westering sun hanging like a ball over the black horizon of the desolate summit. We rode as far as a deep fissure filled with frozen snow, with a ledge beyond, threw ourselves from our mules, jumped the fissure, and more than 800 feet below yawne.l the inaccessible blackness and horror of the crater of Mokuaweoweo, six miles in circumference, and 11,000 feet long by 8,000 wide. The mystery was solved, for at one end of the crater, in a deep gorge of its own, above the level of the rest of the area, there was the lonely fire, the reflection of which, for six weeks, has been seen for 100 miles.

Nearly opposite us, a thing of beauty, a perfect fountain of pure yellow fire, unlike the gory gleam of Kilauea, was regularly playing in several united but independent jets, throwing up its glorious incandescence, to a height, as we afterwards ascertained, of from 150 to 300 feet, and attaining at one time 600! You cannot imagine such a beautiful sight. The sunset gold was not purer than the living fire. The distance which we were from it, divested it of the inevitable horrors which surround it. It was all beauty. For the last two miles of the ascent, we had heard a distant vibrating roar: there, at the crater's edge, it was a glorious sound, the roar of an ocean at dispeace, mingled with the hollow murmur of surf echoing in sea caves, booming

on, rising and falling, like the thunder music of windward Hawaii.

We sat on the ledge outside the fissure for some time,
and Mr. Green actually proposed to pitch the tent there,
but I dissuaded him, on the ground that an earthquake
might send the whole thing tumbling into the crater;
nor was this a whimsical objection, for during the night
there were two such falls, and after breakfast, another
quite near us.

We had travelled for two days under a strong impression that the fires had died out, so you can imagine the
sort of stupor of satisfaction with which we feasted on
the glorious certainty. Yes, it was glorious, that far-off
fire-fountain, and the lurid cracks in the slow-moving,
black-crusted flood, which passed calmly down from the
higher level to the grand area of the crater.

This area, over two miles long, and a mile and a half
wide, with precipitous sides 800 feet deep, and a broad
second shelf about 300 feet below the one we occupied,
at that time appeared a dark grey, tolerably level lake,
with great black blotches, and yellow and white stains, the
whole much fissured. No steam or smoke proceeded
from any part of the level surface, and it had the
unnaturally dead look which follows the action of fire.
A ledge, or false beach, which must mark a once higher
level of the lava, skirts the lake, at an elevation of
thirty feet probably, and this fringed the area with various
signs of present volcanic action, steaming sulphur banks,
and heavy jets of smoke. The other side, above the
crater, has a ridgy broken look, giving the false impres-

sion of a mountainous region beyond. At this time the luminous fountain, and the red cracks in the river of lava which proceeded from it, were the only fires visible in the great area of blackness. In former days people have descended to the floor of the crater, but owing to the breaking away of the accessible part of the precipice, a descent now is not feasible, though I doubt not that a man might even now get down, if he went up with suitable tackle, and sufficient assistance.

The one disappointment was that this extraordinary fire-fountain was not only 800 feet below us, but nearly three-quarters of a mile from us, and that it was impossible to get any nearer to it. Those who have made the ascent before have found themselves obliged either to camp on the very spot we occupied, or a little below it.

The natives pitched the tent as near to the crater as was safe, with one pole in a crack, and the other in the great fissure, which was filled to within three feet of the top with snow and ice. As the opening of the tent was on the crater side, we could not get in or out without going down into this *crevasse*. The tent walls were held down with stones to make it as snug as possible, but *snug* is a word of the lower earth, and has no meaning on that frozen mountain top. The natural floor was of rough slabs of lava, laid partly edgewise, so that a newly macadamised road would have been as soft a bed. The natives spread the horse blankets over it, and I arranged the camping blankets, made my own part of the tent as comfortable as possible by putting my inverted saddle down for a pillow, put on my last reserve of warm

clothing, took the food out of the saddle bags, and then
felt how impossible it was to exert myself in the rarified
air, or even to upbraid Mr. Green for having forgotten
the tea, of which I had reminded him as often as was
consistent with politeness!

This discovery was not made till after we had boiled
the kettle, and my dismay was softened by remembering
that as water boils up there at 187°, our tea would have
been worthless. In spite of my objection to stimulants,
and in defiance of the law against giving liquor to
natives, I made a great tin of brandy toddy, of which
all partook, along with tinned·salmon and dough-nuts.
Then the men piled faggots on the fire and began their
everlasting chatter, and Mr. Green and I, huddled up in
blankets, sat on the outer ledge in solemn silence, to
devote ourselves to the volcano.

The sun was just setting: the tooth-like peaks of
Mauna Kea,·cold and snow slashed, which were blushing
red, the next minute turned ghastly against a chilly sky,
and with the disappearance of the sun it became severely
cold; yet we were able to remain there till 9·30, the first
people to whom such a thing has been possible, so
supremely favoured were we by the absence of wind.

When the sun had set, and the brief red glow of the
tropics had vanished, a new world came into being, and
wonder after wonder flashed forth from the previously
lifeless crater. Everywhere through its vast expanse
appeared glints of fire—fires bright and steady, burning
in rows like blast furnaces; fires lone and isolated, unwinking like planets, or twinkling like stars; rows of

little fires marking the margin of the lowest level of the
crater; fire molten in deep *crevasses ;* fire in wavy lines;
fire, calm, stationary, and restful : an incandescent lake
two miles in length beneath a deceptive crust of darkness, and whose depth one dare not fathom even in
thought. Broad in the glare, giving light enough to
read by at a distance of three-quarters of a mile, making
the moon look as blue as an ordinary English sky, its
golden gleam changed to a vivid rose colour, lighting
up the whole of the vast precipices of that part of the
crater with a rosy red, bringing out every detail here,
throwing cliffs and heights into huge black masses there,
rising, falling, never intermitting, leaping in lofty jets
with glorious shapes like wheatsheaves, coruscating, reddening, the most glorious thing beneath the moon was the
fire-fountain of Mokuaweoweo.

By day the cooled crust of the lake had looked black
and even sooty, with a fountain of molten gold playing
upwards from it; by night it was all incandescent, with
black blotches of cooled scum upon it, which were perpetually being devoured. The centre of the lake was at a
white heat, and waves of white hot lava appeared to be
wallowing there as in a whirlpool, and from this centre
the fountain rose, solid at its base, which is estimated
at 150 feet in diameter, but thinning and frittering as it
rose high into the air, and falling from the great altitude
to which it attained, in fiery spray, which made a very
distinct clatter on the fiery surface below. When one jet was
about half high, another rose so as to keep up the action

without intermission; and in the lower part of the
fountain two subsidiary curved jets of great volume continually crossed each other. So, "alone in its glory,"
perennial, self-born, springing up in sparkling light, the
fire-fountain played on as the hours went by.

From the nearer margin of this incandescent lake there
was a mighty but deliberate overflow, a "silent tide" of
fire, passing to the lower level, glowing under and
amidst its crust, with the brightness of metal passing
from a furnace. In the bank of partially cooled and
crusted lava which appears to support the lake, there
were rifts showing the molten lava within. In one place
heavy white vapour blew off in powerful jets from the
edge of the lake, and elsewhere there were frequent jets
and ebullitions of the same, but there was not a trace of
vapour over the burning lake itself. The crusted large
area, with its blowing cones, blotches and rifts of fire, was
nearly all visible, and from the thickness and quietness of
the crust it was obvious that the ocean of lava below was
comparatively at rest, but a dark precipice concealed a
part of the glowing and highly agitated lake, adding
another mystery to its sublimity.

It is probable that the whole interior of this huge
dome is fluid, for the eruptions from this summit crater
do not proceed from its filling up and running over, but
from the mountain sides being unable to bear the enormous pressure; when they give way, high or low, and
bursting, allow the fiery contents to escape. So, in 1855,
the mountain side split open, and the lava gushed forth

for thirteen months in a stream which ran for 60 miles, and flooded Hawaii for 300 square miles.*

From the camping ground, immense cracks parallel with the crater, extend for some distance, and the whole of the compact grey stone of the summit is much fissured. These cracks, like the one by which our tent was pitched, contain water resting on ice. It shows the extreme difference of climate on the two sides of Hawaii, that while vegetation straggles up to a height of 10,000 feet on the windward side in a few miserable blasted forms, it absolutely ceases at a height of 7,000 feet on the leeward.

It was too cold to sit up all night; so by the "fire light" I wrote the enclosed note to you with fingers nearly freezing on the pen, and climbed into the tent.

It is possible that tent life in the East, or in the Rocky Mountains, with beds, tables, travelling knick-knacks of all descriptions, and servants who study their master's whims, may be very charming; but my experience of it having been of the make-shift and non-luxurious kind, is not delectable. A wooden saddle, without stuffing, made a very fair pillow; but the ridges of the lava were severe. I could not spare enough blankets to soften them, and one particularly intractable point persisted in making itself felt. I crowded on everything attainable, two pairs of gloves, with Mr. Gilman's socks over them, and a thick plaid muffled up my face. Mr. Green and the natives, buried in blankets, occupied the other part of the tent. The phrase, "sleeping on the brink of a vol-

* Since white men have inhabited the islands, there have been ten recorded eruptions from the craters of Mauna Loa, and one from Hualalai.

cano," was literally true, for I fell asleep, and fear I
might have been prosaic enough to sleep all night, had it
not been for fleas which had come up in the camping
blankets.   When I woke, it was light enough to see that
the three muffled figures were all asleep, instead of spending the night in shiverings and vertigo, as it appears that
others have done.   Doubtless the bathing of our heads
several times with snow and ice-water had been bene-
ficial.

Circumstances were singular.   It was a strange thing
to sleep on a lava-bed at a height of nearly 14,000 feet,
far away from the nearest dwelling, " in a region," as
Mr. Jarves says, "rarely visited by man," hearing all the
time the roar, clash, and thunder of the mightiest volcano
in the world.   It seemed all a wild dream, as that majestic sound moved on.   There were two loud reports,
followed by a prolonged crash, occasioned by parts of the
crater walls giving way; vibrating rumblings, as if of earthquakes; and then a louder surging of the fiery ocean, and
a series of most imposing detonations.   Creeping over
the sleeping forms, which never stirred even though I
had to kneel upon one of the natives while I untied the
flap of the tent, I crept cautiously into the *crevasse* in
which the snow-water was then hard frozen, and out upon
the projecting ledge.   The four hours in which we had previously watched the volcano had passed like one; but
the lonely hours which followed might have been two
minutes or a year, for time was obliterated.

Coldly the Pole-star shivered above the frozen summit,
and a blue moon, nearly full, withdrew her faded light

into infinite space. The Southern Cross had set. Two peaks below the Pole-star, sharply defined against the sky, were the only signs of any other world than the world of fire and mystery around. It was light, broadly, vividly light; the sun himself, one would have thought, might look pale beside it. But such a light ! The silver index of my thermometer, which had fallen to 23° Fahrenheit, was ruby red; that of the aneroid, which gave the height at 13,803 feet (an error of 43 feet in excess), was the same. The white duck of the tent was rosy, and all the crater walls and the dull-grey ridges which lie around were a vivid rose red.

All Hawaii was sleeping. Our Hilo friends looked out the last thing; saw the glare, and probably wondered how we were " getting on," high up among the stars. Mine were the only mortal eyes which saw what is perhaps the grandest spectacle on earth. Once or twice I felt so overwhelmed by the very sublimity of the loneliness, that I turned to the six animals, which stood shivering in the north wind, without any consciousness than that of cold, hunger, and thirst. It was some relief even to pity them, for pity was at least a human feeling, and a momentary rest from the thrill of the new sensations inspired by the circumstances. The moon herself looked a wan un-familiar thing—not the same moon which floods the palm and mango groves of Hilo with light and tenderness. And those palm and mango groves, and lighted homes, and seas, and ships, and cities, and faces of friends, and all familiar things, and the day before, and the years before, were as things in dreams, coming up out of a vanished past. And would there ever be another day, and would the earth ever be young and green again, and would men buy and sell and strive for gold, and should I ever with a human voice tell living human beings of the things of this midnight ? How far it was from all the world, uplifted above love, hate, and storms of passion, and war, and wreck of thrones, and dissonant clash of human thought, serene in the eternal solitudes !

Things had changed, as they change hourly in craters. The previous loud detonations were probably connected with the evolutions of some " blowing cones," which were now very fierce, and throwing up lava at the comparatively dead end of the crater. Lone stars of fire broke out frequently through the blackened crust. The molten river, flowing from the incandescent lake, had advanced and broadened considerably. That lake itself, whose diameter has been estimated at 800 feet, was rose-red and self-illuminated, and the increased noise was owing to the increased force of the fire-fountain, which was playing regularly at a height of 300 feet, with the cross fountains, like wheat-sheaves, at its lower part. These cross-fountains were the colour of a mixture of blood and fire, and the lower part of the perpendicular jets was the same; but as they rose and thinned, this colour passed into a vivid rose-red, and the spray and splashes were as rubies and flame mingled. For ever falling in fiery masses and fiery foam : accompanied by a thunder-music of its own : companioned only by the solemn stars : exhibiting no other token of its glories to man than the reflection of its fires on mist and smoke ; it burns for

the Creator's eye alone. No foot of mortal can approach it.

Hours passed as I watched the indescribable glories of
the fire-fountain, its beauty of form, and its radiant
reflection on the precipices, eight hundred feet high, which
wall it in, and listened to its surges beating, and the ebb
and flow of its thunder-music. Then a change occurred.
The jets, which for long had been playing at a height of
300 feet, suddenly became quite low, and for a few
seconds appeared as cones of fire wallowing in a sea of
light; then with a roar like the sound of gathering waters,
nearly the whole surface of the lake was lifted up by the
action of some powerful internal force, and rose three times
with its whole radiant mass, in one glorious, upward
burst, to a height, as estimated by the surrounding
cliffs, of six hundred feet, while the earth trembled,
and the moon and stars withdrew abashed into far-off
space. After this the fire-fountain played as before. The
cold had become intense, 11° of frost; and I crept back
into the tent; those words occurring to me with a new
meaning, "dwelling in the light which no man can
approach unto."

We remained in the tent till the sun had slightly warmed
the air, and then attempted to prepare breakfast by the
fire; but no one could eat anything, and the native from
Waimea complained of severe headache, which shortly
became agonizing, and he lay on the ground moaning,
and completely prostrated by mountain sickness. I felt
extreme lassitude, and exhaustion followed the slightest
effort; but the use of snow to the head produced great

relief. The water in our canteens was hard frozen, and the keenness of the cold aggravated the uncomfortable symptoms which accompany pulses at 110°. The native guide was the only person capable of work, so we were late in getting off, and rode four and a half hours to the camping ground, only stopping once to tighten our girths. Not a rope, strap, or buckle, or any of our gear gave way, and though I rode without a crupper, the breeching of a pack mule's saddle kept mine steady.

The descent, to the riders, is far more trying than the ascent, owing to the continued stretch of very steep declivity for eight thousand feet; but our mules never tripped, and came into Ainepo as if they had not travelled at all. The horses were terribly cut, both again in the *a-a* stream, and on the descent. It was sickening to follow them, for at first they left fragments of hide and hair on the rocks, then flesh, and when there was no more hide or flesh to come off their poor heels and fetlocks, blood dripped on every rock, and if they stood still for a few moments, every hoof left a little puddle of gore. We had all the enjoyment and they all the misery. I was much exhausted when we reached the camping-ground, but soon revived under the influence of food; but the poor native, who was really very ill, abandoned himself to wretchedness, and has only recovered to-day.

The belt of cloud which was all radiance above, was all drizzling fog below, and we reached Ainepo in a regular Scotch mist. The ranchmen seemed rather grumpy at our successful ascent, which involved the failure of all their prophecies, and, indeed, we were thoroughly unsatisfactory travellers, arriving fresh and complacent, with neither adventures nor disasters to gladden people's hearts. We started for this ranch seven miles further, soon after dark, and arrived before nine, after the most successful ascent of Mauna Loa ever made.

Without being a Sybarite, I certainly do prefer a comfortable *pulu* bed to one of ridgy lava, and the fire which blazes on this broad hearth to the camp-fire on the frozen top of the volcano. The worthy ranchman expected us, and has treated us very sumptuously, and even Kahélé is being regaled on Chinese sorghum. The Sunday's rest, too, is a luxury, which I wonder that travellers can ever forego. If one is always on the move, even very vivid impressions are hunted out of the memory by the last new thing. Though I am not unduly tired, even had it not been Sunday, I should have liked a day in which to recall and arrange my memories of Mauna Loa before the forty-eight miles' ride to Hilo.

This afternoon, we were sitting under the verandah talking volcanic talk, when there was a loud rumbling, and a severe shock of earthquake, and I have been twice interrupted in writing this letter by other shocks, in which all the frame-work of the house has yawned and closed again. They say that four years ago, at the time of the great "mud flow" which is close by, this house was moved several feet by an earthquake, and that all the cattle walls which surround it were thrown down. The ranchman tells us that on January 7th and 8th, 1873, there was a sudden and tremendous outburst of Mauna Loa. The ground, he says, throbbed and quivered for twenty miles ; a tremendous roaring, like that of a blast furnace, was heard for the same distance, and clouds of black smoke trailed out over the sea for thirty miles.

We have dismissed our guide with encomiums. His charge was $10; but Mr. Green would not allow me to share that, or any part of the expense, or pay anything, but $6 for my own mule. The guide is a goat-hunter, and the chase is very curiously pursued. The hunter catches sight of a flock of goats, and hunts them up the mountain, till, agile and fleet of foot as they are, he actually tires them out, and gets close enough to them to cut their throats for the sake of their skins. If I understand rightly, this young man has captured as many as seventy in a day.

CRATER HOUSE, KILAUEA. June 9th.

This morning Mr. Green left for Kona, and I for Kilauea; the ranchman's native wife and her sister riding with me for several miles to put me on the right track. Kahélé's sociable instincts are so strong, that, before they left me, I dismounted, blindfolded him, and led him round and round several times, a process which so successfully confused his intellects, that he started off in this direction with more alacrity than usual. They certainly put me on a track which could not be mistaken, for it was a narrow, straight path, cut and hammered through a broad horrible a-a stream, whose jagged spikes were the height of the horse. But beyond this lie ten miles of pahoehoe, the lava-flows of ages, with only now and then the vestige of a trail.

Except the perilous crossing of the Hilo gulches in February, this is the most difficult ride I have had—eerie and impressive in every way.   The loneliness was absolute.   For several hours I saw no trace of human beings, except the very rare print of a shod horse's hoof. It is a region for ever " desolate and without inhabitant," trackless, waterless, silent, as if it had passed into the passionless calm of lunar solitudes.   It is composed of rough hummocks of *pahoehoe*, rising out of a sandy desert. Only stunted *ohias*, loaded with crimson tufts, raise them-selves out of cracks : twisted, tortured growths, bearing their bright blossoms under protest, driven unwillingly to be gay by a fiery soil and a fiery sun.   To the left, there was the high, dark wall of an *a-a* stream ; further yet, a tremendous volcanic fissure, at times the bed of a fiery river, and above this the towering dome of Mauna Loa, a brilliant cobalt blue, lined and shaded with indigo where innumerable lava streams had seamed his portentous sides : his whole beauty the effect of atmosphere, on an object in itself hideous.   Ahead and to the right were rolling miles of a *pahoehoe* sea, bounded by the unseen Pacific 3,000 feet below, with countless craters, fissures emitting vapour, and all other concomitants of volcanic action ; bounded to the north by the vast crater of Kilauea. On all this deadly region the sun poured his tropic light and heat from one of the bluest skies I ever saw.

The direction given me on leaving Kapapala was, that after the natives left me I was to keep a certain crater on the south-east till I saw the smoke of Kilauea ; but there were many craters.   Horses cross the sand and hummocks

as nearly as possible on a bee line ; but the lava rarely
indicates that anything has passed over it, and this morning a strong breeze had rippled the sand, completely
obliterating the hoof-marks of the last traveller, and at
times I feared that losing myself, as many others have
done, I should go mad with thirst.   I examined the sand
narrowly for hoof-marks, and every now and then found
one, but always had the disappointment of finding that it
was made by an unshod horse, therefore not a ridden one.
Finding eyesight useless, I dismounted often, and felt with
my finger along the rolling lava for the slightest marks
of abrasion, which might show that shod animals had
passed that way, got up into an *ohia* to look out for
the smoke of Kilauea, and after three hours came out
upon what I here learn is the old track, disused because
of the insecurity of the ground.

It runs quite close to the edge of the crater, there 1,000
feet in depth, and gives a magnificent view of the whole
area, with the pit and the blowing cones.   But the region
through which the trail led was rather an alarming one,
being hollow and porous, all cracks and fissures,
nefariously concealed by scrub and ferns.   I found a place,
as I thought, free from risk, and gave Kahélé a feed of
oats on my plaid, but before he had finished them there
was a rumbling and vibration, and he went into the ground
above his knees, so snatching up the plaid and jumping
on him I galloped away, convinced that that crack was
following me !   However, either the crack thought better
of it, or Kahélé travelled faster, for in another half-hour
I arrived where the whole region steams, smokes, and

fumes with sulphur, and was kindly welcomed here by Mr. Gilman, where he and the old Chinaman appear to be alone.

After a seven hours' ride the quiet and the log fire are very pleasant, and the host is a most intelligent and sympathising listener. It is a solemn night, for the earth quakes, and the sound of Halemaumau is like the surging of the sea.

HILO. *June 11th.*

Once more I am among palm and mango groves, and friendly faces, and sounds of softer surges than those of Kilauea. I had a dreary ride yesterday, as the rain was incessant, and I saw neither man, bird, or beast the whole way. Kahélé was so heavily loaded that I rode the thirty miles at a foot's pace, and he became so tired that I had to walk.

It has been a splendid week, with every circumstance favourable, nothing sordid or worrying to disturb the impressions received, kindness and goodwill everywhere, a travelling companion whose consideration, endurance, and calmness were beyond all praise, and at the end the cordial welcomes of my Hawaiian " home."

I. L. B.

LETTER XXX.*

I LANDED in Kealakakua Bay on a black lava block, on which tradition says that Captain Cook fell, struck with his death-wound, a century ago. The morning sun was flaming above the walls of lava 1,000 feet in height which curve round the dark bay, the green deep water rolled shorewards in lazy undulations, canoes piled full of pineapples poised themselves on the swell, ancient coco-palms glassed themselves in still waters—it was hot, silent, tropical.

The disturbance which made the bay famous is known to every schoolboy; how the great explorer, long supposed by the natives to be their vanished god *Lono*, betrayed his earthly lineage by groaning when he was wounded, and was then dispatched outright. A cocoanut stump, faced by a sheet of copper recording the circumstance, is the great circumnavigator's monument. A few miles

---

* Several letters are omitted here, as they contain repetitions of journeys and circumstances which have been amply detailed before. I went to the Kona district for a few days only, intending to return to friends on Kauai and Maui ; but owing to an alteration in the sailings of the *Kilauea*, was detained there for a month, and afterwards, owing to uncertainties connected with the San Francisco steamers, was obliged to leave the Islands abruptly, after a residence of nearly seven months.

beyond, is the enclosure of Haunaunau, the City of Refuge for western Hawaii. In this district there is a lava road ascribed to Umi, a legendary king, who is said to have lived 500 years ago. It is very perfect, well defined on both sides with kerb-stones, and greatly resembles the chariot ways in Pompeii. Near it are several structures formed of four stones, three being set upright, and the fourth forming the roof. In a northerly direction is the place where Liholiho, the king who died in England, excited by drink and the persuasions of Kaahumanu, broke *tabu*, and made an end of the superstitions of heathenism. Not far off is the battle field on which the adherents of the idols rallied their forces against the iconoclasts, and were miserably and finally defeated. Recent lava streams have descended on each side of the bay, and from the bare black rock of the landing a flow may be traced up the steep ascent as far as a precipice, over which it falls in waves and twists, a cataract of stone. A late lava river passed through the magnificent forest on the southerly slope, and the impressions of the stems of coco and fan palms are stamped clearly on the smooth rock. The rainfall in Kona is heavy, but there is no standing water, and only one stream in a distance of 100 miles.

This district is famous for oranges, coffee, pineapples, and silence. A flaming palm-fringed shore with a prolific strip of table land 1,500 feet above it, a dense timber belt eight miles in breadth, and a volcano smoking somewhere between that and the heavens, and glaring through the trees at night, are the salient points of Kona if any-

thing about it be salient. It is a region where falls
not

> ". . . Hail or any snow,
> Or ever wind blows loudly."

Wind indeed, is a thing unknown. The scarcely audible
whisper of soft airs through the trees morning and
evening, rain drops falling gently, and the murmur of
drowsy surges far below, alone break the stillness. No
ripple ever disturbs the great expanse of ocean which
gleams through the still, thick trees. Rose in the sweet
cool morning, gold in the sweet cool evening, but always
dreaming; and white sails come and go, no larger than a
butterfly's wing on the horizon, of ships drifting on
ocean currents, dreaming too! Nothing surely can ever
happen here : it is so dumb and quiet, and people speak
in hushed thin voices, and move as in a lethargy,
dreaming too! No heat, cold, or wind, nothing empha-
sised or italicised, it is truly a region of endless after-
noons, "a land where all things always seem the same."
Life is dead, and existence is a languid swoon.

This is the only regular boarding house on Hawaii.
The company is accidental and promiscuous. The conversation consists of speculations, varied and repeated with
the hours, as to the arrivals and departures of the
Honolulu schooners *Uilama* and *Prince*, who they will
bring, who they will take, and how long their respective
passages will be. A certain amount of local gossip is
also hashed up at each meal, and every stranger who has
travelled through Hawaii for the last ten years is picked
to pieces and worn threadbare, and his purse, weight,

entertainers, and habits are thoroughly canvassed. On whatever subject the conversation begins it always ends in dollars; but even that most stimulating of all topics only arouses a languid interest among my fellow dreamers. I spend most of my time in riding in the forests, or along the bridle path which trails along the height, among grass and frame-houses, almost smothered by trees and trailers.

Many of these are inhabited by white men, who, having drifted to these shores, have married native women, and are rearing a dusky race, of children who speak the maternal tongue only, and grow up with native habits. Some of these men came for health, others landed from whalers, but of all it is true that infatuated by the ease and lusciousness of this languid region,

> " They sat them down upon the yellow sand,
>   Between the sun and moon upon the shore ;
> And sweet it was to dream of Fatherland,
>   .   .   .   ; but evermore
> Most weary seem'd the sea, weary the oar,
>   Weary the wandering fields of barren foam.
> Then some one said, " We will return no more."

They have enough and more, and a life free from toil, but the obvious tendency of these marriages is to sink the white man to the level of native feelings and habits.

There are two or three educated residents, and there is a small English church with daily service, conducted by a resident clergyman.

The beauty of this part of Kona is wonderful. The interminable forest is richer and greener than anything I

have yet seen, but penetrable only by narrow tracks
which have been made for hauling timber. The trees
are so dense, and so matted together with trailers, that
no ray of noon-day sun brightens the moist tangle of
exquisite mosses and ferns which covers the ground.
Yams with their burnished leaves, and the Polypodium
spectrum, wind round every tree stem, and the heavy *ié*,
which here attains gigantic proportions, links the tops of
the tallest trees together by its stout knotted coils.
Hothouse flowers grow in rank profusion round every
house, and tea-roses, fuchsias, geraniums fifteen feet high,
Nile lilies, Chinese lantern plants, begonias, lantanas,
hibiscus, passion-flowers, Cape jasmine, the hoya, the
tuberose, the beautiful but overpoweringly sweet ginger
plant, and a hundred others : while the whole district is
overrun with the Datura brugmansia (?) here an arborescent shrub fourteen feet high, bearing seventy great trumpet-shaped white blossoms at a time, which at night vie
with those of the night-blowing Cereus in filling the
air with odours.

Pineapples and melons grow like weeds among the
grass, and everything that is good for food flourishes.
Nothing can keep under the redundancy of nature in
Kona; everything is profuse, fervid, passionate, vivified
and pervaded by sunshine. The earth is restless in her
productiveness, and forces up her hothouse growth perpetually, so that the miracle of Jonah's gourd is almost
repeated nightly. All decay is hurried out of sight, and
through the glowing year flowers blossom and fruits
ripen; ferns are always uncurling their young fronds and

bananas unfolding their great shining leaves, and spring blends her everlasting youth and promise with the fulfilment and maturity of summer.

"Never comes the trader, never floats a European flag,
  Slides the bird o'er lustrous woodland, swings the trailer from the crag :
  Droops the heavy-blossom'd bower, hangs the heavy-fruited tree—
  Summer isles of Eden lying in dark purple spheres of sea."

HUALALAI. *July 28th.*

I very soon left the languid life of Kona for this sheep station, 6000 feet high on the desolate slope of the dead volcano of Hualalai, (" offspring of the shining sun,") on the invitation of its hospitable owner, who said if I " could eat his rough fare, and live his rough life, his house and horses were at my disposal." He is married to a very attractive native woman who eats at his table, but does not know a word of English, but they are both away at a wool-shed eight miles off, shearing sheep.

This house is in the great volcanic wilderness of which I wrote from Kalaieha, a desert of drouth and barrenness. There is no permanent track, and on the occasions when I have ridden up here alone, the directions given me have been to steer for an ox bone, and from that to a dwarf *ohia*. There is no coming or going ; it is seventeen miles from the nearest settlement, and looks across a desert valley to Mauna Loa. Woody trailers, harsh hard grass in tufts, the Asplenium trichomanes in rifts, the Pellea ternifolia in sand, and some *ohia* and *mamané* scrub in hollow places sheltered from the wind, all hard, crisp, unlovely growths, contrast with the lavish greenery

428 HAWAII. [LETTER XXX.

below. A brisk cool wind blows all day; every afternoon a dense fog brings the horizon within 200 feet, but
it clears off with frost at dark, and the flames of the
volcano light the whole southern sky.

My companions are an amiable rheumatic native
woman, and a crone who must have lived a century, much
shrivelled and tattooed, and nearly childish. She talks to
herself in weird tones, stretches her lean limbs by the fire
most of the day, and in common with most of the old people
has a prejudice against clothes, and prefers huddling herself up in a blanket to wearing the ordinary dress of her
sex. There is also a dog, but he does not understand
English, and for some time I have not spoken any but
Hawaiian words. I have plenty to do, and find this a
very satisfactory life.

I came up to within eight miles of this house with a
laughing, holiday-making rout of twelve natives, who rode
madly along the narrow forest trail at full gallop, up and
down the hills, through mire and over stones, leaping
over the trunks of prostrate trees, and stooping under
branches with loud laughter, challenging me to reckless
races over difficult ground, and when they found that the
wahine haole was not to be thrown from her horse they
patted me approvingly, and crowned me with *leis* of
mailé. I became acquainted with some of these at
Kilauea in the winter, and since I came to Kona they
have been very kind to me.

I thoroughly like living among them, taking meals
with them on their mats, and eating "two fingered"
poi as if I had been used to it all my life. Their mirth-

fulness and kindliness are most winning; their horses, food, clothes, and time are all bestowed on one so freely, and one lives amongst them with a most restful sense of absolute security. They have many faults, but living alone among them in their houses as I have done so often on Hawaii, I have never seen or encountered a dis-agreeable thing. But the more I see of them the more impressed I am with their carelessness and love of pleasure, their lack of ambition and a sense of responsi-bility, and the time which they spend in doing nothing but talking and singing as they bask in the sun, though spasmodically and under excitement they are capable of tremendous exertions in canoeing, surf-riding, and lassoing cattle.

While down below I joined three natives for the pur-pose of seeing this last sport. They all rode shod horses, and had lassoes of ox hide attached to the horns of their saddles. I sat for an hour on horseback on a rocky hill while they hunted the woods; then I heard the deep voices of bulls, and a great burst of cattle appeared, with hunters in pursuit, but the herd vanished over a dip of the hill side, and the natives joined me. By this time I wished myself safely at home, partly because my unshod horse was not fit for galloping over lava and rough ground, and I asked the men where I should stay to be out of danger. The leader replied, " Oh, just keep close behind me!" I had thought of some safe view-point, not of galloping on an unshod horse with a ruck of half maddened cattle, but it was the safest plan, and there was no time to be lost, for as we rode slowly down, we sighted the herd dodging across the open to regain the shelter of the wood, and much on the alert.

Putting our horses into a gallop we dashed down the hill till we were close up with the chase; then another tremendous gallop, and a brief wild rush, the grass shaking with the surge of cattle and horses. There was much whirling of tails and tearing up of the earth—a lasso spun three or four times round the head of the native who rode in front of me, and almost simultaneously a fine red bullock lay prostrate on the earth, nearly strangled, with his foreleg noosed to his throat. The other natives dismounted, and put two lassoes round his horns, slipping the first into the same position, and vaulted into their saddles before he was on his legs.

He got up, shook himself, put his head down, and made a mad blind rush, but his captors were too dexterous for him, and in that and each succeeding rush he was foiled. As he tore wildly from side to side, the natives dodged under the lasso, slipping it over their heads, and swung themselves over their saddles, hanging in one stirrup, to aid their trained horses to steady themselves as the bullock tugged violently against them. He was escorted thus for a mile, his strength failing with each useless effort, his tongue hanging out, blood and foam dropping from his mouth and nostrils, his flanks covered with foam and sweat, till blind and staggering, he was led to a tree, where he was at once stabbed, and two hours afterwards a part of him was served at table. The natives were surprised that I avoided seeing his death, as the native women greatly enjoy such a spectacle. This mode of killing an animal while heated and terrified, doubtless accounts for the dark colour and hardness of Hawaiian beef.

Numbers of the natives are expert with the lasso, and besides capturing with it wild and half wild cattle, they catch horses with it, and since I came here my host caught a sheep with it, singling out the one he wished to kill, from the rest of the galloping flock with an unerring aim. It takes a whole ox hide cut into strips to make a good lasso.

One of my native friends tells me that a native man who attended on me in one of my earlier expeditions has since been "prayed to death." One often hears this phrase, and it appears that the superstition which it represents has by no means died out. There are persons who are believed to have the lives of others in their hands, and their services are procured by offerings of white fowls, brown hogs, and *awa*, as well as money, by any one who has a grudge against another. Several other instances have been told me of persons who have actually died under the influence of the terror and despair produced by being told that the *kahuna* was "praying them to death." I cannot learn whether these over efficacious prayers are supposed to be addressed to the true God, or to the ancient Hawaiian divinities. The natives are very superstitious, and the late king, who was both educated and intelligent, was much under the dominion of a sorceress.

I have made the ascent of Hualalai twice from here, the first time guided by my host and hostess, and the second time rather adventurously alone. Forests of *koa*, sandal-wood, and *ohia*, with an undergrowth of raspberries and ferns clothe its base, the fragrant *mailé*, and the graceful sarsaparilla vine, with its clustered coral-coloured buds, nearly smother many of the trees, and in several places the heavy *ié* forms the semblance of triumphal arches over the track. This forest terminates abruptly on the great volcanic wilderness, with its starved growth of unsightly scrub. But Hualalai, though 10,000 feet in

height, is covered with Pteris aquilina, *mamané*, coarse bunch grass, and *pukeavé* to its very summit, which is crowned by a small, solitary, blossoming *ohia*.

For two hours before reaching the top, the way lies over countless flows and beds of lava, much disintegrated, and almost entirely of the kind called *pahoehoe*. Countless pit craters extend over the whole mountain, all of them covered outside, and a few inside, with scraggy vegetation. The edges are often very ragged and picturesque. The depth varies from 300 to 700 feet, and the diameter from 700 to 1,200. The walls of some are of a smooth grey stone, the bottoms flat, and very deep

in sand, but others resemble the tufa cones of Mauna
Kea.   They are so crowded together in some places as
to be divided only by a ridge so narrow that two mules
can scarcely walk abreast upon it.   The mountain was
split by an earthquake in 1868, and a great fissure, with
much treacherous ground about it, extends for some distance across it.   It is very striking from every point of
view on this side, being a complete wilderness of craters,
and over 150 lateral cones have been counted.

The object of my second ascent was to visit one of the
grandest of the summit craters, which we had not reached
previously owing to fog.   This crater is bordered by a
narrow and very fantastic ridge of rock, in or on which
there is a mound about 60 feet high, formed of fragments
of black, orange, blue, red, and golden lava, with a cavity
or blow-hole in the centre, estimated by Brigham as
having a diameter of 25 feet, and a depth of 1800.   The
interior is dark brown, much grooved horizontally, and as
smooth and regular as if turned.   There are no steam
cracks or signs of heat anywhere.   Superb caves or
lava-bubbles abound at a height of 6000 feet.   These are
moist with ferns, and the drip from their roofs is the
water supply of this porous region.

Hualalai, owing to the vegetation sparsely sprinkled
over it, looks as if it had been quiet for ages, but it has
only slept since 1801, when there was a tremendous
eruption from it, which flooded several villages, destroyed
many plantations and fishponds, filled up a deep bay 20
miles in extent, and formed the present coast.   The
terrified inhabitants threw living hogs into the stream,
and tried to propitiate the anger of the gods by more

costly offerings, but without effect, till King Kamehameha, attended by a large retinue of priests and chiefs, cut off some of his hair, which was considered sacred, and threw it into the torrent, which in two days ceased to run.   This circumstance gave him a greatly increased ascendancy, from his supposed influence with the deities of the volcanoes.

I have explored the country pretty thoroughly for many miles round, but have not seen anything striking, except the remains of an immense *heiau* in the centre of the desert tableland, said to have been built in a day by the compulsory labour of 25,000 people : a lonely white man who lives among the lava, and believes he has dis-covered the secret of perpetual motion : and the lava-flow from Mauna Loa, which reached the sea 40 miles from its exit from the mountain.

I was riding through the brushwood with a native, and not able to see two yards in any direction, when emerging from the thick scrub, we came upon the torrent of 1859 within six feet of us, a huge, straggling, coal-black river, broken up into streams in our vicinity, but on the whole, presenting an iridescent uphill expanse a mile wide. We had reached one of the divergent streams to which it had been said after its downward course of 9000 feet, "Hitherto shalt thou come and no further," while the main body had pursued its course to the ocean.   What-ever force impelled it had ceased to act, and the last towering wave of fire had halted just there, and lies a black arrested surge 10 feet high, with tender ferns at its feet, and a scarcely singed *ohia* bending over it.   The flow, so far as we scrambled up it, is heaped in great surges of a fierce black, fiercely reflecting the torrid sun, cracked, and stained yellow and white, and its broad glistening surface forms an awful pathway to the dome-like crest of Mauna Loa, now throbbing with internal fires, and crowned with a white smoke wreath, that betokens the action of the same forces which produced this gigantic inundation. Close to us the main river had parted above and united below a small *mamané* tree with bracken under its shadow, and there are several oases of the same kind.

I have twice been down to the larger world of the woolshed, when tired of strips of dried mutton and my own society. The hospitality there is as great as the accommodation is small. The first time, I slept on the floor of the shed with some native women who were up there, and was kept awake all night by the magnificence of the light on the volcano. The second time, several of us slept in a small, dark grass-wigwam, only intended as a temporary shelter, the lowliest dwelling in every sense of the word that I ever occupied. That evening was the finest I have seen on the islands; there was a less abrupt transition from day to night, and the three great mountains and the desert were etherealised and glorified by a lingering rose and violet light. When darkness came on, our great camp fire was hardly redder than the glare from the volcano, and its leaping flames illuminated as motley a group as you would wish to see; the native shearers, who, after shearing eighty sheep each in a day, washed, and changed their clothes before eating; a negro goatherd with a native wife and swarthy children, two native women, my host and myself, all engaged in the rough cooking befitting the region, toasting strips of jerked

mutton on sticks, broiling wild bullock on the coals,
baking *kalo* under ground, and rolls in a rough stone
oven, and all speaking that base mixture of English and
Hawaiian which is current coin here. The meal was not
less rude than the cookery. We ate it on the floor of the
wigwam, with an old tin, with some fat in it, for a lamp,
and a bit of rope for a wick, which kept tumbling into the
fat and leaving us in darkness.

The next day I came up here alone, driving a pack-
horse, and with a hind-quarter of sheep tied to my saddle.
It is really difficult to find the way over this desert,
though I have been several times across. When a breeze
ripples the sand between the lava hummocks, the footprints are obliterated, and there are few landmarks except
the "ox bone" and the "small *ohia*." It is a strange
life up here on the mountain side, but I like it, and never
yearn after civilization. The one drawback is my ignorance of the language, which not only places me sometimes in grotesque difficulties, but deprives me of much
interest. I don't know what day it is, or how long I have
been here, and quite understand how possible it would be
to fall into an indolent and aimless life, in which time is
of no account.

THE RECTORY, KONA.
August 1st.

I left Hualalai yesterday morning, and dined with my
kind host and hostess in the wigwam. It was the last
taste of the wild Hawaiian life I have learned to love so
well, the last meal on a mat, the last exercise of skill in
eating "two-fingered" *poi*. I took leave gratefully of
those who had been so truly kind to me, and with the

friendly *aloha* from kindly lips in my ears, regretfully
left the purple desert in which I have lived so serenely,
and plunged into the forest gloom.   Half way down, I met
a string of my native acquaintances, who, as the courteous
custom is, threw over me *leis* of *mailé* and roses, and
since I arrived here, others have called to wish me good
bye, bringing presents of figs, cocoa-nuts and bananas.

This is one of the stations of the " Honolulu Mission,"
and Mr. Davies, the clergyman, has, besides Sunday and
daily services, a day-school for boys and girls.   The
Sunday attendance at church, so far as I have seen, consists of three adults, though the white population within
four miles is considerable, and at another station on
Maui, the congregation was composed solely of the family
of a planter.   Clerical reinforcements are expected from
England shortly; but from what I have seen and heard
everywhere, I do not think that the coming clergy, even
if inspired by the same devotion and disinterestedness as
Bishop Willis, will make any sensible progress among the
people.

In truth, I believe that the " Honolulu *Mission*," from
the first, has been a mistake.   As such, strictly speaking,
there is no room for it, for all the natives are nominal
Christians, and are connected more or less with the
Congregational denomination.   To attempt to proselytize
them to the English Church, or to unsettle their religious
relations in any way, would, on the whole, be a hopeless,
as well as an invidious task, and would not improbably
result in driving some among them into the greater
apparent unity of the Church of Rome.   Those who believe in the oneness of the invisible church, and that all

who hold "one Lord, one faith, one baptism," are within the pale of salvation, may well hesitate before expending energy, men, money, and time on proselytizing efforts.

Among the whites who have sunk into the mire of an indolent and godless, if not an openly immoral life, there is an undoubted field for Evangelistic effort; but it is very doubtful, I think, whether this class can be reached by services which appeal to higher culture and instincts than it possesses, and, indeed, generally, the island Episcopalians are not in sympathy with the "symbolism" and "high ritual" which from the first have been outstanding features of this "mission." The education of the young in the principles of the Prayer Book is aimed at by the Bishop and his coadjutors, but in spite of zeal and devotion, I doubt whether the English Church on these islands can ever be anything but a pining and sickly exotic.

Kona looks supremely beautiful, a languid dream of all fair things. Yet truly my heart warms to nothing so much as to a row of fat English cabbages which grow in the rectory garden, with a complacent, self-asserting John Bullism about them. It is best to leave the islands now. I love them better every day, and dreams of Fatherland are growing fainter in this perfumed air and under this glittering sky. A little longer, and I too should say, like all who have made their homes here under the deep banana shade,—

> " We will return no more,
> . . . . our island home
> Is far beyond the wave, we will no longer roam."

I. L. B.

LETTER XXXI.

My fate is lying at the wharf in the shape of the Pacific
Mail Steamer *Costa Rica,* and soon to me Hawaii-nei
will be but a dream. "Summer isles of Eden!" My
heart warms towards them as I leave them, for they have
been more like home than any part of the world since
I left England. The moonlight is trickling through
misty algarobas, and feathery tamarinds and palms, and
shines on glossy leaves of breadfruit and citron; a cool
breeze brings in at my open doors the perfumed air and
the soft murmur of the restful sea, and this beautiful
Honolulu, whose lights are twinkling through the purple
night, is at last, as it was at first, Paradise in the Pacific,
a bright blossom of a summer sea.

I shall be in the Rocky Mountains before you receive
my hastily-written reply to your proposal to come out
here for a year, but I will add a few reasons against it, in
addition to the one which I gave regarding the benefit
which I now hope to derive from a change to a more
stimulating climate. The strongest of all is, that if we
were to stay here for a year, we should just sit down
"between the sun and moon upon the shore," and forget

" our island home," and be content to fall " asleep in a
half dream," and " return no more ! "

Of course you will have gathered from my letters that
there are very many advantages here. Indeed, the
mosquitoes of the leeward coast, to whose attacks one
becomes inured in a few months, are the only physical
drawback. The open-air life is most conducive to health,
and the climate is absolutely perfect, owing to its
equability and purity. Whether the steady heat of
Honolulu, the languid airs of Hilo, the balmy breezes of
Onomea, the cool bluster of Waimea, or the odorous
stillness of Kona, it is always the same. The grim gloom
of our anomalous winters, the harsh malignant winds of
our springs, and the dismal rains and overpowering heats
of our summers, have no counterpart in the endless
spring-time of Hawaii.

Existence here is unclogged and easy, a small income
goes a long way, and the simplicity, refinement, kindliness, and sociability of the foreign residents, render
society very pleasant. The life here is truer, simpler,
kinder, and happier than ours. The relation between
the foreign and native population is a kindly and happy
one, and the natives, in spite of their faults, are a most
friendly and pleasant people to live among. With a
knowledge of their easily-acquired language, they would
be a ceaseless source of interest, and every white resident
can have the satisfaction of helping them in their
frequent distresses and illnesses.

The sense of security is a very special charm, and one
enjoys it as well in lonely native houses, and solitary days

and nights of travelling, as in the foreign homes, which are never locked throughout the year. There are no burglarious instincts to dread, and there is no such thing as "a broken sleep of fear beneath the stars." The person and property of a white man are everywhere secure, and a white woman is sure of unvarying respect and kindness.

There are no inevitable hardships. The necessaries, and even the luxuries of civilization can be obtained everywhere, and postal communication with America is now regular and rapid.

When I began this letter, a long procession of counter-balancing disadvantages passed through my mind, but they become "beautifully less" as I set them down in black and white. If I put gossip first, it is because I seriously think that it is the canker of the foreign society on the islands. Its extent and universality are grotesque and amusing to a stranger, but to live in it, and share in it, and learn to enjoy it, would be both lowering and hurtful, and you can hardly be long here without being drawn into its vortex. By *gossip* I don't mean scandal or malignant misrepresentations, or reports of petty strifes, intrigues, and jealousies, such as are common in all cliques and communities, but *nuhou*, mere tattle, the perpetual talking about people, and the picking to tatters of every item of personal detail, whether gathered from fact or imagination.

A great deal of this is certainly harmless, and in some measure arises from the intimate friendly relations which exist between the scattered families, but over-indulgence

in it destroys the privacy of individual existence, and is
deteriorating in more ways than one. From the north of
Kauai to the south of Hawaii, everybody knows every
other body's affairs, income, expenditure, sales, purchases,
debts, furniture, clothing, comings, goings, borrowings,
lendings, letters, correspondents, and every thing else :
and when there is nothing new to relate on any one of
these prolific subjects, supposed intentions afford abundant
matter for speculation. All gossip is focussed here, being
imported from every other district, and re-exported, with
additions and embellishments, by every inter-island mail.
The ingenuity with which *nuhou* is circulated is worthy
of a better cause.

Some disadvantages arise from the presence on the
islands of heterogeneous and ill-assorted nationalities.
The Americans, of course, predominate, and even those
who are Hawaiian born, have, as elsewhere, a strongly
national feeling. The far smaller English community
hangs together in a somewhat cliquish fashion, and
possibly cherishes a latent grudge against the Americans
for their paramount influence in island affairs. The
German residents, as everywhere, are cliquish too. Then,
since the establishment of the Honolulu Mission, church
feeling has run rather high, and here, as elsewhere, has a
socially divisive tendency. Then there are drink and
anti-drink, pro and anti-missionary, and pro and anti-
reciprocity-treaty parties, and various other local naggings
of no interest to you.

The civilization is exotic, and owing to various circumstances, the government and constitution are too experi-

mental and provisional in their nature, and possess too few elements of permanence to engross the profound interest of the foreign residents, although for reasons of policy they are well inclined to sustain a barbaric throne. In spite of a king and court, and titles and officials without number, and uniforms stiff with gold lace, and Royal dinner parties with *menus* printed on white silk, Americans, Republicans in feeling, really " run " the government, and in state affairs there is a taint of that combination of obsequious and flippant vulgarity, which none deplore more deeply than the best among the Americans themselves.

It is a decided misfortune to a community to be divided in its national leanings, and to have no great fusing interests within or without itself, such as those which knit vigorous Victoria to the mother country, or distant Oregon to the heart of the Republic at Washington. Except sugar and dollars, one rarely hears any subject spoken about with general interest. The downfall of an administration in England, or any important piece of national legislation, arouses almost no interest in American society here, and the English are ostentatiously apathetic regarding any piece of intelligence specially absorbing to Americans. The papers pick up every piece of gossip which drifts about the islands, and snarl with much wordiness over local matters, but crowd into a small space the movements which affect the masses of mankind, and in the absence of a telegraph one hardly feels the beat of the pulses of the larger world. Those intellectual movements of the West which might provoke

discussion and conversation are not cordially entered
into, partly owing to the difference in theological beliefs,
and partly from an indolence born of the climate, and
the lack of mental stimulus.

After all, the gossip and the absence of large interests
shared in common, are the only specialities which can be
alleged against Hawaii, and I have never seen people
among whom I should so well like to live. The ladies
are most charming, essentially womanly, and fulfil all
domestic and social duties in a way worthy of imitation
everywhere. The kindness and hospitality, too, are
unbounded, and these cover " a multitude of sins."

There are very few strangers here now. It is the
"dead season." I have met with none except Mr.
Nordhoff, who is writing on the islands for *Harper's
Monthly*, and his charming wife and children. She is a
most expert horsewoman, and has adopted the Mexican
saddle even in Honolulu, where few foreign ladies ride
"cavalier fashion."

My friends all urge me to write on Hawaii, on the
ground that I have seen the islands and lived the island
life so thoroughly ; but possibly they expect more indis-
criminate praise than I could conscientiously bestow !

Honolulu is in the midst of the epidemic of letter
writing which sets in on the arrival of the steamer from
" the coast," and people walk and drive as if they really
had business on hand : and the farewell visits to be made
and received, the pleasant presence of Mr. Thompson,
and Mr. and Mrs. Severance, of Hilo, and the hasty
doing of things which have been left to the last, make

me a sharer in the spasmodic bustle, which, were it permanent, would metamorphose this dreamy, bowery, tropical capital. The undeserved and unexpected kindness shown me here, as everywhere on these islands, renders my last impressions even more delightful than my first. The people are as genial as their own sunny skies, and in more frigid regions I shall never sigh for the last without longing for the first. . . . .

S. S. Costa Rica.
August 7th.

We sailed for San Francisco early this afternoon. Everything looked the same as when I landed in January, except that many of the then strange faces among the radiant crowd are now the faces of friends, that I know nearly everyone by sight, and that the pathos of farewell blended with every look and word. The air still rang with laughter and *alohas*, and the rippling music of the Hawaiian tongue ; bananas and pineapples were still piled in fragrant heaps ; the drifts of surf rolled in, as then, over the barrier reef, canoes with outriggers still poised themselves on the blue water ; the coral divers still plied their graceful trade, and the lazy ripples still flashed in light along the palm-fringed shore. The head-ropes were let go, we steamed through the violet channel into the broad Pacific, Lunalilo, who came out so far with Chief Justice Allen, returned to the shore, and when his kindly *aloha* was spoken, the last link with the islands was severed, and half an hour later Honolulu was out of sight. . . . .

. . . . The breeze is freshening, and the *Costa Rica's* head lies nearly due north. The sun is sinking, and on the far horizon the summit peaks of Oahu gleam like amethysts on a golden sea. Farewell for ever, my bright tropic dream ! *Aloha nui* to Hawaii-nei !

I. L. B.

A CHAPTER ON HAWAIIAN AFFAIRS.

A FEW facts concerning the Hawaiian islands may serve to supplement the deficiencies of the foregoing letters. The group is an hereditary and constitutional monarchy. There is a house of nobles appointed by the Crown, which consists of twenty members. The House of Representatives consists of not less than twenty-four, or more than forty members elected biennially. The Legislature fixes the number, and apportions the same. The Houses sit together, and constitute the Legislative Assembly. The property qualification for a representative is, real estate worth $500, or an annual income of $250 from property, and that for an elector is an annual income of $75. The Legislators are paid, and the expense of a session is about $15,000. There are three cabinet ministers appointed by the Crown, of the Interior, Finance, and Foreign Affairs respectively, and an Attorney-General, who may be regarded as a minister of justice. There is a Supreme Court with a Chief Justice and two associate justices, and there are circuit and district judges on all the larger islands, as well as sheriffs, prisons, and police. There is a standing army of sixty men, mainly for the purposes of guard duty, and rendering assistance to the police.

The question of " how to make ends meet " sorely
exercises the little kingdom. All sorts of improvements
involving a largely increased outlay are continually
urged, while at the same time the burden of taxation
presses increasingly heavily, and there is a constant
clamour for the removal of some of the most lucrative
imposts. Indeed, the Hawaiian dog, with his tax and
his " tag," is seldom out of the Legislative Assembly.

What may be termed the *per capita* taxes are, an
annual poll tax of one dollar levied on each male inhabitant between the ages of seventeen and sixty, an
annual road tax of two dollars upon all persons between
seventeen and fifty, and an annual school tax of two
dollars upon all persons between twenty-one and sixty.
There is a direct tax upon property of $\frac{1}{2}$ per cent. upon
its valuation, and specific taxes of a dollar on every
horse above two years old, and a dollar and a half on
each dog. Of the $206,000 raised by internal taxes
during the last biennial period, the horses paid $50,000,
the mules $6,000, and the dogs $19,000!

The indirect taxation in the shape of customs' duties
amounted to $350,000 in the same period. The poor
Hawaiian does not know the blessing of a " Free Breakfast Table."

The islands are large importers. The value of imported goods paying duties was $1,437,000 in 1873, on
which the Hawaiian Treasury received $198,000 as
customs' duties. Twenty-five thousand dollars' worth of
ale, porter, and light wines, and thirty thousand dollars'
worth of spirits, show that the foreign population of 6,000

is more than sufficiently bibulous. The Chinamen, about 2,000 in number, are, or ought to be, responsible for $13,000 worth of opium; and the $34,000 worth of tobacco and cigars is doubtless distributed pretty equally over all the nationalities. Twenty-one thousand gallons of spirits were imported in 1873. The licences to sell spirits brought $18,000 dollars into the treasury in the last biennial period, but those for the sale of *awa* and opium brought in $55,000 during the same time. These licences are confined to Honolulu.

There are two interesting items of customs receipts, a sum of $924, the proceeds of a *per capita* tax of two dollars levied on passengers landing on the islands, for the support of the Queen's Hospital, and a sum of $1,477, the proceeds of a tax levied on seamen for the support of the Marine Hospital. There is a sum of $700 for passports, as no Hawaiian or stranger can leave the kingdom without an official permit.

There are 58 vessels registered under the Hawaiian flag, of which 40 are coasters, and 18 engaged in foreign freighting and whaling.

The value of domestic exports in 1873 was $1,725,507. Among these are bananas, pineapples, *pulu,* cocoanuts, oranges, limes, sandal-wood, tamarinds, betel leaves, shark's fins, *paiai,* whale oil, sperm oil, cocoanut oil, and whalebone. Among other commodities there was exported, of coffee 262,000 lbs., of fungus 57,000 lbs., of pea nuts 58,000 lbs., of cotton 8,000 lb., of rice 941,000lbs. of paddy 507,000lbs., of hides 20,000 packages, of goat skins 66,000, of horns 13,000, and of tallow 609,000 lbs.

The expense of "keeping things going" on the islands
for the two years ending March 1st, 1874, amounted to
$1,193,276, but this included the funeral expenses of
two kings, as well as of two extra sessions of the
Legislature, which amounted to $42,000. The decrease
in the revenue for the same period amounted to $45,000.
The items of Hawaiian expenditure were as follows :—

For Civil List	$47,689.73
„ Permanent Settlements, Queen Emma	12,000.00
„ Legislature and Privy Council.	15,288.50
„ Extra Legislative Expenses.	19,011.87
„ Department of the Judiciary	72,245.64
„ „ of Foreign Affairs and War	78,145.85
„ „ of the Interior	389,009.08
„ „ of Finance	202,117.05
„ „ of the Attorney-General	97,097.00
„ Bureau of Public Instruction	89,432.40
„ Miscellaneous Expenditures	170,474.67
The balance on hand in the Treasury, March 31st, 1874	764.57
	$1,193,276.36

That, under the head Finance, includes the interest on
borrowed money. The funded national debt is $340,000.
Of this sum a portion bears no stated interest, only such
as may arise from the very dubious profits of the
Hawaiian hotel. The interest charges are 12 per cent. on
$25,000, and 9 per cent. on $272,000. The estimates
for the present biennial period involve a large increase of
debt. The present financial position of the kingdom is,
an increasing expenditure and a decreasing revenue.

The statistics of the Judiciary Department for the last

two years present a few features of interest. There were
4,000 convictions out of 5,764 cases brought before the
courts, equal to a fourteenth part of the population. The
total number of offences in the category is 125. Of these
some are decidedly local. Thus, for "furnishing intoxicating liquors to Hawaiians" 92 persons were
punished; for "exhibition of *Hula*," 10; for "selling
awa without licence," 12; for "selling opium without
licence," 24. It is not surprising to those who know the
habits of the people, that the convictions for violations of
the marriage tie, though greatly diminished, should reach
the number of 384, while under the head "Deserting
Husbands and Wives," 67 convictions are recorded. For
"practising medicine without a licence," 56 persons were
punished; for "furious riding," 197; for "cruelty to
animals," 37; for "gaming," 121; for "gross cheating,"
32; for "violating the Sabbath," 61. We must remember
that the returns include foreigners and Chinamen, or else
the reputation for "harmlessness" which Hawaiians
possess would suffer seriously when we read that within
the last two years there were 178 convictions for
"assault," 248 for "assault and battery," 12 for
"assaults with dangerous weapons," 49 for "affray,"
674 for "drunkenness," 87 for "disturbing quiet of the
night," and 13 for "murder." Yet the number of
criminal cases has largely diminished, and taking civil
and criminal together, there has been a decrease of 656
for the last biennial period, as compared with that immediately preceding it.

The administration of justice is confessedly one of the

most efficient departments of Hawaiian affairs. Chief Justice Allen, both as a lawyer and a gentleman, is worthy to fill the highest position in his native country (America), and the Associate Justices, as well as the native and foreign judges throughout the islands, are highly esteemed for honour and uprightness. I never heard an uttered suspicion of venality or unfairness against anyone of them, and apparently the Judiciary Department of Hawaii deserves the same confidence which we repose in our own.

The Educational System has been carefully modelled, and is carried out with tolerable efficiency. Eighty-seven per cent. of the whole school population are actually at school, and the inspector of schools states that a person who cannot read and write is rarely met with. Each common school is graded into two, three, or four classes, according to the intelligence and proficiency of the pupils, and the curriculum of study is as follows :—

CLASS I.—Reading, mental and written arithmetic, geography, penmanship, and composition.

CLASS II.—Reading, mental arithmetic, geography, penmanship.

CLASS III.—Reading, first principles of arithmetic, penmanship.

CLASS IV.—Primer, use of slate and pencil.

The youngest children are not classified until they can put letters together in syllables.

Vocal music is taught wherever competent teachers are found.

The total sum expended on education, including the

grants to "family" and other schools, is about $40,000 a year.*

It has been remarked that the rising race of Hawaiians has an increased contempt for industry in the form of manual labour, and it is proposed by the Board of Education that such labour shall be made a part of common school education, so that on both girls and boys a desire to provide for their own wants in an honest way shall be officially inculcated. There is a Government Reformatory School, and industrial and family schools for both girls and boys are scattered over the islands. The supply of literature in the vernacular is meagre, and few of the natives have any intelligent comprehension of English.

The group has an area of about 4,000,000 acres, of which about 200,000 may be regarded as arable, and 150,000 as specially adapted for the culture of sugar-cane. Sugar, the great staple production, gives employment in its cultivation and manufacture to nearly 4,000 hands. Only a fifteenth part of the estimated arable area is under cultivation. Over 6,000 natives are returned as the possessors of *Kuleanas* or freeholds, but many of these are heavily mortgaged. Many of the larger lands are

* The schools of the kingdom are as follows :—

	Number Schools.	Boys.	Girls.	Total.
Common Schools	196	3193	2329	5522
Government Boarding Schools . . .	3	185	......	185
Government Haw.-Eng. Day Schools .	5	415	246	661
Subsidized Boarding Schools . . .	10	168	191	359
Subsidized Day Schools	9	201	210	411
Independent Boarding Schools . . .	3	14	62	76
Independent Day Schools . . .	16	287	254	541
Total	242	4463	3292	7755

held on lease from the crown or chiefs, and there are difficulties attending the purchase of small properties.

Almost all the roots and fruits of the torrid and temperate zones can be grown upon the islands, and the banana, *kalo*, yam, sweet potato, cocoanut, breadfruit, arrowroot, sugar-cane, strawberry, raspberry, whortleberry, and native apple, are said to be indigenous.

The indigenous *fauna* is small, consisting only of hogs, dogs, rats, and an anomalous bat which flies by day. There are few insects, except such as have been imported, and these, which consist of centipedes, scorpions, cockroaches, mosquitoes, and fleas, are happily confined to certain localities, and the two first have left most of their venom behind them. A small lizard is abundant, but snakes, toads, and frogs have not yet effected a landing.

The ornithology of the islands is scanty. Domestic fowls are supposed to be indigenous. Wild geese are numerous among the mountains of Hawaii, and plovers, snipe, and wild ducks, are found on all the islands. A handsome owl, called the owl-hawk, is common. There is a paroquet with purple feathers, another with scarlet, a woodpecker with variegated plumage of red, green, and yellow, and a small black bird with a single yellow feather under each wing. There are few singing birds, but one of the few has as sweet a note as that of the English thrush. There are very few varieties of moths and butterflies.

The *flora* of the Hawaiian Islands is far scantier than that of the South Sea groups, and cannot compare with that of many other tropical as well as temperate regions. But all the islands are rich in cryptogamous plants, of which there is an almost infinite variety.

Hawaii is still in process of construction, and is subject to volcanic eruptions, earthquakes, and tidal waves. Hurricanes are unknown, and thunderstorms are rare and light.

Under favourable circumstances of moisture, the soil is most prolific, and "patch cultivation" in glens and ravines, as well as on mountain sides, produces astonishing results. A *Kalo* patch of forty square feet will support a man for a year. An acre of favourably situated land will grow a thousand stems of bananas, which will produce annually ten tons of fruit. The sweet potato flourishes on the most unpromising lava, where soil can hardly be said to exist, and in good localities produces 200 barrels to the acre. On dry light soils the Irish potato grows anyhow and anywhere, with no other trouble than that of planting the sets. Most vegetable dyes, drugs, and spices can be raised. Forty diverse fruits present an overflowing cornucopia. The esculents of the temperate zones flourish. The coffee bush produces from three to five pounds of berries the third year after planting. The average yield of sugar is two and a half tons to the acre. Pineapples grow like weeds in some districts, and water melons are almost a drug. The bamboo is known to grow sixteen inches in a day. Wherever there is a sufficient rainfall, the earth teems with plenty.

Yet the Hawaiian Islands can hardly be regarded as a field for emigration, though nature is lavish, and the climate the most delicious and salubrious in the world. Farming, as we understand it, is unknown. The dearth of insectivorous birds seriously affects the cultivation of

a soil naturally bounteous to excess. The narrow gorges
in which terraced "patch cultivation," is so successful,
offer no temptations to a man with the world before him.
The larger areas require labour, and labour is not to be
had. Though wheat and other cereals mature, attacks of
weevil prevent their storage, and all the grain and flour
consumed are imported from California.

Cacao, cinnamon, and allspice, are subject to an apparently
ineradicable blight. The blight which has attacked the
coffee shrub is so severe, that the larger plantations have
been dug up, and coffee is now raised by patch culture,
mainly among the guava scrub which fringes the forests.
Oranges suffer from blight also, and some of the finest
groves have been cut down. Cotton suffers from the
ravages of a caterpillar. The mulberry tree, which, from
its rapid growth, would be invaluable to silk growers, is
covered with a black and white blight. Sheep are at
present successful, but in some localities the spread of a
pestilent "oat-burr" is depreciating the value of their
wool. The forests, which are essential to the well-
being of the islands, are disappearing in some quarters,
owing to the attacks of a grub, as well as the ravages of
cattle.

Cocoanuts, bananas, yams, sweet potatoes, *kalo*, and
breadfruit, the staple food of the native population, are
free from blight, and so are potatoes and rice. Beef
cattle can be raised for almost nothing, and in some
districts beef can be bought for the cent or two per pound
which pays for the cutting up of the carcase. Every one
can live abundantly, and without the "sweat of the
brow," but few can make money, owing to the various

forms of blight, the scarcity of labour, and the lack of a profitable market.

There is little healthy activity in any department of business. The whaling fleet has deserted the islands. A general *pilikia* prevails. Settlements are disappearing, valley lands are falling out of cultivation, Hilo grass and guava scrub are burying the traces of a former population. The natives are rapidly diminishing,* the old in-

* The population by the last census, taken in 1872, is as follows :—

Total number of natives in 1872	.	. . . .	49,044
,,	,,	half-castes in 1872	2,487
,,	,,	Chinese in 1872	1,938
,,	,,	Americans in 1872	889
,,	,,	Hawaiians born of foreign parents, 1872.	849
,,	,,	Britons in 1872	619
,,	,,	Portuguese in 1872	395
,,	,,	Germans in 1872	224
,,	,,	French in 1872	88
,,	,,	other foreigners in 1872	364

Total population in 1872	56,897

Total number of natives, *including half-castes*, in 1866 .	58,765
,, ,, ,, ,, ,, 1872 .	51,531

Decrease since 1866	7,234

The excess of males over females is 6,403 souls.

AREA AND POPULATION OF EACH ISLAND.

	Acres.	Height in Feet.	Population in 1872.
Hawaii . .	2,500,000	13,953	16,001
Maui . . .	400,000	10,200	12,334
Oahu. . .	350,000	3,800	20,671
Kauai . . .	350,000	4,800	4,961
Molokai . .	200,000	2,800	2,349
Lanai . . .	100,000	2,400	343
Niihau . .	70,000	800	233
Kahoolawe . .	30,000	400	——

Total	56,897

dustries are abandoned, and the inherent immorality of the race, the great outstanding cause of its decay, still resists the influence of Christian teaching and example.

An exotic civilization is having a fair trial on the Hawaiian Islands. With the exception of the serious maladies introduced by foreigners in the early days, and the disastrous moral influence exercised by worthless whites, they have suffered none of the wrongs usually inflicted on the feebler by the stronger race. The rights of the natives were in the first instance carefully secured to them, and have since been protected by equal laws, righteously administered. The Hawaiians have been aided towards independence in political matters, and the foreigners who framed the laws and constitution, and have directed Hawaiian affairs, such as Richards, Lee, Judd, Allen, and Wyllie, were men above reproach; and missionary influence, of all others the most friendly to the natives, has predominated for fifty years.

The effects of missionary labour have been scarcely touched upon in the foregoing letters, and here, in preference to giving any opinion of my own, I quote from Mr. R. H. Dana, an Episcopalian, and a barrister of the highest standing in America, well known in this country by his writings, who sums up his investigations on the Sandwich Islands in the following dispassionate words: "It is no small thing to say of the missionaries of the American Board, that in less than forty years they have taught this whole people to read and to write, to cipher and to sew. They have given them an alphabet, grammar, and dictionary; preserved their language from extinction;

given it a literature, and translated into it the Bible, and
works of devotion, science, and entertainment, &c. They
have established schools, reared up native teachers, and
so pressed their work, that now the proportion of inhabitants who can read and write is greater than in New
England. And whereas they found these islanders a nation
of half-naked savages, living in the surf and on the sand,
eating raw fish, fighting among themselves, tyrannized
over by feudal chiefs, and abandoned to sensuality, they
now see them decently clothed, recognizing the law of
marriage, knowing something of accounts, going to school
and public worship more regularly than the people do at
home, and the more elevated of them taking part in conducting the affairs of the constitutional monarchy under
which they live, holding seats on the judicial bench and
in the legislative chambers, and filling posts in the local
magistracies."

If space permitted, the testimony of " Mark Twain,"
given in " Roughing It," might be added to the above, and
the remaining missionaries may well point to the visible
results of their labours, with the one word *Circumspice!*

A CHAPTER ON HAWAIIAN HISTORY.

In the pre-historic days of Hawaii, for 500 years, as the bards sing, before Captain Cook landed, and indeed for some years afterwards, each island had its king, chiefs, and internal dissensions; and incessant wars, with a reckless waste of human life, kept the whole group in turmoil. Chaotic and legendary as early Hawaiian history is, there is enough to show that there must have been regularly organized communities on the islands for a very long period, with a civilization and polity which, though utterly unworthy of Christianity, were enlightened and advanced for Polynesian heathenism.

The kingly office was hereditary, and the king's power absolute. On the different islands the kings and chiefs who together constituted a privileged class, admitted the priesthood to some portion of their privileges, probably with the view of enslaving the people more completely through the agency of religion, and held the lower classes in absolute subserviency by the most rigorous of feudal systems, which included *hana poalima*, or forced labour, and the *tabu*, well known throughout Polynesia.

A very interesting history begins with Kamehameha the Great, the Conqueror, or the Terrible; the "Napoleon of the Pacific," as he has been called. He

united an overmastering ambition to a singular gift of
ruling, and without education, training, or the help of a
single political precedent to guide him, animated not
only by the lust of conquest, but by the desire to create
a nationality, he subjugated every thing that his canoes
could reach, and fused a rabble of savages and chieftain-
cies into a united nation, every individual of which to
this day inherits something of the patriotism of the
Conqueror.

His wars were by no means puny either in proportions
or slaughter, as, for instance, when he meditated the
conquest of Kauai, his expedition included seven thousand
picked warriors, twenty-one schooners, forty swivels, six
mortars, and an abundance of ammunition! His victories
are celebrated in countless *mélés* or unwritten songs,
which are said to be marked by real poetic feeling and
simplicity, and to resemble the Ossianic poems in
majesty and melancholy. He founded the dynasty which
for seventy years has stood as firmly, and exercised its
functions for the welfare of the people on the whole as
efficiently, as any other government.

The king was forty-five years old when, having "no
more worlds to conquer," he devoted himself to the
consolidation of his kingdom. He placed governors on
each island, directly responsible to himself, who nominated chiefs of districts, heads of villages, and all petty
officers; and tax-gatherers, who, for lack of the art of
writing, kept their accounts by a method in use in the
English exchequer in ancient times. He appointed a
council of chiefs, with whom he advised on important

matters, and a council of " wise men " who assisted him
in framing laws, and in regulating concerns of minor
importance. In all matters of national importance, the
governors and high chiefs of the islands met with the
sovereign in consultations. These were conducted with
great privacy, and the results were promulgated through
the islands by heralds whose office was hereditary.

Kamehameha enacted statutes against theft, murder,
and oppression, and though he wielded oppressive and
despotic authority himself, his people enjoyed a golden
age as compared with those that were past. The king,
governors, and chiefs constituted the magistracy, and
there was an appeal from both chiefs and governors to
the king. It was usual for both parties to be heard face
to face in the enclosure in front of the house of the king
or governor, no lawyers were employed, and every man
advocated his own cause, sitting cross-legged before the
judges. Swiftness and decision characterized the redress
of grievances and the administration of justice.

Kamehameha reduced the feudal tenure of land, which
had heretofore been the theory, into absolute practice,
claiming for the crown the sole ownership of the land,
and dividing it among his followers on the conditions of
tribute and military service. The common people were
attached to the soil and transferred with it. A chief
might nominate his wife, or son, or any other person to
succeed him in his possessions, but at his death they
reverted to the king, whose order was required before the
testamentary wish became of any value. There were
some wise regulations generally applicable, concerning

the planting of cocoanut trees, and a law that the water should be conducted over every plantation twice a week in general, and once a week during the dry season. This king constructed immense fish-ponds on the sea coast, and devoted himself to commerce with such success that in one year he exported $400,000 of sandal-wood (felled and shipped at the cost of much suffering to the common people), and on finding that a large proportion of the profit had been dissipated by harbour dues at Canton, he took up the idea and established harbour dues at Honolulu.

From Vancouver Kamehameha learned of the grandeur and power of Christian nations; and in the idea that his people might grow great through Christianity, he asked him, in 1794, that Christian teachers might be sent from England. This request, if ever presented, was disregarded, as was another made by Captain Turnbull in 1803, and this exceptionally great Polynesian died the year before the light of the Gospel shone on Hawaiian shores.

Some persons, it does not appear whether they were English or American, attempted his conversion; but the astute savage, after listening to their eloquent statements of the power of faith, pressed on them as a crucial test to throw themselves from the top of an adjacent precipice, making his reception of their religion contingent on their arrival unhurt at its base. He built large *heiaus*, amongst others the one at Kawaihae, at the dedication of which to his favourite war god eleven human sacrifices were offered. To the end he remained devoted to the state

religion, and the last instances of capital punishment for
breaking *tabu*, a thraldom deeply interwoven with the
religious system, occurred in the last year of his reign,
when one man was put to death for putting on a chief's
girdle, another for eating of a tabooed dish, and a third
for leaving a house under *tabu*, and entering one which
was not so.

His last prayers were to his great red-feathered god
Kukailimoku, and priests bringing idols crowded round
him in his dying agony.   His last words were " *Move on
in my good way and* " —— In the death-room the high
chiefs consulted, and one, to testify his great grief, proposed to eat the body raw, but was overruled by the
majority.   So the flesh was separated from the bones,
and they were tied up in *tapa*, and concealed so
effectually that they have never since been found.   A
holocaust of three hundred dogs gave splendour to his
obsequies.   " These are our gods whom I worship," he
had said to Kotzebue, while showing him one of the
temples.   " Whether I do right or wrong I do not know,
but I follow my faith, which cannot be wicked, as it
commands me never to do wrong."

Kamehameha the Great died in 1819, and his son
Liholiho, who loved whisky and pleasure, was peaceably
crowned king in his room, and by his name.   He, with
the powerful aid of the Queen Dowager Kaahumanu,
abolished *tabu*, and his subjects cast away their idols,
and fell into indifferent scepticsm, the high priest
Hewahewa being the first to light the iconoclastic torch,
having previously given his opinion that there was only

one great *akua* or spirit in *lani*, the heavens. This Kamehameha II. was the king who with his queen, died of measles in London in 1824, after which the *Blonde* frigate was sent to restore their bodies with much ceremony to Hawaiian soil.

Kamehameha III., a minor, another son of the Conqueror, succeeded, and reigned for thirty years, dividing the lands among the nobles and the people, and conferring upon his kingdom an equable constitution. The law officially abolishing idolatry was confirmed by him, and while complete religious toleration otherwise was granted, the Christian faith was established in these words :—" The religion of the Lord Jesus Christ shall continue to be the established national religion of the Hawaiian Islands." His words on July 31st, 1843, when the English colours, wrongfully hoisted, were lowered in favour of the Hawaiian flag, are the national motto :—" The life of the land is established in righteousness." In his reign Hawaiian independence was recognised by Great Britain, France, and America. His Premier for some time was Mr. Wyllie, who with a rare devotion and disinterestedness devoted his life and a large fortune to his adopted country.

Kamehameha IV., a grandson of the Conqueror, succeeded him in 1854. He was a patriotic prince, and strove hard to advance the civilization of his people, and to arrest their decrease by reformatory and sanitary measures. He was the most accomplished prince of his line, and his death in 1863, soon after that of his only child, the Prince of Hawaii, was very deeply regretted.

His widow, Queen Kaleleonalani, or Emma, visited England after his death.

He was succeeded by his brother, a man of a very different stamp, who was buried on January 11, 1873, after a partial outbreak of the orgies wherewith the natives disgraced themselves after the death of a chief in the old heathen days. It is rare to meet with two people successively who hold the same opinion of Kamehameha V. He was evidently a man of some talent and strong will, intensely patriotic, and determined not to be a merely ornamental figure-head of a government administered by foreigners in his name. He ardently desired the encouragement of foreign immigration, and the opening of a free market in America for Hawaiian produce. He ruled, as well as reigned, and though he abrogated the constitution of 1852, and introduced several features of absolutism into the government, on the whole he seems to have done well by his people. He is said to have been regal and dignified, to have worked hard, to have written correct state papers, and to have been capable of the deportment of an educated Christian gentleman, but to have reimbursed himself for this subservience to conventionality by occasionally retiring to an undignified residence on the sea-shore, where he transformed himself into the likeness of one of his half-clad heathen ancestors, debased himself by whisky, and revelled in the *hula-hula*. He is said also to have been so far under the empire of the old superstitions, as to consult an ancient witch on affairs of importance.

He died amidst the rejoicings incident to his birth-day, and on the next day "lay in state in the throne-room of the palace, while his ministers, his staff, and the chiefs of the realm kept watch over him, and sombre *kahilis* waving at his head, beat a rude and silent dead-march for the crowds of people, subjects and aliens, who continuously filed through the apartment, for a curious farewell glance at the last of the Kamehamehas."

His death closed the first era of Hawaiian history, and the orderly succession of one recognised dynasty. No successor to the throne had been proclaimed, and the king left no nearer kin than the Princess Keelikolani, his half-sister, a lady not in the line of regal descent.

Under these novel circumstances, it devolved upon the Legislative Assembly to elect by ballot "some native *Alii* of the kingdom as successor to the throne." The candidates were the High Chief Kalakaua, the present King, and Prince Lunalilo, the late King, but the "Well-Beloved," as Lunalilo was called, was elected unanimously, amidst an outburst of popular enthusiasm.

From his high resolves and generous instincts much was expected, and the unhappy failing, to which, after the most painful struggles, he succumbed, on the solici-tation of some bad or thoughtless foreigners, if it lessened him aught in the public esteem, abated nothing of the wonderful love that was felt for him.

He died, after a lingering illness, on February 3, 1874. Although the event had been expected for some time, its announcement was received with profound sorrow by the whole community, while the native subjects of the deceased sovereign, according to ancient custom, expressed their feelings in loud wailings, which echoed mournfully through the still, red air of early daylight. On the following evening the body was placed on a shrouded bier, and was escorted in solemn procession by the government officials and the late king's staff, to the Iolani Palace, there to lie in state. It was a cloudless moonlight; not a leaf stirred or bird sang, and the crowd, consisting of several thousands, opened to the right and left to let the dismal death-train pass, in a stillness which was only broken by the solemn tramp of the bearers.

The next day the corpse lay in state, in all the splendour that the islands could bestow, dressed in the clothes the king wore when he took the oath of office, and resting on the royal robe of yellow feathers, a fathom square.* Between eight and ten thousand persons passed through the palace during the morning, and foreigners as well as natives wept tears of genuine grief; while in the palace grounds the wailing knew no intermission, and many of the natives spent hours in reciting *kanakaus* in honour of the deceased. At midnight the king's remains were placed in a coffin, his aged father, His Highness Kanaina, who was broken-hearted for his loss, standing by. When the body was raised from the feather robe, he ordered that it should be wrapped in it, and thus be deposited in its resting place.

* Only one robe like this remains, that which is spread over the throne at the opening of Parliament. The one buried with Lunalilo could not be reproduced for one hundred thousand dollars.

" He is the last of our race," he said ; " it belongs to
him." The natives in attendance turned pale at this
command, for the robe was the property of Kekauluohi,
the dead king's mother, and had descended to her from
her kingly ancestors.

Averse through his life to useless parade and display,
Lunalilo left directions for a simple funeral, and that
none of the old heathenish observances should ensue
upon his death. So, amidst unbounded grief, he was
carried to the grave with hymns and anthems, and the
hopes of Hawaii were buried with him.

He died without naming a successor, and thus for the
second time within fourteen months, a king came to be
elected by ballot.

The proceedings at the election of Lunalilo were marked
by an order, regularity, and peaceableness which reflected
extreme credit on the civilization of the Hawaiians, but in
the subsequent period the temper of the people had considerably changed, and they had been affected by influences to which some allusions were made in Letter XIX.

In politics, Lunalilo's views were essentially democratic,
and he showed an almost undue deference to the will of
the people, giving them a year's practical experience of
democracy which they will never forget.

An antagonism to the foreign residents, or rather to
their political influence, had grown rapidly. Some of
the Americans had been unwise in their language, and
the discussion on the proposed cession of Pearl River
increased the popular discontent, and the jealousy of

foreign interference in island affairs. "America gave us the light," said a native pastor, in a sermon which was reported over the islands, "but now that we have the light, we should be left to use it for ourselves." This sentence represented the bulk of the national feeling, which, if partially unenlightened, is intensely, passionately, almost fanatically patriotic.

The biennial election of delegates to the Legislative Assembly occurred shortly before Lunalilo's death, and the rallying-cry, "Hawaii for the Hawaiians," was used with such effect that the most respectable foreign candidates, even in the capital, had not a chance of success, and for the first time in Hawaiian constitutional history a house was elected, consisting, with one exception, of natives. Immediately on the king's death, Kalakaua, who was understood to represent the foreign interest as well as the policy indicated by the popular rallying-cry, and Queen Emma, came forward as candidates ; the walls were placarded with addresses, mass meetings were held, canvassers were busy night and day, promises impossible of fulfilment were made, and for eight days the Hawaiian capital presented those scenes of excitement, wrangling, and mutual misrepresentation which we associate with popular elections elsewhere, and everywhere.

The day of election came, and thirty-nine votes were given for Kalakaua, and six for Emma. On the announcement of this result, a hoarse, indignant roar, mingled with cheers from the crowd without, was heard within the Assembly chamber, and on the committee appointed to convey to Kalakaua the news of his election, attempting to take their seats in a carriage, they were driven back, maimed and bleeding, into the Courthouse; the carriage was torn to pieces, and the spokes of the wheels were distributed as weapons among the rioters. The "gentle children of the sun" were seen under a new aspect; they became furious, the latent savagery came out, the doors of the Hall of Assembly were battered in, the windows were shattered with clubs and volleys of stones, nine of the representatives, who were known to have voted for Kalakaua, were severely injured; the chairs, tables, and furnishings of the rooms were broken up and thrown out of the windows, along with valuable public and private documents; kerosene was demanded to fire the buildings; the police remained neutral, and conflagration and murder would have followed, had not the ministers dispatched an urgent request for assistance to the United States' ships of war, *Portsmouth* and *Tuscarora*, and H. B. M. ship *Tenedos*, which was promptly met by the landing of such a force of sailors and marines as dispersed the rioters.

Seventy arrests were made, the foreign marines held possession of the Courthouse, Palace, and Government offices, Kalakaua took the oath of office in private; the Representatives, with bandaged heads, and arms in slings, limped, and in some instances were supported, to their desks, to be liberated from their duties by the king in person, and in ten days the joint protectorate was withdrawn.

Those who know the natives best were taken by surprise, and are compelled to recognise that a restive, half-sullen, half-defiant spirit is abroad among them, and that the task of governing them may not be the easy thing which it has been since the days of Kamehameha the Great. Nor do the foreign residents, especially the Americans, feel so safe as formerly, without the presence of a man-of-war in the harbour, since the people of Oahu have so unexpectedly developed one of the prominent arts of civilized democracy, cruel, reckless, and unreasoning mobbing.

Of King Kalakaua, who began his reign under such unfortunate auspices, little at present can be said. Island affairs have not settled down into their old quietude, and party spirit, arising out of the election, has not died out among the natives. The king chose his advisers wisely, and made a concession to native feeling by appointing a native named Nahaolelua to a seat in the cabinet as Minister of Finance, but his first arrangement was upset, and a good deal of confusion has subsequently prevailed.

The Queen, Kapiolani, is a Hawaiian lady of high character and extreme amiability, and both King and Queen have been exemplary in their domestic relations.

Kalakaua's first act was to proclaim his brother, Prince Leleiohoku, his successor, investing him at the same time with the title, "His Royal Highness," and his second was to reorganize the military service, with the view of making it an efficient and well-disciplined force.

There is something melancholy in the fact that this small Pacific kingdom has to fall back upon the old world resource of a standing army, as large, in proportion to its population, as that of the German Empire.

Those readers who have become interested in the Sandwich Islands through the foregoing Letters, will join me in the earnest wish that this people, which has advanced from heathenism and barbarism to Christianity and civilization in the short space of a single generation, may enjoy peace and prosperity under King Kalakaua, that the extinction which threatens the nation may be averted, and that under a gracious Divine Providence, Hawaii may still remain the inheritance of the Hawaiians.

THE END.

For Product Safety Concerns and Information please contact our EU
representative GPSR@taylorandfrancis.com
Taylor & Francis Verlag GmbH, Kaufingerstraße 24, 80331 München, Germany

www.ingramcontent.com/pod-product-compliance
Ingram Content Group UK Ltd.
Pitfield, Milton Keynes, MK11 3LW, UK
UKHW021445080625
459435UK00011B/375